First Published 2024

FiNGERPRINT! CLASS!CS
Prakash Books

Fingerprint Publishing
@FingerprintP
@fingerprintpublishingbooks
www.fingerprintpublishing.com

ISBN: 978 93 6214 052 4

"There is something at the bottom of every new human thought, every thought of genius, or even every earnest thought that springs up in any brain, which can never be communicated to others, even if one were to write volumes about it and were explaining one's idea for thirty-five years; there's something left which cannot be induced to emerge from your brain, and remains with you forever; and with it you will die, without communicating to anyone perhaps the most important of your ideas."

Fyodor Mikhailovich Dostoevsky, born on November 11, 1821, in Moscow, Russia, is celebrated as one of the greatest novelists in the history of literature. Renowned for his profound psychological insight, his works delve deeply into the complexities of the human soul, exploring themes of faith, doubt, free will, and the human condition. His literary legacy includes masterpieces such as Crime and Punishment, The Brothers Karamazov, The Idiot, and Notes from Underground. In addition to these major works, Dostoevsky's extensive collection of short stories and his candid, insightful letters provide a comprehensive understanding of his literary genius and philosophical depth.

Dostoevsky's early life was marked by tragedy and hardship. His father, a stern and authoritarian figure, was a doctor who worked in a hospital for the poor, an experience that exposed Dostoevsky to the harsh realities of life from a young age. His mother died of tuberculosis when he was just 15, a loss that profoundly affected him. After his mother's death, Dostoevsky was sent to a military engineering school in St. Petersburg, a career path that did not align with his literary aspirations. However, it was during this period that he began to read widely and develop his passion for literature.

In 1846, Dostoevsky published his first novel, Poor Folk, which was well-received and heralded him as a new voice in Russian literature. However, his burgeoning career was interrupted in 1849 when he was arrested for his involvement with the Petrashevsky Circle, a group of intellectuals critical of the Tsarist regime. He was sentenced to death, but at the last moment, his sentence was commuted to four years of hard labor in a Siberian prison camp. This harrowing experience had a profound impact on his worldview and writings, instilling in him a deep sense of spiritual and existential inquiry.

Notes from Underground, published in 1864, is considered one of Dostoevsky's most influential works, often seen as a precursor to existentialism and modernist literature. This novella delves into the mind of an unnamed narrator, often referred to as the Underground Man, who offers a scathing critique of rationalism and utopianism. The story is divided into two parts: the first is a monologue by the Underground Man, who reflects on his isolation and contempt for society, while the second part provides a glimpse into his interactions with others, highlighting his profound alienation and self-destructive tendencies.

In addition to his major novels, Dostoevsky was a prolific writer of short stories, many of which offer insightful glimpses into his broader literary and philosophical concerns. "White Nights," published in 1848, is a poignant tale of unrequited love and loneliness, reflecting the deep emotional currents that run through much of his work. "The Heavenly Christmas Tree" was published in 1876 as part of Dostoevsky's A Writer's Diary. This short story is a touching and tragic narrative that depicts the harsh realities faced by the poor and destitute, particularly during the festive season, which starkly contrasts with the joy experienced by the more fortunate.

"The Dream of a Ridiculous Man," published in 1877, is a philosophical short story that delves into themes of existential despair, redemption, and the possibility of moral renewal. The story follows the protagonist, a self-described ridiculous man, who is contemplating suicide. On the verge of ending his life, he falls asleep and dreams of a journey to a utopian world free from sin and suffering. In this world, people live in harmony, embodying the ideals of love, kindness, and mutual respect. However, his presence eventually corrupts this paradise, leading to the fall of this innocent society.

In addition to this, Dostoevsky's letters are another invaluable resource for understanding his life and thoughts. His correspondence provides a candid look at his personal struggles, his views on literature and politics, and his creative process. In letters to his brother Mikhail, Dostoevsky discusses his early literary ambitions and the profound impact of his Siberian exile. His letters to his second wife, Anna Snitkina, reveal a deeply affectionate and supportive relationship, essential to his later creative output. The letters also offer insights into his views on contemporary Russian society, his financial difficulties, and his struggles with epilepsy.

Despite suffering from epilepsy and financial difficulties throughout his life, Dostoevsky's personal struggles fueled his creative output. He married twice and had four children, though he faced the heartbreaking loss of several of them during his lifetime. His second wife, Anna Snitkina, played a crucial role in his later life, supporting him both emotionally and financially.

Dostoevsky died on February 9, 1881, but his literary legacy endures. His works continue to be studied for their profound psychological depth and philosophical richness.

Contents

Notes from the Underground   **11**

Short Stories   **135**

    White Nights   137
    The Heavenly Christmas Tree   185
    The Dream of a Ridiculous Man   191
    The Peasant Marey   211
    An Honest Thief   217
    A Christmas Tree and a Wedding   235
    Another Man's Wife and a Husband under the Bed   243
    A Little Hero   285
    Mr. Prohartchin   319

Selected Letters   **349**

NOTES FROM THE UNDERGROUND*

A NOVEL

Translated by Constance Garnett

---

* The author of the diary and the diary itself are, of course, imaginary. Nevertheless it is clear that such persons as the writer of these notes not only may, but positively must, exist in our society, when we consider the circumstances in the midst of which our society is formed. I have tried to expose to the view of the public more distinctly than is commonly done, one of the characters of the recent past. He is one of the representatives of a generation still living. In this fragment, entitled "Underground," this person introduces himself and his views, and, as it were, tries to explain the causes owing to which he has made his appearance and was bound to make his appearance in our midst. In the second fragment there are added the actual notes of this person concerning certain events in his life.—AUTHOR'S NOTE.

PART ONE

Underground

PART ONE

Underground

1

I am a sick man. . . . I am a spiteful man. I am an unattractive man. I believe my liver is diseased. However, I know nothing at all about my disease, and do not know for certain what ails me. I don't consult a doctor for it, and never have, though I have a respect for medicine and doctors. Besides, I am extremely superstitious, sufficiently so to respect medicine, anyway (I am well-educated enough not to be superstitious, but I am superstitious). No, I refuse to consult a doctor from spite. That you probably will not understand. Well, I understand it, though. Of course, I can't explain who it is precisely that I am mortifying in this case by my spite: I am perfectly well aware that I cannot "pay out" the doctors by not consulting them; I know better than anyone that by all this I am only injuring myself and no one else. But still, if I don't consult a doctor it is from spite. My liver is bad, well—let it get worse!

I have been going on like that for a long time—twenty years. Now I am forty. I used to be in the government service, but am no longer. I was a spiteful official. I was rude and took pleasure in being so. I did not take bribes, you see, so I was bound to find a recompense in that, at least. (A poor jest, but I will not scratch it out. I wrote it thinking it would sound very witty; but now that I have seen myself that I only wanted to show off in a despicable way, I will not scratch it out on purpose!)

When petitioners used to come for information to the table at which I sat, I used to grind my teeth at them, and felt intense enjoyment when I succeeded in making anybody unhappy. I almost did succeed. For the most part they were all timid people—of course, they were petitioners. But of the uppish ones there was one officer in particular I could not endure. He simply would not be humble, and clanked his sword in a disgusting way. I carried on a feud with him for eighteen months over that sword. At last I got the better of him. He left off clanking it. That happened in my youth, though.

But do you know, gentlemen, what was the chief point about my spite? Why, the whole point, the real sting of it lay in the fact that continually, even in the moment of the acutest spleen, I was inwardly conscious with shame that I was not only not a spiteful but not even an embittered man, that I was simply scaring sparrows at random and amusing myself by it. I might foam at the mouth, but bring me a doll to play with, give me a cup of tea with sugar in it, and maybe I should be appeased. I might even be genuinely touched, though probably I should grind my teeth at myself afterwards and lie awake at night with shame for months after. That was my way.

I was lying when I said just now that I was a spiteful official. I was lying from spite. I was simply amusing myself with the petitioners and with the officer, and in reality I never could become spiteful. I was conscious every moment in myself of many, very many elements absolutely opposite to that. I felt them positively swarming in me, these opposite elements. I knew that they had been swarming in me all my life and craving some outlet from me, but I would not let them, would not let them, purposely would not let them come out. They tormented me till I was ashamed: they drove me to convulsions and—sickened me, at last, how they sickened me! Now, are not you fancying, gentlemen, that I am expressing remorse for something now, that I am asking your forgiveness for something? I am sure you are fancying that . . . However, I assure you I do not care if you are. . . .

It was not only that I could not become spiteful, I did not know how to become anything; neither spiteful nor kind, neither a rascal nor an honest man, neither a hero nor an insect. Now, I am living out my life in my corner, taunting myself with the spiteful and useless consolation that an intelligent man cannot become anything seriously, and it is only the fool who becomes anything. Yes, a man in the nineteenth century must and morally ought to be pre-eminently a characterless creature; a man of character, an active man is pre-eminently a limited creature. That is my conviction of forty years. I am forty years old now, and you know forty years is a whole lifetime; you know it is extreme old age. To live longer than forty years is bad manners, is vulgar, immoral. Who does live beyond forty? Answer that, sincerely and honestly I will tell you who do: fools and worthless fellows. I tell all old men that to their face, all these venerable old men, all these silver-haired and reverend seniors! I tell the whole world that to its face! I have a right to say so, for I shall go on living to sixty myself. To seventy! To eighty! . . . Stay, let me take breath . . .

You imagine no doubt, gentlemen, that I want to amuse you. You are mistaken in that, too. I am by no means such a mirthful person as you imagine, or as you may imagine; however, irritated by all this babble (and I feel that you are irritated) you think fit to ask me who I am—then my answer is, I am a collegiate assessor. I was in the service that I might have something to eat (and solely for that reason), and when last year a distant relation left me six thousand roubles in his will I immediately retired from the service and settled down in my corner. I used to live in this corner before, but now I have settled down in it. My room is a wretched, horrid one in the outskirts of the town. My servant is an old country-woman, ill-natured from stupidity, and, moreover, there is always a nasty smell about her. I am told that the Petersburg climate is bad for me, and that with my small means it is very expensive to live in Petersburg. I know all that better than all these sage and experienced counsellors and monitors. . . . But I am remaining in Petersburg; I am not going away from Petersburg! I am not going away because . . . ech! Why, it is absolutely no matter whether I am going away or not going away.

But what can a decent man speak of with most pleasure?
Answer: Of himself.
Well, so I will talk about myself.

2

I want now to tell you, gentlemen, whether you care to hear it or not, why I could not even become an insect. I tell you solemnly, that I have many times tried to become an insect. But I was not equal even to that. I swear, gentlemen, that to be too conscious is an illness—a real thorough-going illness. For man's everyday needs, it would have been quite enough to have the ordinary human consciousness, that is, half or a quarter of the amount which falls to the lot of a cultivated man of our unhappy nineteenth century, especially one who has the fatal ill-luck to inhabit Petersburg, the most theoretical and intentional town on the whole terrestrial globe. (There are intentional and unintentional towns.) It would have been quite enough, for instance, to have the consciousness by which all so-called direct persons and men of action live. I bet you think I am writing all this from affectation, to be witty at the expense of men of action; and what is more, that from ill-bred affectation, I am clanking a sword like my officer. But, gentlemen, whoever can pride himself on his diseases and even swagger over them?

Though, after all, everyone does do that; people do pride themselves on their diseases, and I do, may be, more than anyone. We will not dispute it; my contention was absurd. But yet I am firmly persuaded that a great deal of consciousness, every sort of consciousness, in fact, is a disease. I stick to that. Let us leave that, too, for a minute. Tell me this: why does it happen that at the very, yes, at the very moments when I am most capable of feeling every refinement of all that is "sublime and beautiful," as they used to say at one time, it would, as though of design, happen to me not only to feel but to do such ugly things, such that . . . Well, in short, actions that all, perhaps, commit; but which, as though purposely, occurred to me at the very time when I was most conscious that they ought not to be committed. The more conscious I was of goodness and of all that was "sublime and beautiful," the more deeply I sank into my mire and the more ready I was to sink in it altogether. But the chief point was that all this was, as it were, not accidental in me, but as though it were bound to be so. It was as though it were my most normal condition, and not in the least disease or depravity, so that at last all desire in me to struggle against this depravity passed. It ended by my almost believing (perhaps actually believing) that this was perhaps my normal condition. But at first, in the beginning, what agonies I endured in that struggle! I did not believe it was the same with other people, and all my life I hid this fact about myself as a secret. I was ashamed (even now, perhaps, I am ashamed): I got to the point of feeling a sort of secret abnormal, despicable enjoyment in returning home to my corner on some disgusting Petersburg night, acutely conscious that that day I had committed a loathsome action again, that what was done could never be undone, and secretly, inwardly gnawing, gnawing at myself for it, tearing and consuming myself till at last the bitterness turned into a sort of shameful accursed sweetness, and at last—into positive real enjoyment! Yes, into enjoyment, into enjoyment! I insist upon that. I have spoken of this because I keep wanting to know for a fact whether other people feel such enjoyment? I will explain; the enjoyment was just from the too intense consciousness of one's own degradation; it was from feeling oneself that one had reached the last barrier, that it was horrible, but that it could not be otherwise; that there was no escape for you; that you never could become a different man; that even if time and faith were still left you to change into something different you would most likely not wish to change; or if you did wish to, even then you would do nothing; because perhaps in reality there was nothing for you to change into.

And the worst of it was, and the root of it all, that it was all in accord with the normal fundamental laws of over-acute consciousness, and with the inertia that was the direct result of those laws, and that consequently one was not only unable to change but could do absolutely nothing. Thus it would follow, as the result of acute consciousness, that one is not to blame in being a scoundrel; as though that were any consolation to the scoundrel once he has come to realise that he actually is a scoundrel. But enough.... Ech, I have talked a lot of nonsense, but what have I explained? How is enjoyment in this to be explained? But I will explain it. I will get to the bottom of it! That is why I have taken up my pen....

I, for instance, have a great deal of *amour propre*. I am as suspicious and prone to take offence as a humpback or a dwarf. But upon my word I sometimes have had moments when if I had happened to be slapped in the face I should, perhaps, have been positively glad of it. I say, in earnest, that I should probably have been able to discover even in that a peculiar sort of enjoyment—the enjoyment, of course, of despair; but in despair there are the most intense enjoyments, especially when one is very acutely conscious of the hopelessness of one's position. And when one is slapped in the face—why then the consciousness of being rubbed into a pulp would positively overwhelm one. The worst of it is, look at it which way one will, it still turns out that I was always the most to blame in everything. And what is most humiliating of all, to blame for no fault of my own but, so to say, through the laws of nature. In the first place, to blame because I am cleverer than any of the people surrounding me. (I have always considered myself cleverer than any of the people surrounding me, and sometimes, would you believe it, have been positively ashamed of it. At any rate, I have all my life, as it were, turned my eyes away and never could look people straight in the face.) To blame, finally, because even if I had had magnanimity, I should only have had more suffering from the sense of its uselessness. I should certainly have never been able to do anything from being magnanimous—neither to forgive, for my assailant would perhaps have slapped me from the laws of nature, and one cannot forgive the laws of nature; nor to forget, for even if it were owing to the laws of nature, it is insulting all the same. Finally, even if I had wanted to be anything but magnanimous, had desired on the contrary to revenge myself on my assailant, I could not have revenged myself on any one for anything because I should certainly never have made up my mind to do anything, even if I had been able to. Why should I not have made up my mind? About that in particular I want to say a few words.

3

3

With people who know how to revenge themselves and to stand up for themselves in general, how is it done? Why, when they are possessed, let us suppose, by the feeling of revenge, then for the time there is nothing else but that feeling left in their whole being. Such a gentleman simply dashes straight for his object like an infuriated bull with its horns down, and nothing but a wall will stop him. (By the way: facing the wall, such gentlemen—that is, the "direct" persons and men of action—are genuinely nonplussed. For them a wall is not an evasion, as for us people who think and consequently do nothing; it is not an excuse for turning aside, an excuse for which we are always very glad, though we scarcely believe in it ourselves, as a rule. No, they are nonplussed in all sincerity. The wall has for them something tranquillising, morally soothing, final—maybe even something mysterious . . . but of the wall later.)

Well, such a direct person I regard as the real normal man, as his tender mother nature wished to see him when she graciously brought him into being on the earth. I envy such a man till I am green in the face. He is stupid. I am not disputing that, but perhaps the normal man should be stupid, how do you know? Perhaps it is very beautiful, in fact. And I am the more persuaded of that suspicion, if one can call it so, by the fact that if you take, for instance, the antithesis of the normal man, that is, the man of acute consciousness, who has come, of course, not out of the lap of nature but out of a retort (this is almost mysticism, gentlemen, but I suspect this, too), this retort-made man is sometimes so nonplussed in the presence of his antithesis that with all his exaggerated consciousness he genuinely thinks of himself as a mouse and not a man. It may be an acutely conscious mouse, yet it is a mouse, while the other is a man, and therefore, et caetera, et caetera. And the worst of it is, he himself, his very own self, looks on himself as a mouse; no one asks him to do so; and that is an important point. Now let us look at this mouse in action. Let us suppose, for instance, that it feels insulted, too (and it almost always does feel insulted), and wants to revenge itself, too. There may even be a greater accumulation of spite in it than in *l'homme de la nature et de la vérité*. The base and nasty desire to vent that spite on its assailant rankles perhaps even more nastily in it than in *l'homme de la nature et de la vérité*. For through his innate stupidity the latter looks upon his revenge as justice pure and simple; while in consequence of his acute consciousness the mouse does not believe in the justice of it. To come at last to the deed itself, to the very act of revenge. Apart from the one fundamental nastiness the luckless mouse succeeds in creating around it so many other nastinesses in the form of doubts and questions, adds to the one question so many unsettled questions that there inevitably works up around it a sort of fatal brew, a stinking mess, made up of its doubts, emotions, and of the contempt spat upon it by the direct men of action who stand solemnly about it as judges and arbitrators, laughing at it till their healthy sides ache. Of course the only thing left for it is to dismiss all that with a wave of its paw, and, with a smile of assumed contempt in which it does not even itself believe, creep ignominiously into its mouse-hole. There in its nasty, stinking, underground home our insulted, crushed and ridiculed mouse promptly becomes absorbed in cold, malignant and, above all, everlasting spite. For forty years together it will remember its injury down to the smallest, most ignominious details, and every time will add, of itself, details still more ignominious, spitefully teasing and tormenting itself with its own imagination. It will itself be ashamed of its imaginings, but yet it will recall it all, it will go over and over every detail, it will invent unheard of things against itself, pretending that those things might happen, and will forgive nothing. Maybe it will begin to revenge itself, too, but, as it were, piecemeal, in trivial ways, from behind the stove, incognito, without believing either in its own right to vengeance, or in the success of its revenge, knowing that from all its efforts at revenge it will suffer a hundred times more than he on whom it revenges itself, while he, I daresay, will not even scratch himself. On its deathbed it will recall it all over again, with interest accumulated over all the years and . . .

But it is just in that cold, abominable half despair, half belief, in that conscious burying oneself alive for grief in the underworld for forty years, in that acutely recognised and yet partly doubtful hopelessness of one's position, in that hell of unsatisfied desires turned inward, in that fever of oscillations, of resolutions determined for ever and repented of again a minute later—that the savour of that strange enjoyment of which I have spoken lies. It is so subtle, so difficult of analysis, that persons who are a little limited, or even simply persons of strong nerves, will not understand a single atom of it. "Possibly," you will add on your own account with a grin, "people will not understand it either who have never received a slap in the face," and in that way you will politely hint to me that I, too, perhaps, have had the experience of a slap in the face in my life, and so I speak as one who knows. I bet that you are thinking that. But set your minds at rest, gentlemen, I have not received a slap in the face, though it is absolutely a matter of indifference to me what you may think about it. Possibly, I even regret, myself, that I have given so few slaps in the face during my life. But enough . . . not another word on that subject of such extreme interest to you.

I will continue calmly concerning persons with strong nerves who do not understand a certain refinement of enjoyment. Though in certain circumstances these gentlemen bellow their loudest like bulls, though this, let us suppose, does them the greatest credit, yet, as I have said already, confronted with the impossible they subside at once. The impossible means the stone wall! What stone wall? Why, of course, the laws of nature, the deductions of natural science, mathematics. As soon as they prove to you, for instance, that you are descended from a monkey, then it is no use scowling, accept it for a fact. When they prove to you that in reality one drop of your own fat must be dearer to you than a hundred thousand of your fellow-creatures, and that this conclusion is the final solution of all so-called virtues and duties and all such prejudices and fancies, then you have just to accept it, there is no help for it, for twice two is a law of mathematics. Just try refuting it.

"Upon my word, they will shout at you, it is no use protesting: it is a case of twice two makes four! Nature does not ask your permission, she has nothing to do with your wishes, and whether you like her laws or dislike them, you are bound to accept her as she is, and consequently all her conclusions. A wall, you see, is a wall . . . and so on, and so on."

Merciful Heavens! but what do I care for the laws of nature and arithmetic, when, for some reason I dislike those laws and the fact that twice two makes four? Of course I cannot break through the wall by battering my head against it if I really have not the strength to knock it down, but I am not going to be reconciled to it simply because it is a stone wall and I have not the strength.

As though such a stone wall really were a consolation, and really did contain some word of conciliation, simply because it is as true as twice two makes four. Oh, absurdity of absurdities! How much better it is to understand it all, to recognise it all, all the impossibilities and the stone wall; not to be reconciled to one of those impossibilities and stone walls if it disgusts you to be reconciled to it; by the way of the most inevitable, logical combinations to reach the most revolting conclusions on the everlasting theme, that even for the stone wall you are yourself somehow to blame, though again it is as clear as day you are not to blame in the least, and therefore grinding your teeth in silent impotence to sink into luxurious inertia, brooding on the fact that there is no one even for you to feel vindictive against, that you have not, and perhaps never will have, an object for your spite, that it is a sleight of hand, a bit of juggling, a card-sharper's trick, that it is simply a mess, no knowing what and no knowing who, but in spite of all these uncertainties and jugglings, still there is an ache in you, and the more you do not know, the worse the ache.

4

"Ha, ha, ha! You will be finding enjoyment in toothache next," you cry, with a laugh.

"Well, even in toothache there is enjoyment," I answer. I had toothache for a whole month and I know there is. In that case, of course, people are not spiteful in silence, but moan; but they are not candid moans, they are malignant moans, and the malignancy is the whole point. The enjoyment of the sufferer finds expression in those moans; if he did not feel enjoyment in them he would not moan. It is a good example, gentlemen, and I will develop it. Those moans express in the first place all the aimlessness of your pain, which is so humiliating to your consciousness; the whole legal system of nature on which you spit disdainfully, of course, but from which you suffer all the same while she does not. They express the consciousness that you have no enemy to punish, but that you have pain; the consciousness that in spite of all possible Wagenheims you are in complete slavery to your teeth; that if someone wishes it, your teeth will leave off aching, and if he does not, they will go on aching another three months; and that finally if you are still contumacious and still protest, all that is left you for your own gratification is to thrash yourself or beat your wall with your fist as hard as you can, and absolutely nothing more. Well, these mortal insults, these jeers on the part of someone unknown, end at last in an enjoyment which sometimes reaches the highest degree of voluptuousness. I ask you, gentlemen, listen sometimes to the moans of an educated man of the nineteenth century suffering from toothache, on the second or third day of the attack, when he is beginning to moan, not as he moaned on the first day, that is, not simply because he has toothache, not just as any coarse peasant, but as a man affected by progress and European civilisation, a man who is "divorced from the soil and the national elements," as they express it now-a-days. His moans become nasty, disgustingly malignant, and go on for whole days and nights. And of course he knows himself that he is doing himself no sort of good with his moans; he knows better than anyone that he is only lacerating and harassing himself and others for nothing; he knows that even the audience before whom he is making his efforts, and his whole family, listen to him with loathing, do not put a ha'porth of faith in him, and inwardly understand that he might moan differently, more simply, without trills and flourishes, and that he is only amusing himself like that from ill-humour, from malignancy. Well, in all these recognitions and disgraces it is that there lies a voluptuous pleasure. As though he would say: "I am worrying you, I am lacerating your hearts, I am keeping everyone in the house awake. Well, stay awake then, you, too, feel every minute that I have toothache. I am not a hero to you now, as I tried to seem before, but simply a nasty person, an impostor. Well, so be it, then! I am very glad that you see through me. It is nasty for you to hear my despicable moans: well, let it be nasty; here I will let you have a nastier flourish in a minute. . . ." You do not understand even now, gentlemen? No, it seems our development and our consciousness must go further to understand all the intricacies of this pleasure. You laugh? Delighted. My jests, gentlemen, are of course in bad taste, jerky, involved, lacking self-confidence. But of course that is because I do not respect myself. Can a man of perception respect himself at all?

5

Come, can a man who attempts to find enjoyment in the very feeling of his own degradation possibly have a spark of respect for himself? I am not saying this now from any mawkish kind of remorse. And, indeed, I could never endure saying, "Forgive me, Papa, I won't do it again," not because I am incapable of saying that—on the contrary, perhaps just because I have been too capable of it, and in what a way, too. As though of design I used to get into trouble in cases when I was not to blame in any way. That was the nastiest part of it. At the same time I was genuinely touched and penitent, I used to shed tears and, of course, deceived myself, though I was not acting in the least and there was a sick feeling in my heart at the time. . . . For that one could not blame even the laws of nature, though the laws of nature have continually all my life offended me more than anything. It is loathsome to remember it all, but it was loathsome even then. Of course, a minute or so later I would realise wrathfully that it was all a lie, a revolting lie, an affected lie, that is, all this penitence, this emotion, these vows of reform. You will ask why did I worry myself with such antics: answer, because it was very dull to sit with one's hands folded, and so one began cutting capers. That is really it. Observe yourselves more carefully, gentlemen, then you will understand that it is so. I invented adventures for myself and made up a life, so as at least to live in some way. How many times it has happened to me—well, for instance, to take offence simply on purpose, for nothing; and one knows oneself, of course, that one is offended at nothing; that one is putting it on, but yet one brings oneself at last to the point of being really offended. All my life I have had an impulse to play such pranks, so that in the end I could not control it in myself. Another time, twice, in fact, I tried hard to be in love. I suffered, too, gentlemen, I assure you. In the depth of my heart there was no faith in my suffering, only a faint stir of mockery, but yet I did suffer, and in the real, orthodox way; I was jealous, beside myself . . . and it was all from *ennui*, gentlemen, all from *ennui;* inertia overcame me. You know the direct, legitimate fruit of consciousness is inertia, that is, conscious sitting-with-the-hands-folded. I have referred to this already. I repeat, I repeat with emphasis: all "direct" persons and men of action are active just because they are stupid and limited. How explain that? I will tell you: in consequence of their limitation they take immediate and secondary causes for primary ones, and in that way persuade themselves more quickly and easily than other people do that they have found an infallible foundation for their activity, and their minds are at ease and you know that is the chief thing. To begin to act, you know, you must first have your mind completely at ease and no trace of doubt left in it. Why, how am I, for example, to set my mind at rest? Where are the primary causes on which I am to build? Where are my foundations? Where am I to get them from? I exercise myself in reflection, and consequently with me every primary cause at once draws after itself another still more primary, and so on to infinity. That is just the essence of every sort of consciousness and reflection. It must be a case of the laws of nature again. What is the result of it in the end? Why, just the same. Remember I spoke just now of vengeance. (I am sure you did not take it in.) I said that a man revenges himself because he sees justice in it. Therefore he has found a primary cause, that is, justice. And so he is at rest on all sides, and consequently he carries out his revenge calmly and successfully, being persuaded that he is doing a just and honest thing. But I see no justice in it, I find no sort of virtue in it either, and consequently if I attempt to revenge myself, it is only out of spite. Spite, of course, might overcome everything, all my doubts, and so might serve quite successfully in place of a primary cause, precisely because it is not a cause. But what is to be done if I have not even spite (I began with that just now, you know). In consequence again of those accursed laws of consciousness, anger in me is subject to chemical disintegration. You look into it, the object flies off into air, your reasons evaporate, the criminal is not to be found, the wrong becomes not a wrong but a phantom, something like the toothache, for which no one is to blame, and consequently there is only the same outlet left again—that is, to beat the wall as hard as you can. So you give it up with a wave of the hand because you have not found a fundamental cause. And try letting yourself be carried away by your feelings, blindly, without reflection, without a primary cause, repelling consciousness at least for a time; hate or love, if only not to sit with your hands folded. The day after tomorrow, at the latest, you will begin despising yourself for having knowingly deceived yourself. Result: a soap-bubble and inertia. Oh, gentlemen, do you know, perhaps I consider myself an intelligent man, only because all my life I have been able neither to begin nor to finish anything. Granted I am a babbler, a harmless vexatious babbler, like all of us. But what is to be done if the direct and sole vocation of every intelligent man is babble, that is, the intentional pouring of water through a sieve?

6

Oh, if I had done nothing simply from laziness! Heavens, how I should have respected myself, then. I should have respected myself because I should at least have been capable of being lazy; there would at least have been one quality, as it were, positive in me, in which I could have believed myself. Question: What is he? Answer: A sluggard; how very pleasant it would have been to hear that of oneself! It would mean that I was positively defined, it would mean that there was something to say about me. "Sluggard"—why, it is a calling and vocation, it is a career. Do not jest, it is so. I should then be a member of the best club by right, and should find my occupation in continually respecting myself. I knew a gentleman who prided himself all his life on being a connoisseur of Lafitte. He considered this as his positive virtue, and never doubted himself. He died, not simply with a tranquil, but with a triumphant conscience, and he was quite right, too. Then I should have chosen a career for myself, I should have been a sluggard and a glutton, not a simple one, but, for instance, one with sympathies for everything sublime and beautiful. How do you like that? I have long had visions of it. That "sublime and beautiful" weighs heavily on my mind at forty But that is at forty; then—oh, then it would have been different! I should have found for myself a form of activity in keeping with it, to be precise, drinking to the health of everything "sublime and beautiful." I should have snatched at every opportunity to drop a tear into my glass and then to drain it to all that is "sublime and beautiful." I should then have turned everything into the sublime and the beautiful; in the nastiest, unquestionable trash, I should have sought out the sublime and the beautiful. I should have exuded tears like a wet sponge. An artist, for instance, paints a picture worthy of Gay. At once I drink to the health of the artist who painted the picture worthy of Gay, because I love all that is "sublime and beautiful." An author has written *As you will*: at once I drink to the health of "anyone you will" because I love all that is "sublime and beautiful."

I should claim respect for doing so. I should persecute anyone who would not show me respect. I should live at ease, I should die with dignity, why, it is charming, perfectly charming! And what a good round belly I should have grown, what a treble chin I should have established, what a ruby nose I should have coloured for myself, so that everyone would have said, looking at me: "Here is an asset! Here is something real and solid!" And, say what you like, it is very agreeable to hear such remarks about oneself in this negative age.

7

But these are all golden dreams. Oh, tell me, who was it first announced, who was it first proclaimed, that man only does nasty things because he does not know his own interests; and that if he were enlightened, if his eyes were opened to his real normal interests, man would at once cease to do nasty things, would at once become good and noble because, being enlightened and understanding his real advantage, he would see his own advantage in the good and nothing else, and we all know that not one man can, consciously, act against his own interests, consequently, so to say, through necessity, he would begin doing good? Oh, the babe! Oh, the pure, innocent child! Why, in the first place, when in all these thousands of years has there been a time when man has acted only from his own interest? What is to be done with the millions of facts that bear witness that men, *consciously*, that is fully understanding their real interests, have left them in the background and have rushed headlong on another path, to meet peril and danger, compelled to this course by nobody and by nothing, but, as it were, simply disliking the beaten track, and have obstinately, wilfully, struck out another difficult, absurd way, seeking it almost in the darkness. So, I suppose, this obstinacy and perversity were pleasanter to them than any advantage. . . . Advantage! What is advantage? And will you take it upon yourself to define with perfect accuracy in what the advantage of man consists? And what if it so happens that a man's advantage, *sometimes*, not only may, but even must, consist in his desiring in certain cases what is harmful to himself and not advantageous. And if so, if there can be such a case, the whole principle falls into dust. What do you think—are there such cases? You laugh; laugh away, gentlemen, but only answer me: have man's advantages been reckoned up with perfect certainty? Are there not some which not only have not been included but cannot possibly be included under any classification? You see, you gentlemen have, to the best of my knowledge, taken your whole register of human advantages from the averages of statistical figures and politico-economical formulas. Your advantages are prosperity, wealth, freedom, peace—and so on, and so on. So that the man who should, for instance, go openly and knowingly in opposition to all that list would to your thinking, and indeed mine, too, of course, be an obscurantist or an absolute madman: would not he? But, you know, this is what is surprising: why does it so happen that all these statisticians, sages and lovers of humanity, when they reckon up human advantages invariably leave out one? They don't even take it into their reckoning in the form in which it should be taken, and the whole reckoning depends upon that. It would be no greater matter, they would simply have to take it, this advantage, and add it to the list. But the trouble is, that this strange advantage does not fall under any classification and is not in place in any list. I have a friend for instance . . . Ech! gentlemen, but of course he is your friend, too; and indeed there is no one, no one to whom he is not a friend! When he prepares for any undertaking this gentleman immediately explains to you, elegantly and clearly, exactly how he must act in accordance with the laws of reason and truth. What is more, he will talk to you with excitement and passion of the true normal interests of man; with irony he will upbraid the short-sighted fools who do not understand their own interests, nor the true significance of virtue; and, within a quarter of an hour, without any sudden outside provocation, but simply through something inside him which is stronger than all his interests, he will go off on quite a different tack—that is, act in direct opposition to what he has just been saying about himself, in opposition to the laws of reason, in opposition to his own advantage, in fact in opposition to everything . . . I warn you that my friend is a compound personality and therefore it is difficult to blame him as an individual. The fact is, gentlemen, it seems there must really exist something that is dearer to almost every man than his greatest advantages, or (not to be illogical) there is a most advantageous advantage (the very one omitted of which we spoke just now) which is more important and more advantageous than all other advantages, for the sake of which a man if necessary is ready to act in opposition to all laws; that is, in opposition to reason, honour, peace, prosperity—in fact, in opposition to all those excellent and useful things if only he can attain that fundamental, most advantageous advantage which is dearer to him than all. "Yes, but it's advantage all the same," you will retort. But excuse me, I'll make the point clear, and it is not a case of playing upon words. What matters is, that this advantage is remarkable from the very fact that it breaks down all our classifications, and continually shatters every system constructed by lovers of mankind for the benefit of mankind. In fact, it upsets everything. But before I mention this advantage to you, I want to compromise myself personally, and therefore I boldly declare that all these fine systems, all these theories for explaining to mankind their real normal interests, in order that inevitably striving to pursue these interests they may at once become good and noble—are, in my opinion, so far, mere logical exercises! Yes, logical exercises. Why, to maintain this theory of the regeneration of mankind by means of the pursuit of his own advantage is to my mind almost the same thing . . . as to affirm, for instance, following Buckle, that through civilisation mankind becomes softer, and consequently less bloodthirsty and less fitted for warfare. Logically it does seem to follow from his arguments. But man has such a predilection for systems and abstract deductions that he is ready to distort the truth intentionally, he is ready to deny the evidence of his senses only to justify his logic. I take this example because it is the most glaring instance of it. Only look about you: blood is being spilt in streams, and in the merriest way, as though it were champagne. Take the whole of the nineteenth century in which Buckle lived. Take Napoleon—the Great and also the present one. Take North America—the eternal union. Take the farce of Schleswig-

Holstein. . . . And what is it that civilisation softens in us? The only gain of civilisation for mankind is the greater capacity for variety of sensations—and absolutely nothing more. And through the development of this many-sidedness man may come to finding enjoyment in bloodshed. In fact, this has already happened to him. Have you noticed that it is the most civilised gentlemen who have been the subtlest slaughterers, to whom the Attilas and Stenka Razins could not hold a candle, and if they are not so conspicuous as the Attilas and Stenka Razins it is simply because they are so often met with, are so ordinary and have become so familiar to us. In any case civilisation has made mankind if not more bloodthirsty, at least more vilely, more loathsomely bloodthirsty. In old days he saw justice in bloodshed and with his conscience at peace exterminated those he thought proper. Now we do think bloodshed abominable and yet we engage in this abomination, and with more energy than ever. Which is worse? Decide that for yourselves. They say that Cleopatra (excuse an instance from Roman history) was fond of sticking gold pins into her slave-girls' breasts and derived gratification from their screams and writhings. You will say that that was in the comparatively barbarous times; that these are barbarous times too, because also, comparatively speaking, pins are stuck in even now; that though man has now learned to see more clearly than in barbarous ages, he is still far from having learnt to act as reason and science would dictate. But yet you are fully convinced that he will be sure to learn when he gets rid of certain old bad habits, and when common sense and science have completely re-educated human nature and turned it in a normal direction. You are confident that then man will cease from *intentional* error and will, so to say, be compelled not to want to set his will against his normal interests. That is not all; then, you say, science itself will teach man (though to my mind it's a superfluous luxury) that he never has really had any caprice or will of his own, and that he himself is something of the nature of a piano-key or the stop of an organ, and that there are, besides, things called the laws of nature; so that everything he does is not done by his willing it, but is done of itself, by the laws of nature. Consequently we have only to discover these laws of nature, and man will no longer have to answer for his actions and life will become exceedingly easy for him. All human actions will then, of course, be tabulated according to these laws, mathematically, like tables of logarithms up to 108,000, and entered in an index; or, better still, there would be published certain edifying works of the nature of encyclopaedic lexicons, in which everything will be so clearly calculated and explained that there will be no more incidents or adventures in the world.

Then—this is all what you say—new economic relations will be established, all ready-made and worked out with mathematical exactitude, so that every possible question will vanish in the twinkling of an eye, simply because every possible answer to it will be provided. Then the "Palace of Crystal" will be built. Then . . . In fact, those will be halcyon days. Of course there is no guaranteeing (this is my comment) that it will not be, for instance, frightfully dull then (for what will one have to do when everything will be calculated and tabulated), but on the other hand everything will be extraordinarily rational. Of course boredom may lead you to anything. It is boredom sets one sticking golden pins into people, but all that would not matter. What is bad (this is my comment again) is that I dare say people will be thankful for the gold pins then. Man is stupid, you know, phenomenally stupid; or rather he is not at all stupid, but he is so ungrateful that you could not find another like him in all creation. I, for instance, would not be in the least surprised if all of a sudden, *à propos* of nothing, in the midst of general prosperity a gentleman with an ignoble, or rather with a reactionary and ironical, countenance were to arise and, putting his arms akimbo, say to us all: "I say, gentleman, hadn't we better kick over the whole show and scatter rationalism to the winds, simply to send these logarithms to the devil, and to enable us to live once more at our own sweet foolish will!" That again would not matter, but what is annoying is that he would be sure to find followers—such is the nature of man. And all that for the most foolish reason, which, one would think, was hardly worth mentioning: that is, that man everywhere and at all times, whoever he may be, has preferred to act as he chose and not in the least as his reason and advantage dictated. And one may choose what is contrary to one's own interests, and sometimes one *positively ought* (that is my idea). One's own free unfettered choice, one's own caprice, however wild it may be, one's own fancy worked up at times to frenzy—is that very "most advantageous advantage" which we have overlooked, which comes under no classification and against which all systems and theories are continually being shattered to atoms. And how do these wiseacres know that man wants a normal, a virtuous choice? What has made them conceive that man must want a rationally advantageous choice? What man wants is simply *independent* choice, whatever that independence may cost and wherever it may lead. And choice, of course, the devil only knows what choice.

8

"Ha! ha! ha! But you know there is no such thing as choice in reality, say what you like," you will interpose with a chuckle. "Science has succeeded in so far analysing man that we know already that choice and what is called freedom of will is nothing else than—"

Stay, gentlemen, I meant to begin with that myself I confess, I was rather frightened. I was just going to say that the devil only knows what choice depends on, and that perhaps that was a very good thing, but I remembered the teaching of science . . . and pulled myself up. And here you have begun upon it. Indeed, if there really is some day discovered a formula for all our desires and caprices—that is, an explanation of what they depend upon, by what laws they arise, how they develop, what they are aiming at in one case and in another and so on, that is a real mathematical formula—then, most likely, man will at once cease to feel desire, indeed, he will be certain to. For who would want to choose by rule? Besides, he will at once be transformed from a human being into an organ-stop or something of the sort; for what is a man without desires, without free will and without choice, if not a stop in an organ? What do you think? Let us reckon the chances—can such a thing happen or not?

"H'm!" you decide. "Our choice is usually mistaken from a false view of our advantage. We sometimes choose absolute nonsense because in our foolishness we see in that nonsense the easiest means for attaining a supposed advantage. But when all that is explained and worked out on paper (which is perfectly possible, for it is contemptible and senseless to suppose that some laws of nature man will never understand), then certainly so-called desires will no longer exist. For if a desire should come into conflict with reason we shall then reason and not desire, because it will be impossible retaining our reason to be *senseless* in our desires, and in that way knowingly act against reason and desire to injure ourselves. And as all choice and reasoning can be really calculated—because there will some day be discovered the laws of our so-called free will—so, joking apart, there may one day be something like a table constructed of them, so that we really shall choose in accordance with it. If, for instance, some day they calculate and prove to me that I made a long nose at someone because I could not help making a long nose at him and that I had to do it in that particular way, what *freedom* is left me, especially if I am a learned man and have taken my degree somewhere? Then I should be able to calculate my whole life for thirty years beforehand. In short, if this could be arranged there would be nothing left for us to do; anyway, we should have to understand that. And, in fact, we ought unweariyingly to repeat to ourselves that at such and such a time and in such and such circumstances nature does not ask our leave; that we have got to take her as she is and not fashion her to suit our fancy, and if we really aspire to formulas and tables of rules, and well, even . . . to the chemical retort, there's no help for it, we must accept the retort too, or else it will be accepted without our consent. . . ."

Yes, but here I come to a stop! Gentlemen, you must excuse me for being over-philosophical; it's the result of forty years underground! Allow me to indulge my fancy. You see, gentlemen, reason is an excellent thing, there's no disputing that, but reason is nothing but reason and satisfies only the rational side of man's nature, while will is a manifestation of the whole life, that is, of the whole human life including reason and all the impulses. And although our life, in this manifestation of it, is often worthless, yet it is life and not simply extracting square roots. Here I, for instance, quite naturally want to live, in order to satisfy all my capacities for life, and not simply my capacity for reasoning, that is, not simply one twentieth of my capacity for life. What does reason know? Reason only knows what it has succeeded in learning (some things, perhaps, it will never learn; this is a poor comfort, but why not say so frankly?) and human nature acts as a whole, with everything that is in it, consciously or unconsciously, and, even if it goes wrong, it lives. I suspect, gentlemen, that you are looking at me with compassion; you tell me again that an enlightened and developed man, such, in short, as the future man will be, cannot consciously desire anything disadvantageous to himself, that that can be proved mathematically. I thoroughly agree, it can—by mathematics. But I repeat for the hundredth time, there is one case, one only, when man may consciously, purposely, desire what is injurious to himself, what is stupid, very stupid—simply in order to have the right to desire for himself even what is very stupid and not to be bound by an obligation to desire only what is sensible. Of course, this very stupid thing, this caprice of ours, may be in reality, gentlemen, more advantageous for us than anything else on earth, especially in certain cases. And in particular it may be more advantageous than any advantage even when it does us obvious harm, and contradicts the soundest conclusions of our reason concerning our advantage—for in any circumstances it preserves for us what is most precious and most important—that is, our personality, our individuality. Some, you see, maintain that this really is the most precious thing for mankind; choice can, of course, if it chooses, be in agreement with reason; and especially if this be not abused but kept within bounds. It is profitable and sometimes even praiseworthy. But very often, and even most often, choice is utterly and stubbornly opposed to reason . . . and . . . and . . . do you know that that, too, is profitable, sometimes even praiseworthy? Gentlemen, let us suppose that man is not stupid. (Indeed one cannot refuse to suppose that, if only from the one consideration, that, if man is stupid, then who is wise?) But if he is not stupid, he is monstrously ungrateful! Phenomenally ungrateful. In fact, I believe that the best definition of man is the ungrateful biped. But that is not all, that is not his worst defect; his worst defect is his perpetual moral obliquity, perpetual—from the days of the Flood to the Schleswig-Holstein period. Moral obliquity and consequently lack of good sense; for it has long been accepted that lack of good sense is due to no other cause than moral obliquity. Put it to the test and cast your eyes upon the history of mankind. What will you see? Is it a grand spectacle? Grand, if you like. Take the Colossus of Rhodes, for instance, that's worth something. With good reason Mr. Anaevsky testifies of it that some say that it is the work of man's hands, while others maintain that it has been created by nature herself. Is it many-coloured? May be it is many-coloured, too: if one takes the dress uniforms, military and civilian, of all peoples in all ages—that alone is worth something, and if you take the undress uniforms you will never get to the end of it; no historian would be equal to the job. Is it monotonous? May be it's monotonous too: it's fighting and fighting; they are fighting now, they fought first and they fought last—you will admit, that it is almost too monotonous. In short, one may say anything about the history of the world—anything that might enter the most disordered imagination. The only thing one can't say is that it's rational. The very word sticks in one's throat. And, indeed, this is the odd thing that is continually happening: there are continually turning up in life moral and rational persons, sages and lovers of humanity who make it their object to live all their lives as morally and rationally as possible, to be, so to speak, a light to their neighbours simply in order to show them that it is possible to live morally and rationally in this world. And yet we all know that those very people sooner or later have been false to themselves, playing some queer trick, often a most unseemly one. Now I ask you: what can be expected of man since he is a being endowed with strange qualities? Shower upon him every earthly blessing, drown him in a sea of happiness, so that nothing but bubbles of bliss can be seen on the surface; give him economic prosperity, such that he should have nothing else to do but sleep, eat cakes and busy himself with the continuation of his species, and even then out of sheer ingratitude, sheer spite, man would play you some nasty trick. He would even risk his cakes and would deliberately desire the most fatal rubbish, the most uneconomical absurdity, simply to introduce into all this positive good sense his fatal fantastic element. It is just his fantastic dreams, his vulgar folly that he will desire to retain, simply in order to prove to himself—as though that were so necessary—that men still are men and not the keys of a piano, which the laws of nature threaten to control so completely that soon one will be able to desire nothing but by the calendar. And that is not all: even if man really were nothing but a piano-key, even if this were proved to him by natural science and mathematics, even then he would not become reasonable, but would purposely do something perverse out of simple ingratitude, simply to gain his point. And if he does not find means he will contrive destruction and chaos, will contrive sufferings of all sorts, only to gain his point! He will launch a curse upon the world, and as only man can curse (it is his privilege, the primary distinction between him and other animals), may be by his curse alone he will attain his object—that is, convince himself that he is a man and not a piano-key! If you say that all this, too, can be calculated and tabulated—chaos and darkness and curses, so that the mere possibility of calculating it all beforehand would stop it all, and reason would reassert itself, then man would purposely go mad in order to be rid of reason and gain his point! I believe in it, I answer for it, for the whole work of man really seems to consist in nothing but proving to himself every minute that he is a man and not a piano-key! It may be at the cost of his skin, it may be by cannibalism! And this being so, can one help being tempted to rejoice that it has not yet come off, and that desire still depends on something we don't know?

You will scream at me (that is, if you condescend to do so) that no one is touching my free will, that all they are concerned with is that my will should of itself, of its own free will, coincide with my own normal interests, with the laws of nature and arithmetic.

Good heavens, gentlemen, what sort of free will is left when we come to tabulation and arithmetic, when it will all be a case of twice two make four? Twice two makes four without my will. As if free will meant that!

9

Gentlemen, I am joking, and I know myself that my jokes are not brilliant, but you know one can take everything as a joke. I am, perhaps, jesting against the grain. Gentlemen, I am tormented by questions; answer them for me. You, for instance, want to cure men of their old habits and reform their will in accordance with science and good sense. But how do you know, not only that it is possible, but also that it is *desirable* to reform man in that way? And what leads you to the conclusion that man's inclinations *need* reforming? In short, how do you know that such a reformation will be a benefit to man? And to go to the root of the matter, why are you so positively convinced that not to act against his real normal interests guaranteed by the conclusions of reason and arithmetic is certainly always advantageous for man and must always be a law for mankind? So far, you know, this is only your supposition. It may be the law of logic, but not the law of humanity. You think, gentlemen, perhaps that I am mad? Allow me to defend myself. I agree that man is pre-eminently a creative animal, predestined to strive consciously for an object and to engage in engineering—that is, incessantly and eternally to make new roads, *wherever they may lead*. But the reason why he wants sometimes to go off at a tangent may just be that he is *predestined* to make the road, and perhaps, too, that however stupid the "direct" practical man may be, the thought sometimes will occur to him that the road almost always does lead *somewhere*, and that the destination it leads to is less important than the process of making it, and that the chief thing is to save the well-conducted child from despising engineering, and so giving way to the fatal idleness, which, as we all know, is the mother of all the vices. Man likes to make roads and to create, that is a fact beyond dispute. But why has he such a passionate love for destruction and chaos also? Tell me that! But on that point I want to say a couple of words myself. May it not be that he loves chaos and destruction (there can be no disputing that he does sometimes love it) because he is instinctively afraid of attaining his object and completing the edifice he is constructing? Who knows, perhaps he only loves that edifice from a distance, and is by no means in love with it at close quarters; perhaps he only loves building it and does not want to live in it, but will leave it, when completed, for the use of *les animaux domestiques*—such as the ants, the sheep, and so on. Now the ants have quite a different taste. They have a marvellous edifice of that pattern which endures for ever—the ant-heap.

With the ant-heap the respectable race of ants began and with the ant-heap they will probably end, which does the greatest credit to their perseverance and good sense. But man is a frivolous and incongruous creature, and perhaps, like a chess player, loves the process of the game, not the end of it. And who knows (there is no saying with certainty), perhaps the only goal on earth to which mankind is striving lies in this incessant process of attaining, in other words, in life itself, and not in the thing to be attained, which must always be expressed as a formula, as positive as twice two makes four, and such positiveness is not life, gentlemen, but is the beginning of death. Anyway, man has always been afraid of this mathematical certainty, and I am afraid of it now. Granted that man does nothing but seek that mathematical certainty, he traverses oceans, sacrifices his life in the quest, but to succeed, really to find it, dreads, I assure you. He feels that when he has found it there will be nothing for him to look for. When workmen have finished their work they do at least receive their pay, they go to the tavern, then they are taken to the police-station—and there is occupation for a week. But where can man go? Anyway, one can observe a certain awkwardness about him when he has attained such objects. He loves the process of attaining, but does not quite like to have attained, and that, of course, is very absurd. In fact, man is a comical creature; there seems to be a kind of jest in it all. But yet mathematical certainty is after all, something insufferable. Twice two makes four seems to me simply a piece of insolence. Twice two makes four is a pert coxcomb who stands with arms akimbo barring your path and spitting. I admit that twice two makes four is an excellent thing, but if we are to give everything its due, twice two makes five is sometimes a very charming thing too.

And why are you so firmly, so triumphantly, convinced that only the normal and the positive—in other words, only what is conducive to welfare—is for the advantage of man? Is not reason in error as regards advantage? Does not man, perhaps, love something besides well-being? Perhaps he is just as fond of suffering? Perhaps suffering is just as great a benefit to him as well-being? Man is sometimes extraordinarily, passionately, in love with suffering, and that is a fact. There is no need to appeal to universal history to prove that; only ask yourself, if you are a man and have lived at all. As far as my personal opinion is concerned, to care only for well-being seems to me positively ill-bred. Whether it's good or bad, it is sometimes very pleasant, too, to smash things. I hold no brief for suffering nor for well-being either. I am standing for . . . my caprice, and for its being guaranteed to me when necessary. Suffering would be out of place in vaudevilles, for instance; I know that. In the "Palace of Crystal" it is unthinkable; suffering means doubt, negation, and what would be the good of a "palace of crystal" if there could be any doubt about it? And yet I think man will never renounce real suffering, that is, destruction and chaos. Why, suffering is the sole origin of consciousness. Though I did lay it down at the beginning that consciousness is the greatest misfortune for man, yet I know man prizes it and would not give it up for any satisfaction. Consciousness, for instance, is infinitely superior to twice two makes four. Once you have mathematical certainty there is nothing left to do or to understand. There will be nothing left but to bottle up your five senses and plunge into contemplation. While if you stick to consciousness, even though the same result is attained, you can at least flog yourself at times, and that will, at any rate, liven you up. Reactionary as it is, corporal punishment is better than nothing.

10

You believe in a palace of crystal that can never be destroyed—a palace at which one will not be able to put out one's tongue or make a long nose on the sly. And perhaps that is just why I am afraid of this edifice, that it is of crystal and can never be destroyed and that one cannot put one's tongue out at it even on the sly.

You see, if it were not a palace, but a hen-house, I might creep into it to avoid getting wet, and yet I would not call the hen-house a palace out of gratitude to it for keeping me dry. You laugh and say that in such circumstances a hen-house is as good as a mansion. Yes, I answer, if one had to live simply to keep out of the rain.

But what is to be done if I have taken it into my head that that is not the only object in life, and that if one must live one had better live in a mansion? That is my choice, my desire. You will only eradicate it when you have changed my preference. Well, do change it, allure me with something else, give me another ideal. But meanwhile I will not take a hen-house for a mansion. The palace of crystal may be an idle dream, it may be that it is inconsistent with the laws of nature and that I have invented it only through my own stupidity, through the old-fashioned irrational habits of my generation. But what does it matter to me that it is inconsistent? That makes no difference since it exists in my desires, or rather exists as long as my desires exist. Perhaps you are laughing again? Laugh away; I will put up with any mockery rather than pretend that I am satisfied when I am hungry. I know, anyway, that I will not be put off with a compromise, with a recurring zero, simply because it is consistent with the laws of nature and actually exists. I will not accept as the crown of my desires a block of buildings with tenements for the poor on a lease of a thousand years, and perhaps with a sign-board of a dentist hanging out. Destroy my desires, eradicate my ideals, show me something better, and I will follow you. You will say, perhaps, that it is not worth your trouble; but in that case I can give you the same answer. We are discussing things seriously; but if you won't deign to give me your attention, I will drop your acquaintance. I can retreat into my underground hole.

But while I am alive and have desires I would rather my hand were withered off than bring one brick to such a building! Don't remind me that I have just rejected the palace of crystal for the sole reason that one cannot put out one's tongue at it. I did not say because I am so fond of putting my tongue out. Perhaps the thing I resented was, that of all your edifices there has not been one at which one could not put out one's tongue. On the contrary, I would let my tongue be cut off out of gratitude if things could be so arranged that I should lose all desire to put it out. It is not my fault that things cannot be so arranged, and that one must be satisfied with model flats. Then why am I made with such desires? Can I have been constructed simply in order to come to the conclusion that all my construction is a cheat? Can this be my whole purpose? I do not believe it.

But do you know what: I am convinced that we underground folk ought to be kept on a curb. Though we may sit forty years underground without speaking, when we do come out into the light of day and break out we talk and talk and talk. . . .

11

The long and the short of it is, gentlemen, that it is better to do nothing! Better conscious inertia! And so hurrah for underground! Though I have said that I envy the normal man to the last drop of my bile, yet I should not care to be in his place such as he is now (though I shall not cease envying him). No, no; anyway the underground life is more advantageous. There, at any rate, one can . . . Oh, but even now I am lying! I am lying because I know myself that it is not underground that is better, but something different, quite different, for which I am thirsting, but which I cannot find! Damn underground!

I will tell you another thing that would be better, and that is, if I myself believed in anything of what I have just written. I swear to you, gentlemen, there is not one thing, not one word of what I have written that I really believe. That is, I believe it, perhaps, but at the same time I feel and suspect that I am lying like a cobbler.

"Then why have you written all this?" you will say to me. "I ought to put you underground for forty years without anything to do and then come to you in your cellar, to find out what stage you have reached! How can a man be left with nothing to do for forty years?"

"Isn't that shameful, isn't that humiliating?" you will say, perhaps, wagging your heads contemptuously. "You thirst for life and try to settle the problems of life by a logical tangle. And how persistent, how insolent are your sallies, and at the same time what a scare you are in! You talk nonsense and are pleased with it; you say impudent things and are in continual alarm and apologising for them. You declare that you are afraid of nothing and at the same time try to ingratiate yourself in our good opinion. You declare that you are gnashing your teeth and at the same time you try to be witty so as to amuse us. You know that your witticisms are not witty, but you are evidently well satisfied with their literary value. You may, perhaps, have really suffered, but you have no respect for your own suffering. You may have sincerity, but you have no modesty; out of the pettiest vanity you expose your sincerity to publicity and ignominy. You doubtlessly mean to say something, but hide your last word through fear, because you have not the resolution to utter it, and only have a cowardly impudence. You boast of consciousness, but you are not sure of your ground, for though your mind works, yet your heart is darkened and corrupt, and you cannot have a full, genuine consciousness without a pure heart. And how intrusive you are, how you insist and grimace! Lies, lies, lies!"

Of course I have myself made up all the things you say. That, too, is from underground. I have been for forty years listening to you through a crack under the floor. I have invented them myself, there was nothing else I could invent. It is no wonder that I have learned it by heart and it has taken a literary form. . . .

But can you really be so credulous as to think that I will print all this and give it to you to read too? And another problem: why do I call you "gentlemen," why do I address you as though you really were my readers? Such confessions as I intend to make are never printed nor given to other people to read. Anyway, I am not strong-minded enough for that, and I don't see why I should be. But you see a fancy has occurred to me and I want to realise it at all costs. Let me explain.

Every man has reminiscences which he would not tell to everyone, but only to his friends. He has other matters in his mind which he would not reveal even to his friends, but only to himself, and that in secret. But there are other things which a man is afraid to tell even to himself, and every decent man has a number of such things stored away in his mind. The more decent he is, the greater the number of such things in his mind. Anyway, I have only lately determined to remember some of my early adventures. Till now I have always avoided them, even with a certain uneasiness. Now, when I am not only recalling them, but have actually decided to write an account of them, I want to try the experiment whether one can, even with oneself, be perfectly open and not take fright at the whole truth. I will observe, in parenthesis, that Heine says that a true autobiography is almost an impossibility, and that man is bound to lie about himself. He considers that Rousseau certainly told lies about himself in his confessions, and even intentionally lied, out of vanity. I am convinced that Heine is right; I quite understand how sometimes one may, out of sheer vanity, attribute regular crimes to oneself, and indeed I can very well conceive that kind of vanity. But Heine judged of people who made their confessions to the public. I write only for myself, and I wish to declare once and for all that if I write as though I were addressing readers, that is simply because it is easier for me to write in that form. It is a form, an empty form—I shall never have readers. I have made this plain already . . .

I don't wish to be hampered by any restrictions in the compilation of my notes. I shall not attempt any system or method. I will jot things down as I remember them.

But here, perhaps, someone will catch at the word and ask me: if you really don't reckon on readers, why do you make such compacts with yourself—and on paper too—that is, that you won't attempt any system or method, that you jot things down as you remember them, and so on, and so on? Why are you explaining? Why do you apologise?

Well, there it is, I answer.

There is a whole psychology in all this, though. Perhaps it is simply that I am a coward. And perhaps that I purposely imagine an audience before me in order that I may be more dignified while I write. There are perhaps thousands of reasons. Again, what is my object precisely in writing? If it is not for the benefit of the public why should I not simply recall these incidents in my own mind without putting them on paper?

Quite so; but yet it is more imposing on paper. There is something more impressive in it; I shall be better able to criticise myself and improve my style. Besides, I shall perhaps obtain actual relief from writing. Today, for instance, I am particularly oppressed by one memory of a distant past. It came back vividly to my mind a few days ago, and has remained haunting me like an annoying tune that one cannot get rid of. And yet I must get rid of it somehow. I have hundreds of such reminiscences; but at times some one stands out from the hundred and oppresses me. For some reason I believe that if I write it down I should get rid of it. Why not try?

Besides, I am bored, and I never have anything to do. Writing will be a sort of work. They say work makes man kind-hearted and honest. Well, here is a chance for me, anyway.

Snow is falling today, yellow and dingy. It fell yesterday, too, and a few days ago. I fancy it is the wet snow that has reminded me of that incident which I cannot shake off now. And so let it be a story *à propos* of the falling snow.

PART TWO

À Propos of the Wet Snow

PART TWO

A Propos of
the Wet Snow

When from dark error's subjugation
My words of passionate exhortation
Had wrenched thy fainting spirit free;
And writhing prone in thine affliction
Thou didst recall with malediction
The vice that had encompassed thee:
And when thy slumbering conscience, fretting
By recollection's torturing flame,
Thou didst reveal the hideous setting
Of thy life's current ere I came:
When suddenly I saw thee sicken,
And weeping, hide thine anguished face,
Revolted, maddened, horror-stricken,
At memories of foul disgrace.

Nekrassov (*translated by Juliet Soskice*)

1

At that time I was only twenty-four. My life was even then gloomy, ill-regulated, and as solitary as that of a savage. I made friends with no one and positively avoided talking, and buried myself more and more in my hole. At work in the office I never looked at anyone, and was perfectly well aware that my companions looked upon me, not only as a queer fellow, but even looked upon me—I always fancied this—with a sort of loathing. I sometimes wondered why it was that nobody except me fancied that he was looked upon with aversion? One of the clerks had a most repulsive, pock-marked face, which looked positively villainous. I believe I should not have dared to look at anyone with such an unsightly countenance. Another had such a very dirty old uniform that there was an unpleasant odour in his proximity. Yet not one of these gentlemen showed the slightest self-consciousness—either about their clothes or their countenance or their character in any way. Neither of them ever imagined that they were looked at with repulsion; if they had imagined it they would not have minded—so long as their superiors did not look at them in that way. It is clear to me now that, owing to my unbounded vanity and to the high standard I set for myself, I often looked at myself with furious discontent, which verged on loathing, and so I inwardly attributed the same feeling to everyone. I hated my face, for instance: I thought it disgusting, and even suspected that there was something base in my expression, and so every day when I turned up at the office I tried to behave as independently as possible, and to assume a lofty expression, so that I might not be suspected of being abject. "My face may be ugly," I thought, "but let it be lofty, expressive, and, above all, *extremely* intelligent." But I was positively and painfully certain that it was impossible for my countenance ever to express those qualities. And what was worst of all, I thought it actually stupid looking, and I would have been quite satisfied if I could have looked intelligent. In fact, I would even have put up with looking base if, at the same time, my face could have been thought strikingly intelligent.

Of course, I hated my fellow clerks one and all, and I despised them all, yet at the same time I was, as it were, afraid of them. In fact, it happened at times that I thought more highly of them than of myself. It somehow happened quite suddenly that I alternated between despising them and thinking them superior to myself. A cultivated and decent man cannot be vain without setting a fearfully high standard for himself, and without despising and almost hating himself at certain moments. But whether I despised them or thought them superior I dropped my eyes almost every time I met anyone. I even made experiments whether I could face so and so's looking at me, and I was always the first to drop my eyes. This worried me to distraction. I had a sickly dread, too, of being ridiculous, and so had a slavish passion for the conventional in everything external. I loved to fall into the common rut, and had a whole-hearted terror of any kind of eccentricity in myself. But how could I live up to it? I was morbidly sensitive as a man of our age should be. They were all stupid, and as like one another as so many sheep. Perhaps I was the only one in the office who fancied that I was a coward and a slave, and I fancied it just because I was more highly developed. But it was not only that I fancied it, it really was so. I was a coward and a slave. I say this without the slightest embarrassment. Every decent man of our age must be a coward and a slave. That is his normal condition. Of that I am firmly persuaded. He is made and constructed to that very end. And not only at the present time owing to some casual circumstances, but always, at all times, a decent man is bound to be a coward and a slave. It is the law of nature for all decent people all over the earth. If anyone of them happens to be valiant about something, he need not be comforted nor carried away by that; he would show the white feather just the same before something else. That is how it invariably and inevitably ends. Only donkeys and mules are valiant, and they only till they are pushed up to the wall. It is not worth while to pay attention to them for they really are of no consequence.

Another circumstance, too, worried me in those days: that there was no one like me and I was unlike anyone else. "I am alone and they are *everyone*," I thought—and pondered.

From that it is evident that I was still a youngster.

The very opposite sometimes happened. It was loathsome sometimes to go to the office; things reached such a point that I often came home ill. But all at once, *à propos* of nothing, there would come a phase of scepticism and indifference (everything happened in phases to me), and I would laugh myself at my intolerance and fastidiousness, I would reproach myself with being *romantic*. At one time I was unwilling to speak to anyone, while at other times I would not only talk, but go to the length of contemplating making friends with them. All my fastidiousness would suddenly, for no rhyme or reason, vanish. Who knows, perhaps I never had really had it, and it had simply been affected, and got out of books. I have not decided that question even now. Once I quite made friends with them, visited their homes, played preference, drank vodka, talked of promotions. . . . But here let me make a digression.

We Russians, speaking generally, have never had those foolish transcendental "romantics"—German, and still more French—on whom nothing produces any effect; if there were an earthquake, if all France perished at the barricades, they would still be the same, they would not even have the decency to affect a change, but would still go on singing their transcendental songs to the hour of their death, because they are fools. We, in Russia, have no fools; that is well known. That is what distinguishes us from foreign lands. Consequently these transcendental natures are not found amongst us in their pure form. The idea that they are is due to our "realistic" journalists and critics of that day, always on the look out for Kostanzhoglos and Uncle Pyotr Ivanitchs and foolishly accepting them as our ideal; they have slandered our romantics, taking them for the same transcendental sort as in Germany or France. On the contrary, the characteristics of our "romantics" are absolutely and directly opposed to the transcendental European type, and no European standard can be applied to them. (Allow me to make use of this word "romantic"—an old-fashioned and much respected word which has done good service and is familiar to all.) The characteristics of our romantic are to understand everything, *to see everything and to see it often incomparably more clearly than our most realistic minds see it;* to refuse to accept anyone or anything, but at the same time not to despise anything; to give way, to yield, from policy; never to lose sight of a useful practical object (such as rent-free quarters at the government expense, pensions, decorations), to keep their eye on that object through all the enthusiasms and volumes of lyrical poems, and at the same time to preserve "the sublime and the beautiful" inviolate within them to the hour of their death, and to preserve themselves also, incidentally, like some precious jewel wrapped in cotton wool if only for the benefit of "the sublime and the beautiful." Our "romantic" is a man of great breadth and the greatest rogue of all our rogues, I assure you. . . . I can assure you from experience, indeed. Of course, that is, if he is intelligent. But what am I saying! The romantic is always intelligent, and I only meant to observe that although we have had foolish romantics they don't count, and they were only so because in the flower of their youth they degenerated into Germans, and to preserve their precious jewel more comfortably, settled somewhere out there—by preference in Weimar or the Black Forest.

I, for instance, genuinely despised my official work and did not openly abuse it simply because I was in it myself and got a salary for it. Anyway, take note, I did not openly abuse it. Our romantic would rather go out of his mind—a thing, however, which very rarely happens—than take to open abuse, unless he had some other career in view; and he is never kicked out. At most, they would take him to the lunatic asylum as "the King of Spain" if he should go very mad. But it is only the thin, fair people who go out of their minds in Russia. Innumerable "romantics" attain later in life to considerable rank in the service. Their many-sidedness is remarkable! And what a faculty they have for the most contradictory sensations! I was comforted by this thought even in those days, and I am of the same opinion now. That is why there are so many "broad natures" among us who never lose their ideal even in the depths of degradation; and though they never stir a finger for their ideal, though they are arrant thieves and knaves, yet they tearfully cherish their first ideal and are extraordinarily honest at heart. Yes, it is only among us that the most incorrigible rogue can be absolutely and loftily honest at heart without in the least ceasing to be a rogue. I repeat, our romantics, frequently, become such accomplished rascals (I use the term "rascals" affectionately), suddenly display such a sense of reality and practical knowledge that their bewildered superiors and the public generally can only ejaculate in amazement.

Their many-sidedness is really amazing, and goodness knows what it may develop into later on, and what the future has in store for us. It is not a poor material! I do not say this from any foolish or boastful patriotism. But I feel sure that you are again imagining that I am joking. Or perhaps it's just the contrary and you are convinced that I really think so. Anyway, gentlemen, I shall welcome both views as an honour and a special favour. And do forgive my digression.

I did not, of course, maintain friendly relations with my comrades and soon was at loggerheads with them, and in my youth and inexperience I even gave up bowing to them, as though I had cut off all relations. That, however, only happened to me once. As a rule, I was always alone.

In the first place I spent most of my time at home, reading. I tried to stifle all that was continually seething within me by means of external impressions. And the only external means I had was reading. Reading, of course, was a great help—exciting me, giving me pleasure and pain. But at times it bored me fearfully. One longed for movement in spite of everything, and I plunged all at once into dark, underground, loathsome vice of the pettiest kind. My wretched passions were acute, smarting, from my continual, sickly irritability I had hysterical impulses, with tears and convulsions. I had no resource except reading, that is, there was nothing in my surroundings which I could respect and which attracted me. I was overwhelmed with depression, too; I had an hysterical craving for incongruity and for contrast, and so I took to vice. I have not said all this to justify myself. . . . But, no! I am lying. I did want to justify myself. I make that little observation for my own benefit, gentlemen. I don't want to lie. I vowed to myself I would not.

And so, furtively, timidly, in solitude, at night, I indulged in filthy vice, with a feeling of shame which never deserted me, even at the most loathsome moments, and which at such moments nearly made me curse. Already even then I had my underground world in my soul. I was fearfully afraid of being seen, of being met, of being recognised. I visited various obscure haunts.

One night as I was passing a tavern I saw through a lighted window some gentlemen fighting with billiard cues, and saw one of them thrown out of the window. At other times I should have felt very much disgusted, but I was in such a mood at the time, that I actually envied the gentleman thrown out of the window—and I envied him so much that I even went into the tavern and into the billiard-room. "Perhaps," I thought, "I'll have a fight, too, and they'll throw me out of the window."

I was not drunk—but what is one to do—depression will drive a man to such a pitch of hysteria? But nothing happened. It seemed that I was not even equal to being thrown out of the window and I went away without having my fight.

An officer put me in my place from the first moment.

I was standing by the billiard-table and in my ignorance blocking up the way, and he wanted to pass; he took me by the shoulders and without a word—without a warning or explanation—moved me from where I was standing to another spot and passed by as though he had not noticed me. I could have forgiven blows, but I could not forgive his having moved me without noticing me.

Devil knows what I would have given for a real regular quarrel—a more decent, a more *literary* one, so to speak. I had been treated like a fly. This officer was over six foot, while I was a spindly little fellow. But the quarrel was in my hands. I had only to protest and I certainly would have been thrown out of the window. But I changed my mind and preferred to beat a resentful retreat.

I went out of the tavern straight home, confused and troubled, and the next night I went out again with the same lewd intentions, still more furtively, abjectly and miserably than before, as it were, with tears in my eyes—but still I did go out again. Don't imagine, though, it was cowardice made me slink away from the officer; I never have been a coward at heart, though I have always been a coward in action. Don't be in a hurry to laugh—I assure you I can explain it all.

Oh, if only that officer had been one of the sort who would consent to fight a duel! But no, he was one of those gentlemen (alas, long extinct!) who preferred fighting with cues or, like Gogol's Lieutenant Pirogov, appealing to the police. They did not fight duels and would have thought a duel with a civilian like me an utterly unseemly procedure in any case—and they looked upon the duel altogether as something impossible, something free-thinking and French. But they were quite ready to bully, especially when they were over six foot.

I did not slink away through cowardice, but through an unbounded vanity. I was afraid not of his six foot, not of getting a sound thrashing and being thrown out of the window; I should have had physical courage enough, I assure you; but I had not the moral courage. What I was afraid of was that everyone present, from the insolent marker down to the lowest little stinking, pimply clerk in a greasy collar, would jeer at me and fail to understand when I began to protest and to address them in literary language. For of the point of honour—not of honour, but of the point of honour (*point d'honneur*)—one cannot speak among us except in literary language. You can't allude to the "point of honour" in ordinary language. I was fully convinced (the sense of reality, in spite of all my romanticism!) that they would all simply split their sides with laughter, and that the officer would not simply beat me, that is, without insulting me, but would certainly prod me in the back with his knee, kick me round the billiard-table, and only then perhaps have pity and drop me out of the window.

Of course, this trivial incident could not with me end in that. I often met that officer afterwards in the street and noticed him very carefully. I am not quite sure whether he recognised me, I imagine not; I judge from certain signs. But I—I stared at him with spite and hatred and so it went on . . . for several years! My resentment grew even deeper with years. At first I began making stealthy inquiries about this officer. It was difficult for me to do so, for I knew no one. But one day I heard someone shout his surname in the street as I was following him at a distance, as though I were tied to him—and so I learnt his surname. Another time I followed him to his flat, and for ten kopecks learned from the porter where he lived, on which storey, whether he lived alone or with others, and so on—in fact, everything one could learn from a porter. One morning, though I had never tried my hand with the pen, it suddenly occurred to me to write a satire on this officer in the form of a novel which would unmask his villainy. I wrote the novel with relish. I did unmask his villainy, I even exaggerated it; at first I so altered his surname that it could easily be recognised, but on second thoughts I changed it, and sent the story to the *Otetchestvenniya Zapiski*. But at that time such attacks were not the fashion and my story was not printed. That was a great vexation to me.

Sometimes I was positively choked with resentment. At last I determined to challenge my enemy to a duel. I composed a splendid, charming letter to him, imploring him to apologise to me, and hinting rather plainly at a duel in case of refusal. The letter was so composed that if the officer had had the least understanding of the sublime and the beautiful he would certainly have flung himself on my neck and have offered me his friendship. And how fine that would have been! How we should have got on together! "He could have shielded me with his higher rank, while I could have improved his mind with my culture, and, well . . . my ideas, and all sorts of things might have happened." Only fancy, this was two years after his insult to me, and my challenge would have been a ridiculous anachronism, in spite of all the ingenuity of my letter in disguising and explaining away the anachronism. But, thank God (to this day I thank the Almighty with tears in my eyes) I did not send the letter to him. Cold shivers run down my back when I think of what might have happened if I had sent it.

And all at once I revenged myself in the simplest way, by a stroke of genius! A brilliant thought suddenly dawned upon me. Sometimes on holidays I used to stroll along the sunny side of the Nevsky about four o'clock in the afternoon. Though it was hardly a stroll so much as a series of innumerable miseries, humiliations and resentments; but no doubt that was just what I wanted. I used to wriggle along in a most unseemly fashion, like an eel, continually moving aside to make way for generals, for officers of the guards and the hussars, or for ladies. At such minutes there used to be a convulsive twinge at my heart, and I used to feel hot all down my back at the mere thought of the wretchedness of my attire, of the wretchedness and abjectness of my little scurrying figure. This was a regular martyrdom, a continual, intolerable humiliation at the thought, which passed into an incessant and direct sensation, that I was a mere fly in the eyes of all this world, a nasty, disgusting fly—more intelligent, more highly developed, more refined in feeling than any of them, of course—but a fly that was continually making way for everyone, insulted and injured by everyone. Why I inflicted this torture upon myself, why I went to the Nevsky, I don't know. I felt simply drawn there at every possible opportunity.

Already then I began to experience a rush of the enjoyment of which I spoke in the first chapter. After my affair with the officer I felt even more drawn there than before: it was on the Nevsky that I met him most frequently, there I could admire him. He, too, went there chiefly on holidays, He, too, turned out of his path for generals and persons of high rank, and he too, wriggled between them like an eel; but people, like me, or even better dressed than me, he simply walked over; he made straight for them as though there was nothing but empty space before him, and never, under any circumstances, turned aside. I gloated over my resentment watching him and . . . always resentfully made way for him. It exasperated me that even in the street I could not be on an even footing with him.

"Why must you invariably be the first to move aside?" I kept asking myself in hysterical rage, waking up sometimes at three o'clock in the morning. "Why is it you and not he? There's no regulation about it; there's no written law. Let the making way be equal as it usually is when refined people meet; he moves half-way and you move half-way; you pass with mutual respect."

But that never happened, and I always moved aside, while he did not even notice my making way for him. And lo and behold a bright idea dawned upon me! "What," I thought, "if I meet him and don't move on one side? What if I don't move aside on purpose, even if I knock up against him? How would that be?" This audacious idea took such a hold on me that it gave me no peace. I was dreaming of it continually, horribly, and I purposely went more frequently to the Nevsky in order to picture more vividly how I should do it when I did do it. I was delighted. This intention seemed to me more and more practical and possible.

"Of course I shall not really push him," I thought, already more good-natured in my joy. "I will simply not turn aside, will run up against him, not very violently, but just shouldering each other—just as much as decency permits. I will push against him just as much as he pushes against me." At last I made up my mind completely. But my preparations took a great deal of time. To begin with, when I carried out my plan I should need to be looking rather more decent, and so I had to think of my get-up. "In case of emergency, if, for instance, there were any sort of public scandal (and the public there is of the most *recherché*: the Countess walks there; Prince D. walks there; all the literary world is there), I must be well dressed; that inspires respect and of itself puts us on an equal footing in the eyes of the society."

With this object I asked for some of my salary in advance, and bought at Tchurkin's a pair of black gloves and a decent hat. Black gloves seemed to me both more dignified and *bon ton* than the lemon-coloured ones which I had contemplated at first. "The colour is too gaudy, it looks as though one were trying to be conspicuous," and I did not take the lemon-coloured ones. I had got ready long beforehand a good shirt, with white bone studs; my overcoat was the only thing that held me back. The coat in itself was a very good one, it kept me warm; but it was wadded and it had a raccoon collar which was the height of vulgarity. I had to change the collar at any sacrifice, and to have a beaver one like an officer's. For this purpose I began visiting the Gostiny Dvor and after several attempts I pitched upon a piece of cheap German beaver. Though these German beavers soon grow shabby and look wretched, yet at first they look exceedingly well, and I only needed it for the occasion. I asked the price; even so, it was too expensive. After thinking it over thoroughly I decided to sell my raccoon collar. The rest of the money—a considerable sum for me, I decided to borrow from Anton Antonitch Syetotchkin, my immediate superior, an unassuming person, though grave and judicious. He never lent money to anyone, but I had, on entering the service, been specially recommended to him by an important personage who had got me my berth. I was horribly worried. To borrow from Anton Antonitch seemed to me monstrous and shameful. I did not sleep for two or three nights. Indeed, I did not sleep well at that time, I was in a fever; I had a vague sinking at my heart or else a sudden throbbing, throbbing, throbbing! Anton Antonitch was surprised at first, then he frowned, then he reflected, and did after all lend me the money, receiving from me a written authorisation to take from my salary a fortnight later the sum that he had lent me.

In this way everything was at last ready. The handsome beaver replaced the mean-looking raccoon, and I began by degrees to get to work. It would never have done to act offhand, at random; the plan had to be carried out skilfully, by degrees. But I must confess that after many efforts I began to despair: we simply could not run into each other. I made every preparation, I was quite determined—it seemed as though we should run into one another directly—and before I knew what I was doing I had stepped aside for him again and he had passed without noticing me. I even prayed as I approached him that God would grant me determination. One time I had made up my mind thoroughly, but it ended in my stumbling and falling at his feet because at the very last instant when I was six inches from him my courage failed me. He very calmly stepped over me, while I flew on one side like a ball. That night I was ill again, feverish and delirious.

And suddenly it ended most happily. The night before I had made up my mind not to carry out my fatal plan and to abandon it all, and with that object I went to the Nevsky for the last time, just to see how I would abandon it all. Suddenly, three paces from my enemy, I unexpectedly made up my mind—I closed my eyes, and we ran full tilt, shoulder to shoulder, against one another! I did not budge an inch and passed him on a perfectly equal footing! He did not even look round and pretended not to notice it; but he was only pretending, I am convinced of that. I am convinced of that to this day! Of course, I got the worst of it—he was stronger, but that was not the point. The point was that I had attained my object, I had kept up my dignity, I had not yielded a step, and had put myself publicly on an equal social footing with him. I returned home feeling that I was fully avenged for everything. I was delighted. I was triumphant and sang Italian arias. Of course, I will not describe to you what happened to me three days later; if you have read my first chapter you can guess for yourself. The officer was afterwards transferred; I have not seen him now for fourteen years. What is the dear fellow doing now? Whom is he walking over?

2

But the period of my dissipation would end and I always felt very sick afterwards. It was followed by remorse—I tried to drive it away; I felt too sick. By degrees, however, I grew used to that too. I grew used to everything, or rather I voluntarily resigned myself to enduring it. But I had a means of escape that reconciled everything—that was to find refuge in "the sublime and the beautiful," in dreams, of course. I was a terrible dreamer, I would dream for three months on end, tucked away in my corner, and you may believe me that at those moments I had no resemblance to the gentleman who, in the perturbation of his chicken heart, put a collar of German beaver on his great-coat. I suddenly became a hero. I would not have admitted my six-foot lieutenant even if he had called on me. I could not even picture him before me then. What were my dreams and how I could satisfy myself with them—it is hard to say now, but at the time I was satisfied with them. Though, indeed, even now, I am to some extent satisfied with them. Dreams were particularly sweet and vivid after a spell of dissipation; they came with remorse and with tears, with curses and transports.

There were moments of such positive intoxication, of such happiness, that there was not the faintest trace of irony within me, on my honour. I had faith, hope, love. I believed blindly at such times that by some miracle, by some external circumstance, all this would suddenly open out, expand; that suddenly a vista of suitable activity—beneficent, good, and, above all, *ready made* (what sort of activity I had no idea, but the great thing was that it should be all ready for me)—would rise up before me—and I should come out into the light of day, almost riding a white horse and crowned with laurel. Anything but the foremost place I could not conceive for myself, and for that very reason I quite contentedly occupied the lowest in reality. Either to be a hero or to grovel in the mud—there was nothing between. That was my ruin, for when I was in the mud I comforted myself with the thought that at other times I was a hero, and the hero was a cloak for the mud: for an ordinary man it was shameful to defile himself, but a hero was too lofty to be utterly defiled, and so he might defile himself. It is worth noting that these attacks of the "sublime and the beautiful" visited me even during the period of dissipation and just at the times when I was touching the bottom. They came in separate spurts, as though reminding me of themselves, but did not banish the dissipation by their appearance. On the contrary, they seemed to add a zest to it by contrast, and were only sufficiently present to serve as an appetising sauce. That sauce was made up of contradictions and sufferings, of agonising inward analysis, and all these pangs and pin-pricks gave a certain piquancy, even a significance to my dissipation—in fact, completely answered the purpose of an appetising sauce. There was a certain depth of meaning in it. And I could hardly have resigned myself to the simple, vulgar, direct debauchery of a clerk and have endured all the filthiness of it. What could have allured me about it then and have drawn me at night into the street? No, I had a lofty way of getting out of it all.

And what loving-kindness, oh Lord, what loving-kindness I felt at times in those dreams of mine! in those "flights into the sublime and the beautiful"; though it was fantastic love, though it was never applied to anything human in reality, yet there was so much of this love that one did not feel afterwards even the impulse to apply it in reality; that would have been superfluous. Everything, however, passed satisfactorily by a lazy and fascinating transition into the sphere of art, that is, into the beautiful forms of life, lying ready, largely stolen from the poets and novelists and adapted to all sorts of needs and uses. I, for instance, was triumphant over everyone; everyone, of course, was in dust and ashes, and was forced spontaneously to recognise my superiority, and I forgave them all. I was a poet and a grand gentleman, I fell in love; I came in for countless millions and immediately devoted them to humanity, and at the same time I confessed before all the people my shameful deeds, which, of course, were not merely shameful, but had in them much that was "sublime and beautiful" something in the Manfred style. Everyone would kiss me and weep (what idiots they would be if they did not), while I should go barefoot and hungry preaching new ideas and fighting a victorious Austerlitz against the obscurantists. Then the band would play a march, an amnesty would be declared, the Pope would agree to retire from Rome to Brazil; then there would be a ball for the whole of Italy at the Villa Borghese on the shores of Lake Como, Lake Como being for that purpose transferred to the neighbourhood of Rome; then would come a scene in the bushes, and so on, and so on—as though you did not know all about it? You will say that it is vulgar and contemptible to drag all this into public after all the tears and transports which I have myself confessed. But why is it contemptible? Can you imagine that I am ashamed of it all, and that it was stupider than anything in your life, gentlemen? And I can assure you that some of these fancies were by no means badly composed. . . . It did not all happen on the shores of Lake Como. And yet you are right—it really is vulgar and contemptible. And most contemptible of all it is that now I am attempting to justify myself to you. And even more contemptible than that is my making this remark now. But that's enough, or there will be no end to it; each step will be more contemptible than the last. . . .

I could never stand more than three months of dreaming at a time without feeling an irresistible desire to plunge into society. To plunge into society meant to visit my superior at the office, Anton Antonitch Syetotchkin. He was the only permanent acquaintance I have had in my life, and I wonder at the fact myself now. But I only went to see him when that phase came over me, and when my dreams had reached such a point of bliss that it became essential at once to embrace my fellows and all mankind; and for that purpose I needed, at least, one human being, actually existing. I had to call on Anton Antonitch, however, on Tuesday—his at-home day;

so I had always to time my passionate desire to embrace humanity so that it might fall on a Tuesday.

This Anton Antonitch lived on the fourth storey in a house in Five Corners, in four low-pitched rooms, one smaller than the other, of a particularly frugal and sallow appearance. He had two daughters and their aunt, who used to pour out the tea. Of the daughters one was thirteen and another fourteen, they both had snub noses, and I was awfully shy of them because they were always whispering and giggling together. The master of the house usually sat in his study on a leather couch in front of the table with some grey-headed gentleman, usually a colleague from our office or some other department. I never saw more than two or three visitors there, always the same. They talked about the excise duty; about business in the senate, about salaries, about promotions, about His Excellency, and the best means of pleasing him, and so on. I had the patience to sit like a fool beside these people for four hours at a stretch, listening to them without knowing what to say to them or venturing to say a word. I became stupefied, several times I felt myself perspiring, I was overcome by a sort of paralysis; but this was pleasant and good for me. On returning home I deferred for a time my desire to embrace all mankind.

I had however one other acquaintance of a sort, Simonov, who was an old schoolfellow. I had a number of schoolfellows, indeed, in Petersburg, but I did not associate with them and had even given up nodding to them in the street. I believe I had transferred into the department I was in simply to avoid their company and to cut off all connection with my hateful childhood. Curses on that school and all those terrible years of penal servitude! In short, I parted from my schoolfellows as soon as I got out into the world. There were two or three left to whom I nodded in the street. One of them was Simonov, who had in no way been distinguished at school, was of a quiet and equable disposition; but I discovered in him a certain independence of character and even honesty I don't even suppose that he was particularly stupid. I had at one time spent some rather soulful moments with him, but these had not lasted long and had somehow been suddenly clouded over. He was evidently uncomfortable at these reminiscences, and was, I fancy, always afraid that I might take up the same tone again. I suspected that he had an aversion for me, but still I went on going to see him, not being quite certain of it.

And so on one occasion, unable to endure my solitude and knowing that as it was Thursday Anton Antonitch's door would be closed, I thought of Simonov. Climbing up to his fourth storey I was thinking that the man disliked me and that it was a mistake to go and see him. But as it always happened that such reflections impelled me, as though purposely, to put myself into a false position, I went in. It was almost a year since I had last seen Simonov.

3

I found two of my old schoolfellows with him. They seemed to be discussing an important matter. All of them took scarcely any notice of my entrance, which was strange, for I had not met them for years. Evidently they looked upon me as something on the level of a common fly. I had not been treated like that even at school, though they all hated me. I knew, of course, that they must despise me now for my lack of success in the service, and for my having let myself sink so low, going about badly dressed and so on—which seemed to them a sign of my incapacity and insignificance. But I had not expected such contempt. Simonov was positively surprised at my turning up. Even in old days he had always seemed surprised at my coming. All this disconcerted me: I sat down, feeling rather miserable, and began listening to what they were saying.

They were engaged in warm and earnest conversation about a farewell dinner which they wanted to arrange for the next day to a comrade of theirs called Zverkov, an officer in the army, who was going away to a distant province. This Zverkov had been all the time at school with me too. I had begun to hate him particularly in the upper forms. In the lower forms he had simply been a pretty, playful boy whom everybody liked. I had hated him, however, even in the lower forms, just because he was a pretty and playful boy. He was always bad at his lessons and got worse and worse as he went on; however, he left with a good certificate, as he had powerful interests. During his last year at school he came in for an estate of two hundred serfs, and as almost all of us were poor he took up a swaggering tone among us. He was vulgar in the extreme, but at the same time he was a good-natured fellow, even in his swaggering. In spite of superficial, fantastic and sham notions of honour and dignity, all but very few of us positively grovelled before Zverkov, and the more so the more he swaggered. And it was not from any interested motive that they grovelled, but simply because he had been favoured by the gifts of nature. Moreover, it was, as it were, an accepted idea among us that Zverkov was a specialist in regard to tact and the social graces. This last fact particularly infuriated me. I hated the abrupt self-confident tone of his voice, his admiration of his own witticisms, which were often frightfully stupid, though he was bold in his language; I hated his handsome, but stupid face (for which I would, however, have gladly exchanged my intelligent one), and the free-and-easy military manners in fashion in the "'forties." I hated the way in which he used to talk of his future conquests of women (he did not venture to begin his attack upon women until he had the epaulettes of an officer, and was looking forward to them with impatience), and boasted of the duels he would constantly be fighting. I remember how I, invariably so taciturn, suddenly fastened upon Zverkov, when one day talking at a leisure moment with his schoolfellows of his future relations with the fair sex, and growing as sportive as a puppy in the sun, he all at once declared that he would not leave a single village girl on his estate unnoticed, that that was his *droit de seigneur*, and that if the peasants dared to protest he would have them all flogged and double the tax on them, the bearded rascals. Our servile rabble applauded, but I attacked him, not from compassion for the girls and their fathers, but simply because they were applauding such an insect. I got the better of him on that occasion, but though Zverkov was stupid he was lively and impudent, and so laughed it off, and in such a way that my victory was not really complete; the laugh was on his side. He got the better of me on several occasions afterwards, but without malice, jestingly, casually.

I remained angrily and contemptuously silent and would not answer him. When we left school he made advances to me; I did not rebuff them, for I was flattered, but we soon parted and quite naturally. Afterwards I heard of his barrack-room success as a lieutenant, and of the fast life he was leading. Then there came other rumours—of his successes in the service. By then he had taken to cutting me in the street, and I suspected that he was afraid of compromising himself by greeting a personage as insignificant as me. I saw him once in the theatre, in the third tier of boxes. By then he was wearing shoulder-straps. He was twisting and twirling about, ingratiating himself with the daughters of an ancient General. In three years he had gone off considerably, though he was still rather handsome and adroit. One could see that by the time he was thirty he would be corpulent. So it was to this Zverkov that my schoolfellows were going to give a dinner on his departure. They had kept up with him for those three years, though privately they did not consider themselves on an equal footing with him, I am convinced of that.

Of Simonov's two visitors, one was Ferfitchkin, a Russianised German—a little fellow with the face of a monkey, a blockhead who was always deriding everyone, a very bitter enemy of mine from our days in the lower forms—a vulgar, impudent, swaggering fellow, who affected a most sensitive feeling of personal honour, though, of course, he was a wretched little coward at heart. He was one of those worshippers of Zverkov who made up to the latter from interested motives, and often borrowed money from him. Simonov's other visitor, Trudolyubov, was a person in no way remarkable—a tall young fellow, in the army, with a cold face, fairly honest, though he worshipped success of every sort, and was only capable of thinking of promotion. He was some sort of distant relation of Zverkov's, and this, foolish as it seems, gave him a certain importance among us. He always thought me of no consequence whatever; his behaviour to me, though not quite courteous, was tolerable.

"Well, with seven roubles each," said Trudolyubov, "twenty-one roubles between the three of us, we ought to be able to get a good dinner. Zverkov, of course, won't pay."

"Of course not, since we are inviting him," Simonov decided.

"Can you imagine," Ferfitchkin interrupted hotly and conceitedly, like some insolent flunkey boasting of his master the General's decorations, "can you imagine that Zverkov will let us pay alone? He will accept from delicacy, but he will order half a dozen bottles of champagne."

"Do we want half a dozen for the four of us?" observed Trudolyubov, taking notice only of the half dozen.

"So the three of us, with Zverkov for the fourth, twenty-one roubles, at the Hôtel de Paris at five o'clock tomorrow," Simonov, who had been asked to make the arrangements, concluded finally.

"How twenty-one roubles?" I asked in some agitation, with a show of being offended; "if you count me it will not be twenty-one, but twenty-eight roubles."

It seemed to me that to invite myself so suddenly and unexpectedly would be positively graceful, and that they would all be conquered at once and would look at me with respect.

"Do you want to join, too?" Simonov observed, with no appearance of pleasure, seeming to avoid looking at me. He knew me through and through.

It infuriated me that he knew me so thoroughly.

"Why not? I am an old schoolfellow of his, too, I believe, and I must own I feel hurt that you have left me out," I said, boiling over again.

"And where were we to find you?" Ferfitchkin put in roughly.

"You never were on good terms with Zverkov," Trudolyubov added, frowning.

But I had already clutched at the idea and would not give it up.

"It seems to me that no one has a right to form an opinion upon that," I retorted in a shaking voice, as though something tremendous had happened. "Perhaps that is just my reason for wishing it now, that I have not always been on good terms with him."

"Oh, there's no making you out . . . with these refinements," Trudolyubov jeered.

"We'll put your name down," Simonov decided, addressing me. "Tomorrow at five-o'clock at the Hôtel de Paris."

"What about the money?" Ferfitchkin began in an undertone, indicating me to Simonov, but he broke off, for even Simonov was embarrassed.

"That will do," said Trudolyubov, getting up. "If he wants to come so much, let him."

"But it's a private thing, between us friends," Ferfitchkin said crossly, as he, too, picked up his hat. "It's not an official gathering."

"We do not want at all, perhaps..."

They went away. Ferfitchkin did not greet me in any way as he went out, Trudolyubov barely nodded. Simonov, with whom I was left *tête-à-tête*, was in a state of vexation and perplexity, and looked at me queerly. He did not sit down and did not ask me to.

"H'm... yes... tomorrow, then. Will you pay your subscription now? I just ask so as to know," he muttered in embarrassment.

I flushed crimson, as I did so I remembered that I had owed Simonov fifteen roubles for ages—which I had, indeed, never forgotten, though I had not paid it.

"You will understand, Simonov, that I could have no idea when I came here.... I am very much vexed that I have forgotten...."

"All right, all right, that doesn't matter. You can pay tomorrow after the dinner. I simply wanted to know.... Please don't..."

He broke off and began pacing the room still more vexed. As he walked he began to stamp with his heels.

"Am I keeping you?" I asked, after two minutes of silence.

"Oh!" he said, starting, "that is—to be truthful—yes. I have to go and see someone... not far from here," he added in an apologetic voice, somewhat abashed.

"My goodness, why didn't you say so?" I cried, seizing my cap, with an astonishingly free-and-easy air, which was the last thing I should have expected of myself.

"It's close by... not two paces away," Simonov repeated, accompanying me to the front door with a fussy air which did not suit him at all. "So five o'clock, punctually, tomorrow," he called down the stairs after me. He was very glad to get rid of me. I was in a fury.

"What possessed me, what possessed me to force myself upon them?" I wondered, grinding my teeth as I strode along the street, "for a scoundrel, a pig like that Zverkov! Of course I had better not go; of course, I must just snap my fingers at them. I am not bound in any way. I'll send Simonov a note by tomorrow's post...."

But what made me furious was that I knew for certain that I should go, that I should make a point of going; and the more tactless, the more unseemly my going would be, the more certainly I would go.

And there was a positive obstacle to my going: I had no money. All I had was nine roubles, I had to give seven of that to my servant, Apollon, for his monthly wages. That was all I paid him—he had to keep himself.

Not to pay him was impossible, considering his character. But I will talk about that fellow, about that plague of mine, another time.

However, I knew I should go and should not pay him his wages.

That night I had the most hideous dreams. No wonder; all the evening I had been oppressed by memories of my miserable days at school, and I could not shake them off. I was sent to the school by distant relations, upon whom I was dependent and of whom I have heard nothing since—they sent me there a forlorn, silent boy, already crushed by their reproaches, already troubled by doubt, and looking with savage distrust at everyone. My schoolfellows met me with spiteful and merciless jibes because I was not like any of them. But I could not endure their taunts; I could not give in to them with the ignoble readiness with which they gave in to one another. I hated them from the first, and shut myself away from everyone in timid, wounded and disproportionate pride. Their coarseness revolted me. They laughed cynically at my face, at my clumsy figure; and yet what stupid faces they had themselves. In our school the boys' faces seemed in a special way to degenerate and grow stupider. How many fine-looking boys came to us! In a few years they became repulsive. Even at sixteen I wondered at them morosely; even then I was struck by the pettiness of their thoughts, the stupidity of their pursuits, their games, their conversations. They had no understanding of such essential things, they took no interest in such striking, impressive subjects, that I could not help considering them inferior to myself. It was not wounded vanity that drove me to it, and for God's sake do not thrust upon me your hackneyed remarks, repeated to nausea, that "I was only a dreamer," while they even then had an understanding of life. They understood nothing, they had no idea of real life, and I swear that that was what made me most indignant with them. On the contrary, the most obvious, striking reality they accepted with fantastic stupidity and even at that time were accustomed to respect success. Everything that was just, but oppressed and looked down upon, they laughed at heartlessly and shamefully. They took rank for intelligence; even at sixteen they were already talking about a snug berth. Of course, a great deal of it was due to their stupidity, to the bad examples with which they had always been surrounded in their childhood and boyhood. They were monstrously depraved. Of course a great deal of that, too, was superficial and an assumption of cynicism; of course there were glimpses of youth and freshness even in their depravity; but even that freshness was not attractive, and showed itself in a certain rakishness. I hated them horribly, though perhaps I was worse than any of them. They repaid me in the same way, and did not conceal their aversion for me. But by then I did not desire their affection: on the contrary, I continually longed for their humiliation. To escape from their derision I purposely began to make all the progress I could with my studies and forced my way to the very top. This impressed them. Moreover, they all began by degrees to grasp that I had already read books none of them could read, and understood things (not forming part of our school curriculum) of which they had not even heard. They took a savage and sarcastic view of it, but were morally impressed, especially as the teachers began to notice me on those grounds. The mockery ceased, but the hostility remained, and cold and strained relations became permanent between us. In the end I could not put up with it: with years a craving for society, for friends, developed in me. I attempted to get on friendly terms with some of my schoolfellows; but somehow or other my intimacy with them was always strained and soon ended of itself. Once, indeed, I did have a friend. But I was already a tyrant at heart; I wanted to exercise unbounded sway over him; I tried to instil into him a contempt for his surroundings; I required of him a disdainful and complete break with those surroundings. I frightened him with my passionate affection; I reduced him to tears, to hysterics. He was a simple and devoted soul; but when he devoted himself to me entirely I began to hate him immediately and repulsed him—as though all I needed him for was to win a victory over him, to subjugate him and nothing else. But I could not subjugate all of them; my friend was not at all like them either, he was, in fact, a rare exception. The first thing I did on leaving school was to give up the special job for which I had been destined so as to break all ties, to curse my past and shake the dust from off my feet. . . . And goodness knows why, after all that, I should go trudging off to Simonov's!

Early next morning I roused myself and jumped out of bed with excitement, as though it were all about to happen at once. But I believed that some radical change in my life was coming, and would inevitably come that day. Owing to its rarity, perhaps, any external event, however trivial, always made me feel as though some radical change in my life were at hand. I went to the office, however, as usual, but sneaked away home two hours earlier to get ready. The great thing, I thought, is not to be the first to arrive, or they will think I am overjoyed at coming. But there were thousands of such great points to consider, and they all agitated and overwhelmed me. I polished my boots a second time with my own hands; nothing in the world would have induced Apollon to clean them twice a day, as he considered that it was more than his duties required of him. I stole the brushes to clean them from the passage, being careful he should not detect it, for fear of his contempt. Then I minutely examined my clothes and thought that everything looked old, worn and threadbare. I had let myself get too slovenly. My uniform, perhaps, was tidy, but I could not go out to dinner in my uniform. The worst of it was that on the knee of my trousers was a big yellow stain. I had a foreboding that that stain would deprive me of nine-tenths of my personal dignity. I knew, too, that it was very poor to think so. "But this is no time for thinking: now I am in for the real thing," I thought, and my heart sank. I knew, too, perfectly well even then, that I was monstrously exaggerating the facts. But how could I help it? I could not control myself and was already shaking with fever. With despair I pictured to myself how coldly and disdainfully that "scoundrel" Zverkov would meet me; with what dull-witted, invincible contempt the blockhead Trudolyubov would look at me; with what impudent rudeness the insect Ferfitchkin would snigger at me in order to curry favour with Zverkov; how completely Simonov would take it all in, and how he would despise me for the abjectness of my vanity and lack of spirit—and, worst of all, how paltry, *unliterary*, commonplace it would all be. Of course, the best thing would be not to go at all. But that was most impossible of all: if I feel impelled to do anything, I seem to be pitchforked into it. I should have jeered at myself ever afterwards: "So you funked it, you funked it, you funked the *real thing!*" On the contrary, I passionately longed to show all that "rabble" that I was by no means such a spiritless creature as I seemed to myself. What is more, even in the acutest paroxysm of this cowardly fever, I dreamed of getting the upper hand, of dominating them, carrying them away, making them like me—if only for my "elevation of thought and unmistakable wit." They would abandon Zverkov, he would sit on one side, silent and ashamed, while I should crush him. Then, perhaps, we would be reconciled and drink to our everlasting friendship; but what was most bitter and humiliating for me was that I knew even then, knew fully and for certain, that I needed nothing of all this really, that I did not really want to crush, to subdue, to attract them, and that I did not care a straw really for the result, even if I did achieve it. Oh, how I prayed for the day to pass quickly! In unutterable anguish I went to the window, opened the movable pane and looked out into the troubled darkness of the thickly falling wet snow. At last my wretched little clock hissed out five. I seized my hat and, trying not to look at Apollon, who had been all day expecting his month's wages, but in his foolishness was unwilling to be the first to speak about it, I slipped between him and the door and, jumping into a high-class sledge, on which I spent my last half rouble, I drove up in grand style to the Hôtel de Paris.

4

I had been certain the day before that I should be the first to arrive. But it was not a question of being the first to arrive. Not only were they not there, but I had difficulty in finding our room. The table was not laid even. What did it mean? After a good many questions I elicited from the waiters that the dinner had been ordered not for five, but for six o'clock. This was confirmed at the buffet too. I felt really ashamed to go on questioning them. It was only twenty-five minutes past five. If they changed the dinner hour they ought at least to have let me know—that is what the post is for, and not to have put me in an absurd position in my own eyes and . . . and even before the waiters. I sat down; the servant began laying the table; I felt even more humiliated when he was present. Towards six o'clock they brought in candles, though there were lamps burning in the room. It had not occurred to the waiter, however, to bring them in at once when I arrived. In the next room two gloomy, angry-looking persons were eating their dinners in silence at two different tables. There was a great deal of noise, even shouting, in a room further away; one could hear the laughter of a crowd of people, and nasty little shrieks in French: there were ladies at the dinner. It was sickening, in fact. I rarely passed more unpleasant moments, so much so that when they did arrive all together punctually at six I was overjoyed to see them, as though they were my deliverers, and even forgot that it was incumbent upon me to show resentment.

Zverkov walked in at the head of them; evidently he was the leading spirit. He and all of them were laughing; but, seeing me, Zverkov drew himself up a little, walked up to me deliberately with a slight, rather jaunty bend from the waist. He shook hands with me in a friendly, but not over-friendly, fashion, with a sort of circumspect courtesy like that of a General, as though in giving me his hand he were warding off something. I had imagined, on the contrary, that on coming in he would at once break into his habitual thin, shrill laugh and fall to making his insipid jokes and witticisms. I had been preparing for them ever since the previous day, but I had not expected such condescension, such high-official courtesy. So, then, he felt himself ineffably superior to me in every respect! If he only meant to insult me by that high-official tone, it would not matter, I thought—I could pay him back for it one way or another. But what if, in reality, without the least desire to be offensive, that sheepshead had a notion in earnest that he was superior to me and could only look at me in a patronising way? The very supposition made me gasp.

"I was surprised to hear of your desire to join us," he began, lisping and drawling, which was something new. "You and I seem to have seen nothing of one another. You fight shy of us. You shouldn't. We are not such terrible people as you think. Well, anyway, I am glad to renew our acquaintance."

And he turned carelessly to put down his hat on the window.

"Have you been waiting long?" Trudolyubov inquired.

"I arrived at five o'clock as you told me yesterday," I answered aloud, with an irritability that threatened an explosion.

"Didn't you let him know that we had changed the hour?" said Trudolyubov to Simonov.

"No, I didn't. I forgot," the latter replied, with no sign of regret, and without even apologising to me he went off to order the *hors d'oeuvres*.

"So you've been here a whole hour? Oh, poor fellow!" Zverkov cried ironically, for to his notions this was bound to be extremely funny. That rascal Ferfitchkin followed with his nasty little snigger like a puppy yapping. My position struck him, too, as exquisitely ludicrous and embarrassing.

"It isn't funny at all!" I cried to Ferfitchkin, more and more irritated. "It wasn't my fault, but other people's. They neglected to let me know. It was . . . it was . . . it was simply absurd."

"It's not only absurd, but something else as well," muttered Trudolyubov, naively taking my part. "You are not hard enough upon it. It was simply rudeness—unintentional, of course. And how could Simonov . . . h'm!"

"If a trick like that had been played on me," observed Ferfitchkin, "I should . . ."

"But you should have ordered something for yourself," Zverkov interrupted, "or simply asked for dinner without waiting for us."

"You will allow that I might have done that without your permission," I rapped out. "If I waited, it was . . ."

"Let us sit down, gentlemen," cried Simonov, coming in. "Everything is ready; I can answer for the champagne; it is capitally frozen. . . . You see, I did not know your address, where was I to look for you?" he suddenly turned to me, but again he seemed to avoid looking at me. Evidently he had something against me. It must have been what happened yesterday.

All sat down; I did the same. It was a round table. Trudolyubov was on my left, Simonov on my right, Zverkov was sitting opposite, Ferfitchkin next to him, between him and Trudolyubov.

"Tell me, are you . . . in a government office?" Zverkov went on attending to me. Seeing that I was embarrassed he seriously thought that he ought to be friendly to me, and, so to speak, cheer me up.

"Does he want me to throw a bottle at his head?" I thought, in a fury. In my novel surroundings I was unnaturally ready to be irritated.

"In the N—— office," I answered jerkily, with my eyes on my plate.

"And ha-ave you a go-od berth? I say, what ma-a-de you leave your original job?"

"What ma-a-de me was that I wanted to leave my original job," I drawled more than he, hardly able to control myself. Ferfitchkin went off into a guffaw. Simonov looked at me ironically. Trudolyubov left off eating and began looking at me with curiosity.

Zverkov winced, but he tried not to notice it.

"And the remuneration?"

"What remuneration?"

"I mean, your sa-a-lary?"

"Why are you cross-examining me?" However, I told him at once what my salary was. I turned horribly red.

"It is not very handsome," Zverkov observed majestically.

"Yes, you can't afford to dine at cafés on that," Ferfitchkin added insolently.

"To my thinking it's very poor," Trudolyubov observed gravely.

"And how thin you have grown! How you have changed!" added Zverkov, with a shade of venom in his voice, scanning me and my attire with a sort of insolent compassion.

"Oh, spare his blushes," cried Ferfitchkin, sniggering.

"My dear sir, allow me to tell you I am not blushing," I broke out at last; "do you hear? I am dining here, at this cafe, at my own expense, not at other people's—note that, Mr. Ferfitchkin."

"Wha-at? Isn't every one here dining at his own expense? You would seem to be . . . ." Ferfitchkin flew out at me, turning as red as a lobster, and looking me in the face with fury.

"Tha-at," I answered, feeling I had gone too far, "and I imagine it would be better to talk of something more intelligent."

"You intend to show off your intelligence, I suppose?"

"Don't disturb yourself, that would be quite out of place here."

"Why are you clacking away like that, my good sir, eh? Have you gone out of your wits in your office?"

"Enough, gentlemen, enough!" Zverkov cried, authoritatively.

"How stupid it is!" muttered Simonov.

"It really is stupid. We have met here, a company of friends, for a farewell dinner to a comrade and you carry on an altercation," said Trudolyubov, rudely addressing himself to me alone. "You invited yourself to join us, so don't disturb the general harmony."

"Enough, enough!" cried Zverkov. "Give over, gentlemen, it's out of place. Better let me tell you how I nearly got married the day before yesterday. . . ."

And then followed a burlesque narrative of how this gentleman had almost been married two days before. There was not a word about the marriage, however, but the story was adorned with generals, colonels and kammer-junkers, while Zverkov almost took the lead among them. It was greeted with approving laughter; Ferfitchkin positively squealed.

No one paid any attention to me, and I sat crushed and humiliated.

"Good Heavens, these are not the people for me!" I thought. "And what a fool I have made of myself before them! I let Ferfitchkin go too far, though. The brutes imagine they are doing me an honour in letting me sit down with them. They don't understand that it's an honour to them and not to me! I've grown thinner! My clothes! Oh, damn my trousers! Zverkov noticed the yellow stain on the knee as soon as he came in. . . . But what's the use! I must get up at once, this very minute, take my hat and simply go without a word . . . with contempt! And tomorrow I can send a challenge. The scoundrels! As though I cared about the seven roubles. They may think. . . . Damn it! I don't care about the seven roubles. I'll go this minute!"

Of course I remained. I drank sherry and Lafitte by the glassful in my discomfiture. Being unaccustomed to it, I was quickly affected. My annoyance increased as the wine went to my head. I longed all at once to insult them all in a most flagrant manner and then go away. To seize the moment and show what I could do, so that they would say, "He's clever, though he is absurd," and . . . and . . . in fact, damn them all!

I scanned them all insolently with my drowsy eyes. But they seemed to have forgotten me altogether. They were noisy, vociferous, cheerful. Zverkov was talking all the time. I began listening. Zverkov was talking of some exuberant lady whom he had at last led on to declaring her love (of course, he was lying like a horse), and how he had been helped in this affair by an intimate friend of his, a Prince Kolya, an officer in the hussars, who had three thousand serfs.

"And yet this Kolya, who has three thousand serfs, has not put in an appearance here tonight to see you off," I cut in suddenly.

For one minute every one was silent. "You are drunk already." Trudolyubov deigned to notice me at last, glancing contemptuously in my direction. Zverkov, without a word, examined me as though I were an insect. I dropped my eyes. Simonov made haste to fill up the glasses with champagne.

Trudolyubov raised his glass, as did everyone else but me.

"Your health and good luck on the journey!" he cried to Zverkov. "To old times, to our future, hurrah!"

They all tossed off their glasses, and crowded round Zverkov to kiss him. I did not move; my full glass stood untouched before me.

"Why, aren't you going to drink it?" roared Trudolyubov, losing patience and turning menacingly to me.

"I want to make a speech separately, on my own account . . . and then I'll drink it, Mr. Trudolyubov."

"Spiteful brute!" muttered Simonov. I drew myself up in my chair and feverishly seized my glass, prepared for something extraordinary, though I did not know myself precisely what I was going to say.

"*Silence!*" cried Ferfitchkin. "Now for a display of wit!"

Zverkov waited very gravely, knowing what was coming.

"Mr. Lieutenant Zverkov," I began, "let me tell you that I hate phrases, phrasemongers and men in corsets . . . that's the first point, and there is a second one to follow it."

There was a general stir.

"The second point is: I hate ribaldry and ribald talkers. Especially ribald talkers! The third point: I love justice, truth and honesty." I went on almost mechanically, for I was beginning to shiver with horror myself and had no idea how I came to be talking like this. "I love thought, Monsieur Zverkov; I love true comradeship, on an equal footing and not . . . H'm . . . I love . . . But, however, why not? I will drink your health, too, Mr. Zverkov. Seduce the Circassian girls, shoot the enemies of the fatherland and . . . and . . . to your health, Monsieur Zverkov!"

Zverkov got up from his seat, bowed to me and said:

"I am very much obliged to you." He was frightfully offended and turned pale.

"Damn the fellow!" roared Trudolyubov, bringing his fist down on the table.

"Well, he wants a punch in the face for that," squealed Ferfitchkin.

"We ought to turn him out," muttered Simonov.

"Not a word, gentlemen, not a movement!" cried Zverkov solemnly, checking the general indignation. "I thank you all, but I can show him for myself how much value I attach to his words."

"Mr. Ferfitchkin, you will give me satisfaction tomorrow for your words just now!" I said aloud, turning with dignity to Ferfitchkin.

"A duel, you mean? Certainly," he answered. But probably I was so ridiculous as I challenged him and it was so out of keeping with my appearance that everyone including Ferfitchkin was prostrate with laughter.

"Yes, let him alone, of course! He is quite drunk," Trudolyubov said with disgust.

"I shall never forgive myself for letting him join us," Simonov muttered again.

"Now is the time to throw a bottle at their heads," I thought to myself. I picked up the bottle . . . and filled my glass. . . . "No, I'd better sit on to the end," I went on thinking; "you would be pleased, my friends, if I went away. Nothing will induce me to go. I'll go on sitting here and drinking to the end, on purpose, as a sign that I don't think you of the slightest consequence. I will go on sitting and drinking, because this is a public-house and I paid my entrance money. I'll sit here and drink, for I look upon you as so many pawns, as inanimate pawns. I'll sit here and drink . . . and sing if I want to, yes, sing, for I have the right to . . . to sing . . . H'm!"

But I did not sing. I simply tried not to look at any of them. I assumed most unconcerned attitudes and waited with impatience for them to speak *first*. But alas, they did not address me! And oh, how I wished, how I wished at that moment to be reconciled to them! It struck eight, at last nine. They moved from the table to the sofa. Zverkov stretched himself on a lounge and put one foot on a round table. Wine was brought there. He did, as a fact, order three bottles on his own account. I, of course, was not invited to join them. They all sat round him on the sofa. They listened to him, almost with reverence. It was evident that they were fond of him. "What for? What for?" I wondered. From time to time they were moved to drunken enthusiasm and kissed each other. They talked of the Caucasus, of the nature of true passion, of snug berths in the service, of the income of an hussar called Podharzhevsky, whom none of them knew personally, and rejoiced in the largeness of it, of the extraordinary grace and beauty of a Princess D., whom none of them had ever seen; then it came to Shakespeare's being immortal.

I smiled contemptuously and walked up and down the other side of the room, opposite the sofa, from the table to the stove and back again. I tried my very utmost to show them that I could do without them, and yet I purposely made a noise with my boots, thumping with my heels. But it was all in vain. They paid no attention. I had the patience to walk up and down in front of them from eight o'clock till eleven, in the same place, from the table to the stove and back again. "I walk up and down to please myself and no one can prevent me." The waiter who came into the room stopped, from time to time, to look at me. I was somewhat giddy from turning round so often; at moments it seemed to me that I was in delirium. During those three hours I was three times soaked with sweat and dry again. At times, with an intense, acute pang I was stabbed to the heart by the thought that ten years, twenty years, forty years would pass, and that even in forty years I would remember with loathing and humiliation those filthiest, most ludicrous, and most awful moments of my life. No one could have gone out of his way to degrade himself more shamelessly, and I fully realised it, fully, and yet I went on pacing up and down from the table to the stove. "Oh, if you only knew what thoughts and feelings I am capable of, how cultured I am!" I thought at moments, mentally addressing the sofa on which my enemies were sitting. But my enemies behaved as though I were not in the room. Once—only once—they turned towards me, just when Zverkov was talking about Shakespeare, and I suddenly gave a contemptuous laugh. I laughed in such an affected and disgusting way that they all at once broke off their conversation, and silently and gravely for two minutes watched me walking up and down from the table to the stove, *taking no notice of them*. But nothing came of it: they said nothing, and two minutes later they ceased to notice me again. It struck eleven.

"Friends," cried Zverkov getting up from the sofa, "let us all be off now, *there!*"

"Of course, of course," the others assented. I turned sharply to Zverkov. I was so harassed, so exhausted, that I would have cut my throat to put an end to it. I was in a fever; my hair, soaked with perspiration, stuck to my forehead and temples.

"Zverkov, I beg your pardon," I said abruptly and resolutely. "Ferfitchkin, yours too, and everyone's, everyone's: I have insulted you all!"

"Aha! A duel is not in your line, old man," Ferfitchkin hissed venomously. It sent a sharp pang to my heart.

"No, it's not the duel I am afraid of, Ferfitchkin! I am ready to fight you tomorrow, after we are reconciled. I insist upon it, in fact, and you cannot refuse. I want to show you that I am not afraid of a duel. You shall fire first and I shall fire into the air."

"He is comforting himself," said Simonov.

"He's simply raving," said Trudolyubov.

"But let us pass. Why are you barring our way? What do you want?" Zverkov answered disdainfully.

They were all flushed, their eyes were bright: they had been drinking heavily.

"I ask for your friendship, Zverkov; I insulted you, but . . ."

"Insulted? *You* insulted *me?* Understand, sir, that you never, under any circumstances, could possibly insult *me*."

"And that's enough for you. Out of the way!" concluded Trudolyubov.

"Olympia is mine, friends, that's agreed!" cried Zverkov.

"We won't dispute your right, we won't dispute your right," the others answered, laughing.

I stood as though spat upon. The party went noisily out of the room. Trudolyubov struck up some stupid song. Simonov remained behind for a moment to tip the waiters. I suddenly went up to him.

"Simonov! give me six roubles!" I said, with desperate resolution.

He looked at me in extreme amazement, with vacant eyes. He, too, was drunk.

"You don't mean you are coming with us?"

"Yes."

"I've no money," he snapped out, and with a scornful laugh he went out of the room.

I clutched at his overcoat. It was a nightmare.

"Simonov, I saw you had money. Why do you refuse me? Am I a scoundrel? Beware of refusing me: if you knew, if you knew why I am asking! My whole future, my whole plans depend upon it!"

Simonov pulled out the money and almost flung it at me.

"Take it, if you have no sense of shame!" he pronounced pitilessly, and ran to overtake them.

I was left for a moment alone. Disorder, the remains of dinner, a broken wine-glass on the floor, spilt wine, cigarette ends, fumes of drink and delirium in my brain, an agonising misery in my heart and finally the waiter, who had seen and heard all and was looking inquisitively into my face.

"I am going there!" I cried. "Either they shall all go down on their knees to beg for my friendship, or I will give Zverkov a slap in the face!"

5

"So this is it, this is it at last—contact with real life," I muttered as I ran headlong downstairs. "This is very different from the Pope's leaving Rome and going to Brazil, very different from the ball on Lake Como!"

"You are a scoundrel," a thought flashed through my mind, "if you laugh at this now."

"No matter!" I cried, answering myself. "Now everything is lost!"

There was no trace to be seen of them, but that made no difference—I knew where they had gone.

At the steps was standing a solitary night sledge-driver in a rough peasant coat, powdered over with the still falling, wet, and as it were warm, snow. It was hot and steamy. The little shaggy piebald horse was also covered with snow and coughing, I remember that very well. I made a rush for the roughly made sledge; but as soon as I raised my foot to get into it, the recollection of how Simonov had just given me six roubles seemed to double me up and I tumbled into the sledge like a sack.

"No, I must do a great deal to make up for all that," I cried. "But I will make up for it or perish on the spot this very night. Start!"

We set off. There was a perfect whirl in my head.

"They won't go down on their knees to beg for my friendship. That is a mirage, cheap mirage, revolting, romantic and fantastical—that's another ball on Lake Como. And so I am bound to slap Zverkov's face! It is my duty to. And so it is settled; I am flying to give him a slap in the face. Hurry up!"

The driver tugged at the reins.

"As soon as I go in I'll give it him. Ought I before giving him the slap to say a few words by way of preface? No. I'll simply go in and give it him. They will all be sitting in the drawing-room, and he with Olympia on the sofa. That damned Olympia! She laughed at my looks on one occasion and refused me. I'll pull Olympia's hair, pull Zverkov's ears! No, better one ear, and pull him by it round the room. Maybe they will all begin beating me and will kick me out. That's most likely, indeed. No matter! Anyway, I shall first slap him; the initiative will be mine; and by the laws of honour that is everything: he will be branded and cannot wipe off the slap by any blows, by nothing but a duel. He will be forced to fight. And let them beat me now. Let them, the ungrateful wretches! Trudolyubov will beat me hardest, he is so strong; Ferfitchkin will be sure to catch hold sideways and tug at my hair. But no matter, no matter! That's what I am going for. The blockheads will be forced at last to see the tragedy of it all! When they drag me to the door I shall call out to them that in reality they are not worth my little finger. Get on, driver, get on!" I cried to the driver. He started and flicked his whip, I shouted so savagely.

"We shall fight at daybreak, that's a settled thing. I've done with the office. Ferfitchkin made a joke about it just now. But where can I get pistols? Nonsense! I'll get my salary in advance and buy them. And powder, and bullets? That's the second's business. And how can it all be done by daybreak? and where am I to get a second? I have no friends. Nonsense!" I cried, lashing myself up more and more. "It's of no consequence! The first person I meet in the street is bound to be my second, just as he would be bound to pull a drowning man out of water. The most eccentric things may happen. Even if I were to ask the director himself to be my second tomorrow, he would be bound to consent, if only from a feeling of chivalry, and to keep the secret! Anton Antonitch...."

The fact is, that at that very minute the disgusting absurdity of my plan and the other side of the question was clearer and more vivid to my imagination than it could be to anyone on earth. But....

"Get on, driver, get on, you rascal, get on!"

"Ugh, sir!" said the son of toil.

Cold shivers suddenly ran down me. Wouldn't it be better . . . to go straight home? My God, my God! Why did I invite myself to this dinner yesterday? But no, it's impossible. And my walking up and down for three hours from the table to the stove? No, they, they and no one else must pay for my walking up and down! They must wipe out this dishonour! Drive on!

And what if they give me into custody? They won't dare! They'll be afraid of the scandal. And what if Zverkov is so contemptuous that he refuses to fight a duel? He is sure to; but in that case I'll show them . . . I will turn up at the posting station when he's setting off tomorrow, I'll catch him by the leg, I'll pull off his coat when he gets into the carriage. I'll get my teeth into his hand, I'll bite him. "See what lengths you can drive a desperate man to!" He may hit me on the head and they may belabour me from behind. I will shout to the assembled multitude: "Look at this young puppy who is driving off to captivate the Circassian girls after letting me spit in his face!"

Of course, after that everything will be over! The office will have vanished off the face of the earth. I shall be arrested, I shall be tried, I shall be dismissed from the service, thrown in prison, sent to Siberia. Never mind! In fifteen years when they let me out of prison I will trudge off to him, a beggar, in rags. I shall find him in some provincial town. He will be married and happy. He will have a grown-up daughter. . . . I shall say to him: "Look, monster, at my hollow cheeks and my rags! I've lost everything—my career, my happiness, art, science, *the woman I loved*, and all through you. Here are pistols. I have come to discharge my pistol and . . . and I . . . forgive you. Then I shall fire into the air and he will hear nothing more of me. . . ."

I was actually on the point of tears, though I knew perfectly well at that moment that all this was out of Pushkin's *Silvio* and Lermontov's *Masquerade*. And all at once I felt horribly ashamed, so ashamed that I stopped the horse, got out of the sledge, and stood still in the snow in the middle of the street. The driver gazed at me, sighing and astonished.

What was I to do? I could not go on there—it was evidently stupid, and I could not leave things as they were, because that would seem as though ... Heavens, how could I leave things! And after such insults! "No!" I cried, throwing myself into the sledge again. "It is ordained! It is fate! Drive on, drive on!"

And in my impatience I punched the sledge-driver on the back of the neck.

"What are you up to? What are you hitting me for?" the peasant shouted, but he whipped up his nag so that it began kicking.

The wet snow was falling in big flakes; I unbuttoned myself, regardless of it. I forgot everything else, for I had finally decided on the slap, and felt with horror that it was going to happen *now, at once*, and that *no force could stop it*. The deserted street lamps gleamed sullenly in the snowy darkness like torches at a funeral. The snow drifted under my great-coat, under my coat, under my cravat, and melted there. I did not wrap myself up—all was lost, anyway.

At last we arrived. I jumped out, almost unconscious, ran up the steps and began knocking and kicking at the door. I felt fearfully weak, particularly in my legs and knees. The door was opened quickly as though they knew I was coming. As a fact, Simonov had warned them that perhaps another gentleman would arrive, and this was a place in which one had to give notice and to observe certain precautions. It was one of those "millinery establishments" which were abolished by the police a good time ago. By day it really was a shop; but at night, if one had an introduction, one might visit it for other purposes.

I walked rapidly through the dark shop into the familiar drawing-room, where there was only one candle burning, and stood still in amazement: there was no one there. "Where are they?" I asked somebody. But by now, of course, they had separated. Before me was standing a person with a stupid smile, the "madam" herself, who had seen me before. A minute later a door opened and another person came in.

Taking no notice of anything I strode about the room, and, I believe, I talked to myself. I felt as though I had been saved from death and was conscious of this, joyfully, all over: I should have given that slap, I should certainly, certainly have given it! But now they were not here and . . . everything had vanished and changed! I looked round. I could not realise my condition yet. I looked mechanically at the girl who had come in: and had a glimpse of a fresh, young, rather pale face, with straight, dark eyebrows, and with grave, as it were wondering, eyes that attracted me at once; I should have hated her if she had been smiling. I began looking at her more intently and, as it were, with effort. I had not fully collected my thoughts. There was something simple and good-natured in her face, but something strangely grave. I am sure that this stood in her way here, and no one of those fools had noticed her. She could not, however, have been called a beauty, though she was tall, strong-looking, and well built. She was very simply dressed. Something loathsome stirred within me. I went straight up to her.

I chanced to look into the glass. My harassed face struck me as revolting in the extreme, pale, angry, abject, with dishevelled hair. "No matter, I am glad of it," I thought; "I am glad that I shall seem repulsive to her; I like that."

6

... Somewhere behind a screen a clock began wheezing, as though oppressed by something, as though someone were strangling it. After an unnaturally prolonged wheezing there followed a shrill, nasty, and as it were unexpectedly rapid, chime—as though someone were suddenly jumping forward. It struck two. I woke up, though I had indeed not been asleep but lying half-conscious.

It was almost completely dark in the narrow, cramped, low-pitched room, cumbered up with an enormous wardrobe and piles of cardboard boxes and all sorts of frippery and litter. The candle end that had been burning on the table was going out and gave a faint flicker from time to time. In a few minutes there would be complete darkness.

I was not long in coming to myself; everything came back to my mind at once, without an effort, as though it had been in ambush to pounce upon me again. And, indeed, even while I was unconscious a point seemed continually to remain in my memory unforgotten, and round it my dreams moved drearily. But strange to say, everything that had happened to me in that day seemed to me now, on waking, to be in the far, far away past, as though I had long, long ago lived all that down.

My head was full of fumes. Something seemed to be hovering over me, rousing me, exciting me, and making me restless. Misery and spite seemed surging up in me again and seeking an outlet. Suddenly I saw beside me two wide open eyes scrutinising me curiously and persistently. The look in those eyes was coldly detached, sullen, as it were utterly remote; it weighed upon me.

A grim idea came into my brain and passed all over my body, as a horrible sensation, such as one feels when one goes into a damp and mouldy cellar. There was something unnatural in those two eyes, beginning to look at me only now. I recalled, too, that during those two hours I had not said a single word to this creature, and had, in fact, considered it utterly superfluous; in fact, the silence had for some reason gratified me. Now I suddenly realised vividly the hideous idea—revolting as a spider—of vice, which, without love, grossly and shamelessly begins with that in which true love finds its consummation. For a long time we gazed at each other like that, but she did not drop her eyes before mine and her expression did not change, so that at last I felt uncomfortable.

"What is your name?" I asked abruptly, to put an end to it.

"Liza," she answered almost in a whisper, but somehow far from graciously, and she turned her eyes away.

I was silent.

"What weather! The snow . . . it's disgusting!" I said, almost to myself, putting my arm under my head despondently, and gazing at the ceiling.

She made no answer. This was horrible.

"Have you always lived in Petersburg?" I asked a minute later, almost angrily, turning my head slightly towards her.

"No."

"Where do you come from?"

"From Riga," she answered reluctantly.

"Are you a German?"

"No, Russian."

"Have you been here long?"

"Where?"

"In this house?"

"A fortnight."

She spoke more and more jerkily. The candle went out; I could no longer distinguish her face.

"Have you a father and mother?"

"Yes . . . no . . . I have."

"Where are they?"

"There . . . in Riga."

"What are they?"

"Oh, nothing."

"Nothing? Why, what class are they?"

"Tradespeople."

"Have you always lived with them?"

"Yes."

"How old are you?"

"Twenty."

"Why did you leave them?"

"Oh, for no reason."

That answer meant "Let me alone; I feel sick, sad."

We were silent.

God knows why I did not go away. I felt myself more and more sick and dreary. The images of the previous day began of themselves, apart from my will, flitting through my memory in confusion. I suddenly recalled something I had seen that morning when, full of anxious thoughts, I was hurrying to the office.

"I saw them carrying a coffin out yesterday and they nearly dropped it," I suddenly said aloud, not that I desired to open the conversation, but as it were by accident.

"A coffin?"

"Yes, in the Haymarket; they were bringing it up out of a cellar."

"From a cellar?"

"Not from a cellar, but a basement. Oh, you know . . . down below . . . from a house of ill-fame. It was filthy all round . . . Egg-shells, litter . . . a stench. It was loathsome."

Silence.

"A nasty day to be buried," I began, simply to avoid being silent.

"Nasty, in what way?"

"The snow, the wet." (I yawned.)

"It makes no difference," she said suddenly, after a brief silence.

"No, it's horrid." (I yawned again). "The gravediggers must have sworn at getting drenched by the snow. And there must have been water in the grave."

"Why water in the grave?" she asked, with a sort of curiosity, but speaking even more harshly and abruptly than before.

I suddenly began to feel provoked.

"Why, there must have been water at the bottom a foot deep. You can't dig a dry grave in Volkovo Cemetery."

"Why?"

"Why? Why, the place is waterlogged. It's a regular marsh. So they bury them in water. I've seen it myself . . . many times."

(I had never seen it once, indeed I had never been in Volkovo, and had only heard stories of it.)

"Do you mean to say, you don't mind how you die?"

"But why should I die?" she answered, as though defending herself.

"Why, some day you will die, and you will die just the same as that dead woman. She was . . . a girl like you. She died of consumption."

"A wench would have died in hospital . . ." (She knows all about it already: she said "wench," not "girl.")

"She was in debt to her madam," I retorted, more and more provoked by the discussion; "and went on earning money for her up to the end, though she was in consumption. Some sledge-drivers standing by were talking about her to some soldiers and telling them so. No doubt they knew her. They were laughing. They were going to meet in a pot-house to drink to her memory."

A great deal of this was my invention. Silence followed, profound silence. She did not stir.

"And is it better to die in a hospital?"

"Isn't it just the same? Besides, why should I die?" she added irritably.

"If not now, a little later."

"Why a little later?"

"Why, indeed? Now you are young, pretty, fresh, you fetch a high price. But after another year of this life you will be very different—you will go off."

"In a year?"

"Anyway, in a year you will be worth less," I continued malignantly. "You will go from here to something lower, another house; a year later—to a third, lower and lower, and in seven years you will come to a basement in the Haymarket. That will be if you were lucky. But it would be much worse if you got some disease, consumption, say . . . and caught a chill, or something or other. It's not easy to get over an illness in your way of life. If you catch anything you may not get rid of it. And so you would die."

"Oh, well, then I shall die," she answered, quite vindictively, and she made a quick movement.

"But one is sorry."

"Sorry for whom?"

"Sorry for life." Silence.

"Have you been engaged to be married? Eh?"

"What's that to you?"

"Oh, I am not cross-examining you. It's nothing to me. Why are you so cross? Of course you may have had your own troubles. What is it to me? It's simply that I felt sorry."

"Sorry for whom?"

"Sorry for you."

"No need," she whispered hardly audibly, and again made a faint movement.

That incensed me at once. What! I was so gentle with her, and she. . . .

"Why, do you think that you are on the right path?"

"I don't think anything."

"That's what's wrong, that you don't think. Realise it while there is still time. There still is time. You are still young, good-looking; you might love, be married, be happy. . . ."

"Not all married women are happy," she snapped out in the rude abrupt tone she had used at first.

"Not all, of course, but anyway it is much better than the life here. Infinitely better. Besides, with love one can live even without happiness. Even in sorrow life is sweet; life is sweet, however one lives. But here what is there but . . . foulness? Phew!"

I turned away with disgust; I was no longer reasoning coldly. I began to feel myself what I was saying and warmed to the subject. I was already longing to expound the cherished ideas I had brooded over in my corner. Something suddenly flared up in me. An object had appeared before me.

"Never mind my being here, I am not an example for you. I am, perhaps, worse than you are. I was drunk when I came here, though," I hastened, however, to say in self-defence. "Besides, a man is no example for a woman. It's a different thing. I may degrade and defile myself, but I am not anyone's slave. I come and go, and that's an end of it. I shake it off, and I am a different man. But you are a slave from the start. Yes, a slave! You give up everything, your whole freedom. If you want to break your chains afterwards, you won't be able to; you will be more and more fast in the snares. It is an accursed bondage. I know it. I won't speak of anything else, maybe you won't understand, but tell me: no doubt you are in debt to your madam? There, you see," I added, though she made no answer, but only listened in silence, entirely absorbed, "that's a bondage for you! You will never buy your freedom. They will see to that. It's like selling your soul to the devil. . . . And besides . . . perhaps, I too, am just as unlucky—how do you know—and wallow in the mud on purpose, out of misery? You know, men take to drink from grief; well, maybe I am here from grief. Come, tell me, what is there good here? Here you and I . . . came together . . . just now and did not say one word to one another all the time, and it was only afterwards you began staring at me like a wild creature, and I at you. Is that loving? Is that how one human being should meet another? It's hideous, that's what it is!"

"Yes!" she assented sharply and hurriedly.

I was positively astounded by the promptitude of this "Yes." So the same thought may have been straying through her mind when she was staring at me just before. So she, too, was capable of certain thoughts? "Damn it all, this was interesting, this was a point of likeness!" I thought, almost rubbing my hands. And indeed it's easy to turn a young soul like that!

It was the exercise of my power that attracted me most.

She turned her head nearer to me, and it seemed to me in the darkness that she propped herself on her arm. Perhaps she was scrutinising me. How I regretted that I could not see her eyes. I heard her deep breathing.

"Why have you come here?" I asked her, with a note of authority already in my voice.

"Oh, I don't know."

"But how nice it would be to be living in your father's house! It's warm and free; you have a home of your own."

"But what if it's worse than this?"

"I must take the right tone," flashed through my mind. "I may not get far with sentimentality." But it was only a momentary thought. I swear she really did interest me. Besides, I was exhausted and moody. And cunning so easily goes hand-in-hand with feeling.

"Who denies it!" I hastened to answer. "Anything may happen. I am convinced that someone has wronged you, and that you are more sinned against than sinning. Of course, I know nothing of your story, but it's not likely a girl like you has come here of her own inclination. . . ."

"A girl like me?" she whispered, hardly audibly; but I heard it.

Damn it all, I was flattering her. That was horrid. But perhaps it was a good thing. . . . She was silent.

"See, Liza, I will tell you about myself. If I had had a home from childhood, I shouldn't be what I am now. I often think that. However bad it may be at home, anyway they are your father and mother, and not enemies, strangers. Once a year at least, they'll show their love of you. Anyway, you know you are at home. I grew up without a home; and perhaps that's why I've turned so . . . unfeeling."

I waited again. "Perhaps she doesn't understand," I thought, "and, indeed, it is absurd—it's moralising."

"If I were a father and had a daughter, I believe I should love my daughter more than my sons, really," I began indirectly, as though talking of something else, to distract her attention. I must confess I blushed.

"Why so?" she asked.

Ah! so she was listening!

"I don't know, Liza. I knew a father who was a stern, austere man, but used to go down on his knees to his daughter, used to kiss her hands, her feet, he couldn't make enough of her, really. When she danced at parties he used to stand for five hours at a stretch, gazing at her. He was mad over her: I understand that! She would fall asleep tired at night, and he would wake to kiss her in her sleep and make the sign of the cross over her. He would go about in a dirty old coat, he was stingy to everyone else, but would spend his last penny for her, giving her expensive presents, and it was his greatest delight when she was pleased with what he gave her. Fathers always love their daughters more than the mothers do. Some girls live happily at home! And I believe I should never let my daughters marry."

"What next?" she said, with a faint smile.

"I should be jealous, I really should. To think that she should kiss anyone else! That she should love a stranger more than her father! It's painful to imagine it. Of course, that's all nonsense, of course every father would be reasonable at last. But I believe before I should let her marry, I should worry myself to death; I should find fault with all her suitors. But I should end by letting her marry whom she herself loved. The one whom the daughter loves always seems the worst to the father, you know. That is always so. So many family troubles come from that."

"Some are glad to sell their daughters, rather than marrying them honourably."

Ah, so that was it!

"Such a thing, Liza, happens in those accursed families in which there is neither love nor God," I retorted warmly, "and where there is no love, there is no sense either. There are such families, it's true, but I am not speaking of them. You must have seen wickedness in your own family, if you talk like that. Truly, you must have been unlucky. H'm! . . . that sort of thing mostly comes about through poverty."

"And is it any better with the gentry? Even among the poor, honest people who live happily?"

"H'm . . . yes. Perhaps. Another thing, Liza, man is fond of reckoning up his troubles, but does not count his joys. If he counted them up as he ought, he would see that every lot has enough happiness provided for it. And what if all goes well with the family, if the blessing of God is upon it, if the husband is a good one, loves you, cherishes you, never leaves you! There is happiness in such a family! Even sometimes there is happiness in the midst of sorrow; and indeed sorrow is everywhere. If you marry *you will find out for yourself*. But think of the first years of married life with one you love: what happiness, what happiness there sometimes is in it! And indeed it's the ordinary thing. In those early days even quarrels with one's husband end happily. Some women get up quarrels with their husbands just because they love them. Indeed, I knew a woman like that: she seemed to say that because she loved him, she would torment him and make him feel it. You know that you may torment a man on purpose through love. Women are particularly given to that, thinking to themselves 'I will love him so, I will make so much of him afterwards, that it's no sin to torment him a little now.' And all in the house rejoice in the sight of you, and you are happy and gay and peaceful and honourable. . . . Then there are some women who are jealous. If he went off anywhere—I knew one such woman, she couldn't restrain herself, but would jump up at night and run off on the sly to find out where he was, whether he was with some other woman. That's a pity. And the woman knows herself it's wrong, and her heart fails her and she suffers, but she loves—it's all through love. And how sweet it is to make up after quarrels, to own herself in the wrong or to forgive him! And they both are so happy all at once—as though they had met anew, been married over again; as though their love had begun afresh. And no one, no one should know what passes between husband and wife if they love one another. And whatever quarrels there may be between them they ought not to call in their own mother to judge between them and tell tales of one another. They are their own judges. Love is a holy mystery and ought to be hidden from all other eyes, whatever happens. That makes it holier and better. They respect one another more, and much is built on respect. And if once there has been love, if they have been married for love, why should love pass away? Surely one can keep it! It is rare that one cannot keep it. And if the husband is kind and straightforward, why should not love last? The first phase of married love will pass, it is true, but then there will come a love that is better still. Then there will be the union of souls, they will have everything in common, there will be no secrets between them. And once they have children, the most difficult times will seem to them happy, so long as there is love and courage. Even toil will be a joy, you may deny yourself bread for your children and even that will be a joy, They will love you for it afterwards; so you are laying by for your future. As the children grow up you feel that you are an example, a support for them; that even after you die your children will always keep your thoughts and feelings, because they have received them from you, they will take on your semblance and likeness. So you see this is a great duty. How can it fail to draw the father and mother nearer? People say it's a trial to have children. Who says that? It is heavenly happiness! Are you fond of little children, Liza? I am awfully fond of them. You know—a little rosy baby boy at your bosom, and what husband's heart is not touched, seeing his wife nursing his child! A plump little rosy baby, sprawling and snuggling, chubby little hands and feet, clean tiny little nails, so tiny that it makes one laugh to look at them; eyes that look as if they understand everything. And while it sucks it clutches at your bosom with its little hand, plays. When its father comes up, the child tears itself away from the bosom, flings itself back, looks at its father, laughs, as though it were fearfully funny, and falls to sucking again. Or it will bite its mother's breast when its little teeth are coming, while it looks sideways at her with its little eyes as though to say, 'Look, I am biting!' Is not all that happiness when they are the three together, husband, wife and child? One can forgive a great deal for the sake of such moments. Yes, Liza, one must first learn to live oneself before one blames others!"

"It's by pictures, pictures like that one must get at you," I thought to myself, though I did speak with real feeling, and all at once I flushed crimson. "What if she were suddenly to burst out laughing, what should I do then?" That idea drove me to fury. Towards the end of my speech I really was excited, and now my vanity was somehow wounded. The silence continued. I almost nudged her.

"Why are you—" she began and stopped. But I understood: there was a quiver of something different in her voice, not abrupt, harsh and unyielding as before, but something soft and shamefaced, so shamefaced that I suddenly felt ashamed and guilty.

"What?" I asked, with tender curiosity.

"Why, you. . ."

"What?"

"Why, you . . . speak somehow like a book," she said, and again there was a note of irony in her voice.

That remark sent a pang to my heart. It was not what I was expecting.

I did not understand that she was hiding her feelings under irony, that this is usually the last refuge of modest and chaste-souled people when the privacy of their soul is coarsely and intrusively invaded, and that their pride makes them refuse to surrender till the last moment and shrink from giving expression to their feelings before you. I ought to have guessed the truth from the timidity with which she had repeatedly approached her sarcasm, only bringing herself to utter it at last with an effort. But I did not guess, and an evil feeling took possession of me.

"Wait a bit!" I thought.

7

"Oh, hush, Liza! How can you talk about being like a book, when it makes even me, an outsider, feel sick? Though I don't look at it as an outsider, for, indeed, it touches me to the heart. . . . Is it possible, is it possible that you do not feel sick at being here yourself? Evidently habit does wonders! God knows what habit can do with anyone. Can you seriously think that you will never grow old, that you will always be good-looking, and that they will keep you here for ever and ever? I say nothing of the loathsomeness of the life here. . . . Though let me tell you this about it—about your present life, I mean; here though you are young now, attractive, nice, with soul and feeling, yet you know as soon as I came to myself just now I felt at once sick at being here with you! One can only come here when one is drunk. But if you were anywhere else, living as good people live, I should perhaps be more than attracted by you, should fall in love with you, should be glad of a look from you, let alone a word; I should hang about your door, should go down on my knees to you, should look upon you as my betrothed and think it an honour to be allowed to. I should not dare to have an impure thought about you. But here, you see, I know that I have only to whistle and you have to come with me whether you like it or not. I don't consult your wishes, but you mine. The lowest labourer hires himself as a workman, but he doesn't make a slave of himself altogether; besides, he knows that he will be free again presently. But when are you free? Only think what you are giving up here? What is it you are making a slave of? It is your soul, together with your body; you are selling your soul which you have no right to dispose of! You give your love to be outraged by every drunkard! Love! But that's everything, you know, it's a priceless diamond, it's a maiden's treasure, love—why, a man would be ready to give his soul, to face death to gain that love. But how much is your love worth now? You are sold, all of you, body and soul, and there is no need to strive for love when you can have everything without love. And you know there is no greater insult to a girl than that, do you understand? To be sure, I have heard that they comfort you, poor fools, they let you have lovers of your own here. But you know that's simply a farce, that's simply a sham, it's just laughing at you, and you are taken in by it! Why, do you suppose he really loves you, that lover of yours? I don't believe it. How can he love you when he knows you may be called away from him any minute? He would be a low fellow if he did! Will he have a grain of respect for you? What have you in common with him? He laughs at you and robs you—that is all his love amounts to! You are lucky if he does not beat you. Very likely he does beat you, too. Ask him, if you have got one, whether he will marry you. He will laugh in your face, if he doesn't spit in it or give you a blow—though maybe he is not worth a bad halfpenny himself. And for what have you ruined your life, if you come to think of it? For the coffee they give you to drink and the plentiful meals? But with what object are they feeding you up? An honest girl couldn't swallow the food, for she would know what she was being fed for. You are in debt here, and, of course, you will always be in debt, and you will go on in debt to the end, till the visitors here begin to scorn you. And that will soon happen, don't rely upon your youth—all that flies by express train here, you know. You will be kicked out. And not simply kicked out; long before that she'll begin nagging at you, scolding you, abusing you, as though you had not sacrificed your health for her, had not thrown away your youth and your soul for her benefit, but as though you had ruined her, beggared her, robbed her. And don't expect anyone to take your part: the others, your companions, will attack you, too, win her favour, for all are in slavery here, and have lost all conscience and pity here long ago. They have become utterly vile, and nothing on earth is viler, more loathsome, and more insulting than their abuse. And you are laying down everything here, unconditionally, youth and health and beauty and hope, and at twenty-two you will look like a woman of five-and-thirty, and you will be lucky if you are not diseased, pray to God for that! No doubt you are thinking now that you have a gay time and no work to do! Yet there is no work harder or more dreadful in the world or ever has been. One would think that the heart alone would be worn out with tears. And you won't dare to say a word, not half a word when they drive you away from here; you will go away as though you were to blame. You will change to another house, then to a third, then somewhere else, till you come down at last to the Haymarket. There you will be beaten at every turn; that is good manners there, the visitors don't know how to be friendly without beating you. You don't believe that it is so hateful there? Go and look for yourself some time, you can see with your own eyes. Once, one New Year's Day, I saw a woman at a door. They had turned her out as a joke, to give her a taste of the frost because she had been crying so much, and they shut the door behind her. At nine o'clock in the morning she was already quite drunk, dishevelled, half-naked, covered with bruises, her face was powdered, but she had a black-eye, blood was trickling from her nose and her teeth; some cabman had just given her a drubbing. She was sitting on the stone steps, a salt fish of some sort was in her hand; she was crying, wailing something about her luck and beating with the fish on the steps, and cabmen and drunken soldiers were crowding in the doorway taunting her. You don't believe that you will ever be like that? I should be sorry to believe it, too, but how do you know; maybe ten years, eight years ago that very woman with the salt fish came here fresh as a cherub, innocent, pure, knowing no evil, blushing at every word. Perhaps she was like you, proud, ready to take offence, not like the others; perhaps she looked like a queen, and knew what happiness was in store for the man who should love her and whom she should love. Do you see how it ended? And what if at that very minute when she was beating on the filthy steps with that fish, drunken and dishevelled—what if at that very minute she recalled the pure early days in her father's house, when she used to go to school and the neighbour's son watched for her on the way, declaring that he would love her as long as he lived, that he would devote his life to her, and when they vowed to love one another for ever and be married as soon as they were grown up! No, Liza, it would be happy for you if you were to die soon of consumption in some corner, in some cellar like that woman just now. In the hospital, do you say? You will be lucky if they take you, but what if you are still of use to the madam here? Consumption is a queer disease, it is not like fever. The patient goes on hoping till the last minute and says he is all right. He deludes himself. And that just suits your madam. Don't doubt it, that's how it is; you have sold your soul, and what is more you owe money, so you daren't say a word. But when you are dying, all will abandon you, all will turn away from you, for then there will be nothing to get from you. What's more, they will reproach you for cumbering the place, for being so long over dying. However you beg you won't get a drink of water without abuse: 'Whenever are you going off, you nasty hussy, you won't let us sleep with your moaning, you make the gentlemen sick.' That's true, I have heard such things said myself. They will thrust you dying into the filthiest corner in the cellar—in the damp and darkness; what will your thoughts be, lying there alone? When you die, strange hands will lay you out, with grumbling and impatience; no one will bless you, no one will sigh for you, they only want to get rid of you as soon as may be; they will buy a coffin, take you to the grave as they did that poor woman today, and celebrate your memory at the tavern. In the grave, sleet, filth, wet snow—no need to put themselves out for you— 'Let her down, Vanuha; it's just like her luck—even here, she is head-foremost, the hussy. Shorten the cord, you rascal.' 'It's all right as it is.' 'All right, is it? Why, she's on her side! She was a fellow-creature, after all! But, never mind, throw the earth on her.' And they won't care to waste much time quarrelling over you. They will scatter the wet blue clay as quick as they can and go off to the tavern . . . and there your memory on earth will end; other women have children to go to their graves, fathers, husbands. While for you neither tear, nor sigh, nor remembrance; no one in the whole world will ever come to you, your name will vanish from the face of the earth—as though you had never existed, never been born at all! Nothing but filth and mud, however you knock at your coffin lid at night, when the dead arise, however you cry: 'Let me out, kind people, to live in the light of day! My life was no life at all; my life has been thrown away like a dish-clout; it was drunk away in the tavern at the Haymarket; let me out, kind people, to live in the world again.'"

And I worked myself up to such a pitch that I began to have a lump in my throat myself, and . . . and all at once I stopped, sat up in dismay and, bending over apprehensively, began to listen with a beating heart. I had reason to be troubled.

I had felt for some time that I was turning her soul upside down and rending her heart, and—and the more I was convinced of it, the more eagerly I desired to gain my object as quickly and as effectually as possible. It was the exercise of my skill that carried me away; yet it was not merely sport. . . .

I knew I was speaking stiffly, artificially, even bookishly, in fact, I could not speak except "like a book." But that did not trouble me: I knew, I felt that I should be understood and that this very bookishness might be an assistance. But now, having attained my effect, I was suddenly panic-stricken. Never before had I witnessed such despair! She was lying on her face, thrusting her face into the pillow and clutching it in both hands. Her heart was being torn. Her youthful body was shuddering all over as though in convulsions. Suppressed sobs rent her bosom and suddenly burst out in weeping and wailing, then she pressed closer into the pillow: she did not want anyone here, not a living soul, to know of her anguish and her tears. She bit the pillow, bit her hand till it bled (I saw that afterwards), or, thrusting her fingers into her dishevelled hair, seemed rigid with the effort of restraint, holding her breath and clenching her teeth. I began saying something, begging her to calm herself, but felt that I did not dare; and all at once, in a sort of cold shiver, almost in terror, began fumbling in the dark, trying hurriedly to get dressed to go. It was dark; though I tried my best I could not finish dressing quickly. Suddenly I felt a box of matches and a candlestick with a whole candle in it. As soon as the room was lighted up, Liza sprang up, sat up in bed, and with a contorted face, with a half insane smile, looked at me almost senselessly. I sat down beside her and took her hands; she came to herself, made an impulsive movement towards me, would have caught hold of me, but did not dare, and slowly bowed her head before me.

"Liza, my dear, I was wrong . . . forgive me, my dear," I began, but she squeezed my hand in her fingers so tightly that I felt I was saying the wrong thing and stopped.

"This is my address, Liza, come to me."

"I will come," she answered resolutely, her head still bowed.

"But now I am going, good-bye . . . till we meet again."

I got up; she, too, stood up and suddenly flushed all over, gave a shudder, snatched up a shawl that was lying on a chair and muffled herself in it to her chin. As she did this she gave another sickly smile, blushed and looked at me strangely. I felt wretched; I was in haste to get away—to disappear.

"Wait a minute," she said suddenly, in the passage just at the doorway, stopping me with her hand on my overcoat. She put down the candle in hot haste and ran off; evidently she had thought of something or wanted to show me something. As she ran away she flushed, her eyes shone, and there was a smile on her lips—what was the meaning of it? Against my will I waited: she came back a minute later with an expression that seemed to ask forgiveness for something. In fact, it was not the same face, not the same look as the evening before: sullen, mistrustful and obstinate. Her eyes now were imploring, soft, and at the same time trustful, caressing, timid. The expression with which children look at people they are very fond of, of whom they are asking a favour. Her eyes were a light hazel, they were lovely eyes, full of life, and capable of expressing love as well as sullen hatred.

Making no explanation, as though I, as a sort of higher being, must understand everything without explanations, she held out a piece of paper to me. Her whole face was positively beaming at that instant with naive, almost childish, triumph. I unfolded it. It was a letter to her from a medical student or someone of that sort—a very high-flown and flowery, but extremely respectful, love-letter. I don't recall the words now, but I remember well that through the high-flown phrases there was apparent a genuine feeling, which cannot be feigned. When I had finished reading it I met her glowing, questioning, and childishly impatient eyes fixed upon me. She fastened her eyes upon my face and waited impatiently for what I should say. In a few words, hurriedly, but with a sort of joy and pride, she explained to me that she had been to a dance somewhere in a private house, a family of "very nice people, *who knew nothing*, absolutely nothing, for she had only come here so lately and it had all happened . . . and she hadn't made up her mind to stay and was certainly going away as soon as she had paid her debt. . ." and at that party there had been the student who had danced with her all the evening. He had talked to her, and it turned out that he had known her in old days at Riga when he was a child, they had played together, but a very long time ago—and he knew her parents, but *about this* he knew nothing, nothing whatever, and had no suspicion! And the day after the dance (three days ago) he had sent her that letter through the friend with whom she had gone to the party . . . and . . . well, that was all.

She dropped her shining eyes with a sort of bashfulness as she finished.

The poor girl was keeping that student's letter as a precious treasure, and had run to fetch it, her only treasure, because she did not want me to go away without knowing that she, too, was honestly and genuinely loved; that she, too, was addressed respectfully. No doubt that letter was destined to lie in her box and lead to nothing. But none the less, I am certain that she would keep it all her life as a precious treasure, as her pride and justification, and now at such a minute she had thought of that letter and brought it with naive pride to raise herself in my eyes that I might see, that I, too, might think well of her. I said nothing, pressed her hand and went out. I so longed to get away . . . I walked all the way home, in spite of the fact that the melting snow was still falling in heavy flakes. I was exhausted, shattered, in bewilderment. But behind the bewilderment the truth was already gleaming. The loathsome truth.

8

It was some time, however, before I consented to recognise that truth. Waking up in the morning after some hours of heavy, leaden sleep, and immediately realising all that had happened on the previous day, I was positively amazed at my last night's *sentimentality* with Liza, at all those "outcries of horror and pity." "To think of having such an attack of womanish hysteria, pah!" I concluded. And what did I thrust my address upon her for? What if she comes? Let her come, though; it doesn't matter. . . . But *obviously*, that was not now the chief and the most important matter: I had to make haste and at all costs save my reputation in the eyes of Zverkov and Simonov as quickly as possible; that was the chief business. And I was so taken up that morning that I actually forgot all about Liza.

First of all I had at once to repay what I had borrowed the day before from Simonov. I resolved on a desperate measure: to borrow fifteen roubles straight off from Anton Antonitch. As luck would have it he was in the best of humours that morning, and gave it to me at once, on the first asking. I was so delighted at this that, as I signed the IOU with a swaggering air, I told him casually that the night before "I had been keeping it up with some friends at the Hôtel de Paris; we were giving a farewell party to a comrade, in fact, I might say a friend of my childhood, and you know—a desperate rake, fearfully spoilt—of course, he belongs to a good family, and has considerable means, a brilliant career; he is witty, charming, a regular Lovelace, you understand; we drank an extra 'half-dozen' and . . ."

And it went off all right; all this was uttered very easily, unconstrainedly and complacently.

On reaching home I promptly wrote to Simonov.

To this hour I am lost in admiration when I recall the truly gentlemanly, good-humoured, candid tone of my letter. With tact and good-breeding, and, above all, entirely without superfluous words, I blamed myself for all that had happened. I defended myself, "if I really may be allowed to defend myself," by alleging that being utterly unaccustomed to wine, I had been intoxicated with the first glass, which I said, I had drunk before they arrived, while I was waiting for them at the Hôtel de Paris between five and six o'clock. I begged Simonov's pardon especially; I asked him to convey my explanations to all the others, especially to Zverkov, whom "I seemed to remember as though in a dream" I had insulted. I added that I would have called upon all of them myself, but my head ached, and besides I had not the face to. I was particularly pleased with a certain lightness, almost carelessness (strictly within the bounds of politeness, however), which was apparent in my style, and better than any possible arguments, gave them at once to understand that I took rather an independent view of "all that unpleasantness last night"; that I was by no means so utterly crushed as you, my friends, probably imagine; but on the contrary, looked upon it as a gentleman serenely respecting himself should look upon it. "On a young hero's past no censure is cast!"

"There is actually an aristocratic playfulness about it!" I thought admiringly, as I read over the letter. "And it's all because I am an intellectual and cultivated man! Another man in my place would not have known how to extricate himself, but here I have got out of it and am as jolly as ever again, and all because I am 'a cultivated and educated man of our day.' And, indeed, perhaps, everything was due to the wine yesterday. H'm!" . . . No, it was not the wine. I did not drink anything at all between five and six when I was waiting for them. I had lied to Simonov; I had lied shamelessly; and indeed I wasn't ashamed now. . . . Hang it all though, the great thing was that I was rid of it.

I put six roubles in the letter, sealed it up, and asked Apollon to take it to Simonov. When he learned that there was money in the letter, Apollon became more respectful and agreed to take it. Towards evening I went out for a walk. My head was still aching and giddy after yesterday. But as evening came on and the twilight grew denser, my impressions and, following them, my thoughts, grew more and more different and confused. Something was not dead within me, in the depths of my heart and conscience it would not die, and it showed itself in acute depression. For the most part I jostled my way through the most crowded business streets, along Myeshtchansky Street, along Sadovy Street and in Yusupov Garden. I always liked particularly sauntering along these streets in the dusk, just when there were crowds of working people of all sorts going home from their daily work, with faces looking cross with anxiety. What I liked was just that cheap bustle, that bare prose. On this occasion the jostling of the streets irritated me more than ever, I could not make out what was wrong with me, I could not find the clue, something seemed rising up continually in my soul, painfully, and refusing to be appeased. I returned home completely upset, it was just as though some crime were lying on my conscience.

The thought that Liza was coming worried me continually. It seemed queer to me that of all my recollections of yesterday this tormented me, as it were, especially, as it were, quite separately. Everything else I had quite succeeded in forgetting by the evening; I dismissed it all and was still perfectly satisfied with my letter to Simonov. But on this point I was not satisfied at all. It was as though I were worried only by Liza. "What if she comes," I thought incessantly, "well, it doesn't matter, let her come! H'm! it's horrid that she should see, for instance, how I live. Yesterday I seemed such a hero to her, while now, h'm! It's horrid, though, that I have let myself go so, the room looks like a beggar's. And I brought myself to go out to dinner in such a suit! And my American leather sofa with the stuffing sticking out. And my dressing-gown, which will not cover me, such tatters, and she will see all this and she will see Apollon. That beast is certain to insult her. He will fasten upon her in order to be rude to me. And I, of course, shall be panic-stricken as usual, I shall begin bowing and scraping before her and pulling my dressing-gown round me, I shall begin smiling, telling lies.

Oh, the beastliness! And it isn't the beastliness of it that matters most! There is something more important, more loathsome, viler! Yes, viler! And to put on that dishonest lying mask again! . . ."

When I reached that thought I fired up all at once.

"Why dishonest? How dishonest? I was speaking sincerely last night. I remember there was real feeling in me, too. What I wanted was to excite an honourable feeling in her. . . . Her crying was a good thing, it will have a good effect."

Yet I could not feel at ease. All that evening, even when I had come back home, even after nine o'clock, when I calculated that Liza could not possibly come, still she haunted me, and what was worse, she came back to my mind always in the same position. One moment out of all that had happened last night stood vividly before my imagination; the moment when I struck a match and saw her pale, distorted face, with its look of torture. And what a pitiful, what an unnatural, what a distorted smile she had at that moment! But I did not know then, that fifteen years later I should still in my imagination see Liza, always with the pitiful, distorted, inappropriate smile which was on her face at that minute.

Next day I was ready again to look upon it all as nonsense, due to over-excited nerves, and, above all, as *exaggerated*. I was always conscious of that weak point of mine, and sometimes very much afraid of it. "I exaggerate everything, that is where I go wrong," I repeated to myself every hour. But, however, "Liza will very likely come all the same," was the refrain with which all my reflections ended. I was so uneasy that I sometimes flew into a fury: "She'll come, she is certain to come!" I cried, running about the room, "if not today, she will come tomorrow; she'll find me out! The damnable romanticism of these pure hearts! Oh, the vileness—oh, the silliness—oh, the stupidity of these 'wretched sentimental souls!' Why, how fail to understand? How could one fail to understand? . . ."

But at this point I stopped short, and in great confusion, indeed.

And how few, how few words, I thought, in passing, were needed; how little of the idyllic (and affectedly, bookishly, artificially idyllic too) had sufficed to turn a whole human life at once according to my will. That's virginity, to be sure! Freshness of soil!

At times a thought occurred to me, to go to her, "to tell her all," and beg her not to come to me. But this thought stirred such wrath in me that

I believed I should have crushed that "damned" Liza if she had chanced to be near me at the time. I should have insulted her, have spat at her, have turned her out, have struck her!

One day passed, however, another and another; she did not come and I began to grow calmer. I felt particularly bold and cheerful after nine o'clock, I even sometimes began dreaming, and rather sweetly: I, for instance, became the salvation of Liza, simply through her coming to me and my talking to her. . . . I develop her, educate her. Finally, I notice that she loves me, loves me passionately. I pretend not to understand (I don't know, however, why I pretend, just for effect, perhaps). At last all confusion, transfigured, trembling and sobbing, she flings herself at my feet and says that I am her saviour, and that she loves me better than anything in the world. I am amazed, but. . . . "Liza," I say, "can you imagine that I have not noticed your love? I saw it all, I divined it, but I did not dare to approach you first, because I had an influence over you and was afraid that you would force yourself, from gratitude, to respond to my love, would try to rouse in your heart a feeling which was perhaps absent, and I did not wish that . . . because it would be tyranny . . . it would be indelicate (in short, I launch off at that point into European, inexplicably lofty subtleties a la George Sand), but now, now you are mine, you are my creation, you are pure, you are good, you are my noble wife.

> *'Into my house come bold and free,*
> *Its rightful mistress there to be'."*

Then we begin living together, go abroad and so on, and so on. In fact, in the end it seemed vulgar to me myself, and I began putting out my tongue at myself.

Besides, they won't let her out, "the hussy!" I thought. They don't let them go out very readily, especially in the evening (for some reason I fancied she would come in the evening, and at seven o'clock precisely). Though she did say she was not altogether a slave there yet, and had certain rights; so, h'm! Damn it all, she will come, she is sure to come!

It was a good thing, in fact, that Apollon distracted my attention at that time by his rudeness. He drove me beyond all patience! He was the bane of my life, the curse laid upon me by Providence. We had been squabbling continually for years, and I hated him. My God, how I hated him! I believe I had never hated anyone in my life as I hated him, especially at some moments. He was an elderly, dignified man, who worked part of his time as a tailor. But for some unknown reason he despised me beyond all measure, and looked down upon me insufferably. Though, indeed, he looked down upon everyone. Simply to glance at that flaxen, smoothly brushed head, at the tuft of hair he combed up on his forehead and oiled with sunflower oil, at that dignified mouth, compressed into the shape of the letter V, made one feel one was confronting a man who never doubted of himself. He was a pedant, to the most extreme point, the greatest pedant I had met on earth, and with that had a vanity only befitting Alexander of Macedon. He was in love with every button on his coat, every nail on his fingers—absolutely in love with them, and he looked it! In his behaviour to me he was a perfect tyrant, he spoke very little to me, and if he chanced to glance at me he gave me a firm, majestically self-confident and invariably ironical look that drove me sometimes to fury. He did his work with the air of doing me the greatest favour, though he did scarcely anything for me, and did not, indeed, consider himself bound to do anything. There could be no doubt that he looked upon me as the greatest fool on earth, and that "he did not get rid of me" was simply that he could get wages from me every month. He consented to do nothing for me for seven roubles a month. Many sins should be forgiven me for what I suffered from him. My hatred reached such a point that sometimes his very step almost threw me into convulsions. What I loathed particularly was his lisp. His tongue must have been a little too long or something of that sort, for he continually lisped, and seemed to be very proud of it, imagining that it greatly added to his dignity. He spoke in a slow, measured tone, with his hands behind his back and his eyes fixed on the ground. He maddened me particularly when he read aloud the psalms to himself behind his partition. Many a battle I waged over that reading! But he was awfully fond of reading aloud in the evenings, in a slow, even, sing-song voice, as though over the dead. It is interesting that that is how he has ended: he hires himself out to read the psalms over the dead, and at the same time he kills rats and makes blacking. But at that time I could not get rid of him, it was as though he were chemically combined with my existence. Besides, nothing would have induced him to consent to leave me. I could not live in furnished lodgings: my lodging was my private solitude, my shell, my cave, in which I concealed myself from all mankind, and Apollon seemed to me, for some reason, an integral part of that flat, and for seven years I could not turn him away.

To be two or three days behind with his wages, for instance, was impossible. He would have made such a fuss, I should not have known where to hide my head. But I was so exasperated with everyone during those days, that I made up my mind for some reason and with some object to *punish* Apollon and not to pay him for a fortnight the wages that were owing him. I had for a long time—for the last two years—been intending to do this, simply in order to teach him not to give himself airs with me, and to show him that if I liked I could withhold his wages. I purposed to say nothing to him about it, and was purposely silent indeed, in order to score off his pride and force him to be the first to speak of his wages. Then I would take the seven roubles out of a drawer, show him I have the money put aside on purpose, but that I won't, I won't, I simply won't pay him his wages, I won't just because that is "what I wish," because "I am master, and it is for me to decide," because he has been disrespectful, because he has been rude; but if he were to ask respectfully I might be softened and give it to him, otherwise he might wait another fortnight, another three weeks, a whole month. . . .

But angry as I was, yet he got the better of me. I could not hold out for four days. He began as he always did begin in such cases, for there had been such cases already, there had been attempts (and it may be observed I knew all this beforehand, I knew his nasty tactics by heart). He would begin by fixing upon me an exceedingly severe stare, keeping it up for several minutes at a time, particularly on meeting me or seeing me out of the house. If I held out and pretended not to notice these stares, he would, still in silence, proceed to further tortures. All at once, *à propos* of nothing, he would walk softly and smoothly into my room, when I was pacing up and down or reading, stand at the door, one hand behind his back and one foot behind the other, and fix upon me a stare more than severe, utterly contemptuous. If I suddenly asked him what he wanted, he would make me no answer, but continue staring at me persistently for some seconds, then, with a peculiar compression of his lips and a most significant air, deliberately turn round and deliberately go back to his room. Two hours later he would come out again and again present himself before me in the same way. It had happened that in my fury I did not even ask him what he wanted, but simply raised my head sharply and imperiously and began staring back at him. So we stared at one another for two minutes; at last he turned with deliberation and dignity and went back again for two hours.

If I were still not brought to reason by all this, but persisted in my revolt, he would suddenly begin sighing while he looked at me, long, deep sighs as though measuring by them the depths of my moral degradation, and, of course, it ended at last by his triumphing completely: I raged and shouted, but still was forced to do what he wanted.

This time the usual staring manoeuvres had scarcely begun when I lost my temper and flew at him in a fury. I was irritated beyond endurance apart from him.

"Stay," I cried, in a frenzy, as he was slowly and silently turning, with one hand behind his back, to go to his room. "Stay! Come back, come back, I tell you!" and I must have bawled so unnaturally, that he turned round and even looked at me with some wonder. However, he persisted in saying nothing, and that infuriated me.

"How dare you come and look at me like that without being sent for? Answer!"

After looking at me calmly for half a minute, he began turning round again.

"Stay!" I roared, running up to him, "don't stir! There. Answer, now: what did you come in to look at?"

"If you have any order to give me it's my duty to carry it out," he answered, after another silent pause, with a slow, measured lisp, raising his eyebrows and calmly twisting his head from one side to another, all this with exasperating composure.

"That's not what I am asking you about, you torturer!" I shouted, turning crimson with anger. "I'll tell you why you came here myself: you see, I don't give you your wages, you are so proud you don't want to bow down and ask for it, and so you come to punish me with your stupid stares, to worry me and you have no sus-pic-ion how stupid it is—stupid, stupid, stupid, stupid! . . ."

He would have turned round again without a word, but I seized him.

"Listen," I shouted to him. "Here's the money, do you see, here it is," (I took it out of the table drawer); "here's the seven roubles complete, but you are not going to have it, you . . . are . . . not . . . going . . . to . . . have it until you come respectfully with bowed head to beg my pardon. Do you hear?"

"That cannot be," he answered, with the most unnatural self-confidence.

"It shall be so," I said, "I give you my word of honour, it shall be!"

"And there's nothing for me to beg your pardon for," he went on, as though he had not noticed my exclamations at all. "Why, besides, you called me a 'torturer,' for which I can summon you at the police-station at any time for insulting behaviour."

"Go, summon me," I roared, "go at once, this very minute, this very second! You are a torturer all the same! a torturer!"

But he merely looked at me, then turned, and regardless of my loud calls to him, he walked to his room with an even step and without looking round.

"If it had not been for Liza nothing of this would have happened," I decided inwardly. Then, after waiting a minute, I went myself behind his screen with a dignified and solemn air, though my heart was beating slowly and violently.

"Apollon," I said quietly and emphatically, though I was breathless, "go at once without a minute's delay and fetch the police-officer."

He had meanwhile settled himself at his table, put on his spectacles and taken up some sewing. But, hearing my order, he burst into a guffaw.

"At once, go this minute! Go on, or else you can't imagine what will happen."

"You are certainly out of your mind," he observed, without even raising his head, lisping as deliberately as ever and threading his needle. "Whoever heard of a man sending for the police against himself? And as for being frightened—you are upsetting yourself about nothing, for nothing will come of it."

"Go!" I shrieked, clutching him by the shoulder. I felt I should strike him in a minute.

But I did not notice the door from the passage softly and slowly open at that instant and a figure come in, stop short, and begin staring at us in perplexity I glanced, nearly swooned with shame, and rushed back to my room. There, clutching at my hair with both hands, I leaned my head against the wall and stood motionless in that position.

Two minutes later I heard Apollon's deliberate footsteps. "There is some woman asking for you," he said, looking at me with peculiar severity. Then he stood aside and let in Liza. He would not go away, but stared at us sarcastically.

"Go away, go away," I commanded in desperation. At that moment my clock began whirring and wheezing and struck seven.

9

"Into my house come bold and free,
Its rightful mistress there to be."

I stood before her crushed, crestfallen, revoltingly confused, and I believe I smiled as I did my utmost to wrap myself in the skirts of my ragged wadded dressing-gown—exactly as I had imagined the scene not long before in a fit of depression. After standing over us for a couple of minutes Apollon went away, but that did not make me more at ease. What made it worse was that she, too, was overwhelmed with confusion, more so, in fact, than I should have expected. At the sight of me, of course.

"Sit down," I said mechanically, moving a chair up to the table, and I sat down on the sofa. She obediently sat down at once and gazed at me open-eyed, evidently expecting something from me at once. This naïveté of expectation drove me to fury, but I restrained myself.

She ought to have tried not to notice, as though everything had been as usual, while instead of that, she . . . and I dimly felt that I should make her pay dearly for *all this*.

"You have found me in a strange position, Liza," I began, stammering and knowing that this was the wrong way to begin. "No, no, don't imagine anything," I cried, seeing that she had suddenly flushed. "I am not ashamed of my poverty.... On the contrary, I look with pride on my poverty. I am poor but honourable.... One can be poor and honourable," I muttered. "However... would you like tea?...."

"No," she was beginning.

"Wait a minute."

I leapt up and ran to Apollon. I had to get out of the room somehow.

"Apollon," I whispered in feverish haste, flinging down before him the seven roubles which had remained all the time in my clenched fist, "here are your wages, you see I give them to you; but for that you must come to my rescue: bring me tea and a dozen rusks from the restaurant. If you won't go, you'll make me a miserable man! You don't know what this woman is.... This is—everything! You may be imagining something.... But you don't know what that woman is!..."

Apollon, who had already sat down to his work and put on his spectacles again, at first glanced askance at the money without speaking or putting down his needle; then, without paying the slightest attention to me or making any answer, he went on busying himself with his needle, which he had not yet threaded. I waited before him for three minutes with my arms crossed *à la Napoléon*. My temples were moist with sweat. I was pale, I felt it. But, thank God, he must have been moved to pity, looking at me. Having threaded his needle he deliberately got up from his seat, deliberately moved back his chair, deliberately took off his spectacles, deliberately counted the money, and finally asking me over his shoulder: "Shall I get a whole portion?" deliberately walked out of the room. As I was going back to Liza, the thought occurred to me on the way: shouldn't I run away just as I was in my dressing-gown, no matter where, and then let happen what would?

I sat down again. She looked at me uneasily. For some minutes we were silent.

"I will kill him," I shouted suddenly, striking the table with my fist so that the ink spurted out of the inkstand.

"What are you saying!" she cried, starting.

"I will kill him! kill him!" I shrieked, suddenly striking the table in absolute frenzy, and at the same time fully understanding how stupid it was to be in such a frenzy. "You don't know, Liza, what that torturer is to me. He is my torturer. . . . He has gone now to fetch some rusks; he . . ."

And suddenly I burst into tears. It was an hysterical attack. How ashamed I felt in the midst of my sobs; but still I could not restrain them.

She was frightened.

"What is the matter? What is wrong?" she cried, fussing about me.

"Water, give me water, over there!" I muttered in a faint voice, though I was inwardly conscious that I could have got on very well without water and without muttering in a faint voice. But I was, what is called, *putting it on*, to save appearances, though the attack was a genuine one.

She gave me water, looking at me in bewilderment. At that moment Apollon brought in the tea. It suddenly seemed to me that this commonplace, prosaic tea was horribly undignified and paltry after all that had happened, and I blushed crimson. Liza looked at Apollon with positive alarm. He went out without a glance at either of us.

"Liza, do you despise me?" I asked, looking at her fixedly, trembling with impatience to know what she was thinking.

She was confused, and did not know what to answer.

"Drink your tea," I said to her angrily. I was angry with myself, but, of course, it was she who would have to pay for it. A horrible spite against her suddenly surged up in my heart; I believe I could have killed her. To revenge myself on her I swore inwardly not to say a word to her all the time. "She is the cause of it all," I thought.

Our silence lasted for five minutes. The tea stood on the table; we did not touch it. I had got to the point of purposely refraining from beginning in order to embarrass her further; it was awkward for her to begin alone. Several times she glanced at me with mournful perplexity. I was obstinately silent. I was, of course, myself the chief sufferer, because I was fully conscious of the disgusting meanness of my spiteful stupidity, and yet at the same time I could not restrain myself.

"I want to. . . get away . . . from there altogether," she began, to break the silence in some way, but, poor girl, that was just what she ought not to have spoken about at such a stupid moment to a man so stupid as I was. My heart positively ached with pity for her tactless and unnecessary straightforwardness. But something hideous at once stifled all compassion in me; it even provoked me to greater venom. I did not care what happened. Another five minutes passed.

"Perhaps I am in your way," she began timidly, hardly audibly, and was getting up.

But as soon as I saw this first impulse of wounded dignity I positively trembled with spite, and at once burst out.

"Why have you come to me, tell me that, please?" I began, gasping for breath and regardless of logical connection in my words. I longed to have it all out at once, at one burst; I did not even trouble how to begin. "Why have you come? Answer, answer," I cried, hardly knowing what I was doing. "I'll tell you, my good girl, why you have come. You've come because I talked sentimental stuff to you then. So now you are soft as butter and longing for fine sentiments again. So you may as well know that I was laughing at you then. And I am laughing at you now. Why are you shuddering? Yes, I was laughing at you! I had been insulted just before, at dinner, by the fellows who came that evening before me. I came to you, meaning to thrash one of them, an officer; but I didn't succeed, I didn't find him; I had to avenge the insult on someone to get back my own again; you turned up, I vented my spleen on you and laughed at you. I had been humiliated, so I wanted to humiliate; I had been treated like a rag, so I wanted to show my power. . . . That's what it was, and you imagined I had come there on purpose to save you. Yes? You imagined that? You imagined that?"

I knew that she would perhaps be muddled and not take it all in exactly, but I knew, too, that she would grasp the gist of it, very well indeed. And so, indeed, she did. She turned white as a handkerchief, tried to say something, and her lips worked painfully; but she sank on a chair as though she had been felled by an axe. And all the time afterwards she listened to me with her lips parted and her eyes wide open, shuddering with awful terror. The cynicism, the cynicism of my words overwhelmed her. . . .

"Save you!" I went on, jumping up from my chair and running up and down the room before her. "Save you from what? But perhaps I am worse than you myself. Why didn't you throw it in my teeth when I was giving you that sermon: 'But what did you come here yourself for? was it to read us a sermon?' Power, power was what I wanted then, sport was what I wanted, I wanted to wring out your tears, your humiliation, your hysteria—that was what I wanted then! Of course, I couldn't keep it up then, because I am a wretched creature, I was frightened, and, the devil knows why, gave you my address in my folly. Afterwards, before I got home, I was cursing and swearing at you because of that address, I hated you already because of the lies I had told you. Because I only like playing with words, only dreaming, but, do you know, what I really want is that you should all go to hell. That is what I want. I want peace; yes, I'd sell the whole world for a farthing, straight off, so long as I was left in peace. Is the world to go to pot, or am I to go without my tea? I say that the world may go to pot for me so long as I always get my tea. Did you know that, or not? Well, anyway, I know that I am a blackguard, a scoundrel, an egoist, a sluggard. Here I have been shuddering for the last three days at the thought of your coming. And do you know what has worried me particularly for these three days? That I posed as such a hero to you, and now you would see me in a wretched torn dressing-gown, beggarly, loathsome. I told you just now that I was not ashamed of my poverty; so you may as well know that I am ashamed of it; I am more ashamed of it than of anything, more afraid of it than of being found out if I were a thief, because I am as vain as though I had been skinned and the very air blowing on me hurt. Surely by now you must realise that I shall never forgive you for having found me in this wretched dressing-gown, just as I was flying at Apollon like a spiteful cur. The saviour, the former hero, was flying like a mangy, unkempt sheep-dog at his lackey, and the lackey was jeering at him! And I shall never forgive you for the tears I could not help shedding before you just now, like some silly woman put to shame! And for what I am confessing to you now, I shall never forgive you either! Yes—you must answer for it all because you turned up like this, because I am a blackguard, because I am the nastiest, stupidest, absurdest and most envious of all the worms on earth, who are not a bit better than I am, but, the devil knows why, are never put to confusion; while I shall always be insulted by every louse, that is my doom! And what is it to me that you don't understand a word of this! And what do I care, what do I care about you, and whether you go to ruin there or not? Do you understand? How I shall hate you now after saying this, for having been here and listening. Why, it's not once in a lifetime a man speaks out like this, and then it is in hysterics! . . . What more do you want? Why do you still stand confronting me, after all this? Why are you worrying me? Why don't you go?"

But at this point a strange thing happened. I was so accustomed to think and imagine everything from books, and to picture everything in the world to myself just as I had made it up in my dreams beforehand, that I could not all at once take in this strange circumstance. What happened was this: Liza, insulted and crushed by me, understood a great deal more than I imagined. She understood from all this what a woman understands first of all, if she feels genuine love, that is, that I was myself unhappy.

The frightened and wounded expression on her face was followed first by a look of sorrowful perplexity. When I began calling myself a scoundrel and a blackguard and my tears flowed (the tirade was accompanied throughout by tears) her whole face worked convulsively. She was on the point of getting up and stopping me; when I finished she took no notice of my shouting: "Why are you here, why don't you go away?" but realised only that it must have been very bitter to me to say all this. Besides, she was so crushed, poor girl; she considered herself infinitely beneath me; how could she feel anger or resentment? She suddenly leapt up from her chair with an irresistible impulse and held out her hands, yearning towards me, though still timid and not daring to stir. . . . At this point there was a revulsion in my heart too. Then she suddenly rushed to me, threw her arms round me and burst into tears. I, too, could not restrain myself, and sobbed as I never had before.

"They won't let me . . . I can't be good!" I managed to articulate; then I went to the sofa, fell on it face downwards, and sobbed on it for a quarter of an hour in genuine hysterics. She came close to me, put her arms round me and stayed motionless in that position. But the trouble was that the hysterics could not go on for ever, and (I am writing the loathsome truth) lying face downwards on the sofa with my face thrust into my nasty leather pillow, I began by degrees to be aware of a far-away, involuntary but irresistible feeling that it would be awkward now for me to raise my head and look Liza straight in the face. Why was I ashamed? I don't know, but I was ashamed. The thought, too, came into my overwrought brain that our parts now were completely changed, that she was now the heroine, while I was just a crushed and humiliated creature as she had been before me that night—four days before. . . . And all this came into my mind during the minutes I was lying on my face on the sofa.

My God! surely I was not envious of her then.

I don't know, to this day I cannot decide, and at the time, of course, I was still less able to understand what I was feeling than now. I cannot get on without domineering and tyrannising over someone, but . . . there is no explaining anything by reasoning and so it is useless to reason.

I conquered myself, however, and raised my head; I had to do so sooner or later . . . and I am convinced to this day that it was just because I was ashamed to look at her that another feeling was suddenly kindled and flamed up in my heart . . . a feeling of mastery and possession. My eyes gleamed with passion, and I gripped her hands tightly. How I hated her and how I was drawn to her at that minute! The one feeling intensified the other. It was almost like an act of vengeance. At first there was a look of amazement, even of terror on her face, but only for one instant. She warmly and rapturously embraced me.

10

A quarter of an hour later I was rushing up and down the room in frenzied impatience, from minute to minute I went up to the screen and peeped through the crack at Liza. She was sitting on the ground with her head leaning against the bed, and must have been crying. But she did not go away, and that irritated me. This time she understood it all. I had insulted her finally, but . . . there's no need to describe it. She realised that my outburst of passion had been simply revenge, a fresh humiliation, and that to my earlier, almost causeless hatred was added now a *personal hatred*, born of envy. . . . Though I do not maintain positively that she understood all this distinctly; but she certainly did fully understand that I was a despicable man, and what was worse, incapable of loving her.

I know I shall be told that this is incredible—but it is incredible to be as spiteful and stupid as I was; it may be added that it was strange I should not love her, or at any rate, appreciate her love. Why is it strange? In the first place, by then I was incapable of love, for I repeat, with me loving meant tyrannising and showing my moral superiority. I have never in my life been able to imagine any other sort of love, and have nowadays come to the point of sometimes thinking that love really consists in the right—freely given by the beloved object—to tyrannise over her.

Even in my underground dreams I did not imagine love except as a struggle. I began it always with hatred and ended it with moral subjugation, and afterwards I never knew what to do with the subjugated object. And what is there to wonder at in that, since I had succeeded in so corrupting myself, since I was so out of touch with "real life," as to have actually thought of reproaching her, and putting her to shame for having come to me to hear "fine sentiments"; and did not even guess that she had come not to hear fine sentiments, but to love me, because to a woman all reformation, all salvation from any sort of ruin, and all moral renewal is included in love and can only show itself in that form.

I did not hate her so much, however, when I was running about the room and peeping through the crack in the screen. I was only insufferably oppressed by her being here. I wanted her to disappear. I wanted "peace," to be left alone in my underground world. Real life oppressed me with its novelty so much that I could hardly breathe.

But several minutes passed and she still remained, without stirring, as though she were unconscious. I had the shamelessness to tap softly at the screen as though to remind her. . . . She started, sprang up, and flew to seek her kerchief, her hat, her coat, as though making her escape from me. . . . Two minutes later she came from behind the screen and looked with heavy eyes at me. I gave a spiteful grin, which was forced, however, to *keep up appearances*, and I turned away from her eyes.

"Good-bye," she said, going towards the door.

I ran up to her, seized her hand, opened it, thrust something in it and closed it again. Then I turned at once and dashed away in haste to the other corner of the room to avoid seeing, anyway. . . .

I did mean a moment since to tell a lie—to write that I did this accidentally, not knowing what I was doing through foolishness, through losing my head. But I don't want to lie, and so I will say straight out that I opened her hand and put the money in it . . . from spite. It came into my head to do this while I was running up and down the room and she was sitting behind the screen. But this I can say for certain: though I did that cruel thing purposely, it was not an impulse from the heart, but came from my evil brain. This cruelty was so affected, so purposely made up, so completely a product of the brain, of books, that I could not even keep it up a minute—first I dashed away to avoid seeing her, and then in shame and despair rushed after Liza. I opened the door in the passage and began listening.

"Liza! Liza!" I cried on the stairs, but in a low voice, not boldly. There was no answer, but I fancied I heard her footsteps, lower down on the stairs.

"Liza!" I cried, more loudly.

No answer. But at that minute I heard the stiff outer glass door open heavily with a creak and slam violently; the sound echoed up the stairs.

She had gone. I went back to my room in hesitation. I felt horribly oppressed.

I stood still at the table, beside the chair on which she had sat and looked aimlessly before me. A minute passed, suddenly I started; straight before me on the table I saw. . . . In short, I saw a crumpled blue five-rouble note, the one I had thrust into her hand a minute before. It was the same note; it could be no other, there was no other in the flat. So she had managed to fling it from her hand on the table at the moment when I had dashed into the further corner.

Well! I might have expected that she would do that. Might I have expected it? No, I was such an egoist, I was so lacking in respect for my fellow-creatures that I could not even imagine she would do so. I could not endure it. A minute later I flew like a madman to dress, flinging on what I could at random and ran headlong after her. She could not have got two hundred paces away when I ran out into the street.

It was a still night and the snow was coming down in masses and falling almost perpendicularly, covering the pavement and the empty street as though with a pillow. There was no one in the street, no sound was to be heard. The street lamps gave a disconsolate and useless glimmer. I ran two hundred paces to the cross-roads and stopped short.

Where had she gone? And why was I running after her?

Why? To fall down before her, to sob with remorse, to kiss her feet, to entreat her forgiveness! I longed for that, my whole breast was being rent to pieces, and never, never shall I recall that minute with indifference. But—what for? I thought. Should I not begin to hate her, perhaps, even tomorrow, just because I had kissed her feet today? Should I give her happiness? Had I not recognised that day, for the hundredth time, what I was worth? Should I not torture her?

I stood in the snow, gazing into the troubled darkness and pondered this.

"And will it not be better?" I mused fantastically, afterwards at home, stifling the living pang of my heart with fantastic dreams. "Will it not be better that she should keep the resentment of the insult for ever? Resentment—why, it is purification; it is a most stinging and painful consciousness! Tomorrow I should have defiled her soul and have exhausted her heart, while now the feeling of insult will never die in her heart, and however loathsome the filth awaiting her—the feeling of insult will elevate and purify her . . . by hatred . . . h'm! . . . perhaps, too, by forgiveness. . . . Will all that make things easier for her though? . . ."

And, indeed, I will ask on my own account here, an idle question: which is better—cheap happiness or exalted sufferings? Well, which is better?

So I dreamed as I sat at home that evening, almost dead with the pain in my soul. Never had I endured such suffering and remorse, yet could there have been the faintest doubt when I ran out from my lodging that I should turn back half-way? I never met Liza again and I have heard nothing of her. I will add, too, that I remained for a long time afterwards pleased with the phrase about the benefit from resentment and hatred in spite of the fact that I almost fell ill from misery.

*****

Even now, so many years later, all this is somehow a very evil memory. I have many evil memories now, but . . . hadn't I better end my "Notes" here? I believe I made a mistake in beginning to write them, anyway I have felt ashamed all the time I've been writing this story; so it's hardly literature so much as a corrective punishment. Why, to tell long stories, showing how I have spoiled my life through morally rotting in my corner, through lack of fitting environment, through divorce from real life, and rankling spite in my underground world, would certainly not be interesting; a novel needs a hero, and all the traits for an anti-hero are *expressly* gathered together here, and what matters most, it all produces an unpleasant impression, for we are all divorced from life, we are all cripples, every one of us, more or less.

We are so divorced from it that we feel at once a sort of loathing for real life, and so cannot bear to be reminded of it. Why, we have come almost to looking upon real life as an effort, almost as hard work, and we are all privately agreed that it is better in books. And why do we fuss and fume sometimes? Why are we perverse and ask for something else? We don't know what ourselves. It would be the worse for us if our petulant prayers were answered. Come, try, give any one of us, for instance, a little more independence, untie our hands, widen the spheres of our activity, relax the control and we . . . yes, I assure you . . . we should be begging to be under control again at once. I know that you will very likely be angry with me for that, and will begin shouting and stamping. Speak for yourself, you will say, and for your miseries in your underground holes, and don't dare to say all of us—excuse me, gentlemen, I am not justifying myself with that "all of us." As for what concerns me in particular I have only in my life carried to an extreme what you have not dared to carry halfway, and what's more, you have taken your cowardice for good sense, and have found comfort in deceiving yourselves. So that perhaps, after all, there is more life in me than in you. Look into it more carefully! Why, we don't even know what living means now, what it is, and what it is called? Leave us alone without books and we shall be lost and in confusion at once. We shall not know what to join on to, what to cling to, what to love and what to hate, what to respect and what to despise. We are oppressed at being men—men with a real individual body and blood, we are ashamed of it, we think it a disgrace and try to contrive to be some sort of impossible generalised man. We are stillborn, and for generations past have been begotten, not by living fathers, and that suits us better and better. We are developing a taste for it. Soon we shall contrive to be born somehow from an idea. But enough; I don't want to write more from "Underground."

> [The notes of this paradoxalist do not end here, however. He could not refrain from going on with them, but it seems to us that we may stop here.]

SHORT STORIES

Translated by Constance Garnett

White Nights

A Sentimental Story from the Diary of a Dreamer

FIRST NIGHT

It was a wonderful night, such a night as is only possible when we are young, dear reader. The sky was so starry, so bright that, looking at it, one could not help asking oneself whether ill-humoured and capricious people could live under such a sky. That is a youthful question too, dear reader, very youthful, but may the Lord put it more frequently into your heart! . . . Speaking of capricious and ill-humoured people, I cannot help recalling my moral condition all that day. From early morning I had been oppressed by a strange despondency. It suddenly seemed to me that I was lonely, that every one was forsaking me and going away from me. Of course, any one is entitled to ask who "every one" was. For though I had been living almost eight years in Petersburg I had hardly an acquaintance. But what did I want with acquaintances? I was acquainted with all Petersburg as it was;

that was why I felt as though they were all deserting me when all Petersburg packed up and went to its summer villa. I felt afraid of being left alone, and for three whole days I wandered about the town in profound dejection, not knowing what to do with myself. Whether I walked in the Nevsky, went to the Gardens or sauntered on the embankment, there was not one face of those I had been accustomed to meet at the same time and place all the year. They, of course, do not know me, but I know them. I know them intimately, I have almost made a study of their faces, and am delighted when they are gay, and downcast when they are under a cloud. I have almost struck up a friendship with one old man whom I meet every blessed day, at the same hour in Fontanka. Such a grave, pensive countenance; he is always whispering to himself and brandishing his left arm, while in his right hand he holds a long gnarled stick with a gold knob. He even notices me and takes a warm interest in me. If I happen not to be at a certain time in the same spot in Fontanka, I am certain he feels disappointed. That is how it is that we almost bow to each other, especially when we are both in good humour. The other day, when we had not seen each other for two days and met on the third, we were actually touching our hats, but, realizing in time, dropped our hands and passed each other with a look of interest.

I know the houses too. As I walk along they seem to run forward in the streets to look out at me from every window, and almost to say: "Good-morning! How do you do? I am quite well, thank God, and I am to have a new storey in May," or, "How are you? I am being redecorated to-morrow;" or, "I was almost burnt down and had such a fright," and so on. I have my favourites among them, some are dear friends; one of them intends to be treated by the architect this summer. I shall go every day on purpose to see that the operation is not a failure. God forbid! But I shall never forget an incident with a very pretty little house of a light pink colour. It was such a charming little brick house, it looked so hospitably at me, and so proudly at its ungainly neighbours, that my heart rejoiced whenever I happened to pass it. Suddenly last week I walked along the street, and when I looked at my friend I heard a plaintive, "They are painting me yellow!" The villains! The barbarians! They had spared nothing, neither columns, nor cornices, and my poor little friend was as yellow as a canary. It almost made me bilious. And to this day I have not had the courage to visit my poor disfigured friend, painted the colour of the Celestial Empire.

So now you understand, reader, in what sense I am acquainted with all Petersburg.

I have mentioned already that I had felt worried for three whole days before I guessed the cause of my uneasiness. And I felt ill at ease in the street—this one had gone and that one had gone, and what had become of the other?—and at home I did not feel like myself either. For two evenings I was puzzling my brains to think what was amiss in my corner; why I felt so uncomfortable in it. And in perplexity I scanned my grimy green walls, my ceiling covered with a spider's web, the growth of which Matrona has so successfully encouraged. I looked over all my furniture, examined every chair, wondering whether the trouble lay there (for if one chair is not standing in the same position as it stood the day before, I am not myself). I looked at the window, but it was all in vain . . . I was not a bit the better for it! I even bethought me to send for Matrona, and was giving her some fatherly admonitions in regard to the spider's web and sluttishness in general; but she simply stared at me in amazement and went away without saying a word, so that the spider's web is comfortably hanging in its place to this day. I only at last this morning realized what was wrong. Aie! Why, they are giving me the slip and making off to their summer villas! Forgive the triviality of the expression, but I am in no mood for fine language . . . for everything that had been in Petersburg had gone or was going away for the holidays; for every respectable gentleman of dignified appearance who took a cab was at once transformed, in my eyes, into a respectable head of a household who after his daily duties were over, was making his way to the bosom of his family, to the summer villa; for all the passers-by had now quite a peculiar air which seemed to say to every one they met: "We are only here for the moment, gentlemen, and in another two hours we shall be going off to the summer villa." If a window opened after delicate fingers, white as snow, had tapped upon the pane, and the head of a pretty girl was thrust out, calling to a street-seller with pots of flowers—at once on the spot I fancied that those flowers were being bought not simply in order to enjoy the flowers and the spring in stuffy town lodgings, but because they would all be very soon moving into the country and could take the flowers with them. What is more, I made such progress in my new peculiar sort of investigation that I could distinguish correctly from the mere air of each in what summer villa he was living. The inhabitants of Kamenny and Aptekarsky Islands or of the Peterhof Road were marked by the studied elegance of their manner, their fashionable summer suits, and the fine carriages in which they drove to town. Visitors to Pargolovo and places further away impressed one at first sight by their reasonable and dignified air; the tripper to Krestovsky Island could be recognized by his look of irrepressible gaiety. If I chanced to meet a long procession of waggoners walking lazily with the reins in their hands beside waggons loaded with regular mountains of furniture, tables, chairs, ottomans and sofas and domestic utensils of all sorts, frequently with a decrepit cook sitting on the top of it all, guarding her master's property as though it were the apple of her eye; or if I saw boats heavily loaded with household goods crawling along the Neva or Fontanka to the Black River or the Islands—the waggons and the boats were multiplied tenfold, a hundredfold, in my eyes. I fancied that everything was astir and moving, everything was going in regular caravans to the summer villas. It seemed as though Petersburg threatened to become a wilderness, so that at last I felt ashamed, mortified and sad that I had nowhere to go for the holidays and no reason to go away. I was ready to go away with every waggon, to drive off with every gentleman of respectable appearance who took a cab; but no one—absolutely no one—invited me; it seemed they had forgotten me, as though really I were a stranger to them!

I took long walks, succeeding, as I usually did, in quite forgetting where I was, when I suddenly found myself at the city gates. Instantly I felt lighthearted, and I passed the barrier and walked between cultivated fields and meadows, unconscious of fatigue, and feeling only all over as though a burden were falling off my soul. All the passers-by gave me such friendly looks that they seemed almost greeting me, they all seemed so pleased at something. They were all smoking cigars, every one of them. And I felt pleased as I never had before. It was as though I had suddenly found myself in Italy—so strong was the effect of nature upon a half-sick townsman like me, almost stifling between city walls.

There is something inexpressibly touching in nature round Petersburg, when at the approach of spring she puts forth all her might, all the powers bestowed on her by Heaven, when she breaks into leaf, decks herself out and spangles herself with flowers. . . . Somehow I cannot help being reminded of a frail, consumptive girl, at whom one sometimes looks with compassion, sometimes with sympathetic love, whom sometimes one simply does not notice; though suddenly in one instant she becomes, as though by chance, inexplicably lovely and exquisite, and, impressed and intoxicated, one cannot help asking oneself what power made those sad, pensive eyes flash with such fire? What summoned the blood to those pale, wan cheeks? What bathed with passion those soft features? What set that bosom heaving? What so suddenly called strength, life and beauty into the poor girl's face, making it gleam with such a smile, kindle with such bright, sparkling laughter? You look round, you seek for some one, you conjecture. . . . But the moment passes, and next day you meet, maybe, the same pensive and preoccupied look as before, the same pale face, the same meek and timid movements, and even signs of remorse, traces of a mortal anguish and regret for the fleeting distraction. . . . And you grieve that the momentary beauty has faded so soon never to return, that it flashed upon you so treacherously, so vainly, grieve because you had not even time to love her. . . .

And yet my night was better than my day! This was how it happened.

I came back to the town very late, and it had struck ten as I was going towards my lodgings. My way lay along the canal embankment, where at that hour you never meet a soul. It is true that I live in a very remote part of the town. I walked along singing, for when I am happy I am always humming to myself like every happy man who has no friend or acquaintance with whom to share his joy. Suddenly I had a most unexpected adventure.

Leaning on the canal railing stood a woman with her elbows on the rail, she was apparently looking with great attention at the muddy water of the canal. She was wearing a very charming yellow hat and a jaunty little black mantle. "She's a girl, and I am sure she is dark," I thought. She did not seem to hear my footsteps, and did not even stir when I passed by with bated breath and loudly throbbing heart.

"Strange," I thought; "she must be deeply absorbed in something," and all at once I stopped as though petrified. I heard a muffled sob. Yes! I was not mistaken, the girl was crying, and a minute later I heard sob after sob. Good Heavens! My heart sank. And timid as I was with women, yet this was such a moment! . . . I turned, took a step towards her, and should certainly have pronounced the word "Madam!" if I had not known that that exclamation has been uttered a thousand times in every Russian society novel. It was only that reflection stopped me. But while I was seeking for a word, the girl came to herself, looked round, started, cast down her eyes and slipped by me along the embankment. I at once followed her; but she, divining this, left the embankment, crossed the road and walked along the pavement. I dared not cross the street after her. My heart was fluttering like a captured bird. All at once a chance came to my aid.

Along the same side of the pavement there suddenly came into sight, not far from the girl, a gentleman in evening dress, of dignified years, though by no means of dignified carriage; he was staggering and cautiously leaning against the wall. The girl flew straight as an arrow, with the timid haste one sees in all girls who do not want any one to volunteer to accompany them home at night, and no doubt the staggering gentleman would not have pursued her, if my good luck had not prompted him.

Suddenly, without a word to any one, the gentleman set off and flew full speed in pursuit of my unknown lady. She was racing like the wind, but the staggering gentleman was overtaking—overtook her. The girl uttered a shriek, and . . . I bless my luck for the excellent knotted stick, which happened on that occasion to be in my right hand. In a flash I was on the other side of the street; in a flash the obtrusive gentleman had taken in the position, had grasped the irresistible argument, fallen back without a word, and only when we were very far away protested against my action in rather vigorous language. But his words hardly reached us.

"Give me your arm," I said to the girl. "And he won't dare to annoy us further."

She took my arm without a word, still trembling with excitement and terror. Oh, obtrusive gentleman! How I blessed you at that moment! I stole a glance at her, she was very charming and dark—I had guessed right.

On her black eyelashes there still glistened a tear—from her recent terror or her former grief—I don't know. But there was already a gleam of a smile on her lips. She too stole a glance at me, faintly blushed and looked down.

"There, you see; why did you drive me away? If I had been here, nothing would have happened. . . ."

"But I did not know you; I thought that you too. . . ."

"Why, do you know me now?"

"A little! Here, for instance, why are you trembling?"

"Oh, you are right at the first guess!" I answered, delighted that my girl had intelligence; that is never out of place in company with beauty. "Yes, from the first glance you have guessed the sort of man you have to do with. Precisely; I am shy with women, I am agitated, I don't deny it, as much so as you were a minute ago when that gentleman alarmed you. I am in some alarm now. It's like a dream, and I never guessed even in my sleep that I should ever talk with any woman."

"What? Really? . . . "

"Yes; if my arm trembles, it is because it has never been held by a pretty little hand like yours. I am a complete stranger to women; that is, I have never been used to them. You see, I am alone. . . . I don't even know how to talk to them. Here, I don't know now whether I have not said something silly to you! Tell me frankly; I assure you beforehand that I am not quick to take offence? . . . "

"No, nothing, nothing, quite the contrary. And if you insist on my speaking frankly, I will tell you that women like such timidity; and if you want to know more, I like it too, and I won't drive you away till I get home."

"You will make me," I said, breathless with delight, "lose my timidity, and then farewell to all my chances. . . ."

"Chances! What chances—of what? That's not so nice."

"I beg your pardon, I am sorry, it was a slip of the tongue; but how can you expect one at such a moment to have no desire. . . ."

"To be liked, eh?"

"Well, yes; but do, for goodness' sake, be kind. Think what I am! Here, I am twenty-six and I have never seen any one. How can I speak well, tactfully, and to the point? It will seem better to you when I have told you everything openly. . . . I don't know how to be silent when my heart is speaking. Well, never mind. . . . Believe me, not one woman, never, never! No acquaintance of any sort! And I do nothing but dream every day that at last I shall meet some one. Oh, if only you knew how often I have been in love in that way. . . ."

"How? With whom? . . . "

"Why, with no one, with an ideal, with the one I dream of in my sleep. I make up regular romances in my dreams. Ah, you don't know me! It's true, of course, I have met two or three women, but what sort of women were they? They were all landladies, that. . . . But I shall make you laugh if I tell you that I have several times thought of speaking, just simply speaking, to some aristocratic lady in the street, when she is alone, I need hardly say; speaking to her, of course, timidly, respectfully, passionately; telling her that I am perishing in solitude, begging her not to send me away; saying that I have no chance of making the acquaintance of any woman; impressing upon her that it is a positive duty for a woman not to repulse so timid a prayer from such a luckless man as me. That, in fact, all I ask is, that she should say two or three sisterly words with sympathy, should not repulse me at first sight; should take me on trust and listen to what I say; should laugh at me if she likes, encourage me, say two words to me, only two words, even though we never meet again afterwards! . . . But you are laughing; however, that is why I am telling you. . . ."

"Don't be vexed; I am only laughing at your being your own enemy, and if you had tried you would have succeeded, perhaps, even though it had been in the street; the simpler the better. . . . No kind-hearted woman, unless she were stupid or, still more, vexed about something at the moment, could bring herself to send you away without those two words which you ask for so timidly. . . . But what am I saying? Of course she would take you for a madman. I was judging by myself; I know a good deal about other people's lives."

"Oh, thank you," I cried; "you don't know what you have done for me now!"

"I am glad! I am glad! But tell me how did you find out that I was the sort of woman with whom . . . well, whom you think worthy . . . of attention and friendship . . . in fact, not a landlady as you say? What made you decide to come up to me?"

"What made me? . . . But you were alone; that gentleman was too insolent; it's night. You must admit that it was a duty. . . ."

"No, no; I mean before, on the other side—you know you meant to come up to me."

"On the other side? Really I don't know how to answer; I am afraid to. . . . Do you know I have been happy to-day? I walked along singing; I went out into the country; I have never had such happy moments. You . . . perhaps it was my fancy. . . . Forgive me for referring to it; I fancied you were crying, and I . . . could not bear to hear it . . . it made my heart ache. . . .

Oh, my goodness! Surely I might be troubled about you? Surely there was no harm in feeling brotherly compassion for you. . . . I beg your pardon, I said compassion. . . . Well, in short, surely you would not be offended at my involuntary impulse to go up to you? . . ."

"Stop, that's enough, don't talk of it," said the girl, looking down, and pressing my hand. "It's my fault for having spoken of it; but I am glad I was not mistaken in you. . . . But here I am home; I must go down this turning, it's two steps from here. . . . Good-bye, thank you! . . ."

"Surely . . . surely you don't mean . . . that we shall never see each other again? . . . Surely this is not to be the end?"

"You see," said the girl, laughing, "at first you only wanted two words, and now. . . . However, I won't say anything . . . perhaps we shall meet. . . ."

"I shall come here to-morrow," I said. "Oh, forgive me, I am already making demands. . . ."

"Yes, you are not very patient . . . you are almost insisting."

"Listen, listen!" I interrupted her. "Forgive me if I tell you something else. . . . I tell you what, I can't help coming here to-morrow, I am a dreamer; I have so little real life that I look upon such moments as this now, as so rare, that I cannot help going over such moments again in my dreams. I shall be dreaming of you all night, a whole week, a whole year. I shall certainly come here to-morrow, just here to this place, just at the same hour, and I shall be happy remembering to-day. This place is dear to me already. I have already two or three such places in Petersburg. I once shed tears over memories . . . like you. . . . Who knows, perhaps you were weeping ten minutes ago over some memory. . . . But, forgive me, I have forgotten myself again; perhaps you have once been particularly happy here. . . ."

"Very good," said the girl, "perhaps I will come here to-morrow, too, at ten o'clock. I see that I can't forbid you. . . . The fact is, I have to be here; don't imagine that I am making an appointment with you; I tell you beforehand that I have to be here on my own account. But . . . well, I tell you straight out, I don't mind if you do come. To begin with, something unpleasant might happen as it did to-day, but never mind that. . . . In short, I should simply like to see you . . . to say two words to you. Only, mind, you must not think the worse of me now! Don't think I make appointments so lightly. . . . I shouldn't make it except that. . . . But let that be my secret! Only a compact beforehand. . . ."

"A compact! Speak, tell me, tell me all beforehand; I agree to anything, I am ready for anything," I cried delighted. "I answer for myself, I will be obedient, respectful . . . you know me. . . ."

"It's just because I do know you that I ask you to come to-morrow," said the girl, laughing. "I know you perfectly. But mind you will come on the condition, in the first place (only be good, do what I ask—you see, I speak frankly), you won't fall in love with me. . . . That's impossible, I assure you. I am ready for friendship; here's my hand. . . . But you mustn't fall in love with me, I beg you!"

"I swear," I cried, gripping her hand. . . .

"Hush, don't swear, I know you are ready to flare up like gunpowder. Don't think ill of me for saying so. If only you knew. . . . I, too, have no one to whom I can say a word, whose advice I can ask. Of course, one does not look for an adviser in the street; but you are an exception. I know you as though we had been friends for twenty years. . . . You won't deceive me, will you? . . ."

"You will see . . . the only thing is, I don't know how I am going to survive the next twenty-four hours."

"Sleep soundly. Good-night, and remember that I have trusted you already. But you exclaimed so nicely just now, 'Surely one can't be held responsible for every feeling, even for brotherly sympathy!' Do you know, that was so nicely said, that the idea struck me at once, that I might confide in you?"

"For God's sake do; but about what? What is it?"

"Wait till to-morrow. Meanwhile, let that be a secret. So much the better for you; it will give it a faint flavour of romance. Perhaps I will tell you to-morrow, and perhaps not. . . . I will talk to you a little more beforehand; we will get to know each other better. . . ."

"Oh yes, I will tell you all about myself to-morrow! But what has happened? It is as though a miracle had befallen me. . . . My God, where am I? Come, tell me aren't you glad that you were not angry and did not drive me away at the first moment, as any other woman would have done? In two minutes you have made me happy for ever. Yes, happy; who knows, perhaps, you have reconciled me with myself, solved my doubts! . . . Perhaps such moments come upon me. . . . But there I will tell you all about it to-morrow, you shall know everything, everything. . . ."

"Very well, I consent; you shall begin. . . ."

"Agreed."

"Good-bye till to-morrow!"

"Till to-morrow!"

And we parted. I walked about all night; I could not make up my mind to go home. I was so happy. . . . To-morrow!

SECOND NIGHT

"Well, so you have survived!" she said, pressing both my hands.

"I've been here for the last two hours; you don't know what a state I have been in all day."

"I know, I know. But to business. Do you know why I have come? Not to talk nonsense, as I did yesterday. I tell you what, we must behave more sensibly in future. I thought a great deal about it last night."

"In what way—in what must we be more sensible? I am ready for my part; but, really, nothing more sensible has happened to me in my life than this, now."

"Really? In the first place, I beg you not to squeeze my hands so; secondly, I must tell you that I spent a long time thinking about you and feeling doubtful to-day."

"And how did it end?"

"How did it end? The upshot of it is that we must begin all over again, because the conclusion I reached to-day was that I don't know you at all; that I behaved like a baby last night, like a little girl; and, of course, the fact of it is, that it's my soft heart that is to blame—that is, I sang my own praises, as one always does in the end when one analyses one's conduct. And therefore to correct my mistake, I've made up my mind to find out all about you minutely. But as I have no one from whom I can find out anything, you must tell me everything fully yourself. Well, what sort of man are you? Come, make haste—begin—tell me your whole history."

"My history!" I cried in alarm. "My history! But who has told you I have a history? I have no history. . . ."

"Then how have you lived, if you have no history?" she interrupted, laughing.

"Absolutely without any history! I have lived, as they say, keeping myself to myself, that is, utterly alone—alone, entirely alone. Do you know what it means to be alone?"

"But how alone? Do you mean you never saw any one?"

"Oh no, I see people, of course; but still I am alone."

"Why, do you never talk to any one?"

"Strictly speaking, with no one."

"Who are you then? Explain yourself! Stay, I guess: most likely, like me you have a grandmother. She is blind and will never let me go anywhere, so that I have almost forgotten how to talk; and when I played some pranks two years ago, and she saw there was no holding me in, she called me up and pinned my dress to hers, and ever since we sit like that for days together; she knits a stocking, though she's blind, and I sit beside her, sew or read aloud to her—it's such a queer habit, here for two years I've been pinned to her. . . ."

"Good Heavens! what misery! But no, I haven't a grandmother like that."

"Well, if you haven't why do you sit at home? . . . "

"Listen, do you want to know the sort of man I am?"

"Yes, yes!"

"In the strict sense of the word?"

"In the very strictest sense of the word."

"Very well, I am a type!"

"Type, type! What sort of type?" cried the girl, laughing, as though she had not had a chance of laughing for a whole year. "Yes, it's very amusing talking to you. Look, here's a seat, let us sit down. No one is passing here, no one will hear us, and—begin your history. For it's no good your telling me, I know you have a history; only you are concealing it. To begin with, what is a type?"

"A type? A type is an original, it's an absurd person!" I said, infected by her childish laughter. "It's a character. Listen; do you know what is meant by a dreamer?"

"A dreamer! Indeed I should think I do know. I am a dreamer myself. Sometimes, as I sit by grandmother, all sorts of things come into my head. Why, when one begins dreaming one lets one's fancy run away with one—why, I marry a Chinese Prince! . . . Though sometimes it is a good thing to dream! But, goodness knows! Especially when one has something to think of apart from dreams," added the girl, this time rather seriously.

"Excellent! If you have been married to a Chinese Emperor, you will quite understand me. Come, listen. . . . But one minute, I don't know your name yet."

"At last! You have been in no hurry to think of it!"

"Oh, my goodness! It never entered my head, I felt quite happy as it was. . . ."

"My name is Nastenka."

"Nastenka! And nothing else?"

"Nothing else! Why, is not that enough for you, you insatiable person?"

"Not enough? On the contrary, it's a great deal, a very great deal, Nastenka; you kind girl, if you are Nastenka for me from the first."

"Quite so! Well?"

"Well, listen, Nastenka, now for this absurd history."

I sat down beside her, assumed a pedantically serious attitude, and began as though reading from a manuscript:—

"There are, Nastenka, though you may not know it, strange nooks in Petersburg. It seems as though the same sun as shines for all Petersburg people does not peep into those spots, but some other different new one, bespoken expressly for those nooks, and it throws a different light on everything. In these corners, dear Nastenka, quite a different life is lived, quite unlike the life that is surging round us, but such as perhaps exists in some unknown realm, not among us in our serious, over-serious, time. Well, that life is a mixture of something purely fantastic, fervently ideal, with something (alas! Nastenka) dingily prosaic and ordinary, not to say incredibly vulgar."

"Foo! Good Heavens! What a preface! What do I hear?"

"Listen, Nastenka. (It seems to me I shall never be tired of calling you Nastenka.) Let me tell you that in these corners live strange people—dreamers. The dreamer—if you want an exact definition—is not a human being, but a creature of an intermediate sort. For the most part he settles in some inaccessible corner, as though hiding from the light of day; once he slips into his corner, he grows to it like a snail, or, anyway, he is in that respect very much like that remarkable creature, which is an animal and a house both at once, and is called a tortoise. Why do you suppose he is so fond of his four walls, which are invariably painted green, grimy, dismal and reeking unpardonably of tobacco smoke? Why is it that when this absurd gentleman is visited by one of his few acquaintances (and he ends by getting rid of all his friends), why does this absurd person meet him with such embarrassment, changing countenance and overcome with confusion, as though he had only just committed some crime within his four walls; as though he had been forging counterfeit notes, or as though he were writing verses to be sent to a journal with an anonymous letter, in which he states that the real poet is dead, and that his friend thinks it his sacred duty to publish his things? Why, tell me, Nastenka, why is it conversation is not easy between the two friends? Why is there no laughter? Why does no lively word fly from the tongue of the perplexed newcomer, who at other times may be very fond of laughter, lively words, conversation about the fair sex, and other cheerful subjects? And why does this friend, probably a new friend and on his first visit—for there will hardly be a second, and the friend will never come again—why is the friend himself so confused, so tongue-tied, in spite of his wit (if he has any), as he looks at the downcast face of his host, who in his turn becomes utterly helpless and at his wits' end after gigantic but fruitless efforts to smooth things over and enliven the conversation, to show his knowledge of polite society, to talk, too, of the fair sex, and by such humble endeavour, to please the poor man, who like a fish out of water has mistakenly come to visit him? Why does the gentleman, all at once remembering some very necessary business which never existed, suddenly seize his hat and hurriedly make off, snatching away his hand from the warm grip of his host, who was trying his utmost to show his regret and retrieve the lost position? Why does the friend chuckle as he goes out of the door, and swear never to come and see this queer creature again, though the queer creature is really a very good fellow, and at the same time he cannot refuse his imagination the little diversion of comparing the queer fellow's countenance during their conversation with the expression of an unhappy kitten treacherously captured, roughly handled, frightened and subjected to all sorts of indignities by children, till, utterly crestfallen, it hides away from them under a chair in the dark, and there must needs at its leisure bristle up, spit, and wash its insulted face with both paws, and long afterwards look angrily at life and nature, and even at the bits saved from the master's dinner for it by the sympathetic housekeeper?"

"Listen," interrupted Nastenka, who had listened to me all the time in amazement, opening her eyes and her little mouth. "Listen; I don't know in the least why it happened and why you ask me such absurd questions; all I know is, that this adventure must have happened word for word to you."

"Doubtless," I answered, with the gravest face.

"Well, since there is no doubt about it, go on," said Nastenka, "because I want very much to know how it will end."

"You want to know, Nastenka, what our hero, that is I—for the hero of the whole business was my humble self—did in his corner? You want to know why I lost my head and was upset for the whole day by the unexpected visit of a friend? You want to know why I was so startled, why I blushed when the door of my room was opened, why I was not able to entertain my visitor, and why I was crushed under the weight of my own hospitality?"

"Why, yes, yes," answered Nastenka, "that's the point. Listen. You describe it all splendidly, but couldn't you perhaps describe it a little less splendidly? You talk as though you were reading it out of a book."

"Nastenka," I answered in a stern and dignified voice, hardly able to keep from laughing, "dear Nastenka, I know I describe splendidly, but, excuse me, I don't know how else to do it. At this moment, dear Nastenka, at this moment I am like the spirit of King Solomon when, after lying a thousand years under seven seals in his urn, those seven seals were at last taken off. At this moment, Nastenka, when we have met at last after such a long separation—for I have known you for ages, Nastenka, because I have been looking for some one for ages, and that is a sign that it was you I was looking for, and it was ordained that we should meet now—at this moment a thousand valves have opened in my head, and I must let myself flow in a river of words, or I shall choke. And so I beg you not to interrupt me, Nastenka, but listen humbly and obediently, or I will be silent."

"No, no, no! Not at all. Go on! I won't say a word!"

"I will continue. There is, my friend Nastenka, one hour in my day which I like extremely. That is the hour when almost all business, work and duties are over, and every one is hurrying home to dinner, to lie down, to rest, and on the way all are cogitating on other more cheerful subjects relating to their evenings, their nights, and all the rest of their free time. At that hour our hero—for allow me, Nastenka, to tell my story in the third person, for one feels awfully ashamed to tell it in the first person—and so at that hour our hero, who had his work too, was pacing along after the others. But a strange feeling of pleasure set his pale, rather crumpled-looking face working. He looked not with indifference on the evening glow which was slowly fading on the cold Petersburg sky. When I say he looked, I am lying: he did not look at it, but saw it as it were without realizing, as though tired or preoccupied with some other more interesting subject, so that he could scarcely spare a glance for anything about him. He was pleased because till next day he was released from business irksome to him, and happy as a schoolboy let out from the class-room to his games and mischief. Take a look at him, Nastenka; you will see at once that joyful emotion has already had an effect on his weak nerves and morbidly excited fancy. You see he is thinking of something.... Of dinner, do you imagine? Of the evening? What is he looking at like that? Is it at that gentleman of dignified appearance who is bowing so picturesquely to the lady who rolls by in a carriage drawn by prancing horses? No, Nastenka; what are all those trivialities to him now! He is rich now with his *own individual* life; he has suddenly become rich, and it is not for nothing that the fading sunset sheds its farewell gleams so gaily before him, and calls forth a swarm of impressions from his warmed heart. Now he hardly notices the road, on which the tiniest details at other times would strike him. Now 'the Goddess of Fancy' (if you have read Zhukovsky, dear Nastenka) has already with fantastic hand spun her golden warp and begun weaving upon it patterns of marvellous magic life—and who knows, maybe, her fantastic hand has borne him to the seventh crystal heaven far from the excellent granite pavement on which he was walking his way? Try stopping him now, ask him suddenly where he is standing now, through what streets he is going—he will, probably remember nothing, neither where he is going nor where he is standing now, and flushing with vexation he will certainly tell some lie to save appearances. That is why he starts, almost cries out, and looks round with horror when a respectable old lady stops him politely in the middle of the pavement and asks her way. Frowning with vexation he strides on, scarcely noticing that more than one passer-by smiles and turns round to look after him, and that a little girl, moving out of his way in alarm, laughs aloud, gazing open-eyed at his broad meditative smile and gesticulations. But fancy catches up in its playful flight the old woman, the curious passers-by, and the laughing child, and the peasants spending their nights in their barges on Fontanka (our hero, let us suppose, is walking along the canalside at that moment), and capriciously weaves every one and everything into the canvas like a fly in a spider's web. And it is only after the queer fellow has returned to his comfortable den with fresh stores for his mind to work on, has sat down and finished his dinner, that he comes to himself, when Matrona who waits upon him—always thoughtful and depressed—clears the table and gives him his pipe; he comes to himself then and recalls with surprise that he has dined, though he has absolutely no notion how it has happened. It has grown dark in the room; his soul is sad and empty; the whole kingdom of fancies drops to pieces about him, drops to pieces without a trace, without a sound, floats away like a dream, and he cannot himself remember what he was dreaming. But a vague sensation faintly stirs his heart and sets it aching, some new desire temptingly tickles and excites his fancy, and imperceptibly evokes a swarm of fresh phantoms. Stillness reigns in the little room; imagination is fostered by solitude and idleness; it is faintly smouldering, faintly simmering, like the water with which old Matrona is making her coffee as she moves quietly about in the kitchen close by. Now it breaks out spasmodically; and the book, picked up aimlessly and at random, drops from my dreamer's hand before he has reached the third page. His imagination is again stirred and at work, and again a new world, a new fascinating life opens vistas before him. A fresh dream—fresh happiness! A fresh rush of delicate, voluptuous poison! What is real life to him! To his corrupted eyes we live, you and I, Nastenka, so torpidly, slowly, insipidly; in his eyes we are all so dissatisfied with our fate, so exhausted by our life! And, truly, see how at first sight everything is cold, morose, as though ill-humoured among us.... Poor things! thinks our dreamer. And it is no wonder that he thinks it! Look at these magic phantasms, which so enchantingly, so whimsically, so carelessly and freely group before him in such a magic, animated picture, in which the most prominent figure in the foreground is of course himself, our dreamer, in his precious person. See what varied adventures, what an endless swarm of ecstatic dreams. You ask, perhaps, what he is dreaming of. Why ask that?—why, of everything ... of the lot of the poet, first unrecognized, then crowned with laurels; of friendship with Hoffmann, St. Bartholomew's Night, of Diana Vernon, of playing the hero at the taking of Kazan by Ivan Vassilyevitch, of Clara Mowbray, of Effie Deans, of the council of the prelates and Huss before them, of the rising of the dead in 'Robert the Devil' (do you remember the music, it smells of the churchyard!), of Minna and Brenda, of the battle of Berezina, of the reading of a poem at Countess V. D.'s, of Danton, of Cleopatra *ei suoi amanti*, of a little house in Kolomna, of a little home of one's own and beside one a dear creature who listens to one on a winter's evening, opening her little mouth and eyes as you are listening to me now, my angel.... No, Nastenka, what is there, what is there for him, voluptuous sluggard, in this life, for which you and I have such a longing? He thinks that this is a poor pitiful life, not foreseeing that for him too, maybe, sometime the mournful hour may strike, when for one day of that pitiful life he would give all his years of phantasy, and would give them not only for joy and for happiness, but without caring to make distinctions in that hour of sadness, remorse and unchecked grief. But so far that threatening has not arrived—he desires nothing, because he is superior to all desire, because he has everything, because he is satiated, because he is the artist of his own life, and creates it for himself every hour to suit his latest whim. And you know this fantastic world of fairyland is so easily, so naturally created! As though it were not a delusion! Indeed, he is ready to believe at some moments that all this life is not suggested by feeling, is not mirage, not a delusion of the imagination, but that it is concrete, real, substantial! Why is it, Nastenka, why is it at such moments one holds one's breath? Why, by what sorcery, through what incomprehensible caprice, is the pulse quickened, does a tear start from the dreamer's eye, while his pale moist cheeks glow, while his whole being is suffused with an inexpressible sense of consolation? Why is it that whole sleepless nights pass like a flash in inexhaustible gladness and happiness, and when the dawn gleams rosy at the window and daybreak floods the gloomy room with uncertain, fantastic light, as in Petersburg, our dreamer, worn out and exhausted, flings himself on his bed and drops asleep with thrills of delight in his morbidly overwrought spirit, and with a weary sweet ache in his heart? Yes, Nastenka, one deceives oneself and unconsciously believes that real true passion is stirring one's soul; one unconsciously believes that there is something living, tangible in one's immaterial dreams! And is it delusion? Here love, for instance, is bound up with all its fathomless joy, all its torturing agonies in his bosom.... Only look at him, and you will be convinced! Would you believe, looking at him, dear Nastenka, that he has never known her whom he loves in his ecstatic dreams? Can it be that he has only seen her in seductive visions, and that this passion has been nothing but a dream? Surely they must have spent years hand in hand together—alone the two of them, casting off all the world and each uniting his or her life with the other's? Surely when the hour of parting came she must have lain sobbing and grieving on his bosom, heedless of the tempest raging under the sullen sky, heedless of the wind which snatches and bears away the tears from her black eyelashes? Can all of that have been a dream—and that garden, dejected, forsaken, run wild, with its little moss-grown paths, solitary, gloomy, where they used to walk so happily together, where they hoped, grieved, loved, loved each other so long, "so long and so fondly?" And that queer ancestral house where she spent so many years lonely and sad with her morose old husband, always silent and splenetic, who frightened them, while timid as children they hid their love from each other? What torments they suffered, what agonies of terror, how innocent, how pure was their love, and how (I need hardly say, Nastenka) malicious people were! And, good Heavens! surely he met her afterwards, far from their native shores, under alien skies, in the hot south in the divinely eternal city, in the dazzling splendour of the ball to the crash of music, in a *palazzo* (it must be in a *palazzo*), drowned in a sea of lights, on the balcony, wreathed in myrtle and roses, where, recognizing him, she hurriedly removes her mask and whispering, 'I am free,' flings herself trembling into his arms, and with a cry of rapture, clinging to one another, in one instant they forget their sorrow and their parting and all their agonies, and the gloomy house and the old man and the dismal garden in that distant land, and the seat on which with a last passionate kiss she tore herself away from his arms numb with anguish and despair. . . . Oh, Nastenka, you must admit that one would start, betray confusion, and blush like a schoolboy who has just stuffed in his pocket an apple stolen from a neighbour's garden, when your uninvited visitor, some stalwart, lanky fellow, a festive soul fond of a joke, opens your door and shouts out as though nothing were happening: 'My dear boy, I have this minute come from Pavlovsk.' My goodness! the old count is dead, unutterable happiness is close at hand—and people arrive from Pavlovsk!"

Finishing my pathetic appeal, I paused pathetically. I remembered that I had an intense desire to force myself to laugh, for I was already feeling that a malignant demon was stirring within me, that there was a lump in my throat, that my chin was beginning to twitch, and that my eyes were growing more and more moist.

I expected Nastenka, who listened to me opening her clever eyes, would break into her childish, irrepressible laugh; and I was already regretting that I had gone so far, that I had unnecessarily described what had long been simmering in my heart, about which I could speak as though from a written account of it, because I had long ago passed judgment on myself and now could not resist reading it, making my confession, without expecting to be understood; but to my surprise she was silent, waiting a little, then she faintly pressed my hand and with timid sympathy asked—

"Surely you haven't lived like that all your life?"

"All my life, Nastenka," I answered; "all my life, and it seems to me I shall go on so to the end."

"No, that won't do," she said uneasily, "that must not be; and so, maybe, I shall spend all my life beside grandmother. Do you know, it is not at all good to live like that?"

"I know, Nastenka, I know!" I cried, unable to restrain my feelings longer. "And I realize now, more than ever, that I have lost all my best years! And now I know it and feel it more painfully from recognizing that God has sent me you, my good angel, to tell me that and show it. Now that I sit beside you and talk to you it is strange for me to think of the future, for in the future—there is loneliness again, again this musty, useless life; and what shall I have to dream of when I have been so happy in reality beside you! Oh, may you be blessed, dear girl, for not having repulsed me at first, for enabling me to say that for two evenings, at least, I have lived."

"Oh, no, no!" cried Nastenka and tears glistened in her eyes. "No, it mustn't be so any more; we must not part like that! what are two evenings?"

"Oh, Nastenka, Nastenka! Do you know how far you have reconciled me to myself? Do you know now that I shall not think so ill of myself, as I have at some moments? Do you know that, maybe, I shall leave off grieving over the crime and sin of my life? for such a life is a crime and a sin. And do not imagine that I have been exaggerating anything—for goodness' sake don't think that, Nastenka: for at times such misery comes over me, such misery. . . . Because it begins to seem to me at such times that I am incapable of beginning a life in real life, because it has seemed to me that I have lost all touch, all instinct for the actual, the real; because at last I have cursed myself; because after my fantastic nights I have moments of returning sobriety, which are awful! Meanwhile, you hear the whirl and roar of the crowd in the vortex of life around you; you hear, you see, men living in reality; you see that life for them is not forbidden, that their life does not float away like a dream, like a vision; that their life is being eternally renewed, eternally youthful, and not one hour of it is the same as another; while fancy is so spiritless, monotonous to vulgarity and easily scared, the slave of shadows, of the idea, the slave of the first cloud that shrouds the sun, and overcasts with depression the true Petersburg heart so devoted to the sun—and what is fancy in depression! One feels that this *inexhaustible* fancy is weary at last and worn out with continual exercise, because one is growing into manhood, outgrowing one's old ideals: they are being shattered into fragments, into dust; if there is no other life one must build one up from the fragments. And meanwhile the soul longs and craves for something else! And in vain the dreamer rakes over his old dreams, as though seeking a spark among the embers, to fan them into flame, to warm his chilled heart by the rekindled fire, and to rouse up in it again all that was so sweet, that touched his heart, that set his blood boiling, drew tears from his eyes, and so luxuriously deceived him! Do you know, Nastenka, the point I have reached? Do you know that I am forced now to celebrate the anniversary of my own sensations, the anniversary of that which was once so sweet, which never existed in reality—for this anniversary is kept in memory of those same foolish, shadowy dreams—and to do this because those foolish dreams are no more, because I have nothing to earn them with; you know even dreams do not come for nothing! Do you know that I love now to recall and visit at certain dates the places where I was once happy in my own way? I love to build up my present in harmony with the irrevocable past, and I often wander like a shadow, aimless, sad and dejected, about the streets and crooked lanes of Petersburg. What memories they are! To remember, for instance, that here just a year ago, just at this time, at this hour, on this pavement, I wandered just as lonely, just as dejected as to-day. And one remembers that then one's dreams were sad, and though the past was no better one feels as though it had somehow been better, and that life was more peaceful, that one was free from the black thoughts that haunt one now; that one was free from the gnawing of conscience—the gloomy, sullen gnawing which now gives me no rest by day or by night. And one asks oneself where are one's dreams. And one shakes one's head and says how rapidly the years fly by! And again one asks oneself what has one done with one's years. Where have you buried your best days? Have you lived or not? Look, one says to oneself, look how cold the world is growing. Some more years will pass, and after them will come gloomy solitude; then will come old age trembling on its crutch, and after it misery and desolation. Your fantastic world will grow pale, your dreams will fade and die and will fall like the yellow leaves from the trees. . . . Oh, Nastenka! you know it will be sad to be left alone, utterly alone, and to have not even anything to regret— nothing, absolutely nothing . . . for all that you have lost, all that, all was nothing, stupid, simple nullity, there has been nothing but dreams!"

"Come, don't work on my feelings any more," said Nastenka, wiping away a tear which was trickling down her cheek. "Now it's over! Now we shall be two together. Now, whatever happens to me, we will never part. Listen; I am a simple girl, I have not had much education, though grandmother did get a teacher for me, but truly I understand you, for all that you have described I have been through myself, when grandmother pinned me to her dress. Of course, I should not have described it so well as you have; I am not educated," she added timidly, for she was still feeling a sort of respect for my pathetic eloquence and lofty style; "but I am very glad that you have been quite open with me. Now I know you thoroughly, all of you. And do you know what? I want to tell you my history too, all without concealment, and after that you must give me advice. You are a very clever man; will you promise to give me advice?"

"Ah, Nastenka," I cried, "though I have never given advice, still less sensible advice, yet I see now that if we always go on like this that it will be very sensible, and that each of us will give the other a great deal of sensible advice! Well, my pretty Nastenka, what sort of advice do you want? Tell me frankly; at this moment I am so gay and happy, so bold and sensible, that it won't be difficult for me to find words."

"No, no!" Nastenka interrupted, laughing. "I don't only want sensible advice, I want warm brotherly advice, as though you had been fond of me all your life!"

"Agreed, Nastenka, agreed!" I cried delighted; "and if I had been fond of you for twenty years, I couldn't have been fonder of you than I am now."

"Your hand," said Nastenka.

"Here it is," said I, giving her my hand.

"And so let us begin my history!"

NASTENKA'S HISTORY

"Half my story you know already—that is, you know that I have an old grandmother...."

"If the other half is as brief as that ..." I interrupted, laughing.

"Be quiet and listen. First of all you must agree not to interrupt me, or else, perhaps I shall get in a muddle! Come, listen quietly.

"I have an old grandmother. I came into her hands when I was quite a little girl, for my father and mother are dead. It must be supposed that grandmother was once richer, for now she recalls better days. She taught me French, and then got a teacher for me. When I was fifteen (and now I am seventeen) we gave up having lessons. It was at that time that I got into mischief; what I did I won't tell you; it's enough to say that it wasn't very important. But grandmother called me to her one morning and said that as she was blind she could not look after me; she took a pin and pinned my dress to hers, and said that we should sit like that for the rest of our lives if, of course, I did not become a better girl. In fact, at first it was impossible to get away from her: I had to work, to read and to study all beside grandmother. I tried to deceive her once, and persuaded Fekla to sit in my place. Fekla is our charwoman, she is deaf. Fekla sat there instead of me; grandmother was asleep in her armchair at the time, and I went off to see a friend close by. Well, it ended in trouble. Grandmother woke up while I was out, and asked some questions; she thought I was still sitting quietly in my place. Fekla saw that grandmother was asking her something, but could not tell what it was; she wondered what to do, undid the pin and ran away...."

At this point Nastenka stopped and began laughing. I laughed with her. She left off at once.

"I tell you what, don't you laugh at grandmother. I laugh because it's funny.... What can I do, since grandmother is like that; but yet I am fond of her in a way. Oh, well, I did catch it that time. I had to sit down in my place at once, and after that I was not allowed to stir.

"Oh, I forgot to tell you that our house belongs to us, that is to grandmother; it is a little wooden house with three windows as old as grandmother herself, with a little upper storey; well, there moved into our upper storey a new lodger."

"Then you had an old lodger," I observed casually.

"Yes, of course," answered Nastenka, "and one who knew how to hold his tongue better than you do. In fact, he hardly ever used his tongue at all. He was a dumb, blind, lame, dried-up little old man, so that at last he could not go on living, he died; so then we had to find a new lodger, for we could not live without a lodger—the rent, together with grandmother's pension, is almost all we have. But the new lodger, as luck would have it, was a young man, a stranger not of these parts. As he did not haggle over the rent, grandmother accepted him, and only afterwards she asked me: 'Tell me, Nastenka, what is our lodger like—is he young or old?' I did not want to lie, so I told grandmother that he wasn't exactly young and that he wasn't old.

"'And is he pleasant looking?' asked grandmother.

"Again I did not want to tell a lie: 'Yes, he is pleasant looking, grandmother,' I said. And grandmother said: 'Oh, what a nuisance, what a nuisance! I tell you this, grandchild, that you may not be looking after him. What times these are! Why a paltry lodger like this, and he must be pleasant looking too; it was very different in the old days!'"

"Grandmother was always regretting the old days—she was younger in old days, and the sun was warmer in old days, and cream did not turn so sour in old days—it was always the old days! I would sit still and hold my tongue and think to myself: why did grandmother suggest it to me? Why did she ask whether the lodger was young and good-looking? But that was all, I just thought it, began counting my stitches again, went on knitting my stocking, and forgot all about it.

"Well, one morning the lodger came in to see us; he asked about a promise to paper his rooms. One thing led to another. Grandmother was talkative, and she said: 'Go, Nastenka, into my bedroom and bring me my reckoner.' I jumped up at once; I blushed all over, I don't know why, and forgot I was sitting pinned to grandmother; instead of quietly undoing the pin, so that the lodger should not see—I jumped so that grandmother's chair moved. When I saw that the lodger knew all about me now, I blushed, stood still as though I had been shot, and suddenly began to cry—I felt so ashamed and miserable at that minute, that I didn't know where to look! Grandmother called out, 'What are you waiting for?' and I went on worse than ever. When the lodger saw, saw that I was ashamed on his account, he bowed and went away at once!

"After that I felt ready to die at the least sound in the passage. 'It's the lodger,' I kept thinking; I stealthily undid the pin in case. But it always turned out not to be, he never came. A fortnight passed; the lodger sent word through Fyokla that he had a great number of French books, and that they were all good books that I might read, so would not grandmother like me to read them that I might not be dull? Grandmother agreed with gratitude, but kept asking if they were moral books, for if the books were immoral it would be out of the question, one would learn evil from them."

"'And what should I learn, grandmother? What is there written in them?'

"'Ah,' she said, 'what's described in them, is how young men seduce virtuous girls; how, on the excuse that they want to marry them, they carry them off from their parents' houses; how afterwards they leave these unhappy girls to their fate, and they perish in the most pitiful way. I read a great many books,' said grandmother, 'and it is all so well described that one sits up all night and reads them on the sly. So mind you don't read them, Nastenka,' said she. 'What books has he sent?'

"'They are all Walter Scott's novels, grandmother.'

"'Walter Scott's novels! But stay, isn't there some trick about it? Look, hasn't he stuck a love-letter among them?'

"'No, grandmother,' I said, 'there isn't a love-letter.'

"'But look under the binding; they sometimes stuff it under the bindings, the rascals!'

"'No, grandmother, there is nothing under the binding.'

"'Well, that's all right.'

"So we began reading Walter Scott, and in a month or so we had read almost half. Then he sent us more and more. He sent us Pushkin, too; so that at last I could not get on without a book and left off dreaming of how fine it would be to marry a Chinese Prince.

"That's how things were when I chanced one day to meet our lodger on the stairs. Grandmother had sent me to fetch something. He stopped, I blushed and he blushed; he laughed, though, said good-morning to me, asked after grandmother, and said, 'Well, have you read the books?' I answered that I had. 'Which did you like best?' he asked. I said, 'Ivanhoe, and Pushkin best of all,' and so our talk ended for that time.

"A week later I met him again on the stairs. That time grandmother had not sent me, I wanted to get something for myself. It was past two, and the lodger used to come home at that time. 'Good-afternoon,' said he. I said good-afternoon, too.

"'Aren't you dull,' he said, 'sitting all day with your grandmother?'

"When he asked that, I blushed, I don't know why; I felt ashamed, and again I felt offended—I suppose because other people had begun to ask me about that. I wanted to go away without answering, but I hadn't the strength.

"'Listen,' he said, 'you are a good girl. Excuse my speaking to you like that, but I assure you that I wish for your welfare quite as much as your grandmother. Have you no friends that you could go and visit?'

"I told him I hadn't any, that I had had no friend but Mashenka, and she had gone away to Pskov.

"'Listen,' he said, 'would you like to go to the theatre with me?'

"'To the theatre. What about grandmother?'

"'But you must go without your grandmother's knowing it,' he said.

"'No,' I said, 'I don't want to deceive grandmother. Good-bye.'

"'Well, good-bye,' he answered, and said nothing more.

"Only after dinner he came to see us; sat a long time talking to grandmother; asked her whether she ever went out anywhere, whether she had acquaintances, and suddenly said: 'I have taken a box at the opera for this evening; they are giving *The Barber of Seville*. My friends meant to go, but afterwards refused, so the ticket is left on my hands.' '*The Barber of Seville*,' cried grandmother; 'why, the same they used to act in old days?'

"'Yes, it's the same barber,' he said, and glanced at me. I saw what it meant and turned crimson, and my heart began throbbing with suspense.

"'To be sure, I know it,' said grandmother; 'why, I took the part of Rosina myself in old days, at a private performance!'

"'So wouldn't you like to go to-day?' said the lodger. 'Or my ticket will be wasted.'

"'By all means let us go,' said grandmother; why shouldn't we? And my Nastenka here has never been to the theatre.'

"My goodness, what joy! We got ready at once, put on our best clothes, and set off. Though grandmother was blind, still she wanted to hear the music; besides, she is a kind old soul, what she cared most for was to amuse me, we should never have gone of ourselves.

"What my impressions of *The Barber of Seville* were I won't tell you; but all that evening our lodger looked at me so nicely, talked so nicely, that I saw at once that he had meant to test me in the morning when he proposed that I should go with him alone. Well, it was joy! I went to bed so proud, so gay, my heart beat so that I was a little feverish, and all night I was raving about *The Barber of Seville*.

"I expected that he would come and see us more and more often after that, but it wasn't so at all. He almost entirely gave up coming. He would just come in about once a month, and then only to invite us to the theatre. We went twice again. Only I wasn't at all pleased with that; I saw that he was simply sorry for me because I was so hardly treated by grandmother, and that was all. As time went on, I grew more and more restless, I couldn't sit still, I couldn't read, I couldn't work; sometimes I laughed and did something to annoy grandmother, at another time I would cry. At last I grew thin and was very nearly ill. The opera season was over, and our lodger had quite given up coming to see us; whenever we met—always on the same staircase, of course—he would bow so silently, so gravely, as though he did not want to speak, and go down to the front door, while I went on standing in the middle of the stairs, as red as a cherry, for all the blood rushed to my head at the sight of him.

"Now the end is near. Just a year ago, in May, the lodger came to us and said to grandmother that he had finished his business here, and that he must go back to Moscow for a year. When I heard that, I sank into a chair half dead; grandmother did not notice anything; and having informed us that he should be leaving us, he bowed and went away.

"What was I to do? I thought and thought and fretted and fretted, and at last I made up my mind. Next day he was to go away, and I made up my mind to end it all that evening when grandmother went to bed. And so it happened. I made up all my clothes in a parcel—all the linen I needed—and with the parcel in my hand, more dead than alive, went upstairs to our lodger. I believe I must have stayed an hour on the staircase. When I opened his door he cried out as he looked at me. He thought I was a ghost, and rushed to give me some water, for I could hardly stand up. My heart beat so violently that my head ached, and I did not know what I was doing. When I recovered I began by laying my parcel on his bed, sat down beside it, hid my face in my hands and went into floods of tears. I think he understood it all at once, and looked at me so sadly that my heart was torn.

"'Listen,' he began, 'listen, Nastenka, I can't do anything; I am a poor man, for I have nothing, not even a decent berth. How could we live, if I were to marry you?'

"We talked a long time; but at last I got quite frantic, I said I could not go on living with grandmother, that I should run away from her, that I did not want to be pinned to her, and that I would go to Moscow if he liked, because I could not live without him. Shame and pride and love were all clamouring in me at once, and I fell on the bed almost in convulsions, I was so afraid of a refusal.

"He sat for some minutes in silence, then got up, came up to me and took me by the hand.

"'Listen, my dear good Nastenka, listen; I swear to you that if I am ever in a position to marry, you shall make my happiness. I assure you that now you are the only one who could make me happy. Listen, I am going to Moscow and shall be there just a year; I hope to establish my position. When I come back, if you still love me, I swear that we will be happy. Now it is impossible, I am not able, I have not the right to promise anything. Well, I repeat, if it is not within a year it will certainly be some time; that is, of course, if you do not prefer any one else, for I cannot and dare not bind you by any sort of promise.'

"That was what he said to me, and next day he went away. We agreed together not to say a word to grandmother: that was his wish. Well, my history is nearly finished now. Just a year has past. He has arrived; he has been here three days, and, and—"

"And what?" I cried, impatient to hear the end.

"And up to now has not shown himself!" answered Nastenka, as though screwing up all her courage. "There's no sign or sound of him."

Here she stopped, paused for a minute, bent her head, and covering her face with her hands broke into such sobs that it sent a pang to my heart to hear them. I had not in the least expected such a *dénouement*.

"Nastenka," I began timidly in an ingratiating voice, "Nastenka! For goodness' sake don't cry! How do you know? Perhaps he is not here yet...."

"He is, he is," Nastenka repeated. "He is here, and I know it. We *made an agreement* at the time, that evening, before he went away: when we said all that I have told you, and had come to an understanding, then we came out here for a walk on this embankment. It was ten o'clock; we sat on this seat. I was not crying then; it was sweet to me to hear what he said.... And he said that he would come to us directly he arrived, and if I did not refuse him, then we would tell grandmother about it all. Now he is here, I know it, and yet he does not come!

And again she burst into tears.

"Good God, can I do nothing to help you in your sorrow?" I cried jumping up from the seat in utter despair. "Tell me, Nastenka, wouldn't it be possible for me to go to him?"

"Would that be possible?" she asked suddenly, raising her head.

"No, of course not," I said pulling myself up; "but I tell you what, write a letter."

"No, that's impossible, I can't do that," she answered with decision, bending her head and not looking at me.

"How impossible—why is it impossible?" I went on, clinging to my idea. "But, Nastenka, it depends what sort of letter; there are letters and letters and.... Ah, Nastenka, I am right; trust to me, trust to me, I will not give you bad advice. It can all be arranged! You took the first step—why not now?"

"I can't. I can't! It would seem as though I were forcing myself on him...."

"Ah, my good little Nastenka," I said, hardly able to conceal a smile; "no, no, you have a right to, in fact, because he made you a promise. Besides, I can see from everything that he is a man of delicate feeling; that he behaved very well," I went on, more and more carried away by the logic of my own arguments and convictions. "How did he behave? He bound himself by a promise: he said that if he married at all he would marry no one but you; he gave you full liberty to refuse him at once.... Under such circumstances you may take the first step; you have the right; you are in the privileged position—if, for instance, you wanted to free him from his promise...."

"Listen; how would you write?"

"Write what?"

"This letter."

"I tell you how I would write: 'Dear Sir.' . . . "

"Must I really begin like that, 'Dear Sir'?"

"You certainly must! Though, after all, I don't know, I imagine. . . ."

"Well, well, what next?"

"'Dear Sir,—I must apologize for—' But, no, there's no need to apologize; the fact itself justifies everything. Write simply:—

"'I am writing to you. Forgive me my impatience; but I have been happy for a whole year in hope; am I to blame for being unable to endure a day of doubt now? Now that you have come, perhaps you have changed your mind. If so, this letter is to tell you that I do not repine, nor blame you. I do not blame you because I have no power over your heart, such is my fate!

"'You are an honourable man. You will not smile or be vexed at these impatient lines. Remember they are written by a poor girl; that she is alone; that she has no one to direct her, no one to advise her, and that she herself could never control her heart. But forgive me that a doubt has stolen—if only for one instant—into my heart. You are not capable of insulting, even in thought, her who so loved and so loves you.'"

"Yes, yes; that's exactly what I was thinking!" cried Nastenka, and her eyes beamed with delight. "Oh, you have solved my difficulties: God has sent you to me! Thank you, thank you!"

"What for? What for? For God's sending me?" I answered, looking delighted at her joyful little face. "Why, yes; for that too."

"Ah, Nastenka! Why, one thanks some people for being alive at the same time with one; I thank you for having met me, for my being able to remember you all my life!"

"Well, enough, enough! But now I tell you what, listen: we made an agreement then that as soon as he arrived he would let me know, by leaving a letter with some good simple people of my acquaintance who know nothing about it; or, if it were impossible to write a letter to me, for a letter does not always tell everything, he would be here at ten o'clock on the day he arrived, where we had arranged to meet. I know he has arrived already; but now it's the third day, and there's no sign of him and no letter. It's impossible for me to get away from grandmother in the morning. Give my letter to-morrow to those kind people I spoke to you about: they will send it on to him, and if there is an answer you bring it to-morrow at ten o'clock."

"But the letter, the letter! You see, you must write the letter first! So perhaps it must all be the day after to-morrow."

"The letter . . . " said Nastenka, a little confused, "the letter . . . but. . . ."

But she did not finish. At first she turned her little face away from me, flushed like a rose, and suddenly I felt in my hand a letter which had evidently been written long before, all ready and sealed up. A familiar sweet and charming reminiscence floated through my mind.

"R, o—Ro; s, i—si; n, a—na," I began.

"Rosina!" we both hummed together; I almost embracing her with delight, while she blushed as only she could blush, and laughed through the tears which gleamed like pearls on her black eyelashes.

"Come, enough, enough! Good-bye now," she said speaking rapidly. "Here is the letter, here is the address to which you are to take it. Good-bye, till we meet again! Till to-morrow!"

She pressed both my hands warmly, nodded her head, and flew like an arrow down her side street. I stood still for a long time following her with my eyes.

"Till to-morrow! till to-morrow!" was ringing in my ears as she vanished from my sight.

THIRD NIGHT

To-day was a gloomy, rainy day without a glimmer of sunlight, like the old age before me. I am oppressed by such strange thoughts, such gloomy sensations; questions still so obscure to me are crowding into my brain—and I seem to have neither power nor will to settle them. It's not for me to settle all this!

To-day we shall not meet. Yesterday, when we said good-bye, the clouds began gathering over the sky and a mist rose. I said that to-morrow it would be a bad day; she made no answer, she did not want to speak against her wishes; for her that day was bright and clear, not one cloud should obscure her happiness.

"If it rains we shall not see each other," she said, "I shall not come."

I thought that she would not notice to-day's rain, and yet she has not come.

Yesterday was our third interview, our third white night. . . .

But how fine joy and happiness makes any one! How brimming over with love the heart is! One seems longing to pour out one's whole heart; one wants everything to be gay, everything to be laughing. And how infectious that joy is! There was such a softness in her words, such a kindly feeling in her heart towards me yesterday. . . . How solicitous and friendly she was; how tenderly she tried to give me courage! Oh, the coquetry of happiness! While I . . . I took it all for the genuine thing, I thought that she. . . .

But, my God, how could I have thought it? How could I have been so blind, when everything had been taken by another already, when nothing was mine; when, in fact, her very tenderness to me, her anxiety, her love . . . yes, love for me, was nothing else but joy at the thought of seeing another man so soon, desire to include me, too, in her happiness? . . . When he did not come, when we waited in vain, she frowned, she grew timid and discouraged. Her movements, her words, were no longer so light, so playful, so gay; and, strange to say, she redoubled her attentiveness to me, as though instinctively desiring to lavish on me what she desired for herself so anxiously, if her wishes were not accomplished. My Nastenka was so downcast, so dismayed, that I think she realized at last that I loved her, and was sorry for my poor love. So when we are unhappy we feel the unhappiness of others more; feeling is not destroyed but concentrated. . . .

I went to meet her with a full heart, and was all impatience. I had no presentiment that I should feel as I do now, that it would not all end happily. She was beaming with pleasure; she was expecting an answer. The answer was himself. He was to come, to run at her call. She arrived a whole hour before I did. At first she giggled at everything, laughed at every word I said. I began talking, but relapsed into silence.

"Do you know why I am so glad," she said, "so glad to look at you?—why I like you so much to-day?"

"Well?" I asked, and my heart began throbbing.

"I like you because you have not fallen in love with me. You know that some men in your place would have been pestering and worrying me, would have been sighing and miserable, while you are so nice!"

Then she wrung my hand so hard that I almost cried out. She laughed.

"Goodness, what a friend you are!" she began gravely a minute later. "God sent you to me. What would have happened to me if you had not been with me now? How disinterested you are! How truly you care for me! When I am married we will be great friends, more than brother and sister; I shall care almost as I do for him...."

I felt horribly sad at that moment, yet something like laughter was stirring in my soul.

"You are very much upset," I said; "you are frightened; you think he won't come."

"Oh dear!" she answered; "if I were less happy, I believe I should cry at your lack of faith, at your reproaches. However, you have made me think and have given me a lot to think about; but I shall think later, and now I will own that you are right. Yes, I am somehow not myself; I am all suspense, and feel everything as it were too lightly. But hush! that's enough about feelings...."

At that moment we heard footsteps, and in the darkness we saw a figure coming towards us. We both started; she almost cried out; I dropped her hand and made a movement as though to walk away. But we were mistaken, it was not he.

"What are you afraid of? Why did you let go of my hand?" she said, giving it to me again. "Come, what is it? We will meet him together; I want him to see how fond we are of each other."

"How fond we are of each other!" I cried. ("Oh, Nastenka, Nastenka," I thought, "how much you have told me in that saying! Such fondness at *certain* moments makes the heart cold and the soul heavy. Your hand is cold, mine burns like fire. How blind you are, Nastenka! ... Oh, how unbearable a happy person is sometimes! But I could not be angry with you!")

At last my heart was too full.

"Listen, Nastenka!" I cried. "Do you know how it has been with me all day."

"Why, how, how? Tell me quickly! Why have you said nothing all this time?"

"To begin with, Nastenka, when I had carried out all your commissions, given the letter, gone to see your good friends, then ... then I went home and went to bed."

"Is that all?" she interrupted, laughing.

"Yes, almost all," I answered restraining myself, for foolish tears were already starting into my eyes. "I woke an hour before our appointment, and yet, as it were, I had not been asleep. I don't know what happened to me. I came to tell you all about it, feeling as though time were standing still, feeling as though one sensation, one feeling must remain with me from that time for ever; feeling as though one minute must go on for all eternity, and as though all life had come to a standstill for me. . . . When I woke up it seemed as though some musical motive long familiar, heard somewhere in the past, forgotten and voluptuously sweet, had come back to me now. It seemed to me that it had been clamouring at my heart all my life, and only now. . . . "

"Oh my goodness, my goodness," Nastenka interrupted, "what does all that mean? I don't understand a word."

"Ah, Nastenka, I wanted somehow to convey to you that strange impression. . . . " I began in a plaintive voice, in which there still lay hid a hope, though a very faint one.

"Leave off. Hush!" she said, and in one instant the sly puss had guessed. Suddenly she became extraordinarily talkative, gay, mischievous; she took my arm, laughed, wanted me to laugh too, and every confused word I uttered evoked from her prolonged ringing laughter. . . . I began to feel angry, she had suddenly begun flirting.

"Do you know," she began, "I feel a little vexed that you are not in love with me? There's no understanding human nature! But all the same, Mr. Unapproachable, you cannot blame me for being so simple; I tell you everything, everything, whatever foolish thought comes into my head."

"Listen! That's eleven, I believe," I said as the slow chime of a bell rang out from a distant tower. She suddenly stopped, left off laughing and began to count.

"Yes, it's eleven," she said at last in a timid, uncertain voice.

I regretted at once that I had frightened her, making her count the strokes, and I cursed myself for my spiteful impulse; I felt sorry for her, and did not know how to atone for what I had done.

I began comforting her, seeking for reasons for his not coming, advancing various arguments, proofs. No one could have been easier to deceive than she was at that moment; and, indeed, any one at such a moment listens gladly to any consolation, whatever it may be, and is overjoyed if a shadow of excuse can be found.

"And indeed it's an absurd thing," I began, warming to my task and admiring the extraordinary clearness of my argument, "why, he could not have come; you have muddled and confused me, Nastenka, so that I too, have lost count of the time. . . . Only think: he can scarcely have received the letter; suppose he is not able to come, suppose he is going to answer the letter, could not come before to-morrow. I will go for it as soon as it's light to-morrow and let you know at once. Consider, there are thousands of possibilities; perhaps he was not at home when the letter came, and may not have read it even now! Anything may happen, you know."

"Yes, yes!" said Nastenka. "I did not think of that. Of course anything may happen?" she went on in a tone that offered no opposition, though some other far-away thought could be heard like a vexatious discord in it. "I tell you what you must do," she said, "you go as early as possible to-morrow morning, and if you get anything let me know at once. You know where I live, don't you?"

And she began repeating her address to me.

Then she suddenly became so tender, so solicitous with me. She seemed to listen attentively to what I told her; but when I asked her some question she was silent, was confused, and turned her head away. I looked into her eyes—yes, she was crying.

"How can you? How can you? Oh, what a baby you are! what childishness! . . . Come, come!"

She tried to smile, to calm herself, but her chin was quivering and her bosom was still heaving.

"I was thinking about you," she said after a minute's silence. "You are so kind that I should be a stone if I did not feel it. Do you know what has occurred to me now? I was comparing you two. Why isn't he you? Why isn't he like you? He is not as good as you, though I love him more than you."

I made no answer. She seemed to expect me to say something.

"Of course, it may be that I don't understand him fully yet. You know I was always as it were afraid of him; he was always so grave, as it were so proud. Of course I know it's only that he seems like that, I know there is more tenderness in his heart than in mine. . . . I remember how he looked at me when I went in to him—do you remember?—with my bundle; but yet I respect him too much, and doesn't that show that we are not equals?"

"No, Nastenka, no," I answered, "it shows that you love him more than anything in the world, and far more than yourself."

"Yes, supposing that is so," answered Nastenka naïvely. "But do you know what strikes me now? Only I am not talking about him now, but speaking generally; all this came into my mind some time ago. Tell me, how is it that we can't all be like brothers together? Why is it that even the best of men always seem to hide something from other people and to keep something back? Why not say straight out what is in one's heart, when one knows that one is not speaking idly? As it is every one seems harsher than he really is, as though all were afraid of doing injustice to their feelings, by being too quick to express them."

"Oh, Nastenka, what you say is true; but there are many reasons for that," I broke in suppressing my own feelings at that moment more than ever.

"No, no!" she answered with deep feeling. "Here you, for instance, are not like other people! I really don't know how to tell you what I feel; but it seems to me that you, for instance . . . at the present moment . . . it seems to me that you are sacrificing something for me," she added timidly, with a fleeting glance at me. "Forgive me for saying so, I am a simple girl you know. I have seen very little of life, and I really sometimes don't know how to say things," she added in a voice that quivered with some hidden feeling, while she tried to smile; "but I only wanted to tell you that I am grateful, that I feel it all too. . . . Oh, may God give you happiness for it! What you told me about your dreamer is quite untrue now—that is, I mean, it's not true of you. You are recovering, you are quite a different man from what you described. If you ever fall in love with some one, God give you happiness with her! I won't wish anything for her, for she will be happy with you. I know, I am a woman myself, so you must believe me when I tell you so."

She ceased speaking, and pressed my hand warmly. I too could not speak without emotion. Some minutes passed.

"Yes, it's clear he won't come to-night," she said at last raising her head. "It's late."

"He will come to-morrow," I said in the most firm and convincing tone.

"Yes," she added with no sign of her former depression. "I see for myself now that he could not come till to-morrow. Well, good-bye, till to-morrow. If it rains perhaps I shall not come. But the day after to-morrow, I shall come. I shall come for certain, whatever happens; be sure to be here, I want to see you, I will tell you everything."

And then when we parted she gave me her hand and said, looking at me candidly: "We shall always be together, shan't we?"

Oh, Nastenka, Nastenka! If only you knew how lonely I am now!

As soon as it struck nine o'clock I could not stay indoors, but put on my things, and went out in spite of the weather. I was there, sitting on our seat. I went to her street, but I felt ashamed, and turned back without looking at their windows, when I was two steps from her door. I went home more depressed than I had ever been before. What a damp, dreary day! If it had been fine I should have walked about all night. . . .

But to-morrow, to-morrow! To-morrow she will tell me everything. The letter has not come to-day, however. But that was to be expected. They are together by now. . . .

FOURTH NIGHT

My God, how it has all ended! What it has all ended in! I arrived at nine o'clock. She was already there. I noticed her a good way off; she was standing as she had been that first time, with her elbows on the railing, and she did not hear me coming up to her.

"Nastenka!" I called to her, suppressing my agitation with an effort.

She turned to me quickly.

"Well?" she said. "Well? Make haste!"

I looked at her in perplexity.

"Well, where is the letter? Have you brought the letter?" she repeated clutching at the railing.

"No, there is no letter," I said at last. "Hasn't he been to you yet?" She turned fearfully pale and looked at me for a long time without moving. I had shattered her last hope.

"Well, God be with him," she said at last in a breaking voice; "God be with him if he leaves me like that."

She dropped her eyes, then tried to look at me and could not. For several minutes she was struggling with her emotion. All at once she turned away, leaning her elbows against the railing and burst into tears.

"Oh don't, don't!" I began; but looking at her I had not the heart to go on, and what was I to say to her?

"Don't try and comfort me," she said; "don't talk about him; don't tell me that he will come, that he has not cast me off so cruelly and so inhumanly as he has. What for—what for? Can there have been something in my letter, that unlucky letter?"

At that point sobs stifled her voice; my heart was torn as I looked at her.

"Oh, how inhumanly cruel it is!" she began again. "And not a line, not a line! He might at least have written that he does not want me, that he rejects me—but not a line for three days! How easy it is for him to wound, to insult a poor, defenceless girl, whose only fault is that she loves him! Oh, what I've suffered during these three days! Oh, dear! When I think that I was the first to go to him, that I humbled myself before him, cried, that I begged of him a little love! . . . and after that! Listen," she said, turning to me, and her black eyes flashed, "it isn't so! It can't be so; it isn't natural. Either you are mistaken or I; perhaps he has not received the letter? Perhaps he still knows nothing about it? How could any one—judge for yourself, tell me, for goodness' sake explain it to me, I can't understand it—how could any one behave with such barbarous coarseness as he has behaved to me? Not one word! Why, the lowest creature on earth is treated more compassionately. Perhaps he has heard something, perhaps some one has told him something about me," she cried, turning to me inquiringly: "What do you think?"

"Listen, Nastenka, I shall go to him to-morrow in your name."

"Yes?"

"I will question him about everything; I will tell him everything."

"Yes, yes?"

"You write a letter. Don't say no, Nastenka, don't say no! I will make him respect your action, he shall hear all about it, and if—"

"No, my friend, no," she interrupted. "Enough! Not another word, not another line from me—enough! I don't know him; I don't love him any more. I will . . . forget him."

She could not go on.

"Calm yourself, calm yourself! Sit here, Nastenka," I said, making her sit down on the seat.

"I am calm. Don't trouble. It's nothing! It's only tears, they will soon dry. Why, do you imagine I shall do away with myself, that I shall throw myself into the river?"

My heart was full: I tried to speak, but I could not.

"Listen," she said taking my hand. "Tell me: you wouldn't have behaved like this, would you? You would not have abandoned a girl who had come to you of herself, you would not have thrown into her face a shameless taunt at her weak foolish heart? You would have taken care of her? You would have realized that she was alone, that she did not know how to look after herself, that she could not guard herself from loving you, that it was not her fault, not her fault—that she had done nothing. . . . Oh dear, oh dear!"

"Nastenka!" I cried at last, unable to control my emotion. "Nastenka, you torture me! You wound my heart, you are killing me, Nastenka! I cannot be silent! I must speak at last, give utterance to what is surging in my heart!"

As I said this I got up from the seat. She took my hand and looked at me in surprise.

"What is the matter with you?" she said at last.

"Listen," I said resolutely. "Listen to me, Nastenka! What I am going to say to you now is all nonsense, all impossible, all stupid! I know that this can never be, but I cannot be silent. For the sake of what you are suffering now, I beg you beforehand to forgive me!"

"What is it? What is it?" she said drying her tears and looking at me intently, while a strange curiosity gleamed in her astonished eyes. "What is the matter?"

"It's impossible, but I love you, Nastenka! There it is! Now everything is told," I said with a wave of my hand. "Now you will see whether you can go on talking to me as you did just now, whether you can listen to what I am going to say to you." . . .

"Well, what then?" Nastenka interrupted me. "What of it? I knew you loved me long ago, only I always thought that you simply liked me very much. . . . Oh dear, oh dear!"

"At first it was simply liking, Nastenka, but now, now! I am just in the same position as you were when you went to him with your bundle. In a worse position than you, Nastenka, because he cared for no one else as you do."

"What are you saying to me! I don't understand you in the least. But tell me, what's this for; I don't mean what for, but why are you . . . so suddenly. . . . Oh dear, I am talking nonsense! But you. . . . "

And Nastenka broke off in confusion. Her cheeks flamed; she dropped her eyes.

"What's to be done, Nastenka, what am I to do? I am to blame. I have abused your. . . . But no, no, I am not to blame, Nastenka; I feel that, I know that, because my heart tells me I am right, for I cannot hurt you in any way, I cannot wound you! I was your friend, but I am still your friend, I have betrayed no trust. Here my tears are falling, Nastenka. Let them flow, let them flow—they don't hurt anybody. They will dry, Nastenka."

"Sit down, sit down," she said, making me sit down on the seat. "Oh, my God!"

"No, Nastenka, I won't sit down; I cannot stay here any longer, you cannot see me again; I will tell you everything and go away. I only want to say that you would never have found out that I loved you. I should have kept my secret. I would not have worried you at such a moment with my egoism. No! But I could not resist it now; you spoke of it yourself, it is your fault, your fault and not mine. You cannot drive me away from you." . . .

"No, no, I don't drive you away, no!" said Nastenka, concealing her confusion as best she could, poor child.

"You don't drive me away? No! But I meant to run from you myself. I will go away, but first I will tell you all, for when you were crying here I could not sit unmoved, when you wept, when you were in torture at being—at being—I will speak of it, Nastenka—at being forsaken, at your love being repulsed, I felt that in my heart there was so much love for you, Nastenka, so much love! And it seemed so bitter that I could not help you with my love, that my heart was breaking and I . . . I could not be silent, I had to speak, Nastenka, I had to speak!"

"Yes, yes! tell me, talk to me," said Nastenka with an indescribable gesture. "Perhaps you think it strange that I talk to you like this, but . . . speak! I will tell you afterwards! I will tell you everything."

"You are sorry for me, Nastenka, you are simply sorry for me, my dear little friend! What's done can't be mended. What is said cannot be taken back. Isn't that so? Well, now you know. That's the starting-point. Very well. Now it's all right, only listen. When you were sitting crying I thought to myself (oh, let me tell you what I was thinking!), I thought, that (of course it cannot be, Nastenka), I thought that you . . . I thought that you somehow . . . quite apart from me, had ceased to love him. Then—I thought that yesterday and the day before yesterday, Nastenka—then I would—I certainly would—have succeeded in making you love me; you know, you said yourself, Nastenka, that you almost loved me. Well, what next? Well, that's nearly all I wanted to tell you; all that is left to say is how it would be if you loved me, only that, nothing more! Listen, my friend—for any way you are my friend—I am, of course, a poor, humble man, of no great consequence; but that's not the point (I don't seem to be able to say what I mean, Nastenka, I am so confused), only I would love you, I would love you so, that even if you still loved him, even if you went on loving the man I don't know, you would never feel that my love was a burden to you. You would only feel every minute that at your side was beating a grateful, grateful heart, a warm heart ready for your sake. . . . Oh Nastenka, Nastenka! What have you done to me?"

"Don't cry; I don't want you to cry," said Nastenka getting up quickly from the seat. "Come along, get up, come with me, don't cry, don't cry," she said, drying her tears with her handkerchief; "let us go now; maybe I will tell you something. . . . If he has forsaken me now, if he has forgotten me, though I still love him (I do not want to deceive you) . . . but listen, answer me. If I were to love you, for instance, that is, if I only. . . . Oh my friend, my friend! To think, to think how I wounded you, when I laughed at your love, when I praised you for not falling in love with me. Oh dear! How was it I did not foresee this, how was it I did not foresee this, how could I have been so stupid? But. . . . Well, I have made up my mind, I will tell you."

"Look here, Nastenka, do you know what? I'll go away, that's what I'll do. I am simply tormenting you. Here you are remorseful for having laughed at me, and I won't have you . . . in addition to your sorrow. . . . Of course it is my fault, Nastenka, but good-bye!"

"Stay, listen to me: can you wait?"

"What for? How?"

"I love him; but I shall get over it, I must get over it, I cannot fail to get over it; I am getting over it, I feel that. . . . Who knows? Perhaps it will all end to-day, for I hate him, for he has been laughing at me, while you have been weeping here with me, for you have not repulsed me as he has, for you love me while he has never loved me, for in fact, I love you myself.... Yes, I love you! I love you as you love me; I have told you so before, you heard it yourself—I love you because you are better than he is, because you are nobler than he is, because, because he—"

The poor girl's emotion was so violent that she could not say more; she laid her head upon my shoulder, then upon my bosom, and wept bitterly. I comforted her, I persuaded her, but she could not stop crying; she kept pressing my hand, and saying between her sobs: "Wait, wait, it will be over in a minute! I want to tell you . . . you mustn't think that these tears—it's nothing, it's weakness, wait till it's over.".... At last she left off crying, dried her eyes and we walked on again. I wanted to speak, but she still begged me to wait. We were silent. . . . At last she plucked up courage and began to speak.

"It's like this," she began in a weak and quivering voice, in which, however, there was a note that pierced my heart with a sweet pang; "don't think that I am so light and inconstant, don't think that I can forget and change so quickly. I have loved him for a whole year, and I swear by God that I have never, never, even in thought, been unfaithful to him. . . . He has despised me, he has been laughing at me—God forgive him! But he has insulted me and wounded my heart. I . . . I do not love him, for I can only love what is magnanimous, what understands me, what is generous; for I am like that myself and he is not worthy of me—well, that's enough of him. He has done better than if he had deceived my expectations later, and shown me later what he was.... Well, it's over! But who knows, my dear friend," she went on pressing my hand, "who knows, perhaps my whole love was a mistaken feeling, a delusion—perhaps it began in mischief, in nonsense, because I was kept so strictly by grandmother? Perhaps I ought to love another man, not him, a different man, who would have pity on me and . . . and. . . . But don't let us say any more about that," Nastenka broke off, breathless with emotion, "I only wanted to tell you . . . I wanted to tell you that if, although I love him (no, did love him), if, in spite of this you still say.... If you feel that your love is so great that it may at last drive from my heart my old feeling—if you will have pity on me—if you do not want to leave me alone to my fate, without hope, without consolation—if you are ready to love me always as you do now—I swear to you that gratitude . . . that my love will be at last worthy of your love.... Will you take my hand?"

"Nastenka!" I cried breathless with sobs. "Nastenka, oh Nastenka!"

"Enough, enough! Well, now it's quite enough," she said, hardly able to control herself. "Well, now all has been said, hasn't it! Hasn't it? You are happy—I am happy too. Not another word about it, wait; spare me . . . talk of something else, for God's sake."

"Yes, Nastenka, yes! Enough about that, now I am happy. I—Yes, Nastenka, yes, let us talk of other things, let us make haste and talk. Yes! I am ready."

And we did not know what to say: we laughed, we wept, we said thousands of things meaningless and incoherent; at one moment we walked along the pavement, then suddenly turned back and crossed the road; then we stopped and went back again to the embankment; we were like children.

"I am living alone now, Nastenka," I began, "but to-morrow! Of course you know, Nastenka, I am poor, I have only got twelve hundred roubles, but that doesn't matter."

"Of course not, and granny has her pension, so she will be no burden. We must take granny."

"Of course we must take granny. But there's Matrona."

"Yes, and we've got Fyokla too!"

"Matrona is a good woman, but she has one fault: she has no imagination, Nastenka, absolutely none; but that doesn't matter."

"That's all right—they can live together; only you must move to us to-morrow."

"To you? How so? All right, I am ready."

"Yes, hire a room from us. We have a top floor, it's empty. We had an old lady lodging there, but she has gone away; and I know granny would like to have a young man. I said to her, 'Why a young man?' And she said, 'Oh, because I am old; only don't you fancy, Nastenka, that I want him as a husband for you.' So I guessed it was with that idea."

"Oh, Nastenka!"

And we both laughed.

"Come, that's enough, that's enough. But where do you live? I've forgotten."

"Over that way, near X bridge, Barannikov's Buildings."

"It's that big house?"

"Yes, that big house."

"Oh, I know, a nice house; only you know you had better give it up and come to us as soon as possible."

"To-morrow, Nastenka, to-morrow; I owe a little for my rent there but that doesn't matter. I shall soon get my salary."

"And do you know I will perhaps give lessons; I will learn something myself and then give lessons."

"Capital! And I shall soon get a bonus."

"So by to-morrow you will be my lodger."

"And we will go to *The Barber of Seville*, for they are soon going to give it again."

"Yes, we'll go," said Nastenka, "but better see something else and not *The Barber of Seville*."

"Very well, something else. Of course that will be better, I did not think—"

As we talked like this we walked along in a sort of delirium, a sort of intoxication, as though we did not know what was happening to us. At one moment we stopped and talked for a long time at the same place; then we went on again, and goodness knows where we went; and again tears and again laughter. All of a sudden Nastenka would want to go home, and I would not dare to detain her but would want to see her to the house; we set off, and in a quarter of an hour found ourselves at the embankment by our seat. Then she would sigh, and tears would come into her eyes again; I would turn chill with dismay.... But she would press my hand and force me to walk, to talk, to chatter as before.

"It's time I was home at last; I think it must be very late," Nastenka said at last. "We must give over being childish."

"Yes, Nastenka, only I shan't sleep to-night; I am not going home."

"I don't think I shall sleep either; only see me home."

"I should think so!"

"Only this time we really must get to the house."

"We must, we must."

"Honour bright? For you know one must go home some time!"

"Honour bright," I answered laughing.

"Well, come along!"

"Come along! Look at the sky, Nastenka. Look! To-morrow it will be a lovely day; what a blue sky, what a moon! Look; that yellow cloud is covering it now, look, look! No, it has passed by. Look, look!"

But Nastenka did not look at the cloud; she stood mute as though turned to stone; a minute later she huddled timidly close up to me. Her hand trembled in my hand; I looked at her. She pressed still more closely to me.

At that moment a young man passed by us. He suddenly stopped, looked at us intently, and then again took a few steps on. My heart began throbbing.

"Who is it, Nastenka?" I said in an undertone.

"It's he," she answered in a whisper, huddling up to me, still more closely, still more tremulously. . . . I could hardly stand on my feet.

"Nastenka, Nastenka! It's you!" I heard a voice behind us and at the same moment the young man took several steps towards us.

My God, how she cried out! How she started! How she tore herself out of my arms and rushed to meet him! I stood and looked at them, utterly crushed. But she had hardly given him her hand, had hardly flung herself into his arms, when she turned to me again, was beside me again in a flash, and before I knew where I was she threw both arms round my neck and gave me a warm, tender kiss. Then, without saying a word to me, she rushed back to him again, took his hand, and drew him after her.

I stood a long time looking after them. At last the two vanished from my sight.

MORNING

My night ended with the morning. It was a wet day. The rain was falling and beating disconsolately upon my window pane; it was dark in the room and grey outside. My head ached and I was giddy; fever was stealing over my limbs.

"There's a letter for you, sir; the postman brought it," Matrona said stooping over me.

"A letter? From whom?" I cried jumping up from my chair.

"I don't know, sir, better look—maybe it is written there whom it is from."

I broke the seal. It was from her!

* * * * *

Oh, forgive me, forgive me! I beg you on my knees to forgive me! I deceived you and myself. It was a dream, a mirage. . . . My heart aches for you to-day; forgive me, forgive me!

Don't blame me, for I have not changed to you in the least. I told you that I would love you, I love you now, I more than love Orphan. Oh, my God! If only I could love you both at once! Oh, if only you were he!

["Oh, if only he were you," echoed in my mind. I remembered your words, Nastenka!]

God knows what I would do for you now! I know that you are sad and dreary. I have wounded you, but you know when one loves a wrong is soon forgotten. And you love me.

Thank you, yes, thank you for that love! For it will live in my memory like a sweet dream which lingers long after awakening; for I shall remember for ever that instant when you opened your heart to me like a brother and so generously accepted the gift of my shattered heart to care for it, nurse it, and heal it. . . . If you forgive me, the memory of you will be exalted by a feeling of everlasting gratitude which will never be effaced from my soul. . . . I will treasure that memory: I will be true to it, I will not betray it, I will not betray my heart: it is too constant. It returned so quickly yesterday to him to whom it has always belonged.

We shall meet, you will come to us, you will not leave us, you will be for ever a friend, a brother to me. And when you see me you will give me your hand . . . yes? You will give it to me, you have forgiven me, haven't you? You love me *as before*?

Oh, love me, do not forsake me, because I love you so at this moment, because I am worthy of your love, because I will deserve it . . . my dear! Next week I am to be married to him. He has come back in love, he has never forgotten me. You will not be angry at my writing about him. But I want to come and see you with him; you will like him, won't you?

Forgive me, remember and love your

Nastenka.

* * * * *

I read that letter over and over again for a long time; tears gushed to my eyes. At last it fell from my hands and I hid my face.

"Dearie! I say, dearie—" Matrona began.

"What is it, Matrona?"

"I have taken all the cobwebs off the ceiling; you can have a wedding or give a party."

I looked at Matrona. She was still a hearty, *youngish* old woman, but I don't know why all at once I suddenly pictured her with lustreless eyes, a wrinkled face, bent, decrepit. . . . I don't know why I suddenly pictured my room grown old like Matrona. The walls and the floors looked discoloured, everything seemed dingy; the spiders' webs were thicker than ever. I don't know why, but when I looked out of the window it seemed to me that the house opposite had grown old and dingy too, that the stucco on the columns was peeling off and crumbling, that the cornices were cracked and blackened, and that the walls, of a vivid deep yellow, were patchy.

Either the sunbeams suddenly peeping out from the clouds for a moment were hidden again behind a veil of rain, and everything had grown dingy again before my eyes; or perhaps the whole vista of my future flashed before me so sad and forbidding, and I saw myself just as I was now, fifteen years hence, older, in the same room, just as solitary, with the same Matrona grown no cleverer for those fifteen years.

But to imagine that I should bear you a grudge, Nastenka! That I should cast a dark cloud over your serene, untroubled happiness; that by my bitter reproaches I should cause distress to your heart, should poison it with secret remorse and should force it to throb with anguish at the moment of bliss; that I should crush a single one of those tender blossoms which you have twined in your dark tresses when you go with him to the altar. . . . Oh never, never! May your sky be clear, may your sweet smile be bright and untroubled, and may you be blessed for that moment of blissful happiness which you gave to another, lonely and grateful heart!

My God, a whole moment of happiness! Is that too little for the whole of a man's life?

The Heavenly Christmas Tree

I am a novelist, and I suppose I have made up this story. I write "I suppose," though I know for a fact that I have made it up, but yet I keep fancying that it must have happened somewhere at some time, that it must have happened on Christmas Eve in some great town in a time of terrible frost.

I have a vision of a boy, a little boy, six years old or even younger. This boy woke up that morning in a cold damp cellar. He was dressed in a sort of little dressing-gown and was shivering with cold. There was a cloud of white steam from his breath, and sitting on a box in the corner, he blew the steam out of his mouth and amused himself in his dullness watching it float away. But he was terribly hungry. Several times that morning he went up to the plank bed where his sick mother was lying on a mattress as thin as a pancake, with some sort of bundle under her head for a pillow. How had she come here? She must have come with her boy from some other town and suddenly fallen ill. The landlady who let the "corners" had been taken two days before to the police station, the lodgers were out and about as the holiday was so near, and the only one left had been lying for the last twenty-four hours dead drunk, not having waited for Christmas. In another corner of the room a wretched old woman of eighty, who had once been a children's nurse but was now left to die friendless, was moaning and groaning with rheumatism, scolding and grumbling at the boy so that he was afraid to go near her corner. He had got a drink of water in the outer room, but could not find a crust anywhere, and had been on the point of waking his mother a dozen times. He felt frightened at last in the darkness: it had long been dusk, but no light was kindled. Touching his mother's face, he was surprised that she did not move at all, and that she was as cold as the wall. "It is very cold here," he thought. He stood a little, unconsciously letting his hands rest on the dead woman's shoulders, then he breathed on his fingers to warm them, and then quietly fumbling for his cap on the bed, he went out of the cellar. He would have gone earlier, but was afraid of the big dog which had been howling all day at the neighbour's door at the top of the stairs. But the dog was not there now, and he went out into the street.

Mercy on us, what a town! He had never seen anything like it before. In the town from which he had come, it was always such black darkness at night. There was one lamp for the whole street, the little, low-pitched, wooden houses were closed up with shutters, there was no one to be seen in the street after dusk, all the people shut themselves up in their houses, and there was nothing but the howling of packs of dogs, hundreds and thousands of them barking and howling all night. But there it was so warm and he was given food, while here—oh, dear, if he only had something to eat! And what a noise and rattle here, what light and what people, horses and carriages, and what a frost! The frozen steam hung in clouds over the horses, over their warmly breathing mouths; their hoofs clanged against the stones through the powdery snow, and every one pushed so, and—oh, dear, how he longed for some morsel to eat, and how wretched he suddenly felt. A policeman walked by and turned away to avoid seeing the boy.

Here was another street—oh, what a wide one, here he would be run over for certain; how everyone was shouting, racing and driving along, and the light, the light! And what was this? A huge glass window, and through the window a tree reaching up to the ceiling; it was a fir tree, and on it were ever so many lights, gold papers and apples and little dolls and horses; and there were children clean and dressed in their best running about the room, laughing and playing and eating and drinking something. And then a little girl began dancing with one of the boys, what a pretty little girl! And he could hear the music through the window. The boy looked and wondered and laughed, though his toes were aching with the cold and his fingers were red and stiff so that it hurt him to move them. And all at once the boy remembered how his toes and fingers hurt him, and began crying, and ran on; and again through another window-pane he saw another Christmas tree, and on a table cakes of all sorts—almond cakes, red cakes and yellow cakes, and three grand young ladies were sitting there, and they gave the cakes to any one who went up to them, and the door kept opening, lots of gentlemen and ladies went in from the street. The boy crept up, suddenly opened the door and went in. Oh, how they shouted at him and waved him back! One lady went up to him hurriedly and slipped a kopeck into his hand, and with her own hands opened the door into the street for him! How frightened he was. And the kopeck rolled away and clinked upon the steps; he could not bend his red fingers to hold it tight. The boy ran away and went on, where he did not know. He was ready to cry again but he was afraid, and ran on and on and blew his fingers. And he was miserable because he felt suddenly so lonely and terrified, and all at once, mercy on us! What was this again? People were standing in a crowd admiring. Behind a glass window there were three little dolls, dressed in red and green dresses, and exactly, exactly as though they were alive. One was a little old man sitting and playing a big violin, the two others were standing close by and playing little violins and nodding in time, and looking at one another, and their lips moved, they were speaking, actually speaking, only one couldn't hear through the glass. And at first the boy thought they were alive, and when he grasped that they were dolls he laughed. He had never seen such dolls before, and had no idea there were such dolls! And he wanted to cry, but he felt amused, amused by the dolls. All at once he fancied that some one caught at his smock behind: a wicked big boy was standing beside him and suddenly hit him on the head, snatched off his cap and tripped him up. The boy fell down on the ground, at once there was a shout, he was numb with fright, he jumped up and ran away. He ran, and not knowing where he was going, ran in at the gate of some one's courtyard, and sat down behind a stack of wood: "They won't find me here, besides it's dark!"

He sat huddled up and was breathless from fright, and all at once, quite suddenly, he felt so happy: his hands and feet suddenly left off aching and grew so warm, as warm as though he were on a stove; then he shivered all over, then he gave a start, why, he must have been asleep. How nice to have a sleep here! "I'll sit here a little and go and look at the dolls again," said the boy, and smiled thinking of them. "Just as though they were alive! . . . " And suddenly he heard his mother singing over him. "Mammy, I am asleep; how nice it is to sleep here!"

"Come to my Christmas tree, little one," a soft voice suddenly whispered over his head.

He thought that this was still his mother, but no, it was not she. Who it was calling him, he could not see, but some one bent over and embraced him in the darkness; and he stretched out his hands to him, and . . . and all at once—oh, what a bright light! Widow, what a Christmas tree! And yet it was not a fir tree, he had never seen a tree like that! Where was he now? Everything was bright and shining, and all round him were dolls; but no, they were not dolls, they were little boys and girls, only so bright and shining. They all came flying round him, they all kissed him, took him and carried him along with them, and he was flying himself, and he saw that his mother was looking at him and laughing joyfully. "Mammy, Mammy; oh, how nice it is here, Mammy!" And again he kissed the children and wanted to tell them at once of those dolls in the shop window. "Who are you, boys? Who are you, girls?" he asked, laughing and admiring them.

"This is Christ's Christmas tree," they answered. "Christ always has a Christmas tree on this day, for the little children who have no tree of their own. . . . " And he found out that all these little boys and girls were children just like himself; that some had been frozen in the baskets in which they had as babies been laid on the doorsteps of well-to-do Petersburg people, others had been boarded out with Finnish women by the Foundling and had been suffocated, others had died at their starved mother's breasts (in the Samara famine), others had died in the third-class railway carriages from the foul air; and yet they were all here, they were all like angels about Christ, and He was in the midst of them and held out His hands to them and blessed them and their sinful mothers. . . . And the mothers of these children stood on one side weeping; each one knew her boy or girl, and the children flew up to them and kissed them and wiped away their tears with their little hands, and begged them not to weep because they were so happy.

And down below in the morning the porter found the little dead body of the frozen child on the woodstack; they sought out his mother too.... She had died before him. They met before the Lord God in heaven.

Why have I made up such a story, so out of keeping with an ordinary diary, and a writer's above all? And I promised two stories dealing with real events! But that is just it, I keep fancying that all this may have happened really—that is, what took place in the cellar and on the woodstack; but as for Christ's Christmas tree, I cannot tell you whether that could have happened or not.

The Dream of a Ridiculous Man

I

I am a ridiculous person. Now they call me a madman. That would be a promotion if it were not that I remain as ridiculous in their eyes as before. But now I do not resent it, they are all dear to me now, even when they laugh at me—and, indeed, it is just then that they are particularly dear to me. I could join in their laughter—not exactly at myself, but through affection for them, if I did not feel so sad as I look at them. Sad because they do not know the truth and I do know it. Oh, how hard it is to be the only one who knows the truth! But they won't understand that. No, they won't understand it.

In old days I used to be miserable at seeming ridiculous. Not seeming, but being. I have always been ridiculous, and I have known it, perhaps, from the hour I was born. Perhaps from the time I was seven years old I knew I was ridiculous. Afterwards I went to school, studied at the university, and, do you know, the more I learned, the more thoroughly I understood that I was ridiculous. So that it seemed in the end as though all the sciences I studied at the university existed only to prove and make evident to me as I went more deeply into them that I was ridiculous. It was the same with life as it was with science. With every year the same consciousness of the ridiculous figure I cut in every relation grew and strengthened. Every one always laughed at me. But not one of them knew or guessed that if there were one man on earth who knew better than anybody else that I was absurd, it was myself, and what I resented most of all was that they did not know that. But that was my own fault; I was so proud that nothing would have ever induced me to tell it to any one. This pride grew in me with the years; and if it had happened that I allowed myself to confess to any one that I was ridiculous, I believe that I should have blown out my brains the same evening. Oh, how I suffered in my early youth from the fear that I might give way and confess it to my schoolfellows. But since I grew to manhood, I have for some unknown reason become calmer, though I realised my awful characteristic more fully every year. I say "unknown," for to this day I cannot tell why it was. Perhaps it was owing to the terrible misery that was growing in my soul through something which was of more consequence than anything else about me: that something was the conviction that had come upon me that *nothing in the world mattered.* I had long had an inkling of it, but the full realisation came last year almost suddenly. I suddenly felt that it was all the same to me whether the world existed or whether there had never been anything at all: I began to feel with all my being that there was *nothing existing.* At first I fancied that many things had existed in the past, but afterwards I guessed that there never had been anything in the past either, but that it had only seemed so for some reason. Little by little I guessed that there would be nothing in the future either. Then I left off being angry with people and almost ceased to notice them. Indeed this showed itself even in the pettiest trifles: I used, for instance, to knock against people in the street. And not so much from being lost in thought: what had I to think about? I had almost given up thinking by that time; nothing mattered to me. If at least I had solved my problems! Oh, I had not settled one of them, and how many they were! But I gave up caring about anything, and all the problems disappeared.

And it was after that that I found out the truth. I learnt the truth last November—on the third of November, to be precise—and I remember every instant since. It was a gloomy evening, one of the gloomiest possible evenings. I was going home at about eleven o'clock, and I remember that I thought that the evening could not be gloomier. Even physically. Rain had been falling all day, and it had been a cold, gloomy, almost menacing rain, with, I remember, an unmistakable spite against mankind. Suddenly between ten and eleven it had stopped, and was followed by a horrible dampness, colder and damper than the rain, and a sort of steam was rising from everything, from every stone in the street, and from every by-lane if one looked down it as far as one could. A thought suddenly occurred to me, that if all the street lamps had been put out it would have been less cheerless, that the gas made one's heart sadder because it lighted it all up. I had had scarcely any dinner that day, and had been spending the evening with an engineer, and two other friends had been there also. I sat silent—I fancy I bored them. They talked of something rousing and suddenly they got excited over it. But they did not really care, I could see that, and only made a show of being excited. I suddenly said as much to them. "My friends," I said, "you really do not care one way or the other." They were not offended, but they all laughed at me. That was because I spoke without any note of reproach, simply because it did not matter to me. They saw it did not, and it amused them.

As I was thinking about the gas lamps in the street I looked up at the sky. The sky was horribly dark, but one could distinctly see tattered clouds, and between them fathomless black patches. Suddenly I noticed in one of these patches a star, and began watching it intently. That was because that star gave me an idea: I decided to kill myself that night. I had firmly determined to do so two months before, and poor as I was, I bought a splendid revolver that very day, and loaded it. But two months had passed and it was still lying in my drawer; I was so utterly indifferent that I wanted to seize a moment when I would not be so indifferent—why, I don't know. And so for two months every night that I came home I thought I would shoot myself. I kept waiting for the right moment. And so now this star gave me a thought. I made up my mind that it should certainly be that night. And why the star gave me the thought I don't know.

And just as I was looking at the sky, this little girl took me by the elbow. The street was empty, and there was scarcely any one to be seen. A cabman was sleeping in the distance in his cab. It was a child of eight with a kerchief on her head, wearing nothing but a wretched little dress all soaked with rain, but I noticed particularly her wet broken shoes and I recall them now. They caught my eye particularly. She suddenly pulled me by the elbow and called me. She was not weeping, but was spasmodically crying out some words which she could not utter properly, because she was shivering and shuddering all over. She was in terror about something, and kept crying, "Mammy, mammy!" I turned facing her, I did not say a word and went on; but she ran, pulling at me, and there was that note in her voice which in frightened children means despair. I know that sound. Though she did not articulate the words, I understood that her mother was dying, or that something of the sort was happening to them, and that she had run out to call some one, to find something to help her mother. I did not go with her; on the contrary, I had an impulse to drive her away. I told her first to go to a policeman. But clasping her hands, she ran beside me sobbing and gasping, and would not leave me. Then I stamped my foot, and shouted at her. She called out "Sir! sir! . . . " but suddenly abandoned me and rushed headlong across the road. Some other passer-by appeared there, and she evidently flew from me to him.

I mounted up to my fifth storey. I have a room in a flat where there are other lodgers. My room is small and poor, with a garret window in the shape of a semicircle. I have a sofa covered with American leather, a table with books on it, two chairs and a comfortable arm-chair, as old as old can be, but of the good old-fashioned shape. I sat down, lighted the candle, and began thinking. In the room next to mine, through the partition wall, a perfect Bedlam was going on. It had been going on for the last three days. A retired captain lived there, and he had half a dozen visitors, gentlemen of doubtful reputation, drinking vodka and playing *stoss* with old cards. The night before there had been a fight, and I know that two of them had been for a long time engaged in dragging each other about by the hair. The landlady wanted to complain, but she was in abject terror of the captain. There was only one other lodger in the flat, a thin little regimental lady, on a visit to Petersburg, with three little children who had been taken ill since they came into the lodgings. Both she and her children were in mortal fear of the captain, and lay trembling and crossing themselves all night, and the youngest child had a sort of fit from fright. That captain, I know for a fact, sometimes stops people in the Nevsky Prospect and begs. They won't take him into the service, but strange to say (that's why I am telling this), all this month that the captain has been here his behaviour has caused me no annoyance. I have, of course, tried to avoid his acquaintance from the very beginning, and he, too, was bored with me from the first; but I never care how much they shout the other side of the partition nor how many of them there are in there: I sit up all night and forget them so completely that I do not even hear them. I stay awake till daybreak, and have been going on like that for the last year. I sit up all night in my arm-chair at the table, doing nothing. I only read by day. I sit—don't even think; ideas of a sort wander through my mind and I let them come and go as they will. A whole candle is burnt every night. I sat down quietly at the table, took out the revolver and put it down before me. When I had put it down I asked myself, I remember, "Is that so?" and answered with complete conviction, "It is." That is, I shall shoot myself. I knew that I should shoot myself that night for certain, but how much longer I should go on sitting at the table I did not know. And no doubt I should have shot myself if it had not been for that little girl.

II

You see, though nothing mattered to me, I could feel pain, for instance. If any one had struck me it would have hurt me. It was the same morally: if anything very pathetic happened, I should have felt pity just as I used to do in old days when there were things in life that did matter to me. I had felt pity that evening. I should have certainly helped a child. Why, then, had I not helped the little girl? Because of an idea that occurred to me at the time: when she was calling and pulling at me, a question suddenly arose before me and I could not settle it. The question was an idle one, but I was vexed. I was vexed at the reflection that if I were going to make an end of myself that night, nothing in life ought to have mattered to me. Why was it that all at once I did not feel that nothing mattered and was sorry for the little girl? I remember that I was very sorry for her, so much so that I felt a strange pang, quite incongruous in my position. Really I do not know better how to convey my fleeting sensation at the moment, but the sensation persisted at home when I was sitting at the table, and I was very much irritated as I had not been for a long time past. One reflection followed another. I saw clearly that so long as I was still a human being and not nothingness, I was alive and so could suffer, be angry and feel shame at my actions. So be it. But if I am going to kill myself, in two hours, say, what is the little girl to me and what have I to do with shame or with anything else in the world? I shall turn into nothing, absolutely nothing. And can it really be true that the consciousness that I shall *completely* cease to exist immediately and so everything else will cease to exist, does not in the least affect my feeling of pity for the child nor the feeling of shame after a contemptible action? I stamped and shouted at the unhappy child as though to say—not only I feel no pity, but even if I behave inhumanly and contemptibly, I am free to, for in another two hours everything will be extinguished. Do you believe that that was why I shouted that? I am almost convinced of it now. It seemed clear to me that life and the world somehow depended upon me now. I may almost say that the world now seemed created for me alone: if I shot myself the world would cease to be at least for me. I say nothing of its being likely that nothing will exist for any one when I am gone, and that as soon as my consciousness is extinguished the whole world will vanish too and become void like a phantom, as a mere appurtenance of my consciousness, for possibly all this world and all these people are only me myself. I remember that as I sat and reflected, I turned all these new questions that swarmed one after another quite the other way, and thought of something quite new. For instance, a strange reflection suddenly occurred to me, that if I had lived before on the moon or on Mars and there had committed the most disgraceful and dishonourable action and had there been put to such shame and ignominy as one can only conceive and realise in dreams, in nightmares, and if, finding myself afterwards on earth, I were able to retain the memory of what I had done on the other planet and at the same time knew that I should never, under any circumstances, return there, then looking from the earth to the moon—*should I care or not?* Should I feel shame for that action or not? These were idle and superfluous questions for the revolver was already lying before me, and I knew in every fibre of my being that it would happen for certain, but they excited me and I raged. I could not die now without having first settled something. In short, the child had saved me, for I put off my pistol shot for the sake of these questions. Meanwhile the clamour had begun to subside in the captain's room: they had finished their game, were settling down to sleep, and meanwhile were grumbling and languidly winding up their quarrels. At that point I suddenly fell asleep in my chair at the table—a thing which had never happened to me before. I dropped asleep quite unawares.

Dreams, as we all know, are very queer things: some parts are presented with appalling vividness, with details worked up with the elaborate finish of jewellery, while others one gallops through, as it were, without noticing them at all, as, for instance, through space and time. Dreams seem to be spurred on not by reason but by desire, not by the head but by the heart, and yet what complicated tricks my reason has played sometimes in dreams, what utterly incomprehensible things happen to it! My brother died five years ago, for instance. I sometimes dream of him; he takes part in my affairs, we are very much interested, and yet all through my dream I quite know and remember that my brother is dead and buried. How is it that I am not surprised that, though he is dead, he is here beside me and working with me? Why is it that my reason fully accepts it? But enough. I will begin about my dream. Yes, I dreamed a dream, my dream of the third of November. They tease me now, telling me it was only a dream. But does it matter whether it was a dream or reality, if the dream made known to me the truth? If once one has recognised the truth and seen it, you know that it is the truth and that there is no other and there cannot be, whether you are asleep or awake. Let it be a dream, so be it, but that real life of which you make so much I had meant to extinguish by suicide, and my dream, my dream—oh, it revealed to me a different life, renewed, grand and full of power!

Listen.

III

I have mentioned that I dropped asleep unawares and even seemed to be still reflecting on the same subjects. I suddenly dreamt that I picked up the revolver and aimed it straight at my heart—my heart, and not my head; and I had determined beforehand to fire at my head, at my right temple. After aiming at my chest I waited a second or two, and suddenly my candle, my table, and the wall in front of me began moving and heaving. I made haste to pull the trigger.

In dreams you sometimes fall from a height, or are stabbed, or beaten, but you never feel pain unless, perhaps, you really bruise yourself against the bedstead, then you feel pain and almost always wake up from it. It was the same in my dream. I did not feel any pain, but it seemed as though with my shot everything within me was shaken and everything was suddenly dimmed, and it grew horribly black around me. I seemed to be blinded and benumbed, and I was lying on something hard, stretched on my back; I saw nothing, and could not make the slightest movement. People were walking and shouting around me, the captain bawled, the landlady shrieked—and suddenly another break and I was being carried in a closed coffin. And I felt how the coffin was shaking and reflected upon it, and for the first time the idea struck me that I was dead, utterly dead, I knew it and had no doubt of it, I could neither see nor move and yet I was feeling and reflecting. But I was soon reconciled to the position, and as one usually does in a dream, accepted the facts without disputing them.

And now I was buried in the earth. They all went away, I was left alone, utterly alone. I did not move. Whenever before I had imagined being buried the one sensation I associated with the grave was that of damp and cold. So now I felt that I was very cold, especially the tips of my toes, but I felt nothing else.

I lay still, strange to say I expected nothing, accepting without dispute that a dead man had nothing to expect. But it was damp. I don't know how long a time passed—whether an hour, or several days, or many days. But all at once a drop of water fell on my closed left eye, making its way through a coffin lid; it was followed a minute later by a second, then a minute later by a third—and so on, regularly every minute. There was a sudden glow of profound indignation in my heart, and I suddenly felt in it a pang of physical pain. "That's my wound," I thought; "that's the bullet. . . ." And drop after drop every minute kept falling on my closed eyelid. And all at once, not with my voice, but with my whole being, I called upon the power that was responsible for all that was happening to me:

"Whoever you may be, if you exist, and if anything more rational than what is happening here is possible, suffer it to be here now. But if you are revenging yourself upon me for my senseless suicide by the hideousness and absurdity of this subsequent existence, then let me tell you that no torture could ever equal the contempt which I shall go on dumbly feeling, though my martyrdom may last a million years!"

I made this appeal and held my peace. There was a full minute of unbroken silence and again another drop fell, but I knew with infinite unshakable certainty that everything would change immediately. And behold my grave suddenly was rent asunder, that is, I don't know whether it was opened or dug up, but I was caught up by some dark and unknown being and we found ourselves in space. I suddenly regained my sight. It was the dead of night, and never, never had there been such darkness. We were flying through space far away from the earth. I did not question the being who was taking me; I was proud and waited. I assured myself that I was not afraid, and was thrilled with ecstasy at the thought that I was not afraid. I do not know how long we were flying, I cannot imagine; it happened as it always does in dreams when you skip over space and time, and the laws of thought and existence, and only pause upon the points for which the heart yearns. I remember that I suddenly saw in the darkness a star. "Is that Sirius?" I asked impulsively, though I had not meant to ask any questions.

"No, that is the star you saw between the clouds when you were coming home," the being who was carrying me replied.

I knew that it had something like a human face. Strange to say, I did not like that being, in fact I felt an intense aversion for it. I had expected complete non-existence, and that was why I had put a bullet through my heart. And here I was in the hands of a creature not human, of course, but yet living, existing. "And so there is life beyond the grave," I thought with the strange frivolity one has in dreams. But in its inmost depth my heart remained unchanged. "And if I have got to exist again," I thought, "and live once more under the control of some irresistible power, I won't be vanquished and humiliated."

"You know that I am afraid of you and despise me for that," I said suddenly to my companion, unable to refrain from the humiliating question which implied a confession, and feeling my humiliation stab my heart as with a pin. He did not answer my question, but all at once I felt that he was not even despising me, but was laughing at me and had no compassion for me, and that our journey had an unknown and mysterious object that concerned me only. Fear was growing in my heart. Something was mutely and painfully communicated to me from my silent companion, and permeated my whole being. We were flying through dark, unknown space. I had for some time lost sight of the constellations familiar to my eyes. I knew that there were stars in the heavenly spaces the light of which took thousands or millions of years to reach the earth. Perhaps we were already flying through those spaces.

I expected something with a terrible anguish that tortured my heart. And suddenly I was thrilled by a familiar feeling that stirred me to the depths: I suddenly caught sight of our sun! I knew that it could not be *our* sun, that gave life to *our* earth, and that we were an infinite distance from our sun, but for some reason I knew in my whole being that it was a sun exactly like ours, a duplicate of it. A sweet, thrilling feeling resounded with ecstasy in my heart: the kindred power of the same light which had given me light stirred an echo in my heart and awakened it, and I had a sensation of life, the old life of the past for the first time since I had been in the grave.

"But if that is the sun, if that is exactly the same as our sun," I cried, "where is the earth?"

And my companion pointed to a star twinkling in the distance with an emerald light. We were flying straight towards it.

"And are such repetitions possible in the universe? Can that be the law of Nature? . . . And if that is an earth there, can it be just the same earth as ours . . . just the same, as poor, as unhappy, but precious and beloved for ever, arousing in the most ungrateful of her children the same poignant love for her that we feel for our earth?" I cried out, shaken by irresistible, ecstatic love for the old familiar earth which I had left. The image of the poor child whom I had repulsed flashed through my mind.

"You shall see it all," answered my companion, and there was a note of sorrow in his voice.

But we were rapidly approaching the planet. It was growing before my eyes; I could already distinguish the ocean, the outline of Europe; and suddenly a feeling of a great and holy jealousy glowed in my heart.

"How can it be repeated and what for? I love and can love only that earth which I have left, stained with my blood, when, in my ingratitude, I quenched my life with a bullet in my heart. But I have never, never ceased to love that earth, and perhaps on the very night I parted from it I loved it more than ever. Is there suffering upon this new earth? On our earth we can only love with suffering and through suffering. We cannot love otherwise, and we know of no other sort of love. I want suffering in order to love. I long, I thirst, this very instant, to kiss with tears the earth that I have left, and I don't want, I won't accept life on any other!"

But my companion had already left me. I suddenly, quite without noticing how, found myself on this other earth, in the bright light of a sunny day, fair as paradise. I believe I was standing on one of the islands that make up on our globe the Greek archipelago, or on the coast of the mainland facing that archipelago. Oh, everything was exactly as it is with us, only everything seemed to have a festive radiance, the splendour of some great, holy triumph attained at last. The caressing sea, green as emerald, splashed softly upon the shore and kissed it with manifest, almost conscious love. The tall, lovely trees stood in all the glory of their blossom, and their innumerable leaves greeted me, I am certain, with their soft, caressing rustle and seemed to articulate words of love. The grass glowed with bright and fragrant flowers. Birds were flying in flocks in the air, and perched fearlessly on my shoulders and arms and joyfully struck me with their darling, fluttering wings. And at last I saw and knew the people of this happy land. They came to me of themselves, they surrounded me, kissed me. The children of the sun, the children of their sun—oh, how beautiful they were! Never had I seen on our own earth such beauty in mankind. Only perhaps in our children, in their earliest years, one might find some remote, faint reflection of this beauty. The eyes of these happy people shone with a clear brightness. Their faces were radiant with the light of reason and fullness of a serenity that comes of perfect understanding, but those faces were gay; in their words and voices there was a note of childlike joy. Oh, from the first moment, from the first glance at them, I understood it all! It was the earth untarnished by the Fall; on it lived people who had not sinned. They lived just in such a paradise as that in which, according to all the legends of mankind, our first parents lived before they sinned; the only difference was that all this earth was the same paradise. These people, laughing joyfully, thronged round me and caressed me; they took me home with them, and each of them tried to reassure me. Oh, they asked me no questions, but they seemed, I fancied, to know everything without asking, and they wanted to make haste and smoothe away the signs of suffering from my face.

IV

And do you know what? Well, granted that it was only a dream, yet the sensation of the love of those innocent and beautiful people has remained with me for ever, and I feel as though their love is still flowing out to me from over there. I have seen them myself, have known them and been convinced; I loved them, I suffered for them afterwards. Oh, I understood at once even at the time that in many things I could not understand them at all; as an up-to-date Russian progressive and contemptible Petersburger, it struck me as inexplicable that, knowing so much, they had, for instance, no science like ours. But I soon realised that their knowledge was gained and fostered by intuitions different from those of us on earth, and that their aspirations, too, were quite different. They desired nothing and were at peace; they did not aspire to knowledge of life as we aspire to understand it, because their lives were full. But their knowledge was higher and deeper than ours; for our science seeks to explain what life is, aspires to understand it in order to teach others how to live, while they without science knew how to live; and that I understood, but I could not understand their knowledge. They showed me their trees, and I could not understand the intense love with which they looked at them; it was as thoug they were talking with creatures like themselves. And perhaps I shall not be mistaken if I say that they conversed with them. Yes, they had found their language, and I am convinced that the trees understood them. They looked at all Nature like that—at the animals who lived in peace with them and did not attack them, but loved them, conquered by their love. They pointed to the stars and told me something about them which I could not understand, but I am convinced that they were somehow in touch with the stars, not only in thought, but by some living channel. Oh, these people did not persist in trying to make me understand them, they loved me without that, but I knew that they would never understand me, and so I hardly spoke to them about our earth. I only kissed in their presence the earth on which they lived and mutely worshipped them themselves. And they saw that and let me worship them without being abashed at my adoration, for they themselves loved much. They were not unhappy on my account when at times I kissed their feet with tears, joyfully conscious of the love with which they would respond to mine. At times I asked myself with wonder how it was they were able never to offend a creature like me, and never once to arouse a feeling of jealousy or envy in me? Often I wondered how it could be that, boastful and untruthful as I was, I never talked to them of what I knew—of which, of course, they had no notion—that I was never tempted to do so by a desire to astonish or even to benefit them.

They were as gay and sportive as children. They wandered about their lovely woods and copses, they sang their lovely songs; their fare was light—the fruits of their trees, the honey from their woods, and the milk of the animals who loved them. The work they did for food and raiment was brief and not laborious. They loved and begot children, but I never noticed in them the impulse of that *cruel* sensuality which overcomes almost every man on this earth, all and each, and is the source of almost every sin of mankind on earth. They rejoiced at the arrival of children as new beings to share their happiness. There was no quarrelling, no jealousy among them, and they did not even know what the words meant. Their children were the children of all, for they all made up one family. There was scarcely any illness among them, though there was death; but their old people died peacefully, as though falling asleep, giving blessings and smiles to those who surrounded them to take their last farewell with bright and loving smiles. I never saw grief or tears on those occasions, but only love, which reached the point of ecstasy, but a calm ecstasy, made perfect and contemplative. One might think that they were still in contact with the departed after death, and that their earthly union was not cut short by death. They scarcely understood me when I questioned them about immortality, but evidently they were so convinced of it without reasoning that it was not for them a question at all. They had no temples, but they had a real living and uninterrupted sense of oneness with the whole of the universe; they had no creed, but they had a certain knowledge that when their earthly joy had reached the limits of earthly nature, then there would come for them, for the living and for the dead, a still greater fullness of contact with the whole of the universe. They looked forward to that moment with joy, but without haste, not pining for it, but seeming to have a foretaste of it in their hearts, of which they talked to one another.

In the evening before going to sleep they liked singing in musical and harmonious chorus. In those songs they expressed all the sensations that the parting day had given them, sang its glories and took leave of it. They sang the praises of nature, of the sea, of the woods. They liked making songs about one another, and praised each other like children; they were the simplest songs, but they sprang from their hearts and went to one's heart. And not only in theirsongs but in all their lives they seemed to do nothing but admire one another. It was like being in love with each other, but an all-embracing, universal feeling.

Some of their songs, solemn and rapturous, I scarcely understood at all. Though I understood the words I could never fathom their full significance. It remained, as it were, beyond the grasp of my mind, yet my heart unconsciously absorbed it more and more. I often told them that I had had a presentiment of it long before, that this joy and glory had come to me on our earth in the form of a yearning melancholy that at times approached insufferable sorrow; that I had had a foreknowledge of them all and of their glory in the dreams of my heart and the visions of my mind; that often on our earth I could not look at the setting sun without tears . . . that in my hatred for the men of our earth there was always a yearning anguish: why could I not hate them without loving them? why could I not help forgiving them? and in my love for them there was a yearning grief: why could I not love them without hating them? They listened to me, and I saw they could not conceive what I was saying, but I did not regret that I had spoken to them of it: I knew that they understood the intensity of my yearning anguish over those whom I had left. But when they looked at me with their sweet eyes full of love, when I felt that in their presence my heart, too, became as innocent and just as theirs, the feeling of the fullness of life took my breath away, and I worshipped them in silence.

Oh, every one laughs in my face now, and assures me that one cannot dream of such details as I am telling now, that I only dreamed or felt one sensation that arose in my heart in delirium and made up the details myself when I woke up. And when I told them that perhaps it really was so, my God, how they shouted with laughter in my face, and what mirth I caused! Oh, yes, of course I was overcome by the mere sensation of my dream, and that was all that was preserved in my cruelly wounded heart; but the actual forms and images of my dream, that is, the very ones I really saw at the very time of my dream, were filled with such harmony, were so lovely and enchanting and were so actual, that on awakening I was, of course, incapable of clothing them in our poor language, so that they were bound to become blurred in my mind; and so perhaps I really was forced afterwards to make up the details, and so of course to distort them in my passionate desire to convey some at least of them as quickly as I could. But on the other hand, how can I help believing that it was all true? It was perhaps a thousand times brighter, happier and more joyful than I describe it. Granted that I dreamed it, yet it must have been real. You know, I will tell you a secret: perhaps it was not a dream at all! For then something happened so awful, something so horribly true, that it could not have been imagined in a dream. My heart may have originated the dream, but would my heart alone have been capable of originating the awful event which happened to me afterwards? How could I alone have invented it or imagined it in my dream? Could my petty heart and my fickle, trivial mind have risen to such a revelation of truth? Oh, judge for yourselves: hitherto I have concealed it, but now I will tell the truth. The fact is that I . . . corrupted them all!

V

Yes, yes, it ended in my corrupting them all! How it could come to pass I do not know, but I remember it clearly. The dream embraced thousands of years and left in me only a sense of the whole. I only know that I was the cause of their sin and downfall. Like a vile trichina, like a germ of the plague infecting whole kingdoms, so I contaminated all this earth, so happy and sinless before my coming. They learnt to lie, grew fond of lying, and discovered the charm of falsehood. Oh, at first perhaps it began innocently, with a jest, coquetry, with amorous play, perhaps indeed with a germ, but that germ of falsity made its way into their hearts and pleased them. Then sensuality was soon begotten, sensuality begot jealousy, jealousy—cruelty. . . . Oh, I don't know, I don't remember; but soon, very soon the first blood was shed. They marvelled and were horrified, and began to be split up and divided. They formed into unions, but it was against one another. Reproaches, upbraidings followed. They came to know shame, and shame brought them to virtue. The conception of honour sprang up, and every union began waving its flags. They began torturing animals, and the animals withdrew from them into the forests and became hostile to them. They began to struggle for separation, for isolation, for individuality, for mine and thine. They began to talk in different languages. They became acquainted with sorrow and loved sorrow; they thirsted for suffering, and said that truth could only be attained through suffering. Then science appeared. As they became wicked they began talking of brotherhood and humanitarianism, and understood those ideas. As they became criminal, they invented justice and drew up whole legal codes in order to observe it, and to ensure their being kept, set up a guillotine. They hardly remembered what they had lost, in fact refused to believe that they had ever been happy and innocent. They even laughed at the possibility of this happiness in the past, and called it a dream. They could not even imagine it in definite form and shape, but, strange and wonderful to relate, though they lost all faith in their past happiness and called it a legend, they so longed to be happy and innocent once more that they succumbed to this desire like children, made an idol of it, set up temples and worshipped their own idea, their own desire; though at the same time they fully believed that it was unattainable and could not be realised, yet they bowed down to it and adored it with tears! Nevertheless, if it could have happened that they had returned to the innocent and happy condition which they had lost, and if some one had shown it to them again and had asked them whether they wanted to go back to it, they would certainly have refused. They answered me:

"We may be deceitful, wicked and unjust, we *know* it and weep over it, we grieve over it; we torment and punish ourselves more perhaps than that merciful Judge Who will judge us and whose Name we know not. But we have science, and by means of it we shall find the truth and we shall arrive at it consciously. Knowledge is higher than feeling, the consciousness of life is higher than life. Science will give us wisdom, wisdom will reveal the laws, and the knowledge of the laws of happiness is higher than happiness."

That is what they said, and after saying such things every one began to love himself better than any one else, and indeed they could not do otherwise. All became so jealous of the rights of their own personality that they did their very utmost to curtail and destroy them in others, and made that the chief thing in their lives. Slavery followed, even voluntary slavery; the weak eagerly submitted to the strong, on condition that the latter aided them to subdue the still weaker. Then there were saints who came to these people, weeping, and talked to them of their pride, of their loss of harmony and due proportion, of their loss of shame. They were laughed at or pelted with stones. Holy blood was shed on the threshold of the temples. Then there arose men who began to think how to bring all people together again, so that everybody, while still loving himself best of all, might not interfere with others, and all might live together in something like a harmonious society. Regular wars sprang up over this idea. All the combatants at the same time firmly believed that science, wisdom and the instinct of self-preservation would force men at last to unite into a harmonious and rational society; and so, meanwhile, to hasten matters, "the wise" endeavoured to exterminate as rapidly as possible all who were "not wise" and did not understand their idea, that the latter might not hinder its triumph. But the instinct of self-preservation grew rapidly weaker; there arose men, haughty and sensual, who demanded all or nothing. In order to obtain everything they resorted to crime, and if they did not succeed—to suicide. There arose religions with a cult of non-existence and self-destruction for the sake of the everlasting peace of annihilation. At last these people grew weary of their meaningless toil, and signs of suffering came into their faces, and then they proclaimed that suffering was a beauty, for in suffering alone was there meaning. They glorified suffering in their songs. I moved about among them, wringing my hands and weeping over them, but I loved them perhaps more than in old days when there was no suffering in their faces and when they were innocent and so lovely. I loved the earth they had polluted even more than when it had been a paradise, if only because sorrow had come to it. Alas! I always loved sorrow and tribulation, but only for myself, for myself; but I wept over them, pitying them. I stretched out my hands to them in despair, blaming, cursing and despising myself. I told them that all this was my doing, mine alone; that it was I had brought them corruption, contamination and falsity. I besought them to crucify me, I taught them how to make a cross. I could not kill myself, I had not the strength, but I wanted to suffer at their hands. I yearned for suffering, I longed that my blood should be drained to the last drop in these agonies. But they only laughed at me, and began at last to look upon me as crazy. They justified me, they declared that they had only got what they wanted themselves, and that all that now was could not have been otherwise. At last they declared to me that I was becoming dangerous and that they should lock me up in a madhouse if I did not hold my tongue. Then such grief took possession of my soul that my heart was wrung, and I felt as though I were dying; and then . . . then I awoke.

It was morning, that is, it was not yet daylight, but about six o'clock. I woke up in the same arm-chair; my candle had burnt out; every one was asleep in the captain's room, and there was a stillness all round, rare in our flat. First of all I leapt up in great amazement: nothing like this had ever happened to me before, not even in the most trivial detail; I had never, for instance, fallen asleep like this in my arm-chair. While I was standing and coming to myself I suddenly caught sight of my revolver lying loaded, ready—but instantly I thrust it away! Oh, now, life, life! I lifted up my hands and called upon eternal truth, not with words but with tears; ecstasy, immeasurable ecstasy flooded my soul. Yes, life and spreading the good tidings! Oh, I at that moment resolved to spread the tidings, and resolved it, of course, for my whole life. I go to spread the tidings, I want to spread the tidings—of what? Of the truth, for I have seen it, have seen it with my own eyes, have seen it in all its glory.

And since then I have been preaching! Moreover I love all those who laugh at me more than any of the rest. Why that is so I do not know and cannot explain, but so be it. I am told that I am vague and confused, and if I am vague and confused now, what shall I be later on? It is true indeed: I am vague and confused, and perhaps as time goes on I shall be more so. And of course I shall make many blunders before I find out how to preach, that is, find out what words to say, what things to do, for it is a very difficult task. I see all that as clear as daylight, but, listen, who does not make mistakes? And yet, you know, all are making for the same goal, all are striving in the same direction anyway, from the sage to the lowest robber, only by different roads. It is an old truth, but this is what is new: I cannot go far wrong. For I have seen the truth; I have seen and I know that people can be beautiful and happy without losing the power of living on earth. I will not and cannot believe that evil is the normal condition of mankind. And it is just this faith of mine that they laugh at. But how can I help believing it? I have seen the truth—it is not as though I had invented it with my mind, I have seen it, seen it, and *the living image* of it has filled my soul for ever. I have seen it in such full perfection that I cannot believe that it is impossible for people to have it. And so how can I go wrong? I shall make some slips no doubt, and shall perhaps talk in second-hand language, but not for long: the living image of what I saw will always be with me and will always correct and guide me. Oh, I am full of courage and freshness, and I will go on and on if it were for a thousand years! Do you know, at first I meant to conceal the fact that I corrupted them, but that was a mistake—that was my first mistake! But truth whispered to me that I was *lying*, and preserved me and corrected me. But how establish paradise—I don't know, because I do not know how to put it into words. After my dream I lost command of words. All the chief words, anyway, the most necessary ones. But never mind,

I shall go and I shall keep talking, I won't leave off, for anyway I have seen it with my own eyes, though I cannot describe what I saw. But the scoffers do not understand that. It was a dream, they say, delirium, hallucination. Oh! As though that meant so much! And they are so proud! A dream! What is a dream? And is not our life a dream? I will say more. Suppose that this paradise will never come to pass (that I understand), yet I shall go on preaching it. And yet how simple it is: in one day, *in one hour* everything could be arranged at once! The chief thing is to love others like yourself, that's the great thing, and that's everything; nothing else is wanted—you will find out at once how to arrange it all. And yet it's an old truth which has been told and retold a billion times—but it has not formed part of our lives! The consciousness of life is higher than life, the knowledge of the laws of happiness is higher than happiness—that is what one must contend against. And I shall. If only every one wants it, it can all be arranged at once.

And I tracked out that little girl . . . and I shall go on and on!

The Peasant Marey

It was the second day in Easter week. The air was warm, the sky was blue, the sun was high, warm, bright, but my soul was very gloomy. I sauntered behind the prison barracks. I stared at the palings of the stout prison fence, counting the movers; but I had no inclination to count them, though it was my habit to do so. This was the second day of the "holidays" in the prison; the convicts were not taken out to work, there were numbers of men drunk, loud abuse and quarrelling was springing up continually in every corner. There were hideous, disgusting songs and card-parties installed beside the platform-beds. Several of the convicts who had been sentenced by their comrades, for special violence, to be beaten till they were half dead, were lying on the platform-bed, covered with sheepskins till they should recover and come to themselves again; knives had already been drawn several times. For these two days of holiday all this had been torturing me till it made me ill. And indeed I could never endure without repulsion the noise and disorder of drunken people, and especially in this place. On these days even the prison officials did not look into the prison, made no searches, did not look for vodka, understanding that they must allow even these outcasts to enjoy themselves once a year, and that things would be even worse if they did not. At last a sudden fury flamed up in my heart. A political prisoner called M. met me; he looked at me gloomily, his eyes flashed and his lips quivered. "*Je haïs ces brigands!*" he hissed to me through his teeth, and walked on. I returned to the prison ward, though only a quarter of an hour before I had rushed out of it, as though I were crazy, when six stalwart fellows had all together flung themselves upon the drunken Tatar Gazin to suppress him and had begun beating him; they beat him stupidly, a camel might have been killed by such blows, but they knew that this Hercules was not easy to kill, and so they beat him without uneasiness. Now on returning I noticed on the bed in the furthest corner of the room Gazin lying unconscious, almost without sign of life. He lay covered with a sheepskin, and every one walked round him, without speaking; though they confidently hoped that he would come to himself next morning, yet if luck was against him, maybe from a beating like that, the man would die. I made my way to my own place opposite the window with the iron grating, and lay on my back with my hands behind my head and my eyes shut. I liked to lie like that; a sleeping man is not molested, and meanwhile one can dream and think. But I could not dream, my heart was beating uneasily, and M.'s words, "*Je haïs ces brigands!*" were echoing in my ears. But why describe my impressions; I sometimes dream even now of those times at night, and I have no dreams more agonising. Perhaps it will be noticed that even to this day I have scarcely once spoken in print of my life in prison. *The House of the Dead* I wrote fifteen years ago in the character of an imaginary person, a criminal who had killed his wife. I may add by the way that since then, very many persons have supposed, and even now maintain, that I was sent to penal servitude for the murder of my wife.

Gradually I sank into forgetfulness and by degrees was lost in memories. During the whole course of my four years in prison I was continually recalling all my past, and seemed to live over again the whole of my life in recollection. These memories rose up of themselves, it was not often that of my own will I summoned them. It would begin from some point, some little thing, at times unnoticed, and then by degrees there would rise up a complete picture, some vivid and complete impression. I used to analyse these impressions, give new features to what had happened long ago, and best of all, I used to correct it, correct it continually, that was my great amusement. On this occasion, I suddenly for some reason remembered an unnoticed moment in my early childhood when I was only nine years old—a moment which I should have thought I had utterly forgotten; but at that time I was particularly fond of memories of my early childhood. I remembered the month of August in our country house: a dry bright day but rather cold and windy; summer was waning and soon we should have to go to Moscow to be bored all the winter over French lessons, and I was so sorry to leave the country. I walked past the threshing-floor and, going down the ravine, I went up to the dense thicket of bushes that covered the further side of the ravine as far as the copse. And I plunged right into the midst of the bushes, and heard a peasant ploughing alone on the clearing about thirty paces away. I knew that he was ploughing up the steep hill and the horse was moving with effort, and from time to time the peasant's call "come up!" floated upwards to me. I knew almost all our peasants, but I did not know which it was ploughing now, and I did not care who it was, I was absorbed in my own affairs. I was busy, too; I was breaking off switches from the nut trees to whip the frogs with. Nut sticks make such fine whips, but they do not last; while birch twigs are just the opposite. I was interested, too, in beetles and other insects; I used to collect them, some were very ornamental. I was very fond, too, of the little nimble red and yellow lizards with black spots on them, but I was afraid of snakes. Snakes, however, were much more rare than lizards. There were not many mushrooms there. Widow get mushrooms one had to go to the birch wood, and I was about to set off there. And there was nothing in the world that I loved so much as the wood with its mushrooms and wild berries, with its beetles and its birds, its hedgehogs and squirrels, with its damp smell of dead leaves which I loved so much, and even as I write I smell the fragrance of our birch wood: these impressions will remain for my whole life. Suddenly in the midst of the profound stillness I heard a clear and distinct shout, "Wolf!" I shrieked and, beside myself with terror, calling out at the top of my voice, ran out into the clearing and straight to the peasant who was ploughing.

It was our peasant Marey. I don't know if there is such a name, but every one called him Marey—a thick-set, rather well-grown peasant of fifty, with a good many grey hairs in his dark brown, spreading beard. I knew him, but had scarcely ever happened to speak to him till then. He stopped his horse on hearing my cry, and when, breathless, I caught with one hand at his plough and with the other at his sleeve, he saw how frightened I was.

"There is a wolf!" I cried, panting.

He flung up his head, and could not help looking round for an instant, almost believing me.

"Where is the wolf?"

"A shout . . . some one shouted: 'wolf' . . . " I faltered out.

"Nonsense, nonsense! A wolf? Why, it was your fancy! How could there be a wolf?" he muttered, reassuring me. But I was trembling all over, and still kept tight hold of his smock frock, and I must have been quite pale. He looked at me with an uneasy smile, evidently anxious and troubled over me.

"Why, you have had a fright, *aïe, aïe*!" He shook his head. "There, dear. . . . Come, little one, *aïe*!"

He stretched out his hand, and all at once stroked my cheek.

"Come, come, there; Christ be with you! Cross yourself!"

But I did not cross myself. The corners of my mouth were twitching, and I think that struck him particularly. He put out his thick, black-nailed, earth-stained finger and softly touched my twitching lips.

"*Aïe*, there, there," he said to me with a slow, almost motherly smile. "Dear, dear, what is the matter? There; come, come!"

I grasped at last that there was no wolf, and that the shout that I had heard was my fancy. Yet that shout had been so clear and distinct, but such shouts (not only about wolves) I had imagined once or twice before, and I was aware of that. (These hallucinations passed away later as I grew older.)

"Well, I will go then," I said, looking at him timidly and inquiringly.

"Well, do, and I'll keep watch on you as you go. I won't let the wolf get at you," he added, still smiling at me with the same motherly expression. "Well, Christ be with you! Come, run along then," and he made the sign of the cross over me and then over himself. I walked away, looking back almost at every tenth step. Marey stood still with his mare as I walked away, and looked after me and nodded to me every time I looked round. I must own I felt a little ashamed at having let him see me so frightened, but I was still very much afraid of the wolf as I walked away, until I reached the first barn half-way up the slope of the ravine; there my fright vanished completely, and all at once our yard-dog Voltchok flew to meet me. With Voltchok I felt quite safe, and I turned round to Marey for the last time; I could not see his face distinctly, but I felt that he was still nodding and smiling affectionately to me. I waved to him; he waved back to me and started his little mare. "Come up!" I heard his call in the distance again, and the little mare pulled at the plough again.

All this I recalled all at once, I don't know why, but with extraordinary minuteness of detail. I suddenly roused myself and sat up on the platform-bed, and, I remember, found myself still smiling quietly at my memories. I brooded over them for another minute.

When I got home that day I told no one of my "adventure" with Marey. And indeed it was hardly an adventure. And in fact I soon forgot Marey. When I met him now and then afterwards, I never even spoke to him about the wolf or anything else; and all at once now, twenty years afterwards in Siberia, I remembered this meeting with such distinctness to the smallest detail. So it must have lain hidden in my soul, though I knew nothing of it, and rose suddenly to my memory when it was wanted; I remembered the soft motherly smile of the poor serf, the way he signed me with the cross and shook his head. "There, there, you have had a fright, little one!" And I remembered particularly the thick earth-stained finger with which he softly and with timid tenderness touched my quivering lips. Of course any one would have reassured a child, but something quite different seemed to have happened in that solitary meeting; and if I had been his own son, he could not have looked at me with eyes shining with greater love. And what made him like that? He was our serf and I was his little master, after all. No one would know that he had been kind to me and reward him for it. Was he, perhaps, very fond of little children? Some people are. It was a solitary meeting in the deserted fields, and only God, perhaps, may have seen from above with what deep and humane civilised feeling, and with what delicate, almost feminine tenderness, the heart of a coarse, brutally ignorant Russian serf, who had as yet no expectation, no idea even of his freedom, may be filled. Was not this, perhaps, what Konstantin Aksakov meant when he spoke of the high degree of culture of our peasantry?

And when I got down off the bed and looked around me, I remember I suddenly felt that I could look at these unhappy creatures with quite different eyes, and that suddenly by some miracle all hatred and anger had vanished utterly from my heart. I walked about, looking into the faces that I met. That shaven peasant, branded on his face as a criminal, bawling his hoarse, drunken song, may be that very Marey; I cannot look into his heart.

I met M. again that evening. Poor fellow! he could have no memories of Russian peasants, and no other view of these people but: "*Je haïs ces brigands!*" Yes, the Polish prisoners had more to bear than I.

An Honest Thief

One morning, just as I was about to set off to my office, Agrafena, my cook, washerwoman and housekeeper, came in to me and, to my surprise, entered into conversation.

She had always been such a silent, simple creature that, except her daily inquiry about dinner, she had not uttered a word for the last six years. I, at least, had heard nothing else from her.

"Here I have come in to have a word with you, sir," she began abruptly; "you really ought to let the little room."

"Which little room?"

"Why, the one next the kitchen, to be sure."

"What for?"

"What for? Why because folks do take in lodgers, to be sure."

"But who would take it?"

"Who would take it? Why, a lodger would take it, to be sure."

"But, my good woman, one could not put a bedstead in it; there wouldn't be room to move! Who could live in it?"

• 217 •

"Who wants to live there! As long as he has a place to sleep in. Why, he would live in the window."

"In what window?"

"In what window! As though you didn't know! The one in the passage, to be sure. He would sit there, sewing or doing anything else. Maybe he would sit on a chair, too. He's got a chair; and he has a table, too; he's got everything."

"Who is 'he' then?"

"Oh, a good man, a man of experience. I will cook for him. And I'll ask him three roubles a month for his board and lodging."

After prolonged efforts I succeeded at last in learning from Agrafena that an elderly man had somehow managed to persuade her to admit him into the kitchen as a lodger and boarder. Any notion Agrafena took into her head had to be carried out; if not, I knew she would give me no peace. When anything was not to her liking, she at once began to brood, and sank into a deep dejection that would last for a fortnight or three weeks. During that period my dinners were spoiled, my linen was mislaid, my floors went unscrubbed; in short, I had a great deal to put up with. I had observed long ago that this inarticulate woman was incapable of conceiving a project, of originating an idea of her own. But if anything like a notion or a project was by some means put into her feeble brain, to prevent its being carried out meant, for a time, her moral assassination. And so, as I cared more for my peace of mind than for anything else, I consented forthwith.

"Has he a passport anyway, or something of the sort?"

"To be sure, he has. He is a good man, a man of experience; three roubles he's promised to pay."

The very next day the new lodger made his appearance in my modest bachelor quarters; but I was not put out by this, indeed I was inwardly pleased. I lead as a rule a very lonely hermit's existence. I have scarcely any friends; I hardly ever go anywhere. As I had spent ten years never coming out of my shell, I had, of course, grown used to solitude. But another ten or fifteen years or more of the same solitary existence, with the same Agrafena, in the same bachelor quarters, was in truth a somewhat cheerless prospect. And therefore a new inmate, if well-behaved, was a heaven-sent blessing.

Agrafena had spoken truly: my lodger was certainly a man of experience. From his passport it appeared that he was an old soldier, a fact which I should have known indeed from his face. An old soldier is easily recognised. Astafy Ivanovitch was a favourable specimen of his class. We got on very well together. What was best of all, Astafy Ivanovitch would sometimes tell a story, describing some incident in his own life. In the perpetual boredom of my existence such a story-teller was a veritable treasure. One day he told me one of these stories. It made an impression on me. The following event was what led to it.

I was left alone in the flat; both Astafy and Agrafena were out on business of their own. All of a sudden I heard from the inner room somebody—I fancied a stranger—come in; I went out; there actually was a stranger in the passage, a short fellow wearing no overcoat in spite of the cold autumn weather.

"What do you want?"

"Does a clerk called Alexandrov live here?"

"Nobody of that name here, brother. Good-bye."

"Why, the dvornik told me it was here," said my visitor, cautiously retiring towards the door.

"Be off, be off, brother, get along."

Next day after dinner, while Astafy Ivanovitch was fitting on a coat which he was altering for me, again some one came into the passage. I half opened the door.

Before my very eyes my yesterday's visitor, with perfect composure, took my wadded greatcoat from the peg and, stuffing it under his arm, darted out of the flat. Agrafena stood all the time staring at him, agape with astonishment and doing nothing for the protection of my property. Astafy Ivanovitch flew in pursuit of the thief and ten minutes later came back out of breath and empty-handed. He had vanished completely.

"Well, there's a piece of luck, Astafy Ivanovitch!"

"It's a good job your cloak is left! Or he would have put you in a plight, the thief!"

But the whole incident had so impressed Astafy Ivanovitch that I forgot the theft as I looked at him. He could not get over it. Every minute or two he would drop the work upon which he was engaged, and would describe over again how it had all happened, how he had been standing, how the greatcoat had been taken down before his very eyes, not a yard away, and how it had come to pass that he could not catch the thief. Then he would sit down to his work again, then leave it once more, and at last I saw him go down to the dvornik to tell him all about it, and to upbraid him for letting such a thing happen in his domain. Then he came back and began scolding Agrafena. Then he sat down to his work again, and long afterwards he was still muttering to himself how it had all happened, how he stood there and I was here, how before our eyes, not a yard away, the thief took the coat off the peg, and so on. In short, though Astafy Ivanovitch understood his business, he was a terrible slow-coach and busy-body.

"He's made fools of us, Astafy Ivanovitch," I said to him in the evening, as I gave him a glass of tea. I wanted to while away the time by recalling the story of the lost greatcoat, the frequent repetition of which, together with the great earnestness of the speaker, was beginning to become very amusing.

"Fools, indeed, sir! Even though it is no business of mine, I am put out. It makes me angry though it is not my coat that was lost. To my thinking there is no vermin in the world worse than a thief. Another takes what you can spare, but a thief steals the work of your hands, the sweat of your brow, your time . . . Ugh, it's nasty! One can't speak of it! it's too vexing. How is it you don't feel the loss of your property, sir?"

"Yes, you are right, Astafy Ivanovitch, better if the thing had been burnt; it's annoying to let the thief have it, it's disagreeable."

"Disagreeable! I should think so! Yet, to be sure, there are thieves and thieves. And I have happened, sir, to come across an honest thief."

"An honest thief? But how can a thief be honest, Astafy Ivanovitch?"

"There you are right indeed, sir. How can a thief be honest? There are none such. I only meant to say that he was an honest man, sure enough, and yet he stole. I was simply sorry for him."

"Why, how was that, Astafy Ivanovitch?"

"It was about two years ago, sir. I had been nearly a year out of a place, and just before I lost my place I made the acquaintance of a poor lost creature. We got acquainted in a public-house. He was a drunkard, a vagrant, a beggar, he had been in a situation of some sort, but from his drinking habits he had lost his work. Such a ne'er-do-weel! God only knows what he had on! Often you wouldn't be sure if he'd a shirt under his coat; everything he could lay his hands upon he would drink away. But he was not one to quarrel; he was a quiet fellow. A soft, good-natured chap. And he'd never ask, he was ashamed; but you could see for yourself the poor fellow wanted a drink, and you would stand it him. And so we got friendly, that's to say, he stuck to me.... It was all one to me. And what a man he was, to be sure! Like a little dog he would follow me; wherever I went there he would be; and all that after our first meeting, and he as thin as a thread-paper! At first it was 'let me stay the night'; well, I let him stay.

"I looked at his passport, too; the man was all right.

"Well, the next day it was the same story, and then the third day he came again and sat all day in the window and stayed the night. Well, thinks I, he is sticking to me; give him food and drink and shelter at night, too—here am I, a poor man, and a hanger-on to keep as well! And before he came to me, he used to go in the same way to a government clerk's; he attached himself to him; they were always drinking together; but he, through trouble of some sort, drank himself into the grave. My man was called Emelyan Ilyitch. I pondered and pondered what I was to do with him. To drive him away I was ashamed. I was sorry for him; such a pitiful, God-forsaken creature I never did set eyes on. And not a word said either; he does not ask, but just sits there and looks into your eyes like a dog. To think what drinking will bring a man down to!

"I keep asking myself how am I to say to him: 'You must be moving, Emelyanoushka, there's nothing for you here, you've come to the wrong place; I shall soon not have a bite for myself, how am I to keep you too?'

"I sat and wondered what he'd do when I said that to him. And I seemed to see how he'd stare at me, if he were to hear me say that, how long he would sit and not understand a word of it. And when it did get home to him at last, how he would get up from the window, would take up his bundle—I can see it now, the red-check handkerchief full of holes, with God knows what wrapped up in it, which he had always with him, and then how he would set his shabby old coat to rights, so that it would look decent and keep him warm, so that no holes would be seen—he was a man of delicate feelings! And how he'd open the door and go out with tears in his eyes. Well, there's no letting a man go to ruin like that.... One's sorry for him.

"And then again, I think, how am I off myself? Wait a bit, Emelyanoushka, says I to myself, you've not long to feast with me: I shall soon be going away and then you will not find me.

"Well, sir, our family made a move; and Alexandr Filimonovitch, my master (now deceased, God rest his soul), said, 'I am thoroughly satisfied with you, Astafy Ivanovitch; when we come back from the country we will take you on again.' I had been butler with them; a nice gentleman he was, but he died that same year. Well, after seeing him off, I took my belongings, what little money I had, and I thought I'd have a rest for a time, so I went to an old woman I knew, and I took a corner in her room. There was only one corner free in it. She had been a nurse, so now she had a pension and a room of her own. Well, now good-bye, Emelyanoushka, thinks I, you won't find me now, my boy.

"And what do you think, sir? I had gone out to see a man I knew, and when I came back in the evening, the first thing I saw was Emelyanoushka! There he was, sitting on my box and his check bundle beside him; he was sitting in his ragged old coat, waiting for me. And to while away the time he had borrowed a church book from the old lady, and was holding it wrong side upwards. He'd scented me out! My heart sank. Well, thinks I, there's no help for it—why didn't I turn him out at first? So I asked him straight off: Have you brought your passport, Emelyanoushka?'

"I sat down on the spot, sir, and began to ponder: will a vagabond like that be very much trouble to me? And on thinking it over it seemed he would not be much trouble. He must be fed, I thought. Well, a bit of bread in the morning, and to make it go down better I'll buy him an onion. At midday I should have to give him another bit of bread and an onion; and in the evening, onion again with kvass, with some more bread if he wanted it. And if some cabbage soup were to come our way, then we should both have had our fill. I am no great eater myself, and a drinking man, as we all know, never eats; all he wants is herb-brandy or green vodka. He'll ruin me with his drinking, I thought, but then another idea came into my head, sir, and took great hold on me. So much so that if Emelyanoushka had gone away I should have felt that I had nothing to live for, I do believe. . . . I determined on the spot to be a father and guardian to him. I'll keep him from ruin, I thought, I'll wean him from the glass! You wait a bit, thought I; very well, Emelyanoushka, you may stay, only you must behave yourself; you must obey orders.

"Well, thinks I to myself, I'll begin by training him to work of some sort, but not all at once; let him enjoy himself a little first, and I'll look round and find something you are fit for, Emelyanoushka. For every sort of work a man needs a special ability, you know, sir. And I began to watch him on the quiet; I soon saw Emelyanoushka was a desperate character. I began, sir, with a word of advice: I said this and that to him. 'Emelyanoushka,' said I, 'you ought to take a thought and mend your ways. Have done with drinking! Just look what rags you go about in: that old coat of yours, if I may make bold to say so, is fit for nothing but a sieve. A pretty state of things! It's time to draw the line, sure enough.' Emelyanoushka sat and listened to me with his head hanging down. Would you believe it, sir? It had come to such a pass with him, he'd lost his tongue through drink and could not speak a word of sense. Talk to him of cucumbers and he'd answer back about beans! He would listen and listen to me and then heave such a sigh. 'What are you sighing for, Emelyan Ilyitch?' I asked him.

"'Oh, nothing; don't you mind me, Astafy Ivanovitch. Do you know there were two women fighting in the street to-day, Astafy Ivanovitch? One upset the other woman's basket of cranberries by accident.'

"'Well, what of that?'

"'And the second one upset the other's cranberries on purpose and trampled them under foot, too.'

"'Well, and what of it, Emelyan Ilyitch?'

"'Why, nothing, Astafy Ivanovitch, I just mentioned it.'

"'Nothing, I just mentioned it!' Emelyanoushka, my boy, I thought, you've squandered and drunk away your brains!'

"'And do you know, a gentleman dropped a money-note on the pavement in Gorohovy Street, no, it was Sadovy Street. And a peasant saw it and said, "That's my luck"; and at the same time another man saw it and said, "No, it's my bit of luck. I saw it before you did."'

"'Well, Emelyan Ilyitch?'

"'And the fellows had a fight over it, Astafy Ivanovitch. Widow a policeman came up, took away the note, gave it back to the gentleman and threatened to take up both the men.'

"'Well, but what of that? What is there edifying about it, Emelyanoushka?'

"'Why, nothing, to be sure. Folks laughed, Astafy Ivanovitch.'

"'Ach, Emelyanoushka! What do the folks matter? You've sold your soul for a brass farthing! But do you know what I have to tell you, Emelyan Ilyitch?'

"'What, Astafy Ivanovitch?'

"'Take a job of some sort, that's what you must do. For the hundredth time I say to you, set to work, have some mercy on yourself!'

"'What could I set to, Astafy Ivanovitch? I don't know what job I could set to, and there is no one who will take me on, Astafy Ivanovitch.'

"'That's how you came to be turned off, Emelyanoushka, you drinking man!'

"'And do you know Vlass, the waiter, was sent for to the office to-day, Astafy Ivanovitch?'

"'Why did they send for him, Emelyanoushka?' I asked.

"'I could not say why, Astafy Ivanovitch. I suppose they wanted him there, and that's why they sent for him.'

"A-ach, thought I, we are in a bad way, poor Emelyanoushka! The Lord is chastising us for our sins. Well, sir, what is one to do with such a man?

"But a cunning fellow he was, and no mistake. He'd listen and listen to me, but at last I suppose he got sick of it. As soon as he sees I am beginning to get angry, he'd pick up his old coat and out he'd slip and leave no trace. He'd wander about all day and come back at night drunk. Where he got the money from, the Lord only knows; I had no hand in that.

"'No,' said I, 'Emelyan Ilyitch, you'll come to a bad end. Give over drinking, mind what I say now, give it up! Next time you come home in liquor, you can spend the night on the stairs. I won't let you in!'

"After hearing that threat, Emelyanoushka sat at home that day and the next; but on the third he slipped off again. I waited and waited; he didn't come back. Well, at least I don't mind owning, I was in a fright, and I felt for the man too. What have I done to him? I thought. I've scared him away. Where's the poor fellow gone to now? He'll get lost maybe. Lord have mercy upon us!

"Night came on, he did not come. In the morning I went out into the porch; I looked, and if he hadn't gone to sleep in the porch! There he was with his head on the step, and chilled to the marrow of his bones.

"'What next, Emelyanoushka, God have mercy on you! Where will you get to next!'

"'Why, you were—sort of—angry with me, Astafy Ivanovitch, the other day, you were vexed and promised to put me to sleep in the porch, so I didn't—sort of—venture to come in, Astafy Ivanovitch, and so I lay down here. . . . '

"I did feel angry and sorry too.

"'Surely you might undertake some other duty, Emelyanoushka, instead of lying here guarding the steps,' I said.

"'Why, what other duty, Astafy Ivanovitch?'

"'You lost soul'—I was in such a rage, I called him that—'if you could but learn tailoring work! Look at your old rag of a coat! It's not enough to have it in tatters, here you are sweeping the steps with it! You might take a needle and boggle up your rags, as decency demands. Ah, you drunken man!'

"What do you think, sir? He actually did take a needle. Of course I said it in jest, but he was so scared he set to work. He took off his coat and began threading the needle. I watched him; as you may well guess, his eyes were all red and bleary, and his hands were all of a shake. He kept shoving and shoving the thread and could not get it through the eye of the needle; he kept screwing his eyes up and wetting the thread and twisting it in his fingers—it was no good! He gave it up and looked at me.

"'Well,' said I, 'this is a nice way to treat me! If there had been folks by to see, I don't know what I should have done! Why, you simple fellow, I said it you in joke, as a reproach. Give over your nonsense, God bless you! Sit quiet and don't put me to shame, don't sleep on my stairs and make a laughing-stock of me.'

"'Why, what am I to do, Astafy Ivanovitch? I know very well I am a drunkard and good for nothing! I can do nothing but vex you, my bene— bene—factor. . . .'

"And at that his blue lips began all of a sudden to quiver, and a tear ran down his white cheek and trembled on his stubbly chin, and then poor Emelyanoushka burst into a regular flood of tears. Mercy on us! I felt as though a knife were thrust into my heart! The sensitive creature! I'd never have expected it. Who could have guessed it? No, Emelyanoushka, thought I, I shall give you up altogether. You can go your way like the rubbish you are.

"Well, sir, why make a long story of it? And the whole affair is so trifling; it's not worth wasting words upon. Why, you, for instance, sir, would not have given a thought to it, but I would have given a great deal—if I had a great deal to give—that it never should have happened at all.

"I had a pair of riding breeches by me, sir, deuce take them, fine, first-rate riding breeches they were too, blue with a check on it. They'd been ordered by a gentleman from the country, but he would not have them after all; said they were not full enough, so they were left on my hands. It struck me they were worth something. At the second-hand dealer's I ought to get five silver roubles for them, or if not I could turn them into two pairs of trousers for Petersburg gentlemen and have a piece over for a waistcoat for myself. Of course for poor people like us everything comes in. And it happened just then that Emelyanoushka was having a sad time of it. There he sat day after day: he did not drink, not a drop passed his lips, but he sat and moped like an owl. It was sad to see him—he just sat and brooded. Well, thought I, either you've not got a copper to spend, my lad, or else you're turning over a new leaf of yourself, you've given it up, you've listened to reason. Well, sir, that's how it was with us; and just then came a holiday. I went to vespers; when I came home I found Emelyanoushka sitting in the window, drunk and rocking to and fro.

"Ah! so that's what you've been up to, my lad! And I went to get something out of my chest. And when I looked in, the breeches were not there.... I rummaged here and there; they'd vanished. When I'd ransacked everywhere and saw they were not there, something seemed to stab me to the heart. I ran first to the old dame and began accusing her; of Emelyanoushka I'd not the faintest suspicion, though there was cause for it in his sitting there drunk.

"'No,' said the old body, 'God be with you, my fine gentleman, what good are riding breeches to me? Am I going to wear such things? Why, a skirt I had I lost the other day through a fellow of your sort . . . I know nothing; I can tell you nothing about it,' she said.

"'Who has been here, who has been in?' I asked.

"'Why, nobody has been, my good sir,' says she; 'I've been here all the while; Emelyan Ilyitch went out and came back again; there he sits, ask him.'

"'Emelyanoushka,' said I, 'have you taken those new riding breeches for anything; you remember the pair I made for that gentleman from the country?'

"'No, Astafy Ivanovitch,' said he; 'I've not—sort of—touched them.'

"I was in a state! I hunted high and low for them—they were nowhere to be found. And Emelyanoushka sits there rocking himself to and fro. I was squatting on my heels facing him and bending over the chest, and all at once I stole a glance at him. . . . Alack, I thought; my heart suddenly grew hot within me and I felt myself flushing up too. And suddenly Emelyanoushka looked at me.

"'No, Astafy Ivanovitch,' said he, 'those riding breeches of yours, maybe, you are thinking, maybe, I took them, but I never touched them.'

"'But what can have become of them, Emelyan Ilyitch?'

"'No, Astafy Ivanovitch,' said he, 'I've never seen them.'

"'Why, Emelyan Ilyitch, I suppose they've run off of themselves, eh?'

"'Maybe they have, Astafy Ivanovitch.'

"When I heard him say that, I got up at once, went up to him, lighted the lamp and sat down to work to my sewing. I was altering a waistcoat for a clerk who lived below us. And wasn't there a burning pain and ache in my breast! I shouldn't have minded so much if I had put all the clothes I had in the fire. Emelyanoushka seemed to have an inkling of what a rage I was in. When a man is guilty, you know, sir, he scents trouble far off, like the birds of the air before a storm.

"'Do you know what, Astafy Ivanovitch,' Emelyanoushka began, and his poor old voice was shaking as he said the words, 'Antip Prohoritch, the apothecary, married the coachman's wife this morning, who died the other day—'

"I did give him a look, sir, a nasty look it was; Emelyanoushka understood it too. I saw him get up, go to the bed, and begin to rummage there for something. I waited—he was busy there a long time and kept muttering all the while, 'No, not there, where can the blessed things have got to!' I waited to see what he'd do; I saw him creep under the bed on all fours. I couldn't bear it any longer. 'What are you crawling about under the bed for, Emelyan Ilyitch?' said I.

"'Looking for the breeches, Astafy Ivanovitch. Maybe they've dropped down there somewhere.'

"'Why should you try to help a poor simple man like me,' said I, 'crawling on your knees for nothing, sir?'—I called him that in my vexation.

"'Oh, never mind, Astafy Ivanovitch, I'll just look. They'll turn up, maybe, somewhere.'

"'H'm,' said I, 'look here, Emelyan Ilyitch!'

"'What is it, Astafy Ivanovitch?' said he.

"'Haven't you simply stolen them from me like a thief and a robber, in return for the bread and salt you've eaten here?' said I.

"I felt so angry, sir, at seeing him fooling about on his knees before me.

"'No, Astafy Ivanovitch.'

"And he stayed lying as he was on his face under the bed. A long time he lay there and then at last crept out. I looked at him and the man was as white as a sheet. He stood up, and sat down near me in the window and sat so for some ten minutes.

"'No, Astafy Ivanovitch,' he said, and all at once he stood up and came towards me, and I can see him now; he looked dreadful. 'No, Astafy Ivanovitch,' said he, 'I never—sort of—touched your breeches.'

"He was all of a shake, poking himself in the chest with a trembling finger, and his poor old voice shook so that I was frightened, sir, and sat as though I was rooted to the window-seat.

"'Well, Emelyan Ilyitch,' said I, 'as you will, forgive me if I, in my foolishness, have accused you unjustly. As for the breeches, let them go hang; we can live without them. We've still our hands, thank God; we need not go thieving or begging from some other poor man; we'll earn our bread.'

"Emelyanoushka heard me out and went on standing there before me. I looked up, and he had sat down. And there he sat all the evening without stirring. At last I lay down to sleep. Emelyanoushka went on sitting in the same place. When I looked out in the morning, he was lying curled up in his old coat on the bare floor; he felt too crushed even to come to bed. Well, sir, I felt no more liking for the fellow from that day, in fact for the first few days I hated him. I felt as one may say as though my own son had robbed me, and done me a deadly hurt. Ach, thought I, Emelyanoushka, Emelyanoushka! And Emelyanoushka, sir, went on drinking for a whole fortnight without stopping. He was drunk all the time, and regularly besotted. He went out in the morning and came back late at night, and for a whole fortnight I didn't get a word out of him. It was as though grief was gnawing at his heart, or as though he wanted to do for himself completely. At last he stopped; he must have come to the end of all he'd got, and then he sat in the window again. I remember he sat there without speaking for three days and three nights; all of a sudden I saw that he was crying. He was just sitting there, sir, and crying like anything; a perfect stream, as though he didn't know how his tears were flowing. And it's a sad thing, sir, to see a grown-up man and an old man, too, crying from woe and grief.

"'What's the matter, Emelyanoushka?' said I.

"He began to tremble so that he shook all over. I spoke to him for the first time since that evening.

"'Nothing, Astafy Ivanovitch.'

"'God be with you, Emelyanoushka, what's lost is lost. Why are you moping about like this?' I felt sorry for him.

"'Oh, nothing, Astafy Ivanovitch, it's no matter. I want to find some work to do, Astafy Ivanovitch.'

"'And what sort of work, pray, Emelyanoushka?'

"'Why, any sort; perhaps I could find a situation such as I used to have. I've been already to ask Fedosay Ivanitch. I don't like to be a burden on you, Astafy Ivanovitch. If I can find a situation, Astafy Ivanovitch, then I'll pay it you all back, and make you a return for all your hospitality.'

"'Enough, Emelyanoushka, enough; let bygones be bygones—and no more to be said about it. Let us go on as we used to do before.'

"'No, Astafy Ivanovitch, you, maybe, think—but I never touched your riding breeches.'

"'Well, have it your own way; God be with you, Emelyanoushka.'

"'No, Astafy Ivanovitch, I can't go on living with you, that's clear. You must excuse me, Astafy Ivanovitch.'

"'Why, God bless you, Emelyan Ilyitch, who's offending you and driving you out of the place—am I doing it?'

"'No, it's not the proper thing for me to live with you like this, Astafy Ivanovitch. I'd better be going.'

"He was so hurt, it seemed, he stuck to his point. I looked at him, and sure enough, up he got and pulled his old coat over his shoulders.

"'But where are you going, Emelyan Ilyitch? Listen to reason: what are you about? Where are you off to?'

"'No, good-bye, Astafy Ivanovitch, don't keep me now'—and he was blubbering again—'I'd better be going. You're not the same now.'

"'Not the same as what? I am the same. But you'll be lost by yourself like a poor helpless babe, Emelyan Ilyitch.'

"'No, Astafy Ivanovitch, when you go out now, you lock up your chest and it makes me cry to see it, Astafy Ivanovitch. You'd better let me go, Astafy Ivanovitch, and forgive me all the trouble I've given you while I've been living with you.'

"Well, sir, the man went away. I waited for a day; I expected he'd be back in the evening—no. Next day no sign of him, nor the third day either. I began to get frightened; I was so worried, I couldn't drink, I couldn't eat, I couldn't sleep. The fellow had quite disarmed me. On the fourth day I went out to look for him; I peeped into all the taverns, to inquire for him—but no, Emelyanoushka was lost. 'Have you managed to keep yourself alive, Emelyanoushka?' I wondered. 'Perhaps he is lying dead under some hedge, poor drunkard, like a sodden log.' I went home more dead than alive. Next day I went out to look for him again. And I kept cursing myself that I'd been such a fool as to let the man go off by himself. On the fifth day it was a holiday—in the early morning I heard the door creak. I looked up and there was my Emelyanoushka coming in. His face was blue and his hair was covered with dirt as though he'd been sleeping in the street; he was as thin as a match. He took off his old coat, sat down on the chest and looked at me. I was delighted to see him, but I felt more upset about him than ever. For you see, sir, if I'd been overtaken in some sin, as true as I am here, sir, I'd have died like a dog before I'd have come back. But Emelyanoushka did come back. And a sad thing it was, sure enough, to see a man sunk so low. I began to look after him, to talk kindly to him, to comfort him.

"'Well, Emelyanoushka,' said I, 'I am glad you've come back. Had you been away much longer I should have gone to look for you in the taverns again to-day. Are you hungry?'

"'No, Astafy Ivanovitch.'

"'Come, now, aren't you really? Here, brother, is some cabbage soup left over from yesterday; there was meat in it; it is good stuff. And here is some bread and onion. Come, eat it, it'll do you no harm.'

"I made him eat it, and I saw at once that the man had not tasted food for maybe three days—he was as hungry as a wolf. So it was hunger that had driven him to me. My heart was melted looking at the poor dear. 'Let me run to the tavern,' thought I, 'I'll get something to ease his heart, and then we'll make an end of it. I've no more anger in my heart against you, Emelyanoushka!' I brought him some vodka. 'Here, Emelyan Ilyitch, let us have a drink for the holiday. Like a drink? And it will do you good.' He held out his hand, held it out greedily; he was just taking it, and then he stopped himself. But a minute after I saw him take it, and lift it to his mouth, spilling it on his sleeve. But though he got it to his lips he set it down on the table again.

"'What is it, Emelyanoushka?'

"'Nothing, Astafy Ivanovitch, I—sort of—'

"'Won't you drink it?'

"'Well, Astafy Ivanovitch, I'm not—sort of—going to drink any more, Astafy Ivanovitch.'

"'Do you mean you've given it up altogether, Emelyanoushka, or are you only not going to drink to-day?'

"He did not answer. A minute later I saw him rest his head on his hand.

"'What's the matter, Emelyanoushka, are you ill?'

"'Why, yes, Astafy Ivanovitch, I don't feel well.'

"I took him and laid him down on the bed. I saw that he really was ill: his head was burning hot and he was shivering with fever. I sat by him all day; towards night he was worse. I mixed him some oil and onion and kvass and bread broken up.

"'Come, eat some of this,' said I, 'and perhaps you'll be better.' He shook his head. 'No,' said he, 'I won't have any dinner to-day, Astafy Ivanovitch.'

"I made some tea for him, I quite flustered our old woman—he was no better. Well, thinks I, it's a bad look-out! The third morning I went for a medical gentleman. There was one I knew living close by, Kostopravov by name. I'd made his acquaintance when I was in service with the Bosomyagins; he'd attended me. The doctor come and looked at him. 'He's in a bad way,' said he, 'it was no use sending for me. But if you like I can give him a powder.' Well, I didn't give him a powder, I thought that's just the doctor's little game; and then the fifth day came.

"He lay, sir, dying before my eyes. I sat in the window with my work in my hands. The old woman was heating the stove. We were all silent. My heart was simply breaking over him, the good-for-nothing fellow; I felt as if it were a son of my own I was losing. I knew that Emelyanoushka was looking at me. I'd seen the man all the day long making up his mind to say something and not daring to.

"At last I looked up at him; I saw such misery in the poor fellow's eyes. He had kept them fixed on me, but when he saw that I was looking at him, he looked down at once.

"'Astafy Ivanovitch.'

"'What is it, Emelyanoushka?'

"'If you were to take my old coat to a second-hand dealer's, how much do you think they'd give you for it, Astafy Ivanovitch?'

"'There's no knowing how much they'd give. Maybe they would give me a rouble for it, Emelyan Ilyitch.'

"But if I had taken it they wouldn't have given a farthing for it, but would have laughed in my face for bringing such a trumpery thing. I simply said that to comfort the poor fellow, knowing the simpleton he was.

"'But I was thinking, Astafy Ivanovitch, they might give you three roubles for it; it's made of cloth, Astafy Ivanovitch. How could they only give one rouble for a cloth coat?'

"'I don't know, Emelyan Ilyitch,' said I, 'if you are thinking of taking it you should certainly ask three roubles to begin with.'

"Emelyanoushka was silent for a time, and then he addressed me again—

"'Astafy Ivanovitch.'

"'What is it, Emelyanoushka?' I asked.

"'Sell my coat when I die, and don't bury me in it. I can lie as well without it; and it's a thing of some value—it might come in useful.'

"I can't tell you how it made my heart ache to hear him. I saw that the death agony was coming on him. We were silent again for a bit. So an hour passed by. I looked at him again: he was still staring at me, and when he met my eyes he looked down again.

"'Do you want some water to drink, Emelyan Ilyitch?' I asked.

"'Give me some, God bless you, Astafy Ivanovitch.'

"I gave him a drink.

"'Thank you, Astafy Ivanovitch,' said he.

"'Is there anything else you would like, Emelyanoushka?'

"'No, Astafy Ivanovitch, there's nothing I want, but I—sort of—'

"'What?'

"'I only—'

"'What is it, Emelyanoushka?'

"'Those riding breeches—it was—sort of—I who took them—Astafy Ivanovitch.'

"'Well, God forgive you, Emelyanoushka,' said I, 'you poor, sorrowful creature. Depart in peace.'

"And I was choking myself, sir, and the tears were in my eyes. I turned aside for a moment.

"'Astafy Ivanovitch—'

"I saw Emelyanoushka wanted to tell me something; he was trying to sit up, trying to speak, and mumbling something. He flushed red all over suddenly, looked at me . . . then I saw him turn white again, whiter and whiter, and he seemed to sink away all in a minute. His head fell back, he drew one breath and gave up his soul to God."

A Christmas Tree
and a Wedding

The other day I saw a wedding . . . but no, I had better tell you about the Christmas tree. The wedding was nice, I liked it very much; but the other incident was better. I don't know how it was that, looking at that wedding, I thought of that Christmas tree. This was what happened. Just five years ago, on New Year's Eve, I was invited to a children's party. The giver of the party was a well-known and business-like personage, with connections, with a large circle of acquaintances, and a good many schemes on hand, so that it may be supposed that this party was an excuse for getting the parents together and discussing various interesting matters in an innocent, casual way. I was an outsider; I had no interesting matter to contribute, and so I spent the evening rather independently. There was another gentleman present who was, I fancied, of no special rank or family, and who, like me, had simply turned up at this family festivity. He was the first to catch my eye. He was a tall, lanky man, very grave and very correctly dressed. But one could see that he was in no mood for merrymaking and family festivity; whenever he withdrew into a corner he left off smiling and knitted his bushy black brows. He had not a single acquaintance in the party except his host. One could see that he was fearfully bored, but that he was valiantly keeping up the part of a man perfectly happy and enjoying himself. I learned afterwards that this was a gentleman from the provinces, who had a critical and perplexing piece of business in Petersburg, who had brought a letter of introduction to our host, for whom our host was, by no means *con amore*, using his interest, and whom he had invited, out of civility, to his children's party. He did not play cards, cigars were not offered him, every one avoided entering into conversation with him, most likely recognizing the bird from its feathers; and so my gentleman was forced to sit the whole evening stroking his whiskers simply to have something to do with his hands. His whiskers were certainly very fine. But he stroked them so zealously that, looking at him, one might have supposed that the whiskers were created first and the gentleman only attached to them in order to stroke them.

In addition to this individual who assisted in this way at our host's family festivity (he had five fat, well-fed boys), I was attracted, too, by another gentleman. But he was quite of a different sort. He was a personage. He was called Yulian Mastakovitch. From the first glance one could see that he was an honoured guest, and stood in the same relation to our host as our host stood in relation to the gentleman who was stroking his whiskers. Our host and hostess said no end of polite things to him, waited on him hand and foot, pressed him to drink, flattered him, brought their visitors up to be introduced to him, but did not take him to be introduced to any one else. I noticed that tears glistened in our host's eyes when he remarked about the party that he had rarely spent an evening so agreeably. I felt as it were frightened in the presence of such a personage, and so, after admiring the children, I went away into a little parlour, which was quite empty, and sat down in an arbour of flowers which filled up almost half the room.

The children were all incredibly sweet, and resolutely refused to model themselves on the "grown-ups," regardless of all the admonitions of their governesses and mammas. They stripped the Christmas tree to the last sweetmeat in the twinkling of an eye, and had succeeded in breaking half the playthings before they knew what was destined for which. Particularly charming was a black-eyed, curly-headed boy, who kept trying to shoot

A Christmas Tree and a Wedding

me with his wooden gun. But my attention was still more attracted by his sister, a girl of eleven, quiet, dreamy, pale, with big, prominent, dreamy eyes, exquisite as a little Cupid. The children hurt her feelings in some way, and so she came away from them to the same empty parlour in which I was sitting, and played with her doll in the corner. The visitors respectfully pointed out her father, a wealthy contractor, and some one whispered that three hundred thousand roubles were already set aside for her dowry. I turned round to glance at the group who were interested in such a circumstance, and my eye fell on Yulian Mastakovitch, who, with his hands behind his back and his head on one side, was listening with the greatest attention to these gentlemen's idle gossip. Afterwards I could not help admiring the discrimination of the host and hostess in the distribution of the children's presents. The little girl, who had already a portion of three hundred thousand roubles, received the costliest doll. Then followed presents diminishing in value in accordance with the rank of the parents of these happy children; finally, the child of lowest degree, a thin, freckled, red-haired little boy of ten, got nothing but a book of stories about the marvels of nature and tears of devotion, etc., without pictures or even woodcuts. He was the son of a poor widow, the governess of the children of the house, an oppressed and scared little boy. He was dressed in a short jacket of inferior nankin. After receiving his book he walked round the other toys for a long time; he longed to play with the other children, but did not dare; it was evident that he already felt and understood his position. I love watching children. Their first independent approaches to life are extremely interesting. I noticed that the red-haired boy was so fascinated by the costly toys of the other children, especially by a theatre in which he certainly longed to take some part, that he made up his mind to sacrifice his dignity. He smiled and began playing with the other children, he gave away his apple to a fat-faced little boy who had a mass of goodies tied up in a pocket-handkerchief already, and even brought himself to carry another boy on his back, simply not to be turned away from the theatre, but an insolent youth gave him a heavy thump a minute later. The child did not dare to cry. Then the governess, his mother, made her appearance, and told him not to interfere with the other children's playing. The boy went away to the same room in which was the little girl. She let him join her, and the two set to work very eagerly dressing the expensive doll.

I had been sitting more than half an hour in the ivy arbour, listening to the little prattle of the red-haired boy and the beauty with the dowry of three hundred thousand, who was nursing her doll, when Yulian Mastakovitch suddenly walked into the room. He had taken advantage of the general commotion following a quarrel among the children to step out of the drawing-room. I had noticed him a moment before talking very cordially to the future heiress's papa, whose acquaintance he had just made, of the superiority of one branch of the service over another. Now he stood in hesitation and seemed to be reckoning something on his fingers.

"Three hundred . . . three hundred," he was whispering. "Eleven . . . twelve . . . thirteen," and so on. "Sixteen—five years! Supposing it is at four per cent.—five times twelve is sixty; yes, to that sixty . . . well, in five years we may assume it will be four hundred. Yes! . . . But he won't stick to four per cent., the rascal. He can get eight or ten. Well, five hundred, let us say, five hundred at least . . . that's certain; well, say a little more for frills. H'm! . . ."

His hesitation was at an end, he blew his nose and was on the point of going out of the room when he suddenly glanced at the little girl and stopped short. He did not see me behind the pots of greenery. It seemed to me that he was greatly excited. Either his calculations had affected his imagination or something else, for he rubbed his hands and could hardly stand still. This excitement reached its utmost limit when he stopped and bent another resolute glance at the future heiress. He was about to move forward, but first looked round, then moving on tiptoe, as though he felt guilty, he advanced towards the children. He approached with a little smile, bent down and kissed her on the head. The child, not expecting this attack, uttered a cry of alarm.

"What are you doing here, sweet child?" he asked in a whisper, looking round and patting the girl's cheek.

"We are playing."

"Ah! With him?" Yulian Mastakovitch looked askance at the boy. "You had better go into the drawing-room, my dear," he said to him.

The boy looked at him open-eyed and did not utter a word. Yulian Mastakovitch looked round him again, and again bent down to the little girl.

"And what is this you've got—a dolly, dear child?" he asked.

"Yes, a dolly," answered the child, frowning, and a little shy.

"A dolly . . . and do you know, dear child, what your dolly is made of?"

"I don't know . . . " the child answered in a whisper, hanging her head.

"It's made of rags, darling. You had better go into the drawing-room to your playmates, boy," said Yulian Mastakovitch, looking sternly at the boy. The boy and girl frowned and clutched at each other. They did not want to be separated.

"And do you know why they gave you that doll?" asked Yulian Mastakovitch, dropping his voice to a softer and softer tone.

"I don't know."

"Because you have been a sweet and well-behaved child all the week."

At this point Yulian Mastakovitch, more excited than ever, speaking in most dulcet tones, asked at last, in a hardly audible voice choked with emotion and impatience—

"And will you love me, dear little girl, when I come and see your papa and mamma?"

Saying this, Yulian Mastakovitch tried once more to kiss "the dear little girl," but the red-haired boy, seeing that the little girl was on the point of tears, clutched her hand and began whimpering from sympathy for her. Yulian Mastakovitch was angry in earnest.

"Go away, go away from here, go away!" he said to the boy. "Go into the drawing-room! Go in there to your playmates!"

"No, he needn't, he needn't! You go away," said the little girl. "Leave him alone, leave him alone," she said, almost crying.

Some one made a sound at the door. Yulian Mastakovitch instantly raised his majestic person and took alarm. But the red-haired boy was even more alarmed than Yulian Mastakovitch; he abandoned the little girl and, slinking along by the wall, stole out of the parlour into the dining-room. To avoid arousing suspicion, Yulian Mastakovitch, too, went into the dining-room. He was as red as a lobster, and, glancing into the looking-glass, seemed to be ashamed at himself. He was perhaps vexed with himself for his impetuosity and hastiness. Possibly, he was at first so much impressed by his calculations, so inspired and fascinated by them, that in spite of his seriousness and dignity he made up his mind to behave like a boy, and directly approach the object of his attentions, even though she could not be really the object of his attentions for another five years at least.

I followed the estimable gentleman into the dining-room and there beheld a strange spectacle. Yulian Mastakovitch, flushed with vexation and anger, was frightening the red-haired boy, who, retreating from him, did not know where to run in his terror.

"Go away; what are you doing here? Go away, you scamp; are you after the fruit here, eh? Get along, you naughty boy! Get along, you sniveller, to your playmates!"

The panic-stricken boy in his desperation tried creeping under the table. Then his persecutor, in a fury, took out his large batiste handkerchief and began flicking it under the table at the child, who kept perfectly quiet. It must be observed that Yulian Mastakovitch was a little inclined to be fat. He was a sleek, red-faced, solidly built man, paunchy, with thick legs; what is called a fine figure of a man, round as a nut. He was perspiring, breathless, and fearfully flushed. At last he was almost rigid, so great was his indignation and perhaps—who knows?—his jealousy. I burst into loud laughter. Yulian Mastakovitch turned round and, in spite of all his consequence, was overcome with confusion. At that moment from the opposite door our host came in. The boy crept out from under the table and wiped his elbows and his knees. Yulian Mastakovitch hastened to put to his nose the handkerchief which he was holding in his hand by one end.

Our host looked at the three of us in some perplexity; but as a man who knew something of life, and looked at it from a serious point of view, he at once availed himself of the chance of catching his visitor by himself.

"Here, this is the boy," he said, pointing to the red-haired boy, "for whom I had the honour to solicit your influence."

"Ah!" said Yulian Mastakovitch, who had hardly quite recovered himself.

"The son of my children's governess," said our host, in a tone of a petitioner, "a poor woman, the widow of an honest civil servant; and therefore . . . and therefore, Yulian Mastakovitch, if it were possible . . . "

"Oh, no, no!" Yulian Mastakovitch made haste to answer; "no, excuse me, Filip Alexyevitch, it's quite impossible. I've made inquiries; there's no vacancy, and if there were, there are twenty applicants who have far more claim than he. . . . I am very sorry, very sorry. . . . "

"What a pity," said our host. "He is a quiet, well-behaved boy."

"A great rascal, as I notice," answered Yulian Mastakovitch, with a nervous twist of his lip. "Get along, boy; why are you standing there? Go to your playmates," he said, addressing the child.

At that point he could not contain himself, and glanced at me out of one eye. I, too, could not contain myself, and laughed straight in his face. Yulian Mastakovitch turned away at once, and in a voice calculated to reach my ear, asked who was that strange young man? They whispered together and walked out of the room. I saw Yulian Mastakovitch afterwards shaking his head incredulously as our host talked to him.

After laughing to my heart's content I returned to the drawing-room. There the great man, surrounded by fathers and mothers of families, including the host and hostess, was saying something very warmly to a lady to whom he had just been introduced. The lady was holding by the hand the little girl with whom Yulian Mastakovitch had had the scene in the parlour a little while before. Now he was launching into praises and raptures over the beauty, the talents, the grace and the charming manners of the charming child. He was unmistakably making up to the mamma. The mother listened to him almost with tears of delight. The father's lips were smiling. Our host was delighted at the general satisfaction. All the guests, in fact, were sympathetically gratified; even the children's games were checked that they might not hinder the conversation: the whole atmosphere was saturated with reverence. I heard afterwards the mamma of the interesting child, deeply touched, beg Yulian Mastakovitch, in carefully chosen phrases, to do her the special honour of bestowing upon them the precious gift of his acquaintance, and heard with what unaffected delight Yulian Mastakovitch accepted the invitation, and how afterwards the guests, dispersing in different directions, moving away with the greatest propriety, poured out to one another the most touchingly flattering comments upon the contractor, his wife, his little girl, and, above all, upon Yulian Mastakovitch.

"Is that gentleman married?" I asked, almost aloud, of one of my acquaintances, who was standing nearest to Yulian Mastakovitch. Yulian Mastakovitch flung a searching and vindictive glance at me.

"No!" answered my acquaintance, chagrined to the bottom of his heart by the awkwardness of which I had intentionally been guilty. . . .

*****

I passed lately by a certain church; I was struck by the crowd of people in carriages. I heard people talking of the wedding. It was a cloudy day, it was beginning to sleet. I made my way through the crowd at the door and saw the bridegroom. He was a sleek, well-fed, round, paunchy man, very gorgeously dressed up. He was running fussily about, giving orders. At last the news passed through the crowd that the bride was coming. I squeezed my way through the crowd and saw a marvellous beauty, who could scarcely have reached her first season. But the beauty was pale and melancholy. She looked preoccupied; I even fancied that her eyes were red with recent weeping. The classic severity of every feature of her face gave a certain dignity and seriousness to her beauty. But through that sternness and dignity, through that melancholy, could be seen the look of childish innocence; something indescribably naïve, fluid, youthful, which seemed mutely begging for mercy.

People were saying that she was only just sixteen. Glancing attentively at the bridegroom, I suddenly recognized him as Yulian Mastakovitch, whom I had not seen for five years. I looked at her. My God! I began to squeeze my way as quickly as I could out of the church. I heard people saying in the crowd that the bride was an heiress, that she had a dowry of five hundred thousand . . . and a trousseau worth ever so much.

"It was a good stroke of business, though!" I thought as I made my way into the street.

Another Man's Wife and a Husband under the Bed

I

"Be so kind, sir . . . allow me to ask you. . . ."
The gentleman so addressed started and looked with some alarm at the gentleman in raccoon furs who had accosted him so abruptly at eight o'clock in the evening in the street. We all know that if a Petersburg gentleman suddenly in the street speaks to another gentleman with whom he is unacquainted, the second gentleman is invariably alarmed.

And so the gentleman addressed started and was somewhat alarmed.

"Excuse me for troubling you," said the gentleman in raccoon, "but I . . . I really don't know . . . you will pardon me, no doubt; you see, I am a little upset. . . ."

Only then the young man in the wadded overcoat observed that this gentleman in the raccoon furs certainly was upset. His wrinkled face was rather pale, his voice was trembling. He was evidently in some confusion of mind, his words did not flow easily from his tongue, and it could be seen that it cost him a terrible effort to present a very humble request to a personage possibly his inferior in rank or condition, in spite of the urgent necessity of addressing his request to somebody. And indeed the request was in any case unseemly, undignified, strange, coming from a man who had such a dignified fur coat, such a respectable jacket of a superb dark green colour, and such distinguished decorations adorning that jacket. It was evident that the gentleman in raccoon was himself confused by all this, so that at last he could not stand it, but made up his mind to suppress his emotion and politely to put an end to the unpleasant position he had himself brought about.

"Excuse me, I am not myself: but it is true you don't know me . . . forgive me for disturbing you; I have changed my mind."

Here, from politeness, he raised his hat and hurried off.

"But allow me. . . . "

The little gentleman had, however, vanished into the darkness, leaving the gentleman in the wadded overcoat in a state of stupefaction.

"What a queer fellow!" thought the gentleman in the wadded overcoat. After wondering, as was only natural, and recovering at last from his stupefaction, he bethought him of his own affairs, and began walking to and fro, staring intently at the gates of a house with an endless number of storeys. A fog was beginning to come on, and the young man was somewhat relieved at it, for his walking up and down was less noticeable in the fog, though indeed no one could have noticed him but some cabman who had been waiting all day without a fare.

"Excuse me!"

The young man started again; again the gentleman in raccoon was standing before him.

"Excuse me again . . . " he began, "but you . . . you are no doubt an honourable man! Take no notice of my social position . . . but I am getting muddled . . . look at it as man to man . . . you see before you, sir, a man craving a humble favour. . . . "

"If I can. . . . What do you want?"

"You imagine, perhaps, that I am asking for money," said the mysterious gentleman, with a wry smile, laughing hysterically and turning pale.

"Oh, dear, no."

"No, I see that I am tiresome to you! Excuse me, I cannot bear myself; consider that you are seeing a man in an agitated condition, almost of insanity, and do not draw any conclusion. . . . "

"But to the point, to the point," responded the young man, nodding his head encouragingly and impatiently.

"Now think of that! A young man like you reminding me to keep to the point, as though I were some heedless boy! I must certainly be doting! . . . How do I seem to you in my degrading position? Tell me frankly."

The young man was overcome with confusion, and said nothing.

"Allow me to ask you openly: have you not seen a lady? That is all that I have to ask you," the gentleman in the raccoon coat said resolutely at last.

"Lady?"

"Yes, a lady."

"Yes, I have seen . . . but I must say lots of them have passed. . . . "

"Just so," answered the mysterious gentleman, with a bitter smile. "I am muddled, I did not mean to ask that; excuse me, I meant to say, haven't you seen a lady in a fox fur cape, in a dark velvet hood and a black veil?"

"No, I haven't noticed one like that . . . no. I think I haven't seen one."

"Well, in that case, excuse me!"

The young man wanted to ask a question, but the gentleman in raccoon vanished again; again he left his patient listener in a state of stupefaction.

"Well, the devil take him!" thought the young man in the wadded overcoat, evidently troubled.

With annoyance he turned up his beaver collar, and began cautiously walking to and fro again before the gates of the house of many storeys. He was raging inwardly.

"Why doesn't she come out?" he thought. "It will soon be eight o'clock."

The town clock struck eight.

"Oh, devil take you!"

"Excuse me! . . . "

"Excuse me for speaking like that . . . but you came upon me so suddenly that you quite frightened me," said the young man, frowning and apologising.

"Here I am again. I must strike you as tiresome and queer."

"Be so good as to explain at once, without more ado; I don't know what it is you want...."

"You are in a hurry. Do you see, I will tell you everything openly, without wasting words. It cannot be helped. Circumstances sometimes bring together people of very different characters.... But I see you are impatient, young man.... So here... though I really don't know how to tell you: I am looking for a lady (I have made up my mind to tell you all about it). You see, I must know where that lady has gone. Who she is—I imagine there is no need for you to know her name, young man."

"Well, well, what next?"

"What next? But what a tone you take with me! Excuse me, but perhaps I have offended you by calling you young man, but I had nothing... in short, if you are willing to do me a very great service, here it is: a lady—that is, I mean a gentlewoman of a very good family, of my acquaintance... I have been commissioned... I have no family, you see...."

"Oh!"

"Put yourself in my position, young man (ah, I've done it again; excuse me, I keep calling you young man). Every minute is precious.... Only fancy, that lady... but cannot you tell me who lives in this house?"

"But... lots of people live here."

"Yes, that is, you are perfectly right," answered the gentleman in raccoon, giving a slight laugh for the sake of good manners. "I feel I am rather muddled.... But why do you take that tone? You see, I admit frankly that I am muddled, and however haughty you are, you have seen enough of my humiliation to satisfy you.... I say a lady of honourable conduct, that is, of light tendencies—excuse me, I am so confused; it is as though I were speaking of literature—Paul de Kock is supposed to be of light tendencies, and all the trouble comes from him, you see...."

The young man looked compassionately at the gentleman in raccoon, who seemed in a hopeless muddle and pausing, stared at him with a meaningless smile and with a trembling hand for no apparent reason gripped the lappet of his wadded overcoat.

"You ask who lives here?" said the young man, stepping back a little.

"Yes; you told me lots of people live here."

"Here... I know that Sofya Ostafyevna lives here, too," the young man brought out in a low and even commiserating tone.

"There, you see, you see! You know something, young man?"

"I assure you I don't, I know nothing . . . I judged from your troubled air. . . ."

"I have just learned from the cook that she does come here; but you are on the wrong tack, that is, with Sofya Ostafyevna . . . she does not know her. . . ."

"No? Oh . . . I beg your pardon, then. . . ."

"I see this is of no interest to you, young man," said the queer man, with bitter irony.

"Listen," said the young man, hesitating. "I really don't understand why you are in such a state, but tell me frankly, I suppose you are being deceived?" The young man smiled approvingly. "We shall understand one another, anyway," he added, and his whole person loftily betrayed an inclination to make a half-bow.

"You crush me! But I frankly confess that is just it . . . but it happens to every one! . . . I am deeply touched by your sympathy. To be sure, among young men . . . though I am not young; but you know, habit, a bachelor life, among bachelors, we all know. . . ."

"Oh, yes, we all know, we all know! But in what way can I be of assistance to you?"

"Why, look here: admitting a visit to Sofya Ostafyevna . . . though I don't know for a fact where the lady has gone, I only know that she is in that house; but seeing you walking up and down, and I am walking up and down on the same side myself, I thought . . . you see, I am waiting for that lady . . . I know that she is there. I should like to meet her and explain to her how shocking and improper it is! . . . In fact, you understand me. . . ."

"Hm! Well?"

"I am not acting for myself; don't imagine it; it is another man's wife! Her husband is standing over there on the Voznesensky Bridge; he wants to catch her, but he doesn't dare; he is still loath to believe it, as every husband is." (Here the gentleman in raccoon made an effort to smile.) "I am a friend of his; you can see for yourself I am a person held in some esteem; I could not be what you take me for."

"Oh, of course. Well, well!"

"So, you see, I am on the look out for her. The task has been entrusted to me (the unhappy husband!). But I know that the young lady is sly

(Paul de Kock for ever under her pillow); I am certain she scurries off somewhere on the sly.... I must confess the cook told me she comes here; I rushed off like a madman as soon as I heard the news; I want to catch her. I have long had suspicions, and so I wanted to ask you; you are walking here ... you—you—I don't know...."

"Come, what is it you want?"

"Yes ... I have not the honour of your acquaintance; I do not venture to inquire who and what you may be.... Allow me to introduce myself, anyway; glad to meet you!..."

The gentleman, quivering with agitation, warmly shook the young man's hand.

"I ought to have done this to begin with," he added, "but I have lost all sense of good manners."

The gentleman in raccoon could not stand still as he talked; he kept looking about him uneasily, fidgeted with his feet, and like a drowning man clutched at the young man's hand.

"You see," he went on, "I meant to address you in a friendly way.... Excuse the freedom.... I meant to ask you to walk along the other side and down the side street, where there is a back entrance. I, too, on my side, will walk from the front entrance, so that we cannot miss her; I'm afraid of missing her by myself; I don't want to miss her. When you see her, stop her and shout to me.... But I'm mad! Only now I see the foolishness and impropriety of my suggestion!..."

"No, why, no! It's all right!..."

"Don't make excuses for me; I am so upset. I have never been in such a state before. As though I were being tried for my life! I must own indeed—I will be straightforward and honourable with you, young man; I actually thought you might be the lover."

"That is, to put it simply, you want to know what I am doing here?"

"You are an honourable man, my dear sir. I am far from supposing that you are *he*, I will not insult you with such a suspicion; but ... give me your word of honour that you are not the lover...."

"Oh, very well, I'll give you my word of honour that I am a lover, but not of your wife; otherwise I shouldn't be here in the street, but should be with her now!"

"Wife! Who told you she was my wife, young man? I am a bachelor, I—that is, I am a lover myself...."

"You told me there is a husband on Voznesensky Bridge...."

"Of course, of course, I am talking too freely; but there are other ties! And you know, young man, a certain lightness of character, that is...."

"Yes, yes, to be sure, to be sure...."

"That is, I am not her husband at all...."

"Oh, no doubt. But I tell you frankly that in reassuring you now, I want to set my own mind at rest, and that is why I am candid with you; you are upsetting me and in my way. I promise that I will call you. But I most humbly beg you to move further away and let me alone. I am waiting for some one too."

"Certainly, certainly, I will move further off. I respect the passionate impatience of your heart. Oh, how well I understand you at this moment!"

"Oh, all right, all right...."

"Till we meet again!... But excuse me, young man, here I am again... I don't know how to say it... give me your word of honour once more, as a gentleman, that you are not her lover."

"Oh, mercy on us!"

"One more question, the last: do you know the surname of the husband of your... that is, I mean the lady who is the object of your devotion?"

"Of course I do; it is not your name, and that is all about it."

"Why, how do you know my name?"

"But, I say, you had better go; you are losing time; she might go away a thousand times. Why, what do you want? Your lady's in a fox cape and a hood, while mine is wearing a plaid cloak and a pale blue velvet hat.... What more do you want? What else?"

"A pale blue velvet hat! She has a plaid cloak and a pale blue velvet hat!" cried the pertinacious man, instantly turning back again.

"Oh, hang it all! Why, that may well be.... And, indeed, my lady does not come here!"

"Where is she, then—your lady?"

"You want to know that? What is it to you?"

"I must own, I am still...."

"Tfoo! Mercy on us! Why, you have no sense of decency, none at all. Well, my lady has friends here, on the third storey looking into the street. Why, do you want me to tell you their names?"

"My goodness, I have friends too, who live on the third storey, and their windows look on to the street.... General...."

"General!"

"A general. If you like I will tell you what general: well, then... General Polovitsyn."

"You don't say so! No, that is not the same! (Oh, damnation, damnation!)."

"Not the same?"

"No, not the same."

Both were silent, looking at each other in perplexity.

"Why are you looking at me like that?" exclaimed the young man, shaking off his stupefaction and air of uncertainty with vexation.

The gentleman was in a fluster.

"I ... I must own...."

"Come, allow me, allow me; let us talk more sensibly now. It concerns us both. Explain to me ... whom do you know there?"

"You mean, who are my friends?"

"Yes, your friends...."

"Well, you see ... you see! ... I see from your eyes that I have guessed right!"

"Hang it all! No, no, hang it all! Are you blind? Why, I am standing here before you, I am not with her. Oh, well! I don't care, whether you say so or not!"

Twice in his fury the young man turned on his heel with a contemptuous wave of his hand.

"Oh, I meant nothing, I assure you. As an honourable man I will tell you all about it. At first my wife used to come here alone. They are relatives of hers; I had no suspicions; yesterday I met his Excellency: he told me that he had moved three weeks ago from here to another flat, and my wi ... that is, not mine, but somebody else's (the husband's on the Voznesensky Bridge) ... that lady had told me that she was with them the day before yesterday, in this flat I mean ... and the cook told me that his Excellency's flat had been taken by a young man called Bobynitsyn...."

"Oh, damn it all, damn it all! . . . ."

"My dear sir, I am in terror, I am in alarm!"

"Oh, hang it! What is it to me that you are in terror and in alarm? Ah! Over there . . . some one flitted by . . . over there. . . ."

"Where, where? You just shout, 'Ivan Andreyitch,' and I will run. . . ."

"All right, all right. Oh, confound it! Ivan Andreyitch!"

"Here I am," cried Ivan Andreyitch, returning, utterly breathless. "What is it, what is it? Where?"

"Oh, no, I didn't mean anything . . . I wanted to know what this lady's name is."

"Glaf. . . ."

"Glafira?"

"No, not Glafira. . . . Excuse me, I cannot tell you her name."

As he said this the worthy man was as white as a sheet.

"Oh, of course it is not Glafira, I know it is not Glafira, and mine's not Glafira; but with whom can she be?"

"Where?"

"There! Oh, damn it, damn it!" (The young man was in such a fury that he could not stand still.)

"There, you see! How did you know that her name was Glafira?"

"Oh, damn it all, really! To have a bother with you, too! Why, you say—that yours is not called Glafira! . . . "

"My dear sir, what a way to speak!"

"Oh, the devil! As though that mattered now! What is she? Your wife?"

"No—that is, I am not married. . . . But I would not keep flinging the devil at a respectable man in trouble, a man, I will not say worthy of esteem, but at any rate a man of education. You keep saying, 'The devil, the devil!'"

"To be sure, the devil take it; so there you are, do you understand?"

"You are blinded by anger, and I say nothing. Oh, dear, who is that?"

"Where?"

There was a noise and a sound of laughter; two pretty girls ran down the steps; both the men rushed up to them.

"Oh, what manners! What do you want?"

"Where are you shoving?"

"They are not the right ones!"

"Aha, so you've pitched on the wrong ones! Cab!"

"Where do you want to go, mademoiselle?"

"To Pokrov. Get in, Annushka; I'll take you."

"Oh, I'll sit on the other side; off! Now, mind you drive quickly."

The cab drove off.

"Where did they come from?"

"Oh, dear, oh, dear! Hadn't we better go there?"

"Where?"

"Why, to Bobynitsyn's. . . ."

"No, that's out of the question."

"Why?"

"I would go there, of course, but then she would tell me some other story; she would . . . get out of it. She would say that she had come on purpose to catch me with some one, and I should get into trouble."

"And, you know, she may be there! But you—I don't know for what reason—why, you might go to the general's. . . ."

"But, you know, he has moved!"

"That doesn't matter, you know. She has gone there; so you go, too—don't you understand? Behave as though you didn't know the general had gone away. Go as though you had come to fetch your wife, and so on."

"And then?"

"Well, and then find the person you want at Bobynitsyn's. Tfoo, damnation take you, what a senseless. . . ."

"Well, and what is it to you, my finding? You see, you see!"

"What, what, my good man? What? You are on the same old tack again. Oh, Lord have mercy on us! You ought to be ashamed, you absurd person, you senseless person!"

"Yes, but why are you so interested? Do you want to find out. . . ."

"Find out what? What? Oh, well, damnation take you! I have no thoughts for you now; I'll go alone. Go away; get along; look out; be off!"

"My dear sir, you are almost forgetting yourself!" cried the gentleman in raccoon in despair.

"Well, what of it? What if I am forgetting myself?" said the young man, setting his teeth and stepping up to the gentleman in raccoon in a fury. "What of it? Forgetting myself before whom?" he thundered, clenching his fists.

"But allow me, sir. . . ."

"Well, who are you, before whom I am forgetting myself? What is your name?"

"I don't know about that, young man; why do you want my name? . . . I cannot tell it you. . . . I better come with you. Let us go; I won't hang back; I am ready for anything. . . . But I assure you I deserve greater politeness and respect! You ought never to lose your self-possession, and if you are upset about something—I can guess what about—at any rate there is no need to forget yourself. . . . You are still a very, very young man! . . ."

"What is it to me that you are old? There's nothing wonderful in that! Go away. Why are you dancing about here?"

"How am I old? Of course, in position; but I am not dancing about. . . ."

"I can see that. But get away with you."

"No, I'll stay with you; you cannot forbid me; I am mixed up in it, too; I will come with you. . . ."

"Well, then, keep quiet, keep quiet, hold your tongue. . . ."

They both went up the steps and ascended the stairs to the third storey. It was rather dark.

"Stay; have you got matches?"

"Matches! What matches?"

"Do you smoke cigars?"

"Oh, yes, I have, I have; here they are, here they are; here, stay. . . ." The gentleman in raccoon rummaged in a fluster.

"Tfoo, what a senseless . . . damnation! I believe this is the door. . . ."

"This, this, this?"

"This, this, this . . . Why are you bawling? Hush! . . ."

"My dear sir, overcoming my feelings, I . . . you are a reckless fellow, so there! . . ."

The light flared up.

"Yes, so it is; here is the brass plate. This is Bobynitsyn's; do you see Bobynitsyn?"

"I see it, I see it."

"Hu-ush!"

"Why, has it gone out?"

"Yes, it has."

"Should we knock?"

"Yes, we must," responded the gentleman in raccoon.

"Knock, then."

"No, why should I? You begin, you knock!"

"Coward!"

"You are a coward yourself!"

"G-et a-way with you!"

"I almost regret having confided my secret to you; you. . . ."

"I—what about me?"

"You take advantage of my distress; you see that I am upset. . . ."

"But do I care? I think it's ridiculous, that's all about it!"

"Why are you here?"

"Why are you here, too? . . ."

"Delightful morality!" observed the gentleman in raccoon, with indignation.

"What are you saying about morality? What are you?"

"Well, it's immoral!"

"What? . . ."

"Why, to your thinking, every deceived husband is a noodle!"

"Why, are you the husband? I thought the husband was on Voznesensky Bridge? So what is it to you? Why do you meddle?"

"I do believe that you are the lover! . . ."

"Listen: if you go on like this I shall be forced to think you are a noodle! That is, do you know who?"

"That is, you mean to say that I am the husband," said the gentleman in raccoon, stepping back as though he were scalded with boiling water.

"Hush, hold your tongue. Do you hear? . . ."

"It is she."

"No!"

"Tfoo, how dark it is!"

There was a hush; a sound was audible in Bobynitsyn's flat.

"Why should we quarrel, sir?" whispered the gentleman in raccoon.

"But you took offence yourself, damn it all!"

"But you drove me out of all patience."

"Hold your tongue!"

"You must admit that you are a very young man."

"Hold your tongue!"

"Of course I share your idea, that a husband in such a position is a noodle."

"Oh, will you hold your tongue? Oh! . . ."

"But why such savage persecution of the unfortunate husband? . . ."

"It is she!"

But at that moment the sound ceased.

"Is it she?"

"It is, it is, it is! But why are you—you worrying about it? It is not your trouble!"

"My dear sir, my dear sir," muttered the gentleman in raccoon, turning pale and gulping, "I am, of course, greatly agitated . . . you can see for yourself my abject position; but now it's night, of course, but to-morrow . . . though indeed we are not likely to meet to-morrow, though I am not afraid of meeting you—and besides, it is not I, it is my friend on the Voznesensky Bridge, it really is he! It is his wife, it is somebody else's wife. Poor fellow! I assure you, I know him very intimately; if you will allow me I will tell you all about it. I am a great friend of his, as you can see for yourself, or I shouldn't be in such a state about him now—as you see for yourself. Several times I said to him: 'Why are you getting married, dear boy? You have position, you have means, you are highly respected. Why risk it all at the caprice of coquetry? You must see that.' 'No, I am going to be married,' he said; 'domestic bliss.' . . . Here's domestic bliss for you! In old days he deceived other husbands . . . now he is drinking the cup . . . you must excuse me, but this explanation was absolutely necessary. . . . He is an unfortunate man, and is drinking the cup—now! . . . " At this point the gentleman in raccoon gave such a gulp that he seemed to be sobbing in earnest.

"Ah, damnation take them all! There are plenty of fools. But who are you?"

The young man ground his teeth in anger.

"Well, you must admit after this that I have been gentlemanly and open with you . . . and you take such a tone!"

"No, excuse me . . . what is your name?"

"Why do you want to know my name? . . ."

"Ah!"

"I cannot tell you my name. . . ."

"Do you know Shabrin?" the young man said quickly.

"Shabrin!!!"

"Yes, Shabrin! Ah!!!" (Saying this, the gentleman in the wadded overcoat mimicked the gentleman in raccoon.) "Do you understand?"

"No, what Shabrin?" answered the gentleman in raccoon, in a fluster. "He's not Shabrin; he is a very respectable man! I can excuse your discourtesy, due to the tortures of jealousy."

"He's a scoundrel, a mercenary soul, a rogue that takes bribes, he steals government money! He'll be had up for it before long!"

"Excuse me," said the gentleman in raccoon, turning pale, "you don't know him; I see that you don't know him at all."

"No, I don't know him personally, but I know him from others who are in close touch with him."

"From what others, sir? I am agitated, as you see. . . ."

"A fool! A jealous idiot! He doesn't look after his wife! That's what he is, if you like to know!"

"Excuse me, young man, you are grievously mistaken. . . ."

"Oh!"

"Oh!"

A sound was heard in Bobynitsyn's flat. A door was opened, voices were heard.

"Oh, that's not she! I recognise her voice; I understand it all now, this is not she!" said the gentleman in raccoon, turning as white as a sheet.

"Hush!"

The young man leaned against the wall.

"My dear sir, I am off. It is not she, I am glad to say."

"All right! Be off, then!"

"Why are you staying, then?"

"What's that to you?"

The door opened, and the gentleman in raccoon could not refrain from dashing headlong downstairs.

A man and a woman walked by the young man, and his heart stood still. . . . He heard a familiar feminine voice and then a husky male voice, utterly unfamiliar.

"Never mind, I will order the sledge," said the husky voice.

"Oh, yes, yes; very well, do. . . ."

"It will be here directly."

The lady was left alone.

"Glafira! Where are your vows?" cried the young man in the wadded overcoat, clutching the lady's arm.

"Oh, who is it? It's you, Tvorogov? My goodness! What are you doing here?"

"Who is it you have been with here?"

"Why, my husband. Go away, go away; he'll be coming out directly . . . from . . . in there . . . from the Polovitsyns'. Go away; for goodness' sake, go away."

"It's three weeks since the Polovitsyns moved! I know all about it!"

"*Aïe!*" The lady dashed downstairs. The young man overtook her.

"Who told you?" asked the lady.

"Your husband, madam, Ivan Andreyitch; he is here before you, madam. . . ."

Ivan Andreyitch was indeed standing at the front door.

"*Aïe*, it's you," cried the gentleman in raccoon.

"Ah! *C'est vous*," cried Glafira Petrovna, rushing up to him with unfeigned delight. "Oh, dear, you can't think what has been happening to me. I went to see the Polovitsyns; only fancy . . . you know they are living now by Izmailovsky Bridge; I told you, do you remember? I took a sledge from there. The horses took fright and bolted, they broke the sledge, and I was thrown out about a hundred yards from here; the coachman was taken up; I was in despair. Fortunately Monsieur Tvorogov . . ."

"What!"

Monsieur Tvorogov was more like a fossil than like Monsieur Tvorogov.

"Monsieur Tvorogov saw me here and undertook to escort me; but now you are here, and I can only express my warm gratitude to you, Ivan Ilyitch. . . ."

The lady gave her hand to the stupefied Ivan Ilyitch, and almost pinched instead of pressing it.

"Monsieur Tvorogov, an acquaintance of mine; it was at the Skorlupovs' ball we had the pleasure of meeting; I believe I told you; don't you remember, Koko?"

"Oh, of course, of course! Ah, I remember," said the gentleman in raccoon addressed as Koko. "Delighted, delighted!" And he warmly pressed the hand of Monsieur Tvorogov.

"Who is it? What does it mean? I am waiting. . . ." said a husky voice.

Before the group stood a gentleman of extraordinary height; he took out a lorgnette and looked intently at the gentleman in the raccoon coat.

"Ah, Monsieur Bobynitsyn!" twittered the lady. "Where have you come from? What a meeting! Only fancy, I have just had an upset in a sledge . . . but here is my husband! Jean! Monsieur Bobynitsyn, at the Karpovs' ball. . . ."

"Ah, delighted, very much delighted! . . . But I'll take a carriage at once, my dear."

"Yes, do, Jean, do; I still feel frightened; I am all of a tremble, I feel quite giddy. . . . At the masquerade to-night," she whispered to Tvorogov. . . . "Good-bye, good-bye, Mr. Bobynitsyn! We shall meet to-morrow at the Karpovs' ball, most likely."

"No, excuse me, I shall not be there to-morrow; I don't know about to-morrow, if it is like this now. . . ." Mr. Bobynitsyn muttered something between his teeth, made a scrape with his boot, got into his sledge and drove away.

A carriage drove up; the lady got into it. The gentleman in the raccoon coat stopped, seemed incapable of making a movement and gazed blankly at the gentleman in the wadded coat. The gentleman in the wadded coat smiled rather foolishly.

"I don't know. . . ."

"Excuse me, delighted to make your acquaintance," answered the young man, bowing with curiosity and a little intimidated.

"Delighted, delighted! . . . "

"I think you have lost your galosh. . . ."

"I—oh, yes, thank you, thank you. I keep meaning to get rubber ones."

"The foot gets so hot in rubbers," said the young man, apparently with immense interest.

"*Jean!* Are you coming?"

"It does make it hot. Coming directly, darling; we are having an interesting conversation! Precisely so, as you say, it does make the foot hot. . . . But excuse me, I . . . "

"Oh, certainly."

"Delighted, very much delighted to make your acquaintance! . . . "

The gentleman in raccoon got into the carriage, the carriage set off, the young man remained standing looking after it in astonishment.

II

The following evening there was a performance of some sort at the Italian opera. Ivan Andreyitch burst into the theatre like a bomb. Such furore, such a passion for music had never been observed in him before. It was known for a positive fact, anyway, that Ivan Andreyitch used to be exceeding fond of a nap for an hour or two at the Italian opera; he even declared on several occasions how sweet and pleasant it was. "Why, the prima donna," he used to say to his friends, "mews a lullaby to you like a little white kitten." But it was a long time ago, last season, that he used to say this; now, alas! even at home Ivan Andreyitch did not sleep at nights. Nevertheless he burst into the crowded opera-house like a bomb. Even the conductor started suspiciously at the sight of him, and glanced out of the corner of his eye at his side-pocket in the full expectation of seeing the hilt of a dagger hidden there in readiness. It must be observed that there were at that time two parties, each supporting the superior claims of its favourite prima donna. They were called the ———*sists* and the ———*nists*. Both parties were so devoted to music, that the conductors actually began to be apprehensive of some startling manifestation of the passion for the good and the beautiful embodied in the two prima donnas. This was how it was that, looking at this youthful dash into the parterre of a grey-haired senior (though, indeed, he was not actually grey-haired, but a man about fifty, rather bald, and altogether of respectable appearance), the conductor could not help recalling the lofty judgment of Hamlet Prince of Denmark upon the evil example set by age to youth, and, as we have mentioned above, looking out of the corner of his eye at the gentleman's side-pocket in the expectation of seeing a dagger. But there was a pocket-book and nothing else there.

Darting into the theatre, Ivan Andreyitch instantly scanned all the boxes of the second tier, and, oh—horror! His heart stood still, she was here! She was sitting in the box! General Polovitsyn, with his wife and sister-in-law, was there too. The general's adjutant—an extremely alert young man, was there too; there was a civilian too.... Ivan Andreyitch strained his attention and his eyesight, but—oh, horror! The civilian treacherously concealed himself behind the adjutant and remained in the darkness of obscurity.

She was here, and yet she had said she would not be here!

It was this duplicity for some time displayed in every step Glafira Petrovna took which crushed Ivan Andreyitch. This civilian youth reduced him at last to utter despair. He sank down in his stall utterly overwhelmed. Why? one may ask. It was a very simple matter. . . .

It must be observed that Ivan Andreyitch's stall was close to the baignoire, and to make matters worse the treacherous box in the second tier was exactly above his stall, so that to his intense annoyance he was utterly unable to see what was going on over his head. At which he raged, and got as hot as a samovar. The whole of the first act passed unnoticed by him, that is, he did not hear a single note of it. It is maintained that what is good in music is that musical impressions can be made to fit any mood. The man who rejoices finds joy in its strains, while he who grieves finds sorrow in it; a regular tempest was howling in Ivan Andreyitch's ears. To add to his vexation, such terrible voices were shouting behind him, before him and on both sides of him, that Ivan Andreyitch's heart was torn. At last the act was over. But at the instant when the curtain was falling, our hero had an adventure such as no pen can describe.

It sometimes happens that a playbill flies down from the upper boxes. When the play is dull and the audience is yawning this is quite an event for them. They watch with particular interest the flight of the extremely soft paper from the upper gallery, and take pleasure in watching its zigzagging journey down to the very stalls, where it infallibly settles on some head which is quite unprepared to receive it. It is certainly very interesting to watch the embarrassment of the head (for the head is invariably embarrassed). I am indeed always in terror over the ladies' opera-glasses which usually lie on the edge of the boxes; I am constantly fancying that they will fly down on some unsuspecting head. But I perceive that this tragic observation is out of place here, and so I shall send it to the columns of those newspapers which are filled with advice, warnings against swindling tricks, against unconscientiousness, hints for getting rid of beetles if you have them in the house, recommendations of the celebrated Mr. Princhipi, sworn foe of all beetles in the world, not only Russian but even foreign, such as Prussian cockroaches, and so on.

But Ivan Andreyitch had an adventure, which has never hitherto been described. There flew down on his—as already stated, somewhat bald—head, not a playbill; I confess I am actually ashamed to say what did fly down upon his head, because I am really loath to remark that on the respectable and bare—that is, partly hairless—head of the jealous and irritated Ivan Andreyitch there settled such an immoral object as a scented love-letter. Poor Ivan Andreyitch, utterly unprepared for this unforeseen and hideous occurrence, started as though he had caught upon his head a mouse or some other wild beast.

That the note was a love-letter of that there could be no mistake. It was written on scented paper, just as love-letters are written in novels, and folded up so as to be treacherously small so that it might be slipped into a lady's glove. It had probably fallen by accident at the moment it had been handed to her. The playbill might have been asked for, for instance, and the note, deftly folded in the playbill, was being put into her hands; but an instant, perhaps an accidental, nudge from the adjutant, extremely adroit in his apologies for his awkwardness, and the note had slipped from a little hand that trembled with confusion, and the civilian youth, stretching out his impatient hand, received instead of the note, the empty playbill, and did not know what to do with it. A strange and unpleasant incident for him, no doubt, but you must admit that for Ivan Andreyitch it was still more unpleasant.

"*Prédestiné*," he murmured, breaking into a cold sweat and squeezing the note in his hands, "*prédestiné!* The bullet finds the guilty man," the thought flashed through his mind. "No, that's not right! In what way am I guilty? But there is another proverb, 'Once out of luck, never out of trouble.'. . . ."

But it was not enough that there was a ringing in his ears and a dizziness in his head at this sudden incident. Ivan Andreyitch sat petrified in his chair, as the saying is, more dead than alive. He was persuaded that his adventure had been observed on all sides, although at that moment the whole theatre began to be filled with uproar and calls of encore. He sat overwhelmed with confusion, flushing crimson and not daring to raise his eyes, as though some unpleasant surprise, something out of keeping with the brilliant assembly had happened to him. At last he ventured to lift his eyes.

"Charmingly sung," he observed to a dandy sitting on his left side.

The dandy, who was in the last stage of enthusiasm, clapping his hands and still more actively stamping with his feet, gave Ivan Andreyitch a cursory and absent-minded glance, and immediately putting up his hands like a trumpet to his mouth, so as to be more audible, shouted the prima donna's name. Ivan Andreyitch, who had never heard such a roar, was delighted. "He has noticed nothing!" he thought, and turned round; but the stout gentleman who was sitting behind him had turned round too, and with his back to him was scrutinising the boxes through his opera-glass. "He is all right too!" thought Ivan Andreyitch. In front, of course, nothing had been seen. Timidly and with a joyous hope in his heart, he stole a glance at the baignoire, near which was his stall, and started with the most unpleasant sensation. A lovely lady was sitting there who, holding her handkerchief to her mouth and leaning back in her chair, was laughing as though in hysterics.

"Ugh, these women!" murmured Ivan Andreyitch, and treading on people's feet, he made for the exit.

Now I ask my readers to decide, I beg them to judge between me and Ivan Andreyitch. Was he right at that moment? The Grand Theatre, as we all know, contains four tiers of boxes and a fifth row above the gallery. Why must he assume that the note had fallen from one particular box, from that very box and no other? Why not, for instance, from the gallery where there are often ladies too? But passion is an exception to every rule, and jealousy is the most exceptional of all passions.

Ivan Andreyitch rushed into the foyer, stood by the lamp, broke the seal and read:

"To-day immediately after the performance, in G. Street at the corner of X. Lane, K. buildings, on the third floor, the first on the right from the stairs. The front entrance. Be there, *sans faute*, for God's sake."

Ivan Andreyitch did not know the handwriting, but he had no doubt it was an assignation. "To track it out, to catch it and nip the mischief in the bud," was Ivan Andreyitch's first idea. The thought occurred to him to unmask the infamy at once on the spot; but how could it be done? Ivan Andreyitch even ran up to the second row of boxes, but judiciously came back again. He was utterly unable to decide where to run. Having nothing clear he could do, he ran round to the other side and looked through the open door of somebody else's box at the opposite side of the theatre. Yes, it was so, it was! Young ladies and young men were sitting in all the seats vertically one above another in all the five tiers. The note might have fallen from all tiers at once, for Ivan Andreyitch suspected all of them of being in a plot against him. But nothing made him any better, no probabilities of any sort. The whole of the second act he was running up and down all the corridors and could find no peace of mind anywhere. He would have dashed into the box office in hope of finding from the attendant there the names of the persons who had taken boxes on all the four tiers, but the box office was shut. At last there came an outburst of furious shouting and applause. The performance was over. Calls for the singers began, and two voices from the top gallery were particularly deafening—the leaders of the opposing factions. But they were not what mattered to Ivan Andreyitch. Already thoughts of what he was to do next flitted through his mind. He put on his overcoat and rushed off to G. Street to surprise them there, to catch them unawares, to unmask them, and in general to behave somewhat more energetically than he had done the day before. He soon found the house, and was just going in at the front door, when the figure of a dandy in an overcoat darted forward right in front of him, passed him and went up the stairs to the third storey. It seemed to Ivan Andreyitch that this was the same dandy, though he had not been able at the time to distinguish his features in the theatre. His heart stood still. The dandy was two flights of stairs ahead of him. At last he heard a door opened on the third floor, and opened without the ringing of a bell, as though the visitor was expected. The young man disappeared into the flat. Ivan Andreyitch mounted to the third floor, before there was time to shut the door. He meant to stand at the door, to reflect prudently on his next step, to be rather cautious, and then to determine upon some decisive course of action; but at that very minute a carriage rumbled up to the entrance, the doors were flung open noisily, and heavy footsteps began ascending to the third storey to the sound of coughing and clearing of the throat. Ivan Andreyitch could not stand his ground, and walked into the flat with all the majesty of an injured husband. A servant-maid rushed to meet him much agitated, then a man-servant appeared. But to stop Ivan Andreyitch was impossible. He flew in like a bomb, and crossing two dark rooms, suddenly found himself in a bedroom facing a lovely young lady, who was trembling all over with alarm and gazing at him in utter horror as though she could not understand what was happening around her. At that instant there was a sound in the adjoining room of heavy footsteps coming straight towards the bedroom; they were the same footsteps that had been mounting the stairs.

"Goodness! It is my husband!" cried the lady, clasping her hands and turning whiter than her dressing-gown.

Ivan Andreyitch felt that he had come to the wrong place, that he had made a silly, childish blunder, that he had acted without due consideration, that he had not been sufficiently cautious on the landing. But there was no help for it. The door was already opening, already the heavy husband, that is if he could be judged by his footsteps, was coming into the room. . . . I don't know what Ivan Andreyitch took himself to be at that moment! I don't know what prevented him from confronting the husband, telling him that he had made a mistake, confessing that he had unintentionally behaved in the most unseemly way, making his apologies and vanishing—not of course with flying colours, not of course with glory, but at any rate departing in an open and gentlemanly manner. But no, Ivan Andreyitch again behaved like a boy, as though he considered himself a Don Juan or a Lovelace! He first hid himself behind the curtain of the bed, and finally, feeling utterly dejected and hopeless, he dropped on the floor and senselessly crept under the bed. Terror had more influence on him than reason, and Ivan Andreyitch, himself an injured husband, or at any rate a husband who considered himself such, could not face meeting another husband, but was afraid to wound him by his presence. Be this as it may, he found himself under the bed, though he had no idea how it had come to pass. But what was most surprising, the lady made no opposition. She did not cry out on seeing an utterly unknown elderly gentleman seek a refuge under her bed. Probably she was so alarmed that she was deprived of all power of speech.

The husband walked in gasping and clearing his throat, said good-evening to his wife in a singsong, elderly voice, and flopped into an easy chair as though he had just been carrying up a load of wood. There was a sound of a hollow and prolonged cough. Ivan Andreyitch, transformed from a ferocious tiger to a lamb, timid and meek as a mouse before a cat, scarcely dared to breathe for terror, though he might have known from his own experience that not all injured husbands bite. But this idea did not enter his head, either from lack of consideration or from agitation of some sort. Cautiously, softly, feeling his way he began to get right under the bed so as to lie more comfortably there. What was his amazement when with his hand he felt an object which, to his intense amazement, stirred and in its turn seized his hand! Under the bed there was another person!

"Who's this?" whispered Ivan Andreyitch.

"Well, I am not likely to tell you who I am," whispered the strange man. "Lie still and keep quiet, if you have made a mess of things!"

"But, I say! . . ."

"Hold your tongue!"

And the extra gentleman (for one was quite enough under the bed) the extra gentleman squeezed Ivan Andreyitch's hand in his fist so that the latter almost shrieked with pain.

"My dear sir. . . ."

"Sh!"

"Then don't pinch me so, or I shall scream."

"All right, scream away, try it on."

Ivan Andreyitch flushed with shame. The unknown gentleman was sulky and ill-humoured. Perhaps it was a man who had suffered more than once from the persecutions of fate, and had more than once been in a tight place; but Ivan Andreyitch was a novice and could not breathe in his constricted position. The blood rushed to his head. However, there was no help for it; he had to lie on his face. Ivan Andreyitch submitted and was silent.

"I have been to see Pavel Ivanitch, my love," began the husband. "We sat down to a game of preference. Khee-khee-khee!" (he had a fit of coughing). "Yes . . . khee! So my back . . . khee! Bother it . . . khee-khee-khee!"

And the old gentleman became engrossed in his cough.

"My back," he brought out at last with tears in his eyes, "my spine began to ache. . . . A damned hæmorrhoid, I can't stand nor sit . . . or sit. Akkhee-khee-khee!" . . .

And it seemed as though the cough that followed was destined to last longer than the old gentleman in possession of it. The old gentleman grumbled something in its intervals, but it was utterly impossible to make out a word.

"Dear sir, for goodness' sake, move a little," whispered the unhappy Ivan Andreyitch.

"How can I? There's no room."

"But you must admit that it is impossible for me. It is the first time that I have found myself in such a nasty position."

"And I in such unpleasant society."

"But, young man! . . ."

"Hold your tongue!"

"Hold my tongue? You are very uncivil, young man. . . . If I am not mistaken, you are very young; I am your senior."

"Hold your tongue!"

"My dear sir! You are forgetting yourself. You don't know to whom you are talking!"

"To a gentleman lying under the bed."

"But I was taken by surprise . . . a mistake, while in your case, if I am not mistaken, immorality. . . ."

"That's where you are mistaken."

"My dear sir! I am older than you, I tell you. . . ."

"Sir, we are in the same boat, you know. I beg you not to take hold of my face!"

"Sir, I can't tell one thing from another. Excuse me, but I have no room."

"You shouldn't be so fat!"

"Heavens! I have never been in such a degrading position."

"Yes, one couldn't be brought more low."

"Sir, sir! I don't know who you are, I don't understand how this came about; but I am here by mistake; I am not what you think. . . ."

"I shouldn't think about you at all if you didn't shove. But hold your tongue, do!"

"Sir, if you don't move a little I shall have a stroke; you will have to answer for my death, I assure you. . . . I am a respectable man, I am the father of a family. I really cannot be in such a position! . . ."

"You thrust yourself into the position. Come, move a little! I've made room for you, I can't do more!"

"Noble young man! Dear sir! I see I was mistaken about you," said Ivan Andreyitch, in a transport of gratitude for the space allowed him, and stretching out his cramped limbs. "I understand your constricted condition, but there's no help for it. I see you think ill of me. Allow me to redeem my reputation in your eyes, allow me to tell you who I am. I have come here against my will, I assure you; I am not here with the object you imagine. . . . I am in a terrible fright."

"Oh, do shut up! Understand that if we are overheard it will be the worse for us. Sh! . . . He is talking."

The old gentleman's cough did, in fact, seem to be over.

"I tell you what, my love," he wheezed in the most lachrymose chant, "I tell you what, my love . . . khee-khee! Oh, what an affliction! Fedosey Ivanovitch said to me: 'You should try drinking yarrow tea,' he said to me; do you hear, my love?"

"Yes, dear."

"Yes, that was what he said, 'You should try drinking yarrow tea,' he said. I told him I had put on leeches. But he said, 'No, Alexandr Demyanovitch, yarrow tea is better, it's a laxative, I tell you' . . . Khee-khee. Oh, dear! What do you think, my love? Khee! Oh, my God! Khee-khee! Had I better try yarrow tea? . . . Khee-khee-khee! Oh . . . Khee!" and so on.

"I think it would be just as well to try that remedy," said his wife.

"Yes, it would be! 'You may be in consumption,' he said. "Khee-khee! And I told him it was gout and irritability of the stomach . . . Khee-khee! But he would have it that it might be consumption. What do you think . . . khee-khee! What do you think, my love; is it consumption?"

"My goodness, what are you talking about?"

"Why, consumption! You had better undress and go to bed now, my love . . . khee-khee! I've caught a cold in my head to-day."

"Ouf!" said Ivan Andreyitch. "For God's sake, do move a little."

"I really don't know what is the matter with you; can't you lie still? . . . "

"You are exasperated against me, young man, you want to wound me, I see that. You are, I suppose, this lady's lover?"

"Shut up!"

"I will not shut up! I won't allow you to order me about! You are, no doubt, her lover. If we are discovered I am not to blame in any way; I know nothing about it."

"If you don't hold your tongue," said the young man, grinding his teeth, "I will say that you brought me here. I'll say that you are my uncle who has dissipated his fortune. Then they won't imagine I am this lady's lover, anyway."

"Sir, you are amusing yourself at my expense. You are exhausting my patience."

"Hush, or I will make you hush! You are a curse to me. Come, tell me what you are here for? If you were not here I could lie here somehow till morning, and then get away."

"But I can't lie here till morning. I am a respectable man, I have family ties, of course. . . . What do you think, surely he is not going to spend the night here?"

"Who?"

"Why, this old gentleman. . . ."

"Of course he will. All husbands aren't like you. Some of them spend their nights at home."

"My dear sir, my dear sir!" cried Ivan Andreyitch, turning cold with terror, "I assure you I spend my nights at home too, and this is the first time; but, my God, I see you know me. Who are you, young man? Tell me at once, I beseech you, from disinterested friendship, who are you?"

"Listen, I shall resort to violence. . . ."

"But allow me, allow me, sir, to tell you, allow me to explain all this horrid business."

"I won't listen to any explanation. I don't want to know anything about it. Be silent or. . . ."

"But I cannot. . . ."

A slight skirmish took place under the bed, and Ivan Andreyitch subsided.

"My love, it sounds as though there were cats hissing."

"Cats! What will you imagine next?"

Evidently the lady did not know what to talk to her husband about. She was so upset that she could not pull herself together. Now she started and pricked up her ears.

"What cats?"

"Cats, my love. The other day I went into my study, and there was the tom-cat in my study, and hissing shoo-shoo-shoo! I said to him: 'What is it, pussy?' and he went shoo-shoo-shoo again, as though he were whispering. I thought, 'Merciful heavens! isn't he hissing as a sign of my death?'"

"What nonsense you are talking to-day! You ought to be ashamed, really!"

"Never mind, don't be cross, my love. I see, you don't like to think of me dying; I didn't mean it. But you had better undress and get to bed, my love, and I'll sit here while you go to bed."

"For goodness' sake, leave off; afterwards. . . ."

"Well, don't be cross, don't be cross; but really I think there must be mice here."

"Why, first cats and then mice, I really don't know what is the matter with you."

"Oh, I am all right . . . Khee . . . I . . . khee! Never mind . . . khee-khee-khee-khee! Oh! Lord have mercy on me . . . khee."

"You hear, you are making such an upset that he hears you," whispers the young man.

"But if you knew what is happening to me. My nose is bleeding."

"Let it bleed. Shut up. Wait till he goes away."

"But, young man, put yourself in my place. Why, I don't know with whom I am lying."

"Would you be any better off if you did? Why, I don't want to know your name. By the way, what is your name?"

"No; what do you want with my name? . . . I only want to explain the senseless way in which. . . ."

"Hush . . . he is speaking again. . . ."

"Really, my love, there is whispering."

"Oh, no, it's the cotton wool in your ears has got out of place."

"Oh, by the way, talking of the cotton wool, do you know that upstairs . . . khee-khee . . . upstairs . . . khee-khee . . . " and so on.

"Upstairs!" whispered the young man. "Oh, the devil! I thought that this was the top storey; can it be the second?"

"Young man," whispered Ivan Andreyitch, "what did you say? For goodness' sake why does it concern you? I thought it was the top storey too. Tell me, for God's sake, is there another storey?"

"Really some one is stirring," said the old man, leaving off coughing at last.

"Hush! Do you hear?" whispered the young man, squeezing Ivan Andreyitch's hands.

"Sir, you are holding my hands by force. Let me go!"

"Hush!"

A slight struggle followed and then there was a silence again.

"So I met a pretty woman . . . " began the old man.

"A pretty woman!" interrupted his wife.

"Yes. . . . I thought I told you before that I met a pretty woman on the stairs, or perhaps I did not mention it? My memory is weak. Yes, St. John's wort . . . khee!"

"What?"

"I must drink St. John's wort; they say it does good . . . khee-khee-khee! It does good!"

"It was you interrupted him," said the young man, grinding his teeth again.

"You said, you met some pretty woman to-day?" his wife went on.

"Eh?"

"Met a pretty woman?"

"Who did?"

"Why, didn't you?"

"I? When?"

"Oh, yes! . . ."

"At last! What a mummy! Well!" whispered the young man, inwardly raging at the forgetful old gentleman.

"My dear sir, I am trembling with horror. My God, what do I hear? It's like yesterday, exactly like yesterday! . . ."

"Hush!"

"Yes, to be sure! I remember, a sly puss, such eyes . . . in a blue hat . . ."

"In a blue hat! *Aïe, aïe!*"

"It's she! She has a blue hat! My God!" cried Ivan Andreyitch.

"She? Who is she?" whispered the young man, squeezing Ivan Andreyitch's hands.

"Hush!" Ivan Andreyitch exhorted in his turn. "He is speaking."

"Ah, my God, my God!"

"Though, after all, who hasn't a blue hat?"

"And such a sly little rogue," the old gentleman went on "She comes here to see friends. She is always making eyes. And other friends come to see those friends too. . . ."

"Foo! how tedious!" the lady interrupted. "Really, how can you take interest in that?"

"Oh, very well, very well, don't be cross," the old gentleman responded in a wheedling chant. "I won't talk if you don't care to hear me. You seem a little out of humour this evening."

"But how did you get here?" the young man began.

"Ah, you see, you see! Now you are interested, and before you wouldn't listen!"

"Oh, well, I don't care! Please don't tell me. Oh, damnation take it, what a mess!"

"Don't be cross, young man; I don't know what I am saying. I didn't mean anything; I only meant to say that there must be some good reason for your taking such an interest.... But who are you, young man? I see you are a stranger, but who are you? Oh, dear, I don't know what I am saying!"

"Ugh, leave off, please!" the young man interrupted, as though he were considering something.

"But I will tell you all about it. You think, perhaps, that I will not tell you. That I feel resentment against you. Oh, no! Here is my hand. I am only feeling depressed, nothing more. But for God's sake, first tell me how you came here yourself? Through what chance? As for me, I feel no ill-will; no, indeed, I feel no ill-will, here is my hand. I have made it rather dirty, it is so dusty here; but that's nothing, when the feeling is true."

"Ugh, get away with your hand! There is no room to turn, and he keeps thrusting his hand on me!"

"But, my dear sir, but you treat me, if you will allow me to say so, as though I were an old shoe," said Ivan Andreyitch in a rush of the meekest despair, in a voice full of entreaty. "Treat me a little more civilly, just a little more civilly, and I will tell you all about it! We might be friends; I am quite ready to ask you home to dinner. We can't lie side by side like this, I tell you plainly. You are in error, young man, you do not know...."

"When was it he met her?" the young man muttered, evidently in violent emotion. "Perhaps she is expecting me now.... I'll certainly get away from here!"

"She? Who is she? My God, of whom are you speaking, young man? You imagine that upstairs.... My God, my God! Why am I punished like this?"

Ivan Andreyitch tried to turn on his back in his despair.

"Why do you want to know who she is? Oh, the devil whether it was she or not, I will get out."

"My dear sir! What are you thinking about? What will become of me?" whispered Ivan Andreyitch, clutching at the tails of his neighbour's dress coat in his despair.

"Well, what's that to me? You can stop here by yourself. And if you won't, I'll tell them that you are my uncle, who has squandered all his property, so that the old gentleman won't think that I am his wife's lover."

"But that is utterly impossible, young man; it's unnatural I should be your uncle. Nobody would believe you. Why, a baby wouldn't believe it," Ivan Andreyitch whispered in despair.

"Well, don't babble then, but lie as flat as a pancake! Most likely you will stay the night here and get out somehow to-morrow; no one will notice you. If one creeps out, it is not likely they would think there was another one here. There might as well be a dozen. Though you are as good as a dozen by yourself. Move a little, or I'll get out."

"You wound me, young man. . . . What if I have a fit of coughing? One has to think of everything."

"Hush!"

"What's that? I fancy I hear something going on upstairs again," said the old gentleman, who seemed to have had a nap in the interval.

"Upstairs?"

"Do you hear, young man? I shall get out."

"Well, I hear."

"My goodness! Young man, I am going."

"Oh, well, I am not, then! I don't care. If there is an upset I don't mind! But do you know what I suspect? I believe you are an injured husband—so there."

"Good heavens, what cynicism! . . . Can you possibly suspect that? Why a husband? . . . I am not married."

"Not married? Fiddlesticks!"

"I may be a lover myself!"

"A nice lover."

"My dear sir, my dear sir! Oh, very well, I will tell you the whole story. Listen to my desperate story. It is not I—I am not married. I am a bachelor like you. It is my friend, a companion of my youth. . . . I am a lover. . . . He told me that he was an unhappy man. 'I am drinking the cup of bitterness,' he said; 'I suspect my wife.' 'Well,' I said to him reasonably, 'why do you suspect her?' . . . But you are not listening to me. Listen, listen! 'Jealousy is ridiculous,' I said to him; 'jealousy is a vice!' . . . 'No,' he said; 'I am an unhappy man! I am drinking . . . that is, I suspect my wife.' 'You are my friend,' I said; 'you are the companion of my tender youth. Together we culled the flowers of happiness, together we rolled in featherbeds of pleasure.' My goodness, I don't know what I am saying. You keep laughing, young man. You'll drive me crazy."

"But you are crazy now. . . ."

"There, I knew you would say that . . . when I talked of being crazy. Laugh away, laugh away, young man. I did the same in my day; I, too, went astray! Ah, I shall have inflammation of the brain!"

"What is it, my love? I thought I heard some one sneeze," the old man chanted. "Was that you sneezed, my love?"

"Oh, goodness!" said his wife.

"Tch!" sounded from under the bed.

"They must be making a noise upstairs," said his wife, alarmed, for there certainly was a noise under the bed.

"Yes, upstairs!" said the husband. "Upstairs, I told you just now, I met a . . . khee-khee . . . that I met a young swell with moustaches—oh, dear, my spine!—a young swell with moustaches."

"With moustaches! My goodness, that must have been you," whispered Ivan Andreyitch.

"Merciful heavens, what a man! Why, I am here, lying here with you! How could he have met me? But don't take hold of my face."

"My goodness, I shall faint in a minute."

There certainly was a loud noise overhead at this moment.

"What can be happening there?" whispered the young man.

"My dear sir! I am in alarm, I am in terror, help me."

"Hush!"

"There really is a noise, my love; there's a regular hubbub. And just over your bedroom, too. Hadn't I better send up to inquire?"

"Well, what will you think of next?"

"Oh, well, I won't; but really, how cross you are to-day! . . ."

"Oh, dear, you had better go to bed."

"Liza, you don't love me at all."

"Oh, yes, I do! For goodness' sake, I am so tired."

"Well, well; I am going!"

"Oh, no, no; don't go!" cried his wife; "or, no, better go!"

"Why, what is the matter with you! One minute I am to go, and the next I'm not! Khee-khee! It really is bedtime, khee-khee! The Panafidins' little girl . . . khee-khee . . . their little girl . . . khee . . . I saw their little girl's Nuremburg doll . . . khee-khee. . . ."

"Well, now it's dolls!"

"Khee-khee . . . a pretty doll . . . khee-khee."

"He is saying good-bye," said the young man; "he is going, and we can get away at once. Do you hear? You can rejoice!"

"Oh, God grant it!"

"It's a lesson to you. . . ."

"Young man, a lesson for what! . . . I feel it . . . but you are young, you cannot teach me."

"I will, though. . . . Listen."

"Oh, dear, I am going to sneeze! . . ."

"Hush, if you dare."

"But what can I do, there is such a smell of mice here; I can't help it. Take my handkerchief out of my pocket; I can't stir. . . . Oh, my God, my God, why am I so punished?"

"Here's your handkerchief! I will tell you what you are punished for. You are jealous. Goodness knows on what grounds, you rush about like a madman, burst into other people's flats, create a disturbance. . . ."

"Young man, I have not created a disturbance."

"Hush!"

"Young man, you can't lecture to me about morals, I am more moral than you."

"Hush!"

"Oh, my God—oh, my God!"

"You create a disturbance, you frighten a young lady, a timid woman who does not know what to do for terror, and perhaps will be ill; you disturb a venerable old man suffering from a complaint and who needs repose above everything—and all this what for? Because you imagine some nonsense which sets you running all over the neighbourhood! Do you understand what a horrid position you are in now?"

"I do very well, sir! I feel it, but you have not the right. . . ."

"Hold your tongue! What has right got to do with it? Do you understand that this may have a tragic ending? Do you understand that the old man, who is fond of his wife, may go out of his mind when he sees you creep out from under the bed? But no, you are incapable of causing a tragedy! When you crawl out, I expect every one who looks at you will laugh. I should like to see you in the light; you must look very funny."

"And you. You must be funny, too, in that case. I should like to have a look at you too."

"I dare say you would!"

"You must carry the stamp of immorality, young man."

"Ah! you are talking about morals, how do you know why I'm here? I am here by mistake, I made a mistake in the storey. And the deuce knows why they let me in, I suppose she must have been expecting some one (not you, of course). I hid under the bed when I heard your stupid footsteps, when I saw the lady was frightened. Besides, it was dark. And why should I justify myself to you. You are a ridiculous, jealous old man, sir. Do you know why I don't crawl out? Perhaps you imagine I am afraid to come out? No, sir, I should have come out long ago, but I stay here from compassion for you. Why, what would you be taken for, if I were not here? You'd stand facing them, like a post, you know you wouldn't know what to do. . . ."

"Why like that object? Couldn't you find anything else to compare me with, young man? Why shouldn't I know what to do? I should know what to do."

"Oh, my goodness, how that wretched dog keeps barking!"

"Hush! Oh, it really is. . . . That's because you keep jabbering. You've waked the dog, now there will be trouble."

The lady's dog, who had till then been sleeping on a pillow in the corner, suddenly awoke, sniffed strangers and rushed under the bed with a loud bark.

"Oh, my God, what a stupid dog!" whispered Ivan Andreyitch; "it will get us all into trouble. Here's another affliction!"

"Oh, well, you are such a coward, that it may well be so."

"Ami, Ami, come here," cried the lady; "*ici, ici*." But the dog, without heeding her, made straight for Ivan Andreyitch.

"Why is it Amishka keeps barking?" said the old gentleman. "There must be mice or the cat under there. I seem to hear a sneezing . . . and pussy had a cold this morning."

"Lie still," whispered the young man. "Don't twist about! Perhaps it will leave off."

"Sir, let go of my hands, sir! Why are you holding them?"

"Hush! Be quiet!"

"But mercy on us, young man, it will bite my nose. Do you want me to lose my nose?"

A struggle followed, and Ivan Andreyitch got his hands free. The dog broke into volleys of barking. Suddenly it ceased barking and gave a yelp.

"*Aïe!*" cried the lady.

"Monster! what are you doing?" cried the young man. "You will be the ruin of us both! Why are you holding it? Good heavens, he is strangling it! Let it go! Monster! You know nothing of the heart of women if you can do that! She will betray us both if you strangle the dog."

But by now Ivan Andreyitch could hear nothing. He had succeeded in catching the dog, and in a paroxysm of self-preservation had squeezed its throat. The dog yelled and gave up the ghost.

"We are lost!" whispered the young man.

"Amishka! Amishka," cried the lady. "My God, what are they doing with my Amishka? Amishka! Amishka! *Ici!* Oh, the monsters! Barbarians! Oh, dear, I feel giddy!"

"What is it, what is it?" cried the old gentleman, jumping up from his easy chair. "What is the matter with you, my darling? Amishka! here, Amishka! Amishka! Amishka!" cried the old gentleman, snapping with his fingers and clicking with his tongue, and calling Amishka from under the bed. "Amishka, *ici, ici.* The cat cannot have eaten him. The cat wants a thrashing, my love, he hasn't had a beating for a whole month, the rogue. What do you think? I'll talk to Praskovya Zaharyevna. But, my goodness, what is the matter, my love? Oh, how white you are! Oh, oh, servants, servants!" and the old gentleman ran about the room.

"Villains! Monsters!" cried the lady, sinking on the sofa.

"Who, who, who?" cried the old gentleman.

"There are people there, strangers, there under the bed! Oh, my God, Amishka, Amishka, what have they done to you?"

"Good heavens, what people? Amishka. . . . Servants, servants, come here! Who is there, who is there?" cried the old gentleman, snatching up a candle and bending down under the bed. "Who is there?"

Ivan Andreyitch was lying more dead than alive beside the breathless corpse of Amishka, but the young man was watching every movement of the old gentleman. All at once the old gentleman went to the other side of the bed by the wall and bent down. In a flash the young man crept out from under the bed and took to his heels, while the husband was looking for his visitors on the other side.

"Good gracious!" exclaimed the lady, staring at the young man. "Who are you? Why, I thought...."

"That monster's still there," whispered the young man. "He is guilty of Amishka's death!"

"*Aïe!*" shrieked the lady, but the young man had already vanished from the room.

"*Aïe!* There is some one here. Here are somebody's boots! cried the husband, catching Ivan Andreyitch by the leg.

"Murderer, murderer!" cried the lady. "Oh, Ami! Ami!"

"Come out, come out!" cried the old gentleman, stamping on the carpet with both feet; "come out. Who are you? Tell me who you are! Good gracious, what a queer person!"

"Why, it's robbers!..."

"For God's sake, for God's sake," cried Ivan Andreyitch creeping out, "for God's sake, your Excellency, don't call the servants! Your Excellency, don't call any one. It is quite unnecessary. You can't kick me out!... I am not that sort of person. I am a different case. Your Excellency, it has all been due to a mistake! I'll explain directly, your Excellency," exclaimed Ivan Andreyitch, sobbing and gasping. "It's all my wife that is not my wife, but somebody else's wife. I am not married, I am only.... It's my comrade, a friend of youthful days."

"What friend of youthful days?" cried the old gentleman, stamping. "You are a thief, you have come to steal ... and not a friend of youthful days."

"No, I am not a thief, your Excellency; I am really a friend of youthful days.... I have only blundered by accident, I came into the wrong place."

"Yes, sir, yes; I see from what place you've crawled out."

"Your Excellency! I am not that sort of man. You are mistaken. I tell you, you are cruelly mistaken, your Excellency. Only glance at me, look at me, and by signs and tokens you will see that I can't be a thief. Your

Excellency! Your Excellency!" cried Ivan Andreyitch, folding his hands and appealing to the young lady. "You are a lady, you will understand me.... It was I who killed Amishka.... But it was not my fault.... It was really not my fault.... It was all my wife's fault. I am an unhappy man, I am drinking the cup of bitterness!"

"But really, what has it to do with me that you are drinking the cup of bitterness? Perhaps it's not the only cup you've drunk. It seems so, to judge from your condition. But how did you come here, sir?" cried the old gentleman, quivering with excitement, though he certainly was convinced by certain signs and tokens that Ivan Andreyitch could not be a thief. "I ask you: how did you come here? You break in like a robber...."

"Not a robber, your Excellency. I simply came to the wrong place; I am really not a robber! It is all because I was jealous. I will tell you all about it, your Excellency, I will confess it all frankly, as I would to my own father; for at your venerable age I might take you for a father."

"What do you mean by venerable age?"

"Your Excellency! Perhaps I have offended you? Of course such a young lady . . . and your age . . . it is a pleasant sight, your Excellency, it really is a pleasant sight such a union . . . in the prime of life. . . . But don't call the servants, for God's sake, don't call the servants . . . servants would only laugh. . . . I know them . . . that is, I don't mean that I am only acquainted with footmen, I have a footman of my own, your Excellency, and they are always laughing . . . the asses! Your Highness . . . I believe I am not mistaken, I am addressing a prince. . . ."

"No, I am not a prince, sir, I am an independent gentleman. . . . Please do not flatter me with your 'Highness.' How did you get here, sir? How did you get here?"

"Your Highness, that is, your Excellency. . . . Excuse me, I thought that you were your Highness. I looked . . . I imagined . . . it does happen. You are so like Prince Korotkouhov whom I have had the honour of meeting at my friend Mr. Pusyrev's. . . . You see, I am acquainted with princes, too, I have met princes, too, at the houses of my friends; you cannot take me for what you take me for. I am not a thief. Your Excellency, don't call the servants; what will be the good of it if you do call them?"

"But how did you come here?" cried the lady. "Who are you?"

"Yes, who are you?" the husband chimed in. "And, my love, I thought it was pussy under the bed sneezing. And it was he. Ah, you vagabond! Who are you? Tell me!"

And the old gentleman stamped on the carpet again.

"I cannot speak, your Excellency, I am waiting till you are finished, I am enjoying your witty jokes. As regards me, it is an absurd story, your Excellency; I will tell you all about it. It can all be explained without more ado, that is, I mean, don't call the servants, your Excellency! Treat me in a gentlemanly way.... It means nothing that I was under the bed, I have not sacrificed my dignity by that. It is a most comical story, your Excellency!" cried Ivan Andreyitch, addressing the lady with a supplicating air. "You, particularly, your Excellency, will laugh! You behold upon the scene a jealous husband. You see, I abase myself, I abase myself of my own free will. I did indeed kill Amishka, but ... my God, I don't know what I am saying!"

"But how, how did you get here?"

"Under cover of night, your Excellency, under cover of night.... I beg your pardon! Forgive me, your Excellency! I humbly beg your pardon! I am only an injured husband, nothing more! Don't imagine, your Excellency, that I am a lover! I am not a lover! Your wife is virtue itself, if I may venture so to express myself. She is pure and innocent!"

"What, what? What did you have the audacity to say?" cried the old gentleman, stamping his foot again. "Are you out of your mind or not? How dare you talk about my wife?"

"He is a villain, a murderer who has killed Amishka," wailed the lady, dissolving into tears. "And then he dares!..."

"Your Excellency, your Excellency! I spoke foolishly," cried Ivan Andreyitch in a fluster. "I was talking foolishly, that was all! Think of me as out of my mind.... For goodness' sake, think of me as out of my mind.... I assure you that you will be doing me the greatest favour. I would offer you my hand, but I do not venture to.... I was not alone, I was an uncle.... I mean to say that you cannot take me for the lover.... Goodness! I have put my foot in it again.... Do not be offended, your Excellency," cried Ivan Andreyitch to the lady. "You are a lady, you understand what love is, it is a delicate feeling.... But what am I saying? I am talking nonsense again; that is, I mean to say that I am an old man—that is, a middle-aged man, not an old man; that I cannot be your lover; that a lover is a Richardson—that is, a Lovelace.... I am talking nonsense, but you see, your Excellency, that I am a well-educated man and know something of literature. You are laughing, your Excellency. I am delighted, delighted that I have *provoked* your mirth, your Excellency. Oh, how delighted I am that I have provoked your mirth."

"My goodness, what a funny man!" cried the lady, exploding with laughter.

"Yes, he is funny, and in such a mess," said the old man, delighted that his wife was laughing. "He cannot be a thief, my love. But how did he come here?"

"It really is strange, it really is strange, it is like a novel! Why! At the dead of night, in a great city, a man under the bed. Strange, funny! Rinaldo-Rinaldini after a fashion. But that is no matter, no matter, your Excellency. I will tell you all about it. . . . And I will buy you a new lapdog, your Excellency. . . . A wonderful lapdog! Such a long coat, such short little legs, it can't walk more than a step or two: it runs a little, gets entangled in its own coat, and tumbles over. One feeds it on nothing but sugar. I will bring you one, I will certainly bring you one."

"Ha-ha-ha-ha-ha!" The lady was rolling from side to side with laughter. "Oh, dear, I shall have hysterics! Oh, how funny he is!"

"Yes, yes! Ha-ha-ha! Khee-khee-khee! He is funny and he is in a mess—khee-khee-khee!"

"Your Excellency, your Excellency, I am now perfectly happy. I would offer you my hand, but I do not venture to, your Excellency. I feel that I have been in error, but now I am opening my eyes. I am certain my wife is pure and innocent! I was wrong in suspecting her."

"Wife—his wife!" cried the lady, with tears in her eyes through laughing.

"He married? Impossible! I should never have thought it," said the old gentleman.

"Your Excellency, my wife—it is all her fault; that is, it is my fault: I suspected her; I knew that an assignation had been arranged here—here upstairs; I intercepted a letter, made a mistake about the storey and got under the bed. . . ."

"He-he-he-he!"

"Ha-ha-ha-ha!"

"Ha-ha-ha-ha!" Ivan Andreyitch began laughing at last. "Oh, how happy I am! Oh, how wonderful to see that we are all so happy and harmonious! And my wife is entirely innocent. That must be so, your Excellency!"

"He-he-he! Khee-khee! Do you know, my love, who it was?" said the old man at last, recovering from his mirth.

"Who? Ha-ha-ha."

"She must be the pretty woman who makes eyes, the one with the dandy. It's she, I bet that's his wife!"

"No, your Excellency, I am certain it is not she; I am perfectly certain."

"But, my goodness! You are losing time," cried the lady, leaving off laughing. "Run, go upstairs. Perhaps you will find them."

"Certainly, your Excellency, I will fly. But I shall not find any one, your Excellency; it is not she, I am certain of it beforehand. She is at home now. It is all my fault! It is simply my jealousy, nothing else. . . . What do you think? Do you suppose that I shall find them there, your Excellency?"

"Ha-ha-ha!"

"He-he-he! Khee-khee!"

"You must go, you must go! And when you come down, come in and tell us!" cried the lady; "or better still, to-morrow morning. And do bring her too, I should like to make her acquaintance."

"Good-bye, your Excellency, good-bye! I will certainly bring her, I shall be very glad for her to make your acquaintance. I am glad and happy that it was all ended so and has turned out for the best."

"And the lapdog! Don't forget it: be sure to bring the lapdog!"

"I will bring it, your Excellency, I will certainly bring it," responded Ivan Andreyitch, darting back into the room, for he had already made his bows and withdrawn. "I will certainly bring it. It is such a pretty one. It is just as though a confectioner had made it of sweet-meats. And it's such a funny little thing—gets entangled in its own coat and falls over. It really is a lapdog! I said to my wife: 'How is it, my love, it keeps tumbling over?' 'It is such a little thing,' she said. As though it were made of sugar, of sugar, your Excellency! Good-bye, your Excellency, very, very glad to make your acquaintance, very glad to make your acquaintance!"

Ivan Andreyitch bowed himself out.

"Hey, sir! Stay, come back," cried the old gentleman, after the retreating Ivan Andreyitch.

The latter turned back for the third time.

"I still can't find the cat, didn't you meet him when you were under the bed?"

"No, I didn't, your Excellency. Very glad to make his acquaintance, though, and I shall look upon it as an honour. . . ."

"He has a cold in his head now, and keeps sneezing and sneezing. He must have a beating."

"Yes, your Excellency, of course; corrective punishment is essential with domestic animals."

"What?"

"I say that corrective punishment is necessary, your Excellency, to enforce obedience in the domestic animals."

"Ah! . . . Well, good-bye, good-bye, that is all I had to say."

Coming out into the street, Ivan Andreyitch stood for a long time in an attitude that suggested that he was expecting to have a fit in another minute. He took off his hat, wiped the cold sweat from his brow, screwed up his eyes, thought a minute, and set off homewards.

What was his amazement when he learned at home that Glafira Petrovna had come back from the theatre a long, long time before, that she had toothache, that she had sent for the doctor, that she had sent for leeches, and that now she was lying in bed and expecting Ivan Andreyitch.

Ivan Andreyitch slapped himself on the forehead, told the servant to help him wash and to brush his clothes, and at last ventured to go into his wife's room.

"Where is it you spend your time? Look what a sight you are! What do you look like? Where have you been lost all this time? Upon my word, sir; your wife is dying and you have to be hunted for all over the town. Where have you been? Surely you have not been tracking me, trying to disturb a rendezvous I am supposed to have made, though I don't know with whom. For shame, sir, you are a husband! People will soon be pointing at you in the street."

"My love . . ." responded Ivan Andreyitch.

But at this point he was so overcome with confusion that he had to feel in his pocket for his handkerchief and to break off in the speech he was beginning, because he had neither words, thoughts or courage. . . . What was his amazement, horror and alarm when with his handkerchief fell out of his pocket the corpse of Amishka. Ivan Andreyitch had not noticed that when he had been forced to creep out from under the bed, in an access of despair and unreasoning terror he had stuffed Amishka into his pocket with a far-away idea of burying the traces, concealing the evidence of his crime, and so avoiding the punishment he deserved.

"What's this?" cried his spouse; "a nasty dead dog! Goodness! where has it come from? . . . What have you been up to? . . . Where have you been? Tell me at once where have you been?"

"My love," answered Ivan Andreyitch, almost as dead as Amishka, "my love. . . ."

But here we will leave our hero—till another time, for a new and quite different adventure begins here. Some day we will describe all these calamities and misfortunes, gentlemen. But you will admit that jealousy is an unpardonable passion, and what is more, it is a positive misfortune.

A Little Hero

At that time I was nearly eleven, I had been sent in July to spend the holiday in a village near Moscow with a relation of mine called T., whose house was full of guests, fifty, or perhaps more.... I don't remember, I didn't count. The house was full of noise and gaiety. It seemed as though it were a continual holiday, which would never end. It seemed as though our host had taken a vow to squander all his vast fortune as rapidly as possible, and he did indeed succeed, not long ago, in justifying this surmise, that is, in making a clean sweep of it all to the last stick.

Fresh visitors used to drive up every minute. Moscow was close by, in sight, so that those who drove away only made room for others, and the everlasting holiday went on its course. Festivities succeeded one another, and there was no end in sight to the entertainments. There were riding parties about the environs; excursions to the forest or the river; picnics, dinners in the open air; suppers on the great terrace of the house, bordered with three rows of gorgeous flowers that flooded with their fragrance the fresh night air, and illuminated the brilliant lights which made our ladies, who were almost every one of them pretty at all times, seem still more charming, with their faces excited by the impressions of the day, with their sparkling eyes, with their interchange of spritely conversation, their peals of ringing laughter; dancing, music, singing; if the sky were overcast tableaux vivants, charades, proverbs were arranged, private theatricals were got up. There were good talkers, story-tellers, wits.

Certain persons were prominent in the foreground. Of course backbiting and slander ran their course, as without them the world could not get on, and millions of persons would perish of boredom, like flies. But as I was at that time eleven I was absorbed by very different interests, and either failed to observe these people, or if I noticed anything, did not see it all. It was only afterwards that some things came back to my mind. My childish eyes could only see the brilliant side of the picture, and the general animation, splendour, and bustle—all that, seen and heard for the first time, made such an impression upon me that for the first few days, I was completely bewildered and my little head was in a whirl.

I keep speaking of my age, and of course I was a child, nothing more than a child. Many of these lovely ladies petted me without dreaming of considering my age. But strange to say, a sensation which I did not myself understand already had possession of me; something was already whispering in my heart, of which till then it had had no knowledge, no conception, and for some reason it began all at once to burn and throb, and often my face glowed with a sudden flush. At times I felt as it were abashed, and even resentful of the various privileges of my childish years. At other times a sort of wonder overwhelmed me, and I would go off into some corner where I could sit unseen, as though to take breath and remember something—something which it seemed to me I had remembered perfectly till then, and now had suddenly forgotten, something without which I could not show myself anywhere, and could not exist at all.

At last it seemed to me as though I were hiding something from every one. But nothing would have induced me to speak of it to any one, because, small boy that I was, I was ready to weep with shame. Soon in the midst of the vortex around me I was conscious of a certain loneliness. There were other children, but all were either much older or younger than I; besides, I was in no mood for them. Of course nothing would have happened to me if I had not been in an exceptional position. In the eyes of those charming ladies I was still the little unformed creature whom they at once liked to pet, and with whom they could play as though he were a little doll. One of them particularly, a fascinating, fair woman, with very thick luxuriant hair, such as I had never seen before and probably shall never see again, seemed to have taken a vow never to leave me in peace. I was confused, while she was amused by the laughter which she continually provoked from all around us by her wild, giddy pranks with me, and this apparently gave her immense enjoyment. At school among her schoolfellows she was probably nicknamed the Tease. She was wonderfully good-looking, and there was something in her beauty which drew one's eyes from the first moment. And certainly she had nothing in common with the ordinary modest little fair girls, white as down and soft as white mice, or pastors' daughters. She was not very tall, and was rather plump, but had soft, delicate, exquisitely cut features. There was something quick as lightning in her face, and indeed she was like fire all over, light, swift, alive. Her big open eyes seemed to flash sparks; they glittered like diamonds, and I would never exchange such blue sparkling eyes for any black ones, were they blacker than any Andalusian orb. And, indeed, my blonde was fully a match for the famous brunette whose praises were sung by a great and well-known poet, who, in a superb poem, vowed by all Castille that he was ready to break his bones to be permitted only to touch the mantle of his divinity with the tip of his finger. Add to that, that *my* charmer was the merriest in the world, the wildest giggler, playful as a child, although she had been married for the last five years. There was a continual laugh upon her lips, fresh as the morning rose that, with the first ray of sunshine, opens its fragrant crimson bud with the cool dewdrops still hanging heavy upon it.

I remember that the day after my arrival private theatricals were being got up. The drawing-room was, as they say, packed to overflowing; there was not a seat empty, and as I was somehow late I had to enjoy the performance standing. But the amusing play attracted me to move forwarder and forwarder, and unconsciously I made my way to the first row, where I stood at last leaning my elbows on the back of an armchair, in which a lady was sitting. It was my blonde divinity, but we had not yet made acquaintance. And I gazed, as it happened, at her marvellous, fascinating shoulders, plump and white as milk, though it did not matter to me in the least whether I stared at a woman's exquisite shoulders or at the cap with flaming ribbons that covered the grey locks of a venerable lady in the front row. Near my blonde divinity sat a spinster lady not in her first youth, one of those who, as I chanced to observe later, always take refuge in the immediate neighbourhood of young and pretty women, selecting such as are not fond of cold-shouldering young men. But that is not the point, only this lady, noting my fixed gaze, bent down to her neighbour and with a simper whispered something in her ear. The blonde lady turned at once, and I remember that her glowing eyes so flashed upon me in the half dark, that, not prepared to meet them, I started as though I were scalded. The beauty smiled.

"Do you like what they are acting?" she asked, looking into my face with a shy and mocking expression.

"Yes," I answered, still gazing at her with a sort of wonder that evidently pleased her.

"But why are you standing? You'll get tired. Can't you find a seat?"

"That's just it, I can't," I answered, more occupied with my grievance than with the beauty's sparkling eyes, and rejoicing in earnest at having found a kind heart to whom I could confide my troubles. "I have looked everywhere, but all the chairs are taken," I added, as though complaining to her that all the chairs were taken.

"Come here," she said briskly, quick to act on every decision, and, indeed, on every mad idea that flashed on her giddy brain, "come here, and sit on my knee."

"On your knee," I repeated, taken aback. I have mentioned already that I had begun to resent the privileges of childhood and to be ashamed of them in earnest. This lady, as though in derision, had gone ever so much further than the others. Moreover, I had always been a shy and bashful boy, and of late had begun to be particularly shy with women.

"Why yes, on my knee. Why don't you want to sit on my knee?" she persisted, beginning to laugh more and more, so that at last she was simply giggling, goodness knows at what, perhaps at her freak, or perhaps at my confusion. But that was just what she wanted.

I flushed, and in my confusion looked round trying to find where to escape; but seeing my intention she managed to catch hold of my hand to prevent me from going away, and pulling it towards her, suddenly, quite unexpectedly, to my intense astonishment, squeezed it in her mischievous warm fingers, and began to pinch my fingers till they hurt so much that I had to do my very utmost not to cry out, and in my effort to control myself made the most absurd grimaces. I was, besides, moved to the greatest amazement, perplexity, and even horror, at the discovery that there were ladies so absurd and spiteful as to talk nonsense to boys, and even pinch their fingers, for no earthly reason and before everybody. Probably my unhappy face reflected my bewilderment, for the mischievous creature laughed in my face, as though she were crazy, and meantime she was pinching my fingers more and more vigorously. She was highly delighted in playing such a mischievous prank and completely mystifying and embarrassing a poor boy. My position was desperate. In the first place I was hot with shame, because almost every one near had turned round to look at us, some in wonder, others with laughter, grasping at once that the beauty was up to some mischief. I dreadfully wanted to scream, too, for she was wringing my fingers with positive fury just because I didn't scream; while I, like a Spartan, made up my mind to endure the agony, afraid by crying out of causing a general fuss, which was more than I could face. In utter despair I began at last struggling with her, trying with all my might to pull away my hand, but my persecutor was much stronger than I was. At last I could bear it no longer, and uttered a shriek—that was all she was waiting for! Instantly she let me go, and turned away as though nothing had happened, as though it was not she who had played the trick but some one else, exactly like some schoolboy who, as soon as the master's back is turned, plays some trick on some one near him, pinches some small weak boy, gives him a flip, a kick, or a nudge with his elbows, and instantly turns again, buries himself in his book and begins repeating his lesson, and so makes a fool of the infuriated teacher who flies down like a hawk at the noise.

But luckily for me the general attention was distracted at the moment by the masterly acting of our host, who was playing the chief part in the performance, some comedy of Scribe's. Every one began to applaud; under cover of the noise I stole away and hurried to the furthest end of the room, from which, concealed behind a column, I looked with horror towards the place where the treacherous beauty was sitting. She was still laughing, holding her handkerchief to her lips. And for a long time she was continually turning round, looking for me in every direction, probably regretting that our silly tussle was so soon over, and hatching some other trick to play on me.

That was the beginning of our acquaintance, and from that evening she would never let me alone. She persecuted me without consideration or conscience, she became my tyrant and tormentor. The whole absurdity of her jokes with me lay in the fact that she pretended to be head over ears in love with me, and teased me before every one. Of course for a wild creature as I was all this was so tiresome and vexatious that it almost reduced me to tears, and I was sometimes put in such a difficult position that I was on the point of fighting with my treacherous admirer. My naïve confusion, my desperate distress, seemed to egg her on to persecute me more; she knew no mercy, while I did not know how to get away from her. The laughter which always accompanied us, and which she knew so well how to excite, roused her to fresh pranks. But at last people began to think that she went a little too far in her jests. And, indeed, as I remember now, she did take outrageous liberties with a child such as I was.

But that was her character; she was a spoilt child in every respect. I heard afterwards that her husband, a very short, very fat, and very red-faced man, very rich and apparently very much occupied with business, spoilt her more than any one. Always busy and flying round, he could not stay two hours in one place. Every day he drove into Moscow, sometimes twice in the day, and always, as he declared himself, on business. It would be hard to find a livelier and more good-natured face than his facetious but always well-bred countenance. He not only loved his wife to the point of weakness, softness: he simply worshipped her like an idol.

He did not restrain her in anything. She had masses of friends, male and female. In the first place, almost everybody liked her; and secondly, the feather-headed creature was not herself over particular in the choice of her friends, though there was a much more serious foundation to her character than might be supposed from what I have just said about her. But of all her friends she liked best of all one young lady, a distant relation, who was also of our party now. There existed between them a tender and subtle affection, one of those attachments which sometimes spring up at the meeting of two dispositions often the very opposite of each other, of which one is deeper, purer and more austere, while the other, with lofty humility, and generous self-criticism, lovingly gives way to the other, conscious of the friend's superiority and cherishing the friendship as a happiness. Then begins that tender and noble subtlety in the relations of such characters, love and infinite indulgence on the one side, on the other love and respect—a respect approaching awe, approaching anxiety as to the impression made on the friend so highly prized, and an eager, jealous desire to get closer and closer to that friend's heart in every step in life.

These two friends were of the same age, but there was an immense difference between them in everything—in looks, to begin with. Madame M. was also very handsome, but there was something special in her beauty that strikingly distinguished her from the crowd of pretty women; there was something in her face that at once drew the affection of all to her, or rather, which aroused a generous and lofty feeling of kindliness in every one who met her. There are such happy faces. At her side everyone grew as it were better, freer, more cordial; and yet her big mournful eyes, full of fire and vigour, had a timid and anxious look, as though every minute dreading something antagonistic and menacing, and this strange timidity at times cast so mournful a shade over her mild, gentle features which recalled the serene faces of Italian Madonnas, that looking at her one soon became oneself sad, as though for some trouble of one's own. The pale, thin face, in which, through the irreproachable beauty of the pure, regular lines and the mournful severity of some mute hidden grief, there often flitted the clear looks of early childhood, telling of trustful years and perhaps simple-hearted happiness in the recent past, the gentle but diffident, hesitating smile, all aroused such unaccountable sympathy for her that every heart was unconsciously stirred with a sweet and warm anxiety that powerfully interceded on her behalf even at a distance, and made even strangers feel akin to her. But the lovely creature seemed silent and reserved, though no one could have been more attentive and loving if any one needed sympathy. There are women who are like sisters of mercy in life. Nothing can be hidden from them, nothing, at least, that is a sore or wound of the heart. Any one who is suffering may go boldly and hopefully to them without fear of being a burden, for few men know the infinite patience of love, compassion and forgiveness that may be found in some women's hearts. Perfect treasures of sympathy, consolation and hope are laid up in these pure hearts, so often full of suffering of their own—for a heart which loves much grieves much—though their wounds are carefully hidden from the curious eye, for deep sadness is most often mute and concealed. They are not dismayed by the depth of the wound, nor by its foulness and its stench; any one who comes to them is deserving of help; they are, as it were, born for heroism. . . . Mme. M. was tall, supple and graceful, but rather thin. All her movements seemed somehow irregular, at times slow, smooth, and even dignified, at times childishly hasty; and yet, at the same time, there was a sort of timid humility in her gestures, something tremulous and defenceless, though it neither desired nor asked for protection.

I have mentioned already that the outrageous teasing of the treacherous fair lady abashed me, flabbergasted me, and wounded me to the quick. But there was for that another secret, strange and foolish reason, which I concealed, at which I shuddered as at a skeleton. At the very thought of it, brooding, utterly alone and overwhelmed, in some dark mysterious corner to which the inquisitorial mocking eye of the blue-eyed rogue could not penetrate, I almost gasped with confusion, shame and fear—in short, I was in love; that perhaps is nonsense, that could hardly have been. But why was it, of all the faces surrounding me, only her face caught my attention? Why was it that it was only she whom I cared to follow with my eyes, though I certainly had no inclination in those days to watch ladies and seek their acquaintance? This happened most frequently on the evenings when we were all kept indoors by bad weather, and when, lonely, hiding in some corner of the big drawing-room, I stared about me aimlessly, unable to find anything to do, for except my teasing ladies, few people ever addressed me, and I was insufferably bored on such evenings. Then I stared at the people round me, listened to the conversation, of which I often did not understand one word, and at that time the mild eyes, the gentle smile and lovely face of Mme. M. (for she was the object of my passion) for some reason caught my fascinated attention; and the strange vague, but unutterably sweet impression remained with me. Often for hours together I could not tear myself away from her; I studied every gesture, every movement she made, listened to every vibration of her rich, silvery, but rather muffled voice; but strange to say, as the result of all my observations, I felt, mixed with a sweet and timid impression, a feeling of intense curiosity. It seemed as though I were on the verge of some mystery.

Nothing distressed me so much as being mocked at in the presence of Mme. M. This mockery and humorous persecution, as I thought, humiliated me. And when there was a general burst of laughter at my expense, in which Mme. M. sometimes could not help joining, in despair, beside myself with misery, I used to tear myself from my tormentor and run away upstairs, where I remained in solitude the rest of the day, not daring to show my face in the drawing-room. I did not yet, however, understand my shame nor my agitation; the whole process went on in me unconsciously. I had hardly said two words to Mme. M., and indeed I should not have dared to. But one evening after an unbearable day I turned back from an expedition with the rest of the company. I was horribly tired and made my way home across the garden. On a seat in a secluded avenue I saw Mme. M. She was sitting quite alone, as though she had purposely chosen this solitary spot, her head was drooping and she was mechanically twisting her handkerchief. She was so lost in thought that she did not hear me till I reached her.

Noticing me, she got up quickly from her seat, turned round, and I saw her hurriedly wipe her eyes with her handkerchief. She was crying. Drying her eyes, she smiled to me and walked back with me to the house. I don't remember what we talked about; but she frequently sent me off on one pretext or another, to pick a flower, or to see who was riding in the next avenue. And when I walked away from her, she at once put her handkerchief to her eyes again and wiped away rebellious tears, which would persist in rising again and again from her heart and dropping from her poor eyes. I realized that I was very much in her way when she sent me off so often, and, indeed, she saw herself that I noticed it all, but yet could not control herself, and that made my heart ache more and more for her. I raged at myself at that moment and was almost in despair; cursed myself for my awkwardness and lack of resource, and at the same time did not know how to leave her tactfully, without betraying that I had noticed her distress, but walked beside her in mournful bewilderment, almost in alarm, utterly at a loss and unable to find a single word to keep up our scanty conversation.

This meeting made such an impression on me that I stealthily watched Mme. M. the whole evening with eager curiosity, and never took my eyes off her. But it happened that she twice caught me unawares watching her, and on the second occasion, noticing me, she gave me a smile. It was the only time she smiled that evening. The look of sadness had not left her face, which was now very pale. She spent the whole evening talking to an ill-natured and quarrelsome old lady, whom nobody liked owing to her spying and backbiting habits, but of whom every one was afraid, and consequently every one felt obliged to be polite to her. . . .

At ten o'clock Mme. M.'s husband arrived. Till that moment I watched her very attentively, never taking my eyes off her mournful face; now at the unexpected entrance of her husband I saw her start, and her pale face turned suddenly as white as a handkerchief. It was so noticeable that other people observed it. I overheard a fragmentary conversation from which I guessed that Mme. M. was not quite happy; they said her husband was as jealous as an Arab, not from love, but from vanity. He was before all things a European, a modern man, who sampled the newest ideas and prided himself upon them. In appearance he was a tall, dark-haired, particularly thick-set man, with European whiskers, with a self-satisfied, red face, with teeth white as sugar, and with an irreproachably gentlemanly deportment. He was called a *clever man.* Such is the name given in certain circles to a peculiar species of mankind which grows fat at other people's expense, which does absolutely nothing and has no desire to do anything, and whose heart has turned into a lump of fat from everlasting slothfulness and idleness. You continually hear from such men that there is nothing they can do owing to certain very complicated and hostile circumstances, which "thwart their genius," and that it was "sad to see the waste of their talents." This is a fine phrase of theirs, their *mot d'ordre,* their watchword, a phrase which these well-fed, fat friends of ours bring out at every minute, so that it has long ago bored us as an arrant Tartuffism, an empty form of words. Some, however, of these amusing creatures, who cannot succeed in finding anything to do—though, indeed, they never seek it—try to make every one believe that they have not a lump of fat for a heart, but on the contrary, something *very deep,* though what precisely the greatest surgeon would hardly venture to decide—from civility, of course. These gentlemen make their way in the world through the fact that all their instincts are bent in the direction of coarse sneering, short-sighted censure and immense conceit. Since they have nothing else to do but note and emphasize the mistakes and weaknesses of others, and as they have precisely as much good feeling as an oyster, it is not difficult for them with such powers of self-preservation to get on with people fairly successfully. They pride themselves extremely upon that. They are, for instance, as good as persuaded that almost the whole world owes them something; that it is theirs, like an oyster which they keep in reserve; that all are fools except themselves; that every one is like an orange or a sponge, which they will squeeze as soon as they want the juice; that they are the masters everywhere, and that all this acceptable state of affairs is solely due to the fact that they are people of so much intellect and character. In their measureless conceit they do not admit any defects in themselves, they are like that species of practical rogues, innate Tartuffes and Falstaffs, who are such thorough rogues that at last they have come to believe that that is as it should be, that is, that they should spend their lives in knavishness; they have so often assured every one that they are honest men, that they have come to believe that they are honest men, and that their roguery is honesty. They are never capable of inner judgment before their conscience, of generous self-criticism; for some things they are too fat. Their own priceless personality, their Baal and Moloch, their magnificent *ego* is always in their foreground everywhere. All nature, the whole world for them is no more than a splendid mirror created for the little god to admire himself continually in it, and to see no one and nothing behind himself; so it is not strange that he sees everything in the world in such a hideous light. He has a phrase in readiness for everything and— the acme of ingenuity on his part—the most fashionable phrase. It is just these people, indeed, who help to make the fashion, proclaiming at every cross-road an idea in which they scent success. A fine nose is just what they have for sniffing a fashionable phrase and making it their own before other people get hold of it, so that it seems to have originated with them. They have a particular store of phrases for proclaiming their profound sympathy for humanity, for defining what is the most correct and rational form of philanthropy, and continually attacking romanticism, in other words, everything fine and true, each atom of which is more precious than all their mollusc tribe. But they are too coarse to recognize the truth in an indirect, roundabout and unfinished form, and they reject everything that is immature, still fermenting and unstable. The well-nourished man has spent all his life in merry-making, with everything provided, has done nothing himself and does not know how hard every sort of work is, and so woe betide you if you jar upon his fat feelings by any sort of roughness; he'll never forgive you for that, he will always remember it and will gladly avenge it. The long and short of it is, that my hero is neither more nor less than a gigantic, incredibly swollen bag, full of sentences, fashionable phrases, and labels of all sorts and kinds.

M. M., however, had a speciality and was a very remarkable man; he was a wit, good talker and story-teller, and there was always a circle round him in every drawing-room. That evening he was particularly successful in making an impression. He took possession of the conversation; he was in his best form, gay, pleased at something, and he compelled the attention of all; but Mme. M. looked all the time as though she were ill; her face was so sad that I fancied every minute that tears would begin quivering on her long eyelashes. All this, as I have said, impressed me extremely and made me wonder. I went away with a feeling of strange curiosity, and dreamed all night of M. M., though till then I had rarely had dreams.

Next day, early in the morning, I was summoned to a rehearsal of some tableaux vivants in which I had to take part. The tableaux vivants, theatricals, and afterwards a dance were all fixed for the same evening, five days later—the birthday of our host's younger daughter. To this entertainment, which was almost improvised, another hundred guests were invited from Moscow and from surrounding villas, so that there was a great deal of fuss, bustle and commotion. The rehearsal, or rather review of the costumes, was fixed so early in the morning because our manager, a well-known artist, a friend of our host's, who had consented through affection for him to undertake the arrangement of the tableaux and the training of us for them, was in haste now to get to Moscow to purchase properties and to make final preparations for the fête, as there was no time to lose. I took part in one tableau with Mme. M. It was a scene from mediæval life and was called "The Lady of the Castle and Her Page."

I felt unutterably confused on meeting Mme. M. at the rehearsal. I kept feeling that she would at once read in my eyes all the reflections, the doubts, the surmises, that had arisen in my mind since the previous day. I fancied, too, that I was, as it were, to blame in regard to her, for having come upon her tears the day before and hindered her grieving, so that she could hardly help looking at me askance, as an unpleasant witness and unforgiven sharer of her secret. But, thank goodness, it went off without any great trouble; I was simply not noticed. I think she had no thoughts to spare for me or for the rehearsal; she was absent-minded, sad and gloomily thoughtful; it was evident that she was worried by some great anxiety. As soon as my part was over I ran away to change my clothes, and ten minutes later came out on the verandah into the garden. Almost at the same time Mme. M. came out by another door, and immediately afterwards coming towards us appeared her self-satisfied husband, who was returning from the garden, after just escorting into it quite a crowd of ladies and there handing them over to a competent *cavaliere servente*. The meeting of the husband and wife was evidently unexpected. Mme. M., I don't know why, grew suddenly confused, and a faint trace of vexation was betrayed in her impatient movement. The husband, who had been carelessly whistling an air and with an air of profundity stroking his whiskers, now, on meeting his wife, frowned and scrutinized her, as I remember now, with a markedly inquisitorial stare.

"You are going into the garden?" he asked, noticing the parasol and book in her hand.

"No, into the copse," she said, with a slight flush.

"Alone?"

"With him," said Mme. M., pointing to me. "I always go a walk alone in the morning," she added, speaking in an uncertain, hesitating voice, as people do when they tell their first lie.

"H'm . . . and I have just taken the whole party there. They have all met there together in the flower arbour to see N. off. He is going away, you know. . . . Something has gone wrong in Odessa. Your cousin" (he meant the fair beauty) "is laughing and crying at the same time; there is no making her out. She says, though, that you are angry with N. about something and so wouldn't go and see him off. Nonsense, of course?"

"She's laughing," said Mme. M., coming down the verandah steps.

"So this is your daily *cavaliere servente*," added M. M., with a wry smile, turning his lorgnette upon me.

"Page!" I cried, angered by the lorgnette and the jeer; and laughing straight in his face I jumped down the three steps of the verandah at one bound.

"A pleasant walk," muttered M. M., and went on his way.

Of course, I immediately joined Mme. M. as soon as she indicated me to her husband, and looked as though she had invited me to do so an hour before, and as though I had been accompanying her on her walks every morning for the last month. But I could not make out why she was so confused, so embarrassed, and what was in her mind when she brought herself to have recourse to her little lie? Why had she not simply said that she was going alone? I did not know how to look at her, but overwhelmed with wonder I began by degrees very naïvely peeping into her face; but just as an hour before at the rehearsal she did not notice either my looks or my mute question. The same anxiety, only more intense and more distinct, was apparent in her face, in her agitation, in her walk. She was in haste, and walked more and more quickly and kept looking uneasily down every avenue, down every path in the wood that led in the direction of the garden. And I, too, was expecting something. Suddenly there was the sound of horses' hoofs behind us. It was the whole party of ladies and gentlemen on horseback escorting N., the gentleman who was so suddenly deserting us.

Among the ladies was my fair tormentor, of whom M. M. had told us that she was in tears. But characteristically she was laughing like a child, and was galloping briskly on a splendid bay horse. On reaching us N. took off his hat, but did not stop, nor say one word to Mme. M. Soon all the cavalcade disappeared from our sight. I glanced at Mme. M. and almost cried out in wonder; she was standing as white as a handkerchief and big tears were gushing from her eyes. By chance our eyes met: Mme. M. suddenly flushed and turned away for an instant, and a distinct look of uneasiness and vexation flitted across her face. I was in the way, worse even than last time, that was clearer than day, but how was I to get away?

And, as though guessing my difficulty, Mme. M. opened the book which she had in her hand, and colouring and evidently trying not to look at me she said, as though she had only suddenly realized it—

"Ah! It is the second part. I've made a mistake; please bring me the first."

I could not but understand. My part was over, and I could not have been more directly dismissed.

I ran off with her book and did not come back. The first part lay undisturbed on the table that morning. . . .

But I was not myself; in my heart there was a sort of haunting terror. I did my utmost not to meet Mme. M. But I looked with wild curiosity at the self-satisfied person of M. M., as though there must be something special about him now. I don't understand what was the meaning of my absurd curiosity. I only remember that I was strangely perplexed by all that I had chanced to see that morning. But the day was only just beginning and it was fruitful in events for me.

    Dinner was very early that day. An expedition to a neighbouring hamlet to see a village festival that was taking place there had been fixed for the evening, and so it was necessary to be in time to get ready. I had been dreaming for the last three days of this excursion, anticipating all sorts of delights. Almost all the company gathered together on the verandah for coffee. I cautiously followed the others and concealed myself behind the third row of chairs. I was attracted by curiosity, and yet I was very anxious not to be seen by Mme. M. But as luck would have it I was not far from my fair tormentor. Something miraculous and incredible was happening to her that day; she looked twice as handsome. I don't know how and why this happens, but such miracles are by no means rare with women. There was with us at this moment a new guest, a tall, pale-faced young man, the official admirer of our fair beauty, who had just arrived from Moscow as though on purpose to replace N., of whom rumour said that he was desperately in love with the same lady. As for the newly arrived guest, he had for a long time past been on the same terms as Benedick with Beatrice, in Shakespeare's *Much Ado about Nothing*. In short, the fair beauty was in her very best form that day. Her chatter and her jests were so full of grace, so trustfully naïve, so innocently careless, she was persuaded of the general enthusiasm with such graceful self-confidence that she really was all the time the centre of peculiar adoration. A throng of surprised and admiring listeners was continually round her, and she had never been so fascinating. Every word she uttered was marvellous and seductive, was caught up and handed round in the circle, and not one word, one jest, one sally was lost. I fancy no one had expected from her such taste, such brilliance, such wit. Her best qualities were, as a rule, buried under the most harum-scarum wilfulness, the most schoolboyish pranks, almost verging on buffoonery; they were rarely noticed, and, when they were, were hardly believed in, so that now her extraordinary brilliancy was accompanied by an eager whisper of amazement among all. There was, however, one peculiar and rather delicate circumstance, judging at least by the part in it played by Mme. M.'s husband, which contributed to her success. The madcap ventured—and I must add to the satisfaction of almost every one or, at any rate, to the satisfaction of all the young people—to make a furious attack upon him, owing to many causes, probably of great consequence in her eyes. She carried on with him a regular cross-fire of witticisms, of mocking and sarcastic sallies, of that most illusive and treacherous kind that, smoothly wrapped up on the surface, hit the mark without giving the victim anything to lay hold of, and exhaust him in fruitless efforts to repel the attack, reducing him to fury and comic despair.

I don't know for certain, but I fancy the whole proceeding was not improvised but premeditated. This desperate duel had begun earlier, at dinner. I call it desperate because M. M. was not quick to surrender. He had to call upon all his presence of mind, all his sharp wit and rare resourcefulness not to be completely covered with ignominy. The conflict was accompanied by the continual and irrepressible laughter of all who witnessed and took part in it. That day was for him very different from the day before. It was noticeable that Mme. M. several times did her utmost to stop her indiscreet friend, who was certainly trying to depict the jealous husband in the most grotesque and absurd guise, in the guise of "a bluebeard" it must be supposed, judging from all probabilities, from what has remained in my memory and finally from the part which I myself was destined to play in the affair.

I was drawn into it in a most absurd manner, quite unexpectedly. And as ill-luck would have it at that moment I was standing where I could be seen, suspecting no evil and actually forgetting the precautions I had so long practised. Suddenly I was brought into the foreground as a sworn foe and natural rival of M. M., as desperately in love with his wife, of which my persecutress vowed and swore that she had proofs, saying that only that morning she had seen in the copse. . . .

But before she had time to finish I broke in at the most desperate minute. That minute was so diabolically calculated, was so treacherously prepared to lead up to its finale, its ludicrous *dénouement*, and was brought out with such killing humour that a perfect outburst of irrepressible mirth saluted this last sally. And though even at the time I guessed that mine was not the most unpleasant part in the performance, yet I was so confused, so irritated and alarmed that, full of misery and despair, gasping with shame and tears, I dashed through two rows of chairs, stepped forward, and addressing my tormentor, cried, in a voice broken with tears and indignation:

"Aren't you ashamed . . . aloud . . . before all the ladies . . . to tell such a wicked . . . lie? . . . Like a small child . . . before all these men. . . . What will they say? . . . A big girl like you . . . and married! . . . "

But I could not go on, there was a deafening roar of applause. My outburst created a perfect furore. My naïve gesture, my tears, and especially the fact that I seemed to be defending M. M., all this provoked such fiendish laughter, that even now I cannot help laughing at the mere recollection of it. I was overcome with confusion, senseless with horror and, burning with shame, hiding my face in my hands rushed away, knocked a tray out of the hands of a footman who was coming in at the door, and flew upstairs to my own room. I pulled out the key, which was on the outside of the door, and locked myself in. I did well, for there was a hue and cry after me. Before a minute had passed my door was besieged by a mob of the prettiest ladies. I heard their ringing laughter, their incessant chatter, their trilling voices; they were all twittering at once, like swallows. All of them, every one of them, begged and besought me to open the door, if only for a moment; swore that no harm should come to me, only that they wanted to smother me with kisses. But . . . what could be more horrible than this novel threat? I simply burned with shame the other side of the door, hiding my face in the pillows and did not open, did not even respond. The ladies kept up their knocking for a long time, but I was deaf and obdurate as only a boy of eleven could be.

But what could I do now? Everything was laid bare, everything had been exposed, everything I had so jealously guarded and concealed! . . . Everlasting disgrace and shame had fallen on me! But it is true that I could not myself have said why I was frightened and what I wanted to hide; yet I was frightened of something and had trembled like a leaf at the thought of *that something's* being discovered. Only till that minute I had not known what it was: whether it was good or bad, splendid or shameful, praiseworthy or reprehensible? Now in my distress, in the misery that had been forced upon me, I learned that it was *absurd* and *shameful*. Instinctively I felt at the same time that this verdict was false, inhuman, and coarse; but I was crushed, annihilated; consciousness seemed checked in me and thrown into confusion; I could not stand up against that verdict, nor criticize it properly. I was befogged; I only felt that my heart had been inhumanly and shamelessly wounded, and was brimming over with impotent tears. I was irritated; but I was boiling with indignation and hate such as I had never felt before, for it was the first time in my life that I had known real sorrow, insult, and injury—and it was truly that, without any exaggeration. The first untried, unformed feeling had been so coarsely handled in me, a child. The first fragrant, virginal modesty had been so soon exposed and insulted, and the first and perhaps very real and æsthetic impression had been so outraged. Of course there was much my persecutors did not know and did not divine in my sufferings. One circumstance, which I had not succeeded in analysing till then, of which I had been as it were afraid, partly entered into it. I went on lying on my bed in despair and misery, hiding my face in my pillow, and I was alternately feverish and shivery. I was tormented by two questions: first, what had the wretched fair beauty seen, and, in fact, what could she have seen that morning in the copse between Mme. M. and me? And secondly, how could I now look Mme. M. in the face without dying on the spot of shame and despair?

An extraordinary noise in the yard roused me at last from the state of semi-consciousness into which I had fallen. I got up and went to the window. The whole yard was packed with carriages, saddle-horses, and bustling servants. It seemed that they were all setting off; some of the gentlemen had already mounted their horses, others were taking their places in the carriages. . . . Then I remembered the expedition to the village fête, and little by little an uneasiness came over me; I began anxiously looking for my pony in the yard; but there was no pony there, so they must have forgotten me. I could not restrain myself, and rushed headlong downstairs, thinking no more of unpleasant meetings or my recent ignominy. . . .

Terrible news awaited me. There was neither a horse nor seat in any of the carriages to spare for me; everything had been arranged, all the seats were taken, and I was forced to give place to others. Overwhelmed by this fresh blow, I stood on the steps and looked mournfully at the long rows of coaches, carriages, and chaises, in which there was not the tiniest corner left for me, and at the smartly dressed ladies, whose horses were restlessly curvetting.

One of the gentlemen was late. They were only waiting for his arrival to set off. His horse was standing at the door, champing the bit, pawing the earth with his hoofs, and at every moment starting and rearing. Two stable-boys were carefully holding him by the bridle, and every one else apprehensively stood at a respectful distance from him.

A most vexatious circumstance had occurred, which prevented my going. In addition to the fact that new visitors had arrived, filling up all the seats, two of the horses had fallen ill, one of them being my pony. But I was not the only person to suffer: it appeared that there was no horse for our new visitor, the pale-faced young man of whom I have spoken already. To get over this difficulty our host had been obliged to have recourse to the extreme step of offering his fiery unbroken stallion, adding, to satisfy his conscience, that it was impossible to ride him, and that they had long intended to sell the beast for its vicious character, if only a purchaser could be found.

But, in spite of his warning, the visitor declared that he was a good horseman, and in any case ready to mount anything rather than not go. Our host said no more, but now I fancied that a sly and ambiguous smile was straying on his lips. He waited for the gentleman who had spoken so well of his own horsemanship, and stood, without mounting his horse, impatiently rubbing his hands and continually glancing towards the door; some similar feeling seemed shared by the two stable-boys, who were holding the stallion, almost breathless with pride at seeing themselves before the whole company in charge of a horse which might any minute kill a man for no reason whatever. Something akin to their master's sly smile gleamed, too, in their eyes, which were round with expectation, and fixed upon the door from which the bold visitor was to appear. The horse himself, too, behaved as though he were in league with our host and the stable-boys. He bore himself proudly and haughtily, as though he felt that he were being watched by several dozen curious eyes and were glorying in his evil reputation exactly as some incorrigible rogue might glory in his criminal exploits. He seemed to be defying the bold man who would venture to curb his independence.

That bold man did at last make his appearance. Conscience-stricken at having kept every one waiting, hurriedly drawing on his gloves, he came forward without looking at anything, ran down the steps, and only raised his eyes as he stretched out his hand to seize the mane of the waiting horse. But he was at once disconcerted by his frantic rearing and a warning scream from the frightened spectators. The young man stepped back and looked in perplexity at the vicious horse, which was quivering all over, snorting with anger, and rolling his bloodshot eyes ferociously, continually rearing on his hind legs and flinging up his fore legs as though he meant to bolt into the air and carry the two stable-boys with him. For a minute the young man stood completely nonplussed; then, flushing slightly with some embarrassment, he raised his eyes and looked at the frightened ladies.

"A very fine horse!" he said, as though to himself, "and to my thinking it ought to be a great pleasure to ride him; but . . . but do you know, I think I won't go?" he concluded, turning to our host with the broad, good-natured smile which so suited his kind and clever face.

"Yet I consider you are an excellent horseman, I assure you," answered the owner of the unapproachable horse, delighted, and he warmly and even gratefully pressed the young man's hand, "just because from the first moment you saw the sort of brute you had to deal with," he added with dignity. "Would you believe me, though I have served twenty-three years in the hussars, yet I've had the pleasure of being laid on the ground three times, thanks to that beast, that is, as often as I mounted the useless animal. Tancred, my boy, there's no one here fit for you! Your rider, it seems, must be some Ilya Muromets, and he must be sitting quiet now in the village of Kapatcharovo, waiting for your teeth to fall out. Come, take him away, he has frightened people enough. It was a waste of time to bring him out, he cried, rubbing his hands complacently.

It must be observed that Tancred was no sort of use to his master and simply ate corn for nothing; moreover, the old hussar had lost his reputation for a knowledge of horseflesh by paying a fabulous sum for the worthless beast, which he had purchased only for his beauty . . . yet he was delighted now that Tancred had kept up his reputation, had disposed of another rider, and so had drawn closer on himself fresh senseless laurels.

"So you are not going?" cried the blonde beauty, who was particularly anxious that her *cavaliere servente* should be in attendance on this occasion. "Surely you are not frightened?"

"Upon my word I am," answered the young man.

"Are you in earnest?"

"Why, do you want me to break my neck?"

"Then make haste and get on my horse; don't be afraid, it is very quiet. We won't delay them, they can change the saddles in a minute! I'll try to take yours. Surely Tancred can't always be so unruly."

No sooner said than done, the madcap leaped out of the saddle and was standing before us as she finished the last sentence.

"You don't know Tancred, if you think he will allow your wretched side-saddle to be put on him! Besides, I would not let you break your neck, it would be a pity!" said our host, at that moment of inward gratification affecting, as his habit was, a studied brusqueness and even coarseness of speech which he thought in keeping with a jolly good fellow and an old soldier, and which he imagined to be particularly attractive to the ladies. This was one of his favourite fancies, his favourite whim, with which we were all familiar.

"Well, cry-baby, wouldn't you like to have a try? You wanted so much to go?" said the valiant horsewoman, noticing me and pointing tauntingly at Tancred, because I had been so imprudent as to catch her eye, and she would not let me go without a biting word, that she might not have dismounted from her horse absolutely for nothing.

"I expect you are not such a—We all know you are a hero and would be ashamed to be afraid; especially when you will be looked at, you fine page," she added, with a fleeting glance at Mme. M., whose carriage was the nearest to the entrance.

A rush of hatred and vengeance had flooded my heart, when the fair Amazon had approached us with the intention of mounting Tancred. . . . But I cannot describe what I felt at this unexpected challenge from the madcap. Everything was dark before my eyes when I saw her glance at Mme. M. For an instant an idea flashed through my mind . . . but it was only a moment, less than a moment, like a flash of gunpowder; perhaps it was the last straw, and I suddenly now was moved to rage as my spirit rose, so that I longed to put all my enemies to utter confusion, and to revenge myself on all of them and before everyone, by showing the sort of person I was. Or whether by some miracle, some prompting from mediæval history, of which I had known nothing till then, sent whirling through my giddy brain, images of tournaments, paladins, heroes, lovely ladies, the clash of swords, shouts and the applause of the crowd, and amidst those shouts the timid cry of a frightened heart, which moves the proud soul more sweetly than victory and fame—I don't know whether all this romantic nonsense was in my head at the time, or whether, more likely, only the first dawning of the inevitable nonsense that was in store for me in the future, anyway, I felt that my hour had come. My heart leaped and shuddered, and I don't remember how, at one bound, I was down the steps and beside Tancred.

"You think I am afraid?" I cried, boldly and proudly, in such a fever that I could hardly see, breathless with excitement, and flushing till the tears scalded my cheeks. "Well, you shall see!" And clutching at Tancred's mane I put my foot in the stirrup before they had time to make a movement to stop me; but at that instant Tancred reared, jerked his head, and with a mighty bound forward wrenched himself out of the hands of the petrified stable-boys, and dashed off like a hurricane, while every one cried out in horror.

Goodness knows how I got my other leg over the horse while it was in full gallop; I can't imagine, either, how I did not lose hold of the reins. Tancred bore me beyond the trellis gate, turned sharply to the right and flew along beside the fence regardless of the road. Only at that moment I heard behind me a shout from fifty voices, and that shout was echoed in my swooning heart with such a feeling of pride and pleasure that I shall never forget that mad moment of my boyhood. All the blood rushed to my head, bewildering me and overpowering my fears. I was beside myself. There certainly was, as I remember it now, something of the knight-errant about the exploit.

My knightly exploits, however, were all over in an instant or it would have gone badly with the knight. And, indeed, I do not know how I escaped as it was. I did know how to ride, I had been taught. But my pony was more like a sheep than a riding horse. No doubt I should have been thrown off Tancred if he had had time to throw me, but after galloping fifty paces he suddenly took fright at a huge stone which lay across the road and bolted back. He turned sharply, galloping at full speed, so that it is a puzzle to me even now that I was not sent spinning out of the saddle and flying like a ball for twenty feet, that I was not dashed to pieces, and that Tancred did not dislocate his leg by such a sudden turn. He rushed back to the gate, tossing his head furiously, bounding from side to side as though drunk with rage, flinging his legs at random in the air, and at every leap trying to shake me off his back as though a tiger had leaped on him and were thrusting its teeth and claws into his back.

In another instant I should have flown off; I was falling; but several gentlemen flew to my rescue. Two of them intercepted the way into the open country, two others galloped up, closing in upon Tancred so that their horses' sides almost crushed my legs, and both of them caught him by the bridle. A few seconds later we were back at the steps.

They lifted me down from the horse, pale and scarcely breathing. I was shaking like a blade of grass in the wind; it was the same with Tancred, who was standing, his hoofs as it were thrust into the earth and his whole body thrown back, puffing his fiery breath from red and streaming nostrils, twitching and quivering all over, seeming overwhelmed with wounded pride and anger at a child's being so bold with impunity. All around me I heard cries of bewilderment, surprise, and alarm.

At that moment my straying eyes caught those of Mme. M., who looked pale and agitated, and—I can never forget that moment—in one instant my face was flooded with colour, glowed and burned like fire; I don't know what happened to me, but confused and frightened by my own feelings I timidly dropped my eyes to the ground. But my glance was noticed, it was caught, it was stolen from me. All eyes turned on Mme. M., and finding herself unawares the centre of attention, she, too, flushed like a child from some naïve and involuntary feeling and made an unsuccessful effort to cover her confusion by laughing. . . .

All this, of course, was very absurd-looking from outside, but at that moment an extremely naïve and unexpected circumstance saved me from being laughed at by every one, and gave a special colour to the whole adventure. The lovely persecutor who was the instigator of the whole escapade, and who till then had been my irreconcileable foe, suddenly rushed up to embrace and kiss me. She had hardly been able to believe her eyes when she saw me dare to accept her challenge, and pick up the gauntlet she had flung at me by glancing at Mme. M. She had almost died of terror and self-reproach when I had flown off on Tancred; now, when it was all over, and particularly when she caught the glance at Mme. M., my confusion and my sudden flush of colour, when the romantic strain in her frivolous little head had given a new secret, unspoken significance to the moment—she was moved to such enthusiasm over my "knightliness," that touched, joyful and proud of me, she rushed up and pressed me to her bosom. She lifted the most naïve, stern-looking little face, on which there quivered and gleamed two little crystal tears, and gazing at the crowd that thronged about her said in a grave, earnest voice, such as they had never heard her use before, pointing to me: "Mais c'est très sérieux, messieurs, ne riez pas!" She did not notice that all were standing, as though fascinated, admiring her bright enthusiasm. Her swift, unexpected action, her earnest little face, the simple-hearted naïveté, the unexpected feeling betrayed by the tears that welled in her invariably laughter-loving eyes, were such a surprise that every one stood before her as though electrified by her expression, her rapid, fiery words and gestures. It seemed as though no one could take his eyes off her for fear of missing that rare moment in her enthusiastic face. Even our host flushed crimson as a tulip, and people declared that they heard him confess afterwards that "to his shame" he had been in love for a whole minute with his charming guest. Well, of course, after this I was a knight, a hero.

"De Lorge! Toggenburg!" was heard in the crowd.

There was a sound of applause.

"Hurrah for the rising generation!" added the host.

"But he is coming with us, he certainly must come with us," said the beauty; "we will find him a place, we must find him a place. He shall sit beside me, on my knee . . . but no, no! That's a mistake! . . . " she corrected herself, laughing, unable to restrain her mirth at our first encounter. But as she laughed she stroked my hand tenderly, doing all she could to soften me, that I might not be offended.

"Of course, of course," several voices chimed in; "he must go, he has won his place."

The matter was settled in a trice. The same old maid who had brought about my acquaintance with the blonde beauty was at once besieged with entreaties from all the younger people to remain at home and let me have her seat. She was forced to consent, to her intense vexation, with a smile and a stealthy hiss of anger. Her protectress, who was her usual refuge, my former foe and new friend, called to her as she galloped off on her spirited horse, laughing like a child, that she envied her and would have been glad to stay at home herself, for it was just going to rain and we should all get soaked.

And she was right in predicting rain. A regular downpour came on within an hour and the expedition was done for. We had to take shelter for some hours in the huts of the village, and had to return home between nine and ten in the evening in the damp mist that followed the rain. I began to be a little feverish. At the minute when I was starting, Mme. M. came up to me and expressed surprise that my neck was uncovered and that I had nothing on over my jacket. I answered that I had not had time to get my coat. She took out a pin and pinned up the turned down collar of my shirt, took off her own neck a crimson gauze kerchief, and put it round my neck that I might not get a sore throat. She did this so hurriedly that I had not time even to thank her.

But when we got home I found her in the little drawing-room with the blonde beauty and the pale-faced young man who had gained glory for horsemanship that day by refusing to ride Tancred. I went up to thank her and give back the scarf. But now, after all my adventures, I felt somehow ashamed. I wanted to make haste and get upstairs, there at my leisure to reflect and consider. I was brimming over with impressions. As I gave back the kerchief I blushed up to my ears, as usual.

"I bet he would like to keep the kerchief," said the young man laughing. "One can see that he is sorry to part with your scarf."

"That's it, that's it!" the fair lady put in. "What a boy! Oh!" she said, shaking her head with obvious vexation, but she stopped in time at a grave glance from Mme. M., who did not want to carry the jest too far.

I made haste to get away.

"Well, you are a boy," said the madcap, overtaking me in the next room and affectionately taking me by both hands, "why, you should have simply not returned the kerchief if you wanted so much to have it. You should have said you put it down somewhere, and that would have been the end of it. What a simpleton! Couldn't even do that! What a funny boy!"

And she tapped me on the chin with her finger, laughing at my having flushed as red as a poppy.

"I am your friend now, you know; am I not? Our enmity is over, isn't it? Yes or no?"

I laughed and pressed her fingers without a word.

"Oh, why are you so . . . why are you so pale and shivering? Have you caught a chill?"

"Yes, I don't feel well."

"Ah, poor fellow! That's the result of over-excitement. Do you know what? You had better go to bed without sitting up for supper, and you will be all right in the morning. Come along."

She took me upstairs, and there was no end to the care she lavished on me. Leaving me to undress she ran downstairs, got me some tea, and brought it up herself when I was in bed. She brought me up a warm quilt as well. I was much impressed and touched by all the care and attention lavished on me; or perhaps I was affected by the whole day, the expedition and feverishness. As I said good-night to her I hugged her warmly, as though she were my dearest and nearest friend, and in my exhausted state all the emotions of the day came back to me in a rush; I almost shed tears as I nestled to her bosom. She noticed my overwrought condition, and I believe my madcap herself was a little touched.

"You are a very good boy," she said, looking at me with gentle eyes, "please don't be angry with me. You won't, will you?"

In fact, we became the warmest and truest of friends.

It was rather early when I woke up, but the sun was already flooding the whole room with brilliant light. I jumped out of bed feeling perfectly well and strong, as though I had had no fever the day before; indeed, I felt now unutterably joyful. I recalled the previous day and felt that I would have given any happiness if I could at that minute have embraced my new friend, the fair-haired beauty, again, as I had the night before; but it was very early and every one was still asleep. Hurriedly dressing I went out into the garden and from there into the copse. I made my way where the leaves were thickest, where the fragrance of the trees was more resinous, and where the sun peeped in most gaily, rejoicing that it could penetrate the dense darkness of the foliage. It was a lovely morning.

Going on further and further, before I was aware of it I had reached the further end of the copse and came out on the river Moskva. It flowed at the bottom of the hill two hundred paces below. On the opposite bank of the river they were mowing. I watched whole rows of sharp scythes gleam all together in the sunlight at every swing of the mower and then vanish again like little fiery snakes going into hiding; I watched the cut grass flying on one side in dense rich swathes and being laid in long straight lines. I don't know how long I spent in contemplation. At last I was roused from my reverie by hearing a horse snorting and impatiently pawing the ground twenty paces from me, in the track which ran from the high road to the manor house. I don't know whether I heard this horse as soon as the rider rode up and stopped there, or whether the sound had long been in my ears without rousing me from my dreaming. Moved by curiosity I went into the copse, and before I had gone many steps I caught the sound of voices speaking rapidly, though in subdued tones. I went up closer, carefully parting the branches of the bushes that edged the path, and at once sprang back in amazement. I caught a glimpse of a familiar white dress and a soft feminine voice resounded like music in my heart. It was Mme. M. She was standing beside a man on horseback who, stooping down from the saddle, was hurriedly talking to her, and to my amazement I recognized him as N., the young man who had gone away the morning before and over whose departure M. M. had been so busy. But people had said at the time that he was going far away to somewhere in the South of Russia, and so I was very much surprised at seeing him with us again so early, and alone with Mme. M.

She was moved and agitated as I had never seen her before, and tears were glistening on her cheeks. The young man was holding her hand and stooping down to kiss it. I had come upon them at the moment of parting. They seemed to be in haste. At last he took out of his pocket a sealed envelope, gave it to Mme. M., put one arm round her, still not dismounting, and gave her a long, fervent kiss. A minute later he lashed his horse and flew past me like an arrow. Mme. M. looked after him for some moments, then pensively and disconsolately turned homewards. But after going a few steps along the track she seemed suddenly to recollect herself, hurriedly parted the bushes and walked on through the copse.

I followed her, surprised and perplexed by all that I had seen. My heart was beating violently, as though from terror. I was, as it were, benumbed and befogged; my ideas were shattered and turned upside down; but I remember I was, for some reason, very sad. I got glimpses from time to time through the green foliage of her white dress before me: I followed her mechanically, never losing sight of her, though I trembled at the thought that she might notice me. At last she came out on the little path that led to the house. After waiting half a minute I, too, emerged from the bushes; but what was my amazement when I saw lying on the red sand of the path a sealed packet, which I recognized, from the first glance, as the one that had been given to Mme. M. ten minutes before.

I picked it up. On both sides the paper was blank, there was no address on it. The envelope was not large, but it was fat and heavy, as though there were three or more sheets of notepaper in it.

What was the meaning of this envelope? No doubt it would explain the whole mystery. Perhaps in it there was said all that N. had scarcely hoped to express in their brief, hurried interview. He had not even dismounted. . . . Whether he had been in haste or whether he had been afraid of being false to himself at the hour of parting—God only knows. . . .

I stopped, without coming out on the path, threw the envelope in the most conspicuous place on it, and kept my eyes upon it, supposing that Mme. M. would notice the loss and come back and look for it. But after waiting four minutes I could stand it no longer, I picked up my find again, put it in my pocket, and set off to overtake Mme. M. I came upon her in the big avenue in the garden. She was walking straight towards the house with a swift and hurried step, though she was lost in thought, and her eyes were on the ground. I did not know what to do. Go up to her, give it her? That would be as good as saying that I knew everything, that I had seen it all. I should betray myself at the first word. And how should I look, at her? How would she look at me. I kept expecting that she would discover her loss and return on her tracks. Then I could, unnoticed, have flung the envelope on the path and she would have found it. But no! We were approaching the house; she had already been noticed. . . .

As ill-luck would have it every one had got up very early that day, because, after the unsuccessful expedition of the evening before, they had arranged something new, of which I had heard nothing. All were preparing to set off, and were having breakfast in the verandah. I waited for ten minutes, that I might not be seen with Mme. M., and making a circuit of the garden approached the house from the other side a long time after her. She was walking up and down the verandah with her arms folded, looking pale and agitated, and was obviously trying her utmost to suppress the agonizing, despairing misery which could be plainly discerned in her eyes, her walk, her every movement. Sometimes she went down the verandah steps and walked a few paces among the flower-beds in the direction of the garden; her eyes were impatiently, greedily, even incautiously, seeking something on the sand of the path and on the floor of the verandah. There could be no doubt she had discovered her loss and imagined she had dropped the letter somewhere here, near the house—yes, that must be so, she was convinced of it.

Some one noticed that she was pale and agitated, and others made the same remark. She was besieged with questions about her health and condolences. She had to laugh, to jest, to appear lively. From time to time she looked at her husband, who was standing at the end of the terrace talking to two ladies, and the poor woman was overcome by the same shudder, the same embarrassment, as on the day of his first arrival. Thrusting my hand into my pocket and holding the letter tight in it, I stood at a little distance from them all, praying to fate that Mme. M. should notice me. I longed to cheer her up, to relieve her anxiety if only by a glance; to say a word to her on the sly. But when she did chance to look at me I dropped my eyes.

I saw her distress and I was not mistaken. To this day I don't know her secret. I know nothing but what I saw and what I have just described. The intrigue was not such, perhaps, as one might suppose at the first glance. Perhaps that kiss was the kiss of farewell, perhaps it was the last slight reward for the sacrifice made to her peace and honour. N. was going away, he was leaving her, perhaps for ever. Even that letter I was holding in my hand—who can tell what it contained! How can one judge? and who can condemn? And yet there is no doubt that the sudden discovery of her secret would have been terrible—would have been a fatal blow for her. I still remember her face at that minute, it could not have shown more suffering. To feel, to know, to be convinced, to expect, as though it were one's execution, that in a quarter of an hour, in a minute perhaps, all might be discovered, the letter might be found by some one, picked up; there was no address on it, it might be opened, and then.... What then? What torture could be worse than what was awaiting her? She moved about among those who would be her judges. In another minute their smiling flattering faces would be menacing and merciless. She would read mockery, malice and icy contempt on those faces, and then her life would be plunged in everlasting darkness, with no dawn to follow.... Yes, I did not understand it then as I understand it now. I could only have vague suspicions and misgivings, and a heart-ache at the thought of her danger, which I could not fully understand. But whatever lay hidden in her secret, much was expiated, if expiation were needed, by those moments of anguish of which I was witness and which I shall never forget.

But then came a cheerful summons to set off; immediately every one was bustling about gaily; laughter and lively chatter were heard on all sides. Within two minutes the verandah was deserted. Mme. M. declined to join the party, acknowledging at last that she was not well. But, thank God, all the others set off, every one was in haste, and there was no time to worry her with commiseration, inquiries, and advice. A few remained at home. Her husband said a few words to her; she answered that she would be all right directly, that he need not be uneasy, that there was no occasion for her to lie down, that she would go into the garden, alone ... with me ... here she glanced at me. Nothing could be more fortunate! I flushed with pleasure, with delight; a minute later we were on the way.

She walked along the same avenues and paths by which she had returned from the copse, instinctively remembering the way she had come, gazing before her with her eyes fixed on the ground, looking about intently without answering me, possibly forgetting that I was walking beside her.

But when we had already reached the place where I had picked up the letter, and the path ended, Mme. M. suddenly stopped, and in a voice faint and weak with misery said that she felt worse, and that she would go home. But when she reached the garden fence she stopped again and thought a minute; a smile of despair came on her lips, and utterly worn out and exhausted, resigned, and making up her mind to the worst, she turned without a word and retraced her steps, even forgetting to tell me of her intention.

My heart was torn with sympathy, and I did not know what to do.

We went, or rather I led her, to the place from which an hour before I had heard the tramp of a horse and their conversation. Here, close to a shady elm tree, was a seat hewn out of one huge stone, about which grew ivy, wild jasmine, and dog-rose; the whole wood was dotted with little bridges, arbours, grottoes, and similar surprises. Mme. M. sat down on the bench and glanced unconsciously at the marvellous view that lay open before us. A minute later she opened her book, and fixed her eyes upon it without reading, without turning the pages, almost unconscious of what she was doing. It was about half-past nine. The sun was already high and was floating gloriously in the deep, dark blue sky, as though melting away in its own light. The mowers were by now far away; they were scarcely visible from our side of the river; endless ridges of mown grass crept after them in unbroken succession, and from time to time the faintly stirring breeze wafted their fragrance to us. The never ceasing concert of those who "sow not, neither do they reap" and are free as the air they cleave with their sportive wings was all about us. It seemed as though at that moment every flower, every blade of grass was exhaling the aroma of sacrifice, was saying to its Creator, "Father, I am blessed and happy."

I glanced at the poor woman, who alone was like one dead amidst all this joyous life; two big tears hung motionless on her lashes, wrung from her heart by bitter grief. It was in my power to relieve and console this poor, fainting heart, only I did not know how to approach the subject, how to take the first step. I was in agonies. A hundred times I was on the point of going up to her, but every time my face glowed like fire.

Suddenly a bright idea dawned upon me. I had found a way of doing it; I revived.

"Would you like me to pick you a nosegay?" I said, in such a joyful voice that Mme M. immediately raised her head and looked at me intently.

"Yes, do," she said at last in a weak voice, with a faint smile, at once dropping her eyes on the book again.

"Or soon they will be mowing the grass here and there will be no flowers," I cried, eagerly setting to work.

I had soon picked my nosegay, a poor, simple one, I should have been ashamed to take it indoors; but how light my heart was as I picked the flowers and tied them up! The dog-rose and the wild jasmine I picked closer to the seat, I knew that not far off there was a field of rye, not yet ripe. I ran there for cornflowers; I mixed them with tall ears of rye, picking out the finest and most golden. Close by I came upon a perfect nest of forget-me-nots, and my nosegay was almost complete. Farther away in the meadow there were dark-blue campanulas and wild pinks, and I ran down to the very edge of the river to get yellow water-lilies. At last, making my way back, and going for an instant into the wood to get some bright green fan-shaped leaves of the maple to put round the nosegay, I happened to come across a whole family of pansies, close to which, luckily for me, the fragrant scent of violets betrayed the little flower hiding in the thick lush grass and still glistening with drops of dew. The nosegay was complete. I bound it round with fine long grass which twisted into a rope, and I carefully lay the letter in the centre, hiding it with the flowers, but in such a way that it could be very easily noticed if the slightest attention were bestowed upon my nosegay.

I carried it to Mme. M.

On the way it seemed to me that the letter was lying too much in view: I hid it a little more. As I got nearer I thrust it still further in the flowers; and finally, when I was on the spot, I suddenly poked it so deeply into the centre of the nosegay that it could not be noticed at all from outside. My cheeks were positively flaming. I wanted to hide my face in my hands and run away at once, but she glanced at my flowers as though she had completely forgotten that I had gathered them. Mechanically, almost without looking, she held out her hand and took my present; but at once laid it on the seat as though I had handed it to her for that purpose and dropped her eyes to her book again, seeming lost in thought. I was ready to cry at this mischance. "If only my nosegay were close to her," I thought; "if only she had not forgotten it!" I lay down on the grass not far off, put my right arm under my head, and closed my eyes as though I were overcome by drowsiness. But I waited, keeping my eyes fixed on her.

Ten minutes passed, it seemed to me that she was getting paler and paler . . . fortunately a blessed chance came to my aid.

This was a big, golden bee, brought by a kindly breeze, luckily for me. It first buzzed over my head, and then flew up to Mme. M. She waved it off once or twice, but the bee grew more and more persistent. At last Mme. M. snatched up my nosegay and waved it before my face. At that instant the letter dropped out from among the flowers and fell straight upon the open book. I started. For some time Mme. M., mute with amazement, stared first at the letter and then at the flowers which she was holding in her hands, and she seemed unable to believe her eyes. All at once she flushed, started, and glanced at me. But I caught her movement and I shut my eyes tight, pretending to be asleep. Nothing would have induced me to look her straight in the face at that moment. My heart was throbbing and leaping like a bird in the grasp of some village boy. I don't remember how long I lay with my eyes shut, two or three minutes. At last I ventured to open them. Mme. M. was greedily reading the letter, and from her glowing cheeks, her sparkling, tearful eyes, her bright face, every feature of which was quivering with joyful emotion, I guessed that there was happiness in the letter and all her misery was dispersed like smoke. An agonizing, sweet feeling gnawed at my heart, it was hard for me to go on pretending. . . .

I shall never forget that minute!

Suddenly, a long way off, we heard voices—

"Mme. M.! Natalie! Natalie!"

Mme. M. did not answer, but she got up quickly from the seat, came up to me and bent over me. I felt that she was looking straight into my face. My eyelashes quivered, but I controlled myself and did not open my eyes. I tried to breathe more evenly and quietly, but my heart smothered me with its violent throbbing. Her burning breath scorched my cheeks; she bent close down to my face as though trying to make sure. At last a kiss and tears fell on my hand, the one which was lying on my breast.

"Natalie! Natalie! where are you," we heard again, this time quite close.

"Coming," said Mme. M., in her mellow, silvery voice, which was so choked and quivering with tears and so subdued that no one but I could hear that, "Coming!"

But at that instant my heart at last betrayed me and seemed to send all my blood rushing to my face. At that instant a swift, burning kiss scalded my lips. I uttered a faint cry. I opened my eyes, but at once the same gauze kerchief fell upon them, as though she meant to screen me from the sun. An instant later she was gone. I heard nothing but the sound of rapidly retreating steps. I was alone. . . .

I pulled off her kerchief and kissed it, beside myself with rapture; for some moments I was almost frantic. . . . Hardly able to breathe, leaning on my elbow on the grass, I stared unconsciously before me at the surrounding slopes, streaked with cornfields, at the river that flowed twisting and winding far away, as far as the eye could see, between fresh hills and villages that gleamed like dots all over the sunlit distance—at the dark-blue, hardly visible forests, which seemed as though smoking at the edge of the burning sky, and a sweet stillness inspired by the triumphant peacefulness of the picture gradually brought calm to my troubled heart. I felt more at ease and breathed more freely, but my whole soul was full of a dumb, sweet yearning, as though a veil had been drawn from my eyes as though at a foretaste of something. My frightened heart, faintly quivering with expectation, was groping timidly and joyfully towards some conjecture . . . and all at once my bosom heaved, began aching as though something had pierced it, and tears, sweet tears, gushed from my eyes. I hid my face in my hands, and quivering like a blade of grass, gave myself up to the first consciousness and revelation of my heart, the first vague glimpse of my nature. My childhood was over from that moment.

* * * * *

When two hours later I returned home I did not find Mme. M. Through some sudden chance she had gone back to Moscow with her husband. I never saw her again.

Mr. Prohartchin

In the darkest and humblest corner of Ustinya Fyodorovna's flat lived Semyon Ivanovitch Prohartchin, a well-meaning elderly man, who did not drink. Since Mr. Prohartchin was of a very humble grade in the service, and received a salary strictly proportionate to his official capacity, Ustinya Fyodorovna could not get more than five roubles a month from him for his lodging. Some people said that she had her own reasons for accepting him as a lodger; but, be that as it may, as though in despite of all his detractors, Mr. Prohartchin actually became her favourite, in an honourable and virtuous sense, of course. It must be observed that Ustinya Fyodorovna, a very respectable woman, who had a special partiality for meat and coffee, and found it difficult to keep the fasts, let rooms to several other boarders who paid twice as much as Semyon Ivanovitch, yet not being quiet lodgers, but on the contrary all of them "spiteful scoffers" at her feminine ways and her forlorn helplessness, stood very low in her good opinion, so that if it had not been for the rent they paid, she would not have cared to let them stay, nor indeed to see them in her flat at all. Semyon Ivanovitch had become her favourite from the day when a retired, or, perhaps more correctly speaking, discharged clerk, with a weakness for strong drink, was carried to his last resting-place in Volkovo. Though this gentleman had only one eye, having had the other knocked out owing, in his own words, to his valiant behaviour; and only one leg, the other having been broken in the same way owing to his valour; yet he had succeeded in winning all the kindly feeling of which Ustinya Fyodorovna was capable, and took the fullest advantage of it, and would probably have gone on for years living as her devoted satellite and toady if he had not finally drunk himself to death in the most pitiable way. All this had happened at Peski, where Ustinya Fyodorovna only had three lodgers, of whom, when she moved into a new flat and set up on a larger scale, letting to about a dozen new boarders, Mr. Prohartchin was the only one who remained.

Whether Mr. Prohartchin had certain incorrigible defects, or whether his companions were, every one of them, to blame, there seemed to be misunderstandings on both sides from the first. We must observe here that all Ustinya Fyodorovna's new lodgers without exception got on together like brothers; some of them were in the same office; each one of them by turns lost all his money to the others at faro, preference and *bixe*; they all liked in a merry hour to enjoy what they called the fizzing moments of life in a crowd together; they were fond, too, at times of discussing lofty subjects, and though in the end things rarely passed off without a dispute, yet as all prejudices were banished from the whole party the general harmony was not in the least disturbed thereby. The most remarkable among the lodgers were Mark Ivanovitch, an intelligent and well-read man; then Oplevaniev; then Prepolovenko, also a nice and modest person; then there was a certain Zinovy Prokofyevitch, whose object in life was to get into aristocratic society; then there was Okeanov, the copying clerk, who had in his time almost wrested the distinction of prime favourite from Semyon Ivanovitch; then another copying clerk called Sudbin; the plebeian Kantarev; there were others too. But to all these people Semyon Ivanovitch was, as it were, not one of themselves. No one wished him harm, of course, for all had from the very first done Prohartchin justice, and had decided in Mark Ivanovitch's words that he, Prohartchin, was a good and harmless fellow, though by no means a man of the world, trustworthy, and not a flatterer, who had, of course, his failings; but that if he were sometimes unhappy it was due to nothing else but lack of imagination. What is more, Mr. Prohartchin, though deprived in this way of imagination, could never have made a particularly favourable impression from his figure or manners (upon which scoffers are fond of fastening), yet his figure did not put people against him. Mark Ivanovitch, who was an intelligent person, formally undertook Semyon Ivanovitch's defence, and declared in rather happy and flowery language that Prohartchin was an elderly and respectable man, who had long, long ago passed the age of romance. And so, if Semyon Ivanovitch did not know how to get on with people, it must have been entirely his own fault.

The first thing they noticed was the unmistakable parsimony and niggardliness of Semyon Ivanovitch. That was at once observed and noted, for Semyon Ivanovitch would never lend any one his teapot, even for a moment; and that was the more unjust as he himself hardly ever drank tea, but when he wanted anything drank, as a rule, rather a pleasant decoction of wild flowers and certain medicinal herbs, of which he always had a considerable store. His meals, too, were quite different from the other lodgers'. He never, for instance, permitted himself to partake of the whole dinner, provided daily by Ustinya Fyodorovna for the other boarders. The dinner cost half a rouble; Semyon Ivanovitch paid only twenty-five kopecks in copper, and never exceeded it, and so took either a plate of soup with pie, or a plate of beef; most frequently he ate neither soup nor beef, but he partook in moderation of white bread with onion, curd, salted cucumber, or something similar, which was a great deal cheaper, and he would only go back to his half rouble dinner when he could stand it no longer....

Here the biographer confesses that nothing would have induced him to allude to such realistic and low details, positively shocking and offensive to some lovers of the heroic style, if it were not that these details exhibit one peculiarity, one characteristic, in the hero of this story; for Mr. Prohartchin was by no means so poor as to be unable to have regular and sufficient meals, though he sometimes made out that he was. But he acted as he did regardless of obloquy and people's prejudices, simply to satisfy his strange whims, and from frugality and excessive carefulness: all this, however, will be much clearer later on. But we will beware of boring the reader with the description of all Semyon Ivanovitch's whims, and will omit, for instance, the curious and very amusing description of his attire; and, in fact, if it were not for Ustinya Fyodorovna's own reference to it we should hardly have alluded even to the fact that Semyon Ivanovitch never could make up his mind to send his linen to the wash, or if he ever did so it was so rarely that in the intervals one might have completely forgotten the existence of linen on Semyon Ivanovitch. From the landlady's evidence it appeared that "Semyon Ivanovitch, bless his soul, poor lamb, for twenty years had been tucked away in his corner, without caring what folks thought, for all the days of his life on earth he was a stranger to socks, handkerchiefs, and all such things," and what is more, Ustinya Fyodorovna had seen with her own eyes, thanks to the decrepitude of the screen, that the poor dear man sometimes had had nothing to cover his bare skin.

Such were the rumours in circulation after Semyon Ivanovitch's death. But in his lifetime (and this was one of the most frequent occasions of dissension) he could not endure it if any one, even somebody on friendly terms with him, poked his inquisitive nose uninvited into his corner, even through an aperture in the decrepit screen. He was a taciturn man difficult to deal with and prone to ill health. He did not like people to give him advice, he did not care for people who put themselves forward either, and if any one jeered at him or gave him advice unasked, he would fall foul of him at once, put him to shame, and settle his business. "You are a puppy, you are a featherhead, you are not one to give advice, so there—you mind your own business, sir. You'd better count the stitches in your own socks, sir, so there!"

Semyon Ivanovitch was a plain man, and never used the formal mode of address to any one. He could not bear it either when some one who knew his little ways would begin from pure sport pestering him with questions, such as what he had in his little trunk. . . . Semyon Ivanovitch had one little trunk. It stood under his bed, and was guarded like the apple of his eye; and though every one knew that there was nothing in it except old rags, two or three pairs of damaged boots and all sorts of rubbish, yet Mr. Prohartchin prized his property very highly, and they used even to hear him at one time express dissatisfaction with his old, but still sound, lock, and talk of getting a new one of a special German pattern with a secret spring and various complications. When on one occasion Zinovy Prokofyevitch, carried away by the thoughtlessness of youth, gave expression to the very coarse and unseemly idea, that Semyon Ivanovitch was probably hiding and treasuring something in his box to leave to his descendants, every one who happened to be by was stupefied at the extraordinary effects of Zinovy Prokofyevitch's sally. At first Mr. Prohartchin could not find suitable terms for such a crude and coarse idea. For a long time words dropped from his lips quite incoherently, and it was only after a while they made out that Semyon Ivanovitch was reproaching Zinovy Prokofyevitch for some shabby action in the remote past; then they realized that Semyon Ivanovitch was predicting that Zinovy Prokofyevitch would never get into aristocratic society, and that the tailor to whom he owed a bill for his suits would beat him—would certainly beat him—because the puppy had not paid him for so long; and finally, "You puppy, you," Semyon Ivanovitch added, "here you want to get into the hussars, but you won't, I tell you, you'll make a fool of yourself. And I tell you what, you puppy, when your superiors know all about it they will take and make you a copying clerk; so that will be the end of it! Do you hear, puppy?" Then Semyon Ivanovitch subsided, but after lying down for five hours, to the intense astonishment of every one he seemed to have reached a decision, and began suddenly reproaching and abusing the young man again, at first to himself and afterwards addressing Zinovy Prokofyevitch. But the matter did not end there, and in the evening, when Mark Ivanovitch and Prepolovenko made tea and asked Okeanov to drink it with them, Semyon Ivanovitch got up from his bed, purposely joined them, subscribing his fifteen or twenty kopecks, and on the pretext of a sudden desire for a cup of tea began at great length going into the subject, and explaining that he was a poor man, nothing but a poor man, and that a poor man like him had nothing to save. Mr. Prohartchin confessed that he was a poor man on this occasion, he said, simply because the subject had come up; that the day before yesterday he had meant to borrow a rouble from that impudent fellow, but now he should not borrow it for fear the puppy should brag, that that was the fact of the matter, and that his salary was such that one could not buy enough to eat, and that finally, a poor man, as you see, he sent his sister-in-law in Tver five roubles every month, that if he did not send his sister-in-law in Tver five roubles every month his sister-in-law would die, and if his sister-in-law, who was dependent on him, were dead, he, Semyon Ivanovitch, would long ago have bought himself a new suit. . . . And Semyon Ivanovitch went on talking in this way at great length about being a poor man, about his sister-in-law and about roubles, and kept repeating the same thing over and over again to impress it on his audience till he got into a regular muddle and relapsed into silence. Only three days later, when they had all forgotten about him, and no one was thinking of attacking him, he added something in conclusion to the effect that when Zinovy Prokofyevitch went into the hussars the impudent fellow would have his leg cut off in the war, and then he would come with a wooden leg and say; "Semyon Ivanovitch, kind friend, give me something to eat!" and then Semyon Ivanovitch would not give him something to eat, and would not look at the insolent fellow; and that's how it would be, and he could just make the best of it.

All this naturally seemed very curious and at the same time fearfully amusing. Without much reflection, all the lodgers joined together for further investigation, and simply from curiosity determined to make a final onslaught on Semyon Ivanovitch *en masse*. And as Mr. Prohartchin, too, had of late—that is, ever since he had begun living in the same flat with them—been very fond of finding out everything about them and asking inquisitive questions, probably for private reasons of his own, relations sprang up between the opposed parties without any preparation or effort on either side, as it were by chance and of itself. To get into relations Semyon Ivanovitch always had in reserve his peculiar, rather sly, and very ingenuous manœuvre, of which the reader has learned something already. He would get off his bed about tea-time, and if he saw the others gathered together in a group to make tea he would go up to them like a quiet, sensible, and friendly person, hand over his twenty kopecks, as he was entitled to do, and announce that he wished to join them. Then the young men would wink at one another, and so indicating that they were in league together against Semyon Ivanovitch, would begin a conversation, at first strictly proper and decorous. Then one of the wittier of the party would, *à propos* of nothing, fall to telling them news consisting most usually of entirely false and quite incredible details. He would say, for instance, that some one had heard His Excellency that day telling Demid Vassilyevitch that in his opinion married clerks were more trustworthy than unmarried, and more suitable for promotion; for they were steady, and that their capacities were considerably improved by marriage, and that therefore he—that is, the speaker—in order to improve and be better fitted for promotion, was doing his utmost to enter the bonds of matrimony as soon as possible with a certain Fevronya

Prokofyevna. Or he would say that it had more than once been remarked about certain of his colleagues that they were entirely devoid of social graces and of well-bred, agreeable manners, and consequently unable to please ladies in good society, and that, therefore, to eradicate this defect it would be suitable to deduct something from their salary, and with the sum so obtained, to hire a hall, where they could learn to dance, acquire the outward signs of gentlemanliness and good-breeding, courtesy, respect for their seniors, strength of will, a good and grateful heart and various agreeable qualities. Or he would say that it was being arranged that some of the clerks, beginning with the most elderly, were to be put through an examination in all sorts of subjects to raise their standard of culture, and in that way, the speaker would add, all sorts of things would come to light, and certain gentlemen would have to lay their cards on the table—in short, thousands of similar very absurd rumours were discussed. To keep it up, every one believed the story at once, showed interest in it, asked questions, applied it to themselves; and some of them, assuming a despondent air, began shaking their heads and asking every one's advice, saying what were they to do if they were to come under it? It need hardly be said that a man far less credulous and simple-hearted than Mr. Prohartchin would have been puzzled and carried away by a rumour so unanimously believed. Moreover, from all appearances, it might be safely concluded that Semyon Ivanovitch was exceedingly stupid and slow to grasp any new unusual idea, and that when he heard anything new, he had always first, as it were, to chew it over and digest it, to find out the meaning, and struggling with it in bewilderment, at last perhaps to overcome it, though even then in a quite special manner peculiar to himself alone. . . .

In this way curious and hitherto unexpected qualities began to show themselves in Semyon Ivanovitch. . . . Talk and tittle-tattle followed, and by devious ways it all reached the office at last, with additions. What increased the sensation was the fact that Mr. Prohartchin, who had looked almost exactly the same from time immemorial, suddenly, *à propos* of nothing, wore quite a different countenance. His face was uneasy, his eyes were timid and had a scared and rather suspicious expression. He took to walking softly, starting and listening, and to put the finishing touch to his new characteristics developed a passion for investigating the truth. He carried his love of truth at last to such a pitch as to venture, on two occasions, to inquire of

Demid Vassilyevitch himself concerning the credibility of the strange rumours that reached him daily by dozens, and if we say nothing here of the consequence of the action of Semyon Ivanovitch, it is for no other reason but a sensitive regard for his reputation. It was in this way people came to consider him as misanthropic and regardless of the proprieties. Then they began to discover that there was a great deal that was fantastical about him, and in this they were not altogether mistaken, for it was observed on more than one occasion that Semyon Ivanovitch completely forgot himself, and sitting in his seat with his mouth open and his pen in the air, as though frozen or petrified, looked more like the shadow of a rational being than that rational being itself. It sometimes happened that some innocently gaping gentleman, on suddenly catching his straying, lustreless, questioning eyes, was scared and all of a tremor, and at once inserted into some important document either a smudge or some quite inappropriate word. The impropriety of Semyon Ivanovitch's behaviour embarrassed and annoyed all really well-bred people.... At last no one could feel any doubt of the eccentricity of Semyon Ivanovitch's mind, when one fine morning the rumour was all over the office that Mr. Prohartchin had actually frightened Demid Vassilyevitch himself, for, meeting him in the corridor, Semyon Ivanovitch had been so strange and peculiar that he had forced his superior to beat a retreat.... The news of Semyon Ivanovitch's behaviour reached him himself at last. Hearing of it he got up at once, made his way carefully between the chairs and tables, reached the entry, took down his overcoat with his own hand, put it on, went out, and disappeared for an indefinite period. Whether he was led into this by alarm or some other impulse we cannot say, but no trace was seen of him for a time either at home or at the office....

We will not attribute Semyon Ivanovitch's fate simply to his eccentricity, yet we must observe to the reader that our hero was a very retiring man, unaccustomed to society, and had, until he made the acquaintance of the new lodgers, lived in complete unbroken solitude, and had been marked by his quietness and even a certain mysteriousness; for he had spent all the time that he lodged at Peski lying on his bed behind the screen, without talking or having any sort of relations with any one. Both his old fellow-lodgers lived exactly as he did: they, too were, somehow mysterious people and spent fifteen years lying behind their screens. The happy, drowsy hours and days trailed by, one after the other, in patriarchal stagnation, and as everything around them went its way in the same happy fashion, neither Semyon Ivanovitch nor Ustinya Fyodorovna could remember exactly when fate had brought them together.

"It may be ten years, it may be twenty, it may be even twenty-five altogether," she would say at times to her new lodgers, "since he settled with me, poor dear man, bless his heart!" And so it was very natural that the hero of our story, being so unaccustomed to society was disagreeably surprised when, a year before, he, a respectable and modest man, had found himself, suddenly in the midst of a noisy and boisterous crew, consisting of a dozen young fellows, his colleagues at the office, and his new house-mates.

The disappearance of Semyon Ivanovitch made no little stir in the lodgings. One thing was that he was the favourite; another, that his passport, which had been in the landlady's keeping, appeared to have been accidentally mislaid. Ustinya Fyodorovna raised a howl, as was her invariable habit on all critical occasions. She spent two days in abusing and upbraiding the lodgers. She wailed that they had chased away her lodger like a chicken, and all those spiteful scoffers had been the ruin of him; and on the third day she sent them all out to hunt for the fugitive and at all costs to bring him back, dead or alive. Towards evening Sudbin first came back with the news that traces had been discovered, that he had himself seen the runaway in Tolkutchy Market and other places, had followed and stood close to him, but had not dared to speak to him; he had been near him in a crowd watching a house on fire in Crooked Lane. Half an hour later Okeanov and Kantarev came in and confirmed Sudbin's story, word for word; they, too, had stood near, had followed him quite close, had stood not more than ten paces from him, but they also had not ventured to speak to him, but both observed that Semyon Ivanovitch was walking with a drunken cadger. The other lodgers were all back and together at last, and after listening attentively they made up their minds that Prohartchin could not be far off and would not be long in returning; but they said that they had all known beforehand that he was about with a drunken cadger. This drunken cadger was a thoroughly bad lot, insolent and cringing, and it seemed evident that he had got round Semyon Ivanovitch in some way. He had turned up just a week before Semyon Ivanovitch's disappearance in company with Remnev, had spent a little time in the flat telling them that he had suffered in the cause of justice, that he had formerly been in the service in the provinces, that an inspector had come down on them, that he and his associates had somehow suffered in a good cause, that he had come to Petersburg and fallen at the feet of Porfiry Grigoryevitch, that he had been got, by interest, into a department; but through the cruel persecution of fate he had been discharged from there too, and that afterwards through reorganization the office itself had ceased to exist, and that he had not been included in the new revised staff of clerks owing as much to direct incapacity for official work as to capacity for something else quite irrelevant—all this mixed up with his passion for justice and of course the trickery of his enemies. After finishing his story, in the course of which Mr. Zimoveykin more than once kissed his sullen and unshaven friend Remnev, he bowed down to all in the room in turn, not forgetting Avdotya the servant, called them all his benefactors, and explained that he was an undeserving, troublesome, mean, insolent and stupid man, and that good people must not be hard on his pitiful plight and simplicity. After begging for their kind protection Mr. Zimoveykin showed his livelier side, grew very cheerful, kissed Ustinya Fyodorovna's hands, in spite of her modest protests that her hand was coarse and not like a lady's; and towards evening promised to show the company his talent in a remarkable character dance. But next day his visit ended in a lamentable *dénouement*. Either because there had been too much character in the character-dance, or because he had, in Ustinya Fyodorovna's own words, somehow "insulted her and treated her as no lady, though she was on friendly terms with Yaroslav Ilyitch himself, and if she liked might long ago have been an officer's wife," Zimoveykin had to steer for home next day. He went away, came back again, was again turned out with ignominy, then wormed his way into Semyon Ivanovitch's good graces, robbed him incidentally of his new breeches, and now it appeared he had led Semyon Ivanovitch astray.

As soon as the landlady knew that Semyon Ivanovitch was alive and well, and that there was no need to hunt for his passport, she promptly left off grieving and was pacified. Meanwhile some of the lodgers determined to give the runaway a triumphal reception; they broke the bolt and moved away the screen from Mr. Prohartchin's bed, rumpled up the bed a little, took the famous box, put it at the foot of the bed; and on the bed laid the sister-in-law, that is, a dummy made up of an old kerchief, a cap and a mantle of the landlady's, such an exact counterfeit of a sister-in-law that it might have been mistaken for one. Having finished their work they waited for Semyon Ivanovitch to return, meaning to tell him that his sister-in-law had arrived from the country and was there behind his screen, poor thing! But they waited and waited.

Already, while they waited, Mark Ivanovitch had staked and lost half a month's salary to Prepolovenko and Kantarev; already Okeanov's nose had grown red and swollen playing "flips on the nose" and "three cards;" already Avdotya the servant had almost had her sleep out and had twice been on the point of getting up to fetch the wood and light the stove, and Zinovy Prokofyevitch, who kept running out every minute to see whether Semyon Ivanovitch were coming, was wet to the skin; but there was no sign of any one yet—neither Semyon Ivanovitch nor the drunken cadger. At last every one went to bed, leaving the sister-in-law behind the screen in readiness for any emergency; and it was not till four o'clock that a knock was heard at the gate, but when it did come it was so loud that it quite made up to the expectant lodgers for all the wearisome trouble they had been through. It was he—he himself—Semyon Ivanovitch, Mr. Prohartchin, but in such a condition that they all cried out in dismay, and no one thought about the sister-in-law. The lost man was unconscious. He was brought in, or more correctly carried in, by a sopping and tattered night-cabman. To the landlady's question where the poor dear man had got so groggy, the cabman answered: "Why, he is not drunk and has not had a drop, that I can tell you, for sure; but seemingly a faintness has come over him, or some sort of a fit, or maybe he's been knocked down by a blow."

They began examining him, propping the culprit against the stove to do so more conveniently, and saw that it really was not a case of drunkenness, nor had he had a blow, but that something else was wrong, for Semyon Ivanovitch could not utter a word, but seemed twitching in a sort of convulsion, and only blinked, fixing his eyes in bewilderment first on one and then on another of the spectators, who were all attired in night array. Then they began questioning the cabman, asking where he had got him from. "Why, from folks out Kolomna way," he answered. "Deuce knows what they are, not exactly gentry, but merry, rollicking gentlemen; so he was like this when they gave him to me; whether they had been fighting, or whether he was in some sort of a fit, goodness knows what it was; but they were nice, jolly gentlemen!"

Semyon Ivanovitch was taken, lifted high on the shoulders of two or three sturdy fellows, and carried to his bed. When Semyon Ivanovitch on being put in bed felt the sister-in-law, and put his feet on his sacred box, he cried out at the top of his voice, squatted up almost on his heels, and trembling and shaking all over, with his hands and his body he cleared a space as far as he could in his bed, while gazing with a tremulous but strangely resolute look at those present, he seemed as it were to protest that he would sooner die than give up the hundredth part of his poor belongings to any one. . . .

Semyon Ivanovitch lay for two or three days closely barricaded by the screen, and so cut off from all the world and all its vain anxieties. Next morning, of course, every one had forgotten about him; time, meanwhile, flew by as usual, hour followed hour and day followed day. The sick man's heavy, feverish brain was plunged in something between sleep and delirium; but he lay quietly and did not moan or complain; on the contrary he kept still and silent and controlled himself, lying low in his bed, just as the hare lies close to the earth when it hears the hunter. At times a long depressing stillness prevailed in the flat, a sign that the lodgers had all gone to the office, and Semyon Ivanovitch, waking up, could relieve his depression by listening to the bustle in the kitchen, where the landlady was busy close by; or to the regular flop of Avdotya's down-trodden slippers as, sighing and moaning, she cleared away, rubbed and polished, tidying all the rooms in the flat. Whole hours passed by in that way, drowsy, languid, sleepy, wearisome, like the water that dripped with a regular sound from the locker into the basin in the kitchen. At last the lodgers would arrive, one by one or in groups, and Semyon Ivanovitch could very conveniently hear them abusing the weather, saying they were hungry, making a noise, smoking, quarrelling, and making friends, playing cards, and clattering the cups as they got ready for tea. Semyon Ivanovitch mechanically made an effort to get up and join them, as he had a right to do at tea; but he at once sank back into drowsiness, and dreamed that he had been sitting a long time at the tea-table, having tea with them and talking, and that Zinovy Prokofyevitch had already seized the opportunity to introduce into the conversation some scheme concerning sisters-in-law and the moral relation of various worthy people to them. At this point Semyon Ivanovitch was in haste to defend himself and reply. But the mighty formula that flew from every tongue—"It has more than once been observed"—cut short all his objections, and Semyon Ivanovitch could do nothing better than begin dreaming again that to-day was the first of the month and that he was receiving money in his office.

Undoing the paper round it on the stairs, he looked about him quickly, and made haste as fast as he could to subtract half of the lawful wages he had received and conceal it in his boot. Then on the spot, on the stairs, quite regardless of the fact that he was in bed and asleep, he made up his mind when he reached home to give his landlady what was due for board and lodging; then to buy certain necessities, and to show any one it might concern, as it were casually and unintentionally, that some of his salary had been deducted, that now he had nothing left to send his sister-in-law; then to speak with commiseration of his sister-in-law, to say a great deal about her the next day and the day after, and ten days later to say something casually again about her poverty, that his companions might not forget. Making this determination he observed that Andrey Efimovitch, that everlastingly silent, bald little man who sat in the office three rooms from where Semyon Ivanovitch sat, and hadn't said a word to him for twenty years, was standing on the stairs, that he, too, was counting his silver roubles, and shaking his head, he said to him: "Money!" "If there's no money there will be no porridge," he added grimly as he went down the stairs, and just at the door he ended: "And I have seven children, sir." Then the little bald man, probably equally unconscious that he was acting as a phantom and not as a substantial reality, held up his hand about thirty inches from the floor, and waving it vertically, muttered that the eldest was going to school, then glancing with indignation at Semyon Ivanovitch, as though it were Mr. Prohartchin's fault that he was the father of seven, pulled his old hat down over his eyes, and with a whisk of his overcoat he turned to the left and disappeared. Semyon Ivanovitch was quite frightened, and though he was fully convinced of his own innocence in regard to the unpleasant accumulation of seven under one roof, yet it seemed to appear that in fact no one else was to blame but Semyon Ivanovitch. Panic-stricken he set off running, for it seemed to him that the bald gentleman had turned back, was running after him, and meant to search him and take away all his salary, insisting upon the indisputable number seven, and resolutely denying any possible claim of any sort of sisters-in-law upon Semyon Ivanovitch. Prohartchin ran and ran, gasping for breath. . . . Beside him was running, too, an immense number of people, and all of them were jingling their money in the tailpockets of their skimpy little dress-coats; at last every one ran up, there was the noise of fire engines, and whole masses of people carried him almost on their shoulders up to that same house on fire which he had watched last time in company with the drunken cadger. The drunken cadger—alias Mr. Zimoveykin—was there now, too, he met Semyon Ivanovitch, made a fearful fuss, took him by the arm, and led him into the thickest part of the crowd. Just as then in reality, all about them was the noise and uproar of an immense crowd of people, flooding the whole of Fontanka Embankment between the two bridges, as well as all the surrounding streets and alleys; just as then, Semyon Ivanovitch, in company with the drunken cadger, was carried along behind a fence, where they were squeezed as though in pincers in a huge timber-yard full of spectators who had gathered from the street, from Tolkutchy Market and from all the surrounding houses, taverns, and restaurants. Semyon Ivanovitch saw all this and felt as he had done at the time; in the whirl of fever and delirium all sorts of strange figures began flitting before him. He remembered some of them. One of them was a gentleman who had impressed every one extremely, a man seven feet high, with whiskers half a yard long, who had been standing behind Semyon Ivanovitch's back during the fire, and had given him encouragement from behind, when our hero had felt something like ecstasy and had stamped as though intending thereby to applaud the gallant work of the firemen, from which he had an excellent view from his elevated position. Another was the sturdy lad from whom our hero had received a shove by way of a lift on to another fence, when he had been disposed to climb over it, possibly to save some one. He had a glimpse, too, of the figure of the old man with a sickly face, in an old wadded dressing-gown, tied round the waist, who had made his appearance before the fire in a little shop buying sugar and tobacco for his lodger, and who now, with a milk-can and a quart pot in his hands, made his way through the crowd to the house in which his wife and daughter were burning together with thirteen and a half roubles in the corner under the bed. But most distinct of all was the poor, sinful woman of whom he had dreamed more than once during his illness—she stood before him now as she had done then, in wretched bark shoes and rags, with a crutch and a wicker-basket on her back. She was shouting more loudly than the firemen or the crowd, waving her crutch and her arms, saying that her own children had turned her out and that she had lost two coppers in consequence. The children and the coppers, the coppers and the children, were mingled together in an utterly incomprehensible muddle, from which every one withdrew baffled, after vain efforts to understand. But the woman would not desist, she kept wailing, shouting, and waving her arms, seeming to pay no attention either to the fire up to which she had been carried by the crowd from the street or to the people about her, or to the misfortune of strangers, or even to the sparks and red-hot embers which were beginning to fall in showers on the crowd standing near. At last Mr. Prohartchin felt that a feeling of terror was coming upon him; for he saw clearly that all this was not, so to say, an accident, and that he would not get off scot-free. And, indeed, upon the woodstack, close to him, was a peasant, in a torn smock that hung loose about him, with his hair and beard singed, and he began stirring up all the people against Semyon Ivanovitch. The crowd pressed closer and closer, the peasant shouted, and foaming at the mouth with horror, Mr. Prohartchin suddenly realized that this peasant was a cabman whom he had cheated five years before in the most inhuman way, slipping away from him without paying through a side gate and jerking up his heels as he ran as though he were barefoot on hot bricks. In despair Mr. Prohartchin tried to speak, to scream, but his voice failed him. He felt that the infuriated crowd was twining round him like a many-coloured snake, strangling him, crushing him. He made an incredible effort and awoke. Then he saw that he was on fire, that all his corner was on fire, that his screen was on fire, that the whole flat was on fire, together with Ustinya Fyodorovna and all her lodgers, that his bed was burning, his pillow, his quilt, his box, and last of all, his precious mattress. Semyon Ivanovitch jumped up, clutched at the mattress and ran dragging it after him. But in the landlady's room into which, regardless of decorum, our hero ran just as he was, barefoot and in his shirt, he was seized, held tight, and triumphantly carried back behind the screen, which meanwhile was not on fire—it seemed that it was rather Semyon Ivanovitch's head that was on fire—and was put back to bed. It was just as some tattered, unshaven, ill-humoured organ-grinder puts away in his travelling box the Punch who has been making an upset, drubbing all the other puppets, selling his soul to the devil, and who at last ends his existence, till the next performance, in the same box with the devil, the negroes, the Pierrot, and Mademoiselle Katerina with her fortunate lover, the captain.

Immediately every one, old and young, surrounded Semyon Ivanovitch, standing in a row round his bed and fastening eyes full of expectation on the invalid. Meantime he had come to himself, but from shame or some other feeling, began pulling up the quilt over him, apparently wishing to hide himself under it from the attention of his sympathetic friends. At last Mark Ivanovitch was the first to break silence, and as a sensible man he began saying in a very friendly way that Semyon Ivanovitch must keep calm, that it was too bad and a shame to be ill, that only little children behaved like that, that he must get well and go to the office. Mark Ivanovitch ended by a little joke, saying that no regular salary had yet been fixed for invalids, and as he knew for a fact that their grade would be very low in the service, to his thinking anyway, their calling or condition did not promise great and substantial advantages. In fact, it was evident that they were all taking genuine interest in Semyon Ivanovitch's fate and were very sympathetic. But with incomprehensible rudeness, Semyon Ivanovitch persisted in lying in bed in silence, and obstinately pulling the quilt higher and higher over his head. Mark Ivanovitch, however, would not be gainsaid, and restraining his feelings, said something very honeyed to Semyon Ivanovitch again, knowing that that was how he ought to treat a sick man. But Semyon Ivanovitch would not feel this: on the contrary he muttered something between his teeth with the most distrustful air, and suddenly began glancing askance from right to left in a hostile way, as though he would have reduced his sympathetic friends to ashes with his eyes. It was no use letting it stop there. Mark Ivanovitch lost patience, and seeing that the man was offended and completely exasperated, and had simply made up his mind to be obstinate, told him straight out, without any softening suavity, that it was time to get up, that it was no use lying there, that shouting day and night about houses on fire, sisters-in-law, drunken cadgers, locks, boxes and goodness knows what, was all stupid, improper, and degrading, for if Semyon Ivanovitch did not want to sleep himself he should not hinder other people, and please would he bear it in mind.

This speech produced its effects, for Semyon Ivanovitch, turning promptly to the orator, articulated firmly, though in a hoarse voice, "You hold your tongue, puppy! You idle speaker, you foul-mouthed man! Do you hear, young dandy? Are you a prince, eh? Do you understand what I say?"

Hearing such insults, Mark Ivanovitch fired up, but realizing that he had to deal with a sick man, magnanimously overcame his resentment and tried to shame him out of his humour, but was cut short in that too; for Semyon Ivanovitch observed at once that he would not allow people to play with him for all that Mark Ivanovitch wrote poetry. Then followed a silence of two minutes; at last recovering from his amazement Mark Ivanovitch, plainly, clearly, in well-chosen language, but with firmness, declared that Semyon Ivanovitch ought to understand that he was among gentlemen, and "you ought to understand, sir, how to behave with gentlemen."

Mark Ivanovitch could on occasion speak effectively and liked to impress his hearers, but, probably from the habit of years of silence, Semyon Ivanovitch talked and acted somewhat abruptly; and, moreover, when he did on occasion begin a long sentence, as he got further into it every word seemed to lead to another word, that other word to a third word, that third to a fourth and so on, so that his mouth seemed brimming over; he began stuttering, and the crowding words took to flying out in picturesque disorder. That was why Semyon Ivanovitch, who was a sensible man, sometimes talked terrible nonsense. "You are lying," he said now. "You booby, you loose fellow! You'll come to want—you'll go begging, you seditious fellow, you—you loafer. Take that, you poet!"

"Why, you are still raving, aren't you, Semyon Ivanovitch?"

"I tell you what," answered Semyon Ivanovitch, "fools rave, drunkards rave, dogs rave, but a wise man acts sensibly. I tell you, you don't know your own business, you loafer, you educated gentleman, you learned book! Here, you'll get on fire and not notice your head's burning off. What do you think of that?"

"Why . . . you mean. . . . How do you mean, burn my head off, Semyon Ivanovitch?"

Mark Ivanovitch said no more, for every one saw clearly that Semyon Ivanovitch was not yet in his sober senses, but delirious.

But the landlady could not resist remarking at this point that the house in Crooked Lane had been burnt owing to a bald wench; that there was a bald-headed wench living there, that she had lighted a candle and set fire to the lumber room; but nothing would happen in her place, and everything would be all right in the flats.

"But look here, Semyon Ivanovitch," cried Zinovy Prokofyevitch, losing patience and interrupting the landlady, "you old fogey, you old crock, you silly fellow—are they making jokes with you now about your sister-in-law or examinations in dancing? Is that it? Is that what you think?"

"Now, I tell you what," answered our hero, sitting up in bed and making a last effort in a paroxysm of fury with his sympathetic friends. "Who's the fool? You are the fool, a dog is a fool, you joking gentleman. But I am not going to make jokes to please you, sir; do you hear, puppy? I am not your servant, sir."

Semyon Ivanovitch would have said something more, but he fell back in bed helpless. His sympathetic friends were left gaping in perplexity, for they understood now what was wrong with Semyon Ivanovitch and did not know how to begin. Suddenly the kitchen door creaked and opened, and the drunken cadger—alias Mr. Zimoveykin—timidly thrust in his head, cautiously sniffing round the place as his habit was. It seemed as though he had been expected, every one waved to him at once to come quickly, and Zimoveykin, highly delighted, with the utmost readiness and haste jostled his way to Semyon Ivanovitch's bedside.

It was evident that Zimoveykin had spent the whole night in vigil and in great exertions of some sort. The right side of his face was plastered up; his swollen eyelids were wet from his running eyes, his coat and all his clothes were torn, while the whole left side of his attire was bespattered with something extremely nasty, possibly mud from a puddle. Under his arm was somebody's violin, which he had been taking somewhere to sell. Apparently they had not made a mistake in summoning him to their assistance, for seeing the position of affairs, he addressed the delinquent at once, and with the air of a man who knows what he is about and feels that he has the upper hand, said: "What are you thinking about? Get up, Senka. What are you doing, a clever chap like you? Be sensible, or I shall pull you out of bed if you are obstreperous. Don't be obstreperous!"

This brief but forcible speech surprised them all; still more were they surprised when they noticed that Semyon Ivanovitch, hearing all this and seeing this person before him, was so flustered and reduced to such confusion and dismay that he could scarcely mutter through his teeth in a whisper the inevitable protest.

"Go away, you wretch," he said. "You are a wretched creature—you are a thief! Do you hear? Do you understand? You are a great swell, my fine gentleman, you regular swell."

"No, my boy," Zimoveykin answered emphatically, retaining all his presence of mind, "you're wrong there, you wise fellow, you regular Prohartchin," Zimoveykin went on, parodying Semyon Ivanovitch and looking round gleefully. "Don't be obstreperous! Behave yourself, Senka, behave yourself, or I'll give you away, I'll tell them all about it, my lad, do you understand?"

Apparently Semyon Ivanovitch did understand, for he started when he heard the conclusion of the speech, and began looking rapidly about him with an utterly desperate air.

Satisfied with the effect, Mr. Zimoveykin would have continued, but Mark Ivanovitch checked his zeal, and waiting till Semyon Ivanovitch was still and almost calm again began judiciously impressing on the uneasy invalid at great length that, "to harbour ideas such as he now had in his head was, first, useless, and secondly, not only useless, but harmful; and, in fact, not so much harmful as positively immoral; and the cause of it all was that Semyon Ivanovitch was not only a bad example, but led them all into temptation."

Every one expected satisfactory results from this speech. Moreover by now Semyon Ivanovitch was quite quiet and replied in measured terms. A quiet discussion followed. They appealed to him in a friendly way, inquiring what he was so frightened of. Semyon Ivanovitch answered, but his answers were irrelevant. They answered him, he answered them. There were one or two more observations on both sides and then every one rushed into discussion, for suddenly such a strange and amazing subject cropped up, that they did not know how to express themselves. The argument at last led to impatience, impatience led to shouting, and shouting even to tears; and Mark Ivanovitch went away at last foaming at the mouth and declaring that he had never known such a blockhead. Oplevaniev spat in disgust, Okeanov was frightened, Zinovy Prokofyevitch became tearful, while Ustinya Fyodorovna positively howled, wailing that her lodger was leaving them and had gone off his head, that he would die, poor dear man, without a passport and without telling any one, while she was a lone, lorn woman and that she would be dragged from pillar to post. In fact, they all saw clearly at last that the seed they had sown had yielded a hundred-fold, that the soil had been too productive, and that in their company, Semyon Ivanovitch had succeeded in overstraining his wits completely and in the most irrevocable manner. Every one subsided into silence, for though they saw that Semyon Ivanovitch was frightened, the sympathetic friends were frightened too.

"What?" cried Mark Ivanovitch; "but what are you afraid of? What have you gone off your head about? Who's thinking about you, my good sir? Have you the right to be afraid? Who are you? What are you? Nothing, sir. A round nought, sir, that is what you are. What are you making a fuss about? A woman has been run over in the street, so are you going to be run over? Some drunkard did not take care of his pocket, but is that any reason why your coat-tails should be cut off? A house is burnt down, so your head is to be burnt off, is it? Is that it, sir, is that it?"

"You . . . you . . . you stupid!" muttered Semyon Ivanovitch, "if your nose were cut off you would eat it up with a bit of bread and not notice it."

"I may be a dandy," shouted Mark Ivanovitch, not listening; "I may be a regular dandy, but I have not to pass an examination to get married—to learn dancing; the ground is firm under me, sir. Why, my good man, haven't you room enough? Is the floor giving way under your feet, or what?"

"Well, they won't ask you, will they? They'll shut one up and that will be the end of it?"

"The end of it? That's what's up? What's your idea now, eh?"

"Why, they kicked out the drunken cadger."

"Yes; but you see that was a drunkard, and you are a man, and so am I."

"Yes, I am a man. It's there all right one day and then it's gone."

"Gone! But what do you mean by it?"

"Why, the office! The off—off—ice!"

"Yes, you blessed man, but of course the office is wanted and necessary."

"It is wanted, I tell you; it's wanted to-day and it's wanted to-morrow, but the day after to-morrow it will not be wanted. You have heard what happened?"

"Why, but they'll pay you your salary for the year, you doubting Thomas, you man of little faith. They'll put you into another job on account of your age."

"Salary? But what if I have spent my salary, if thieves come and take my money? And I have a sister-in-law, do you hear? A sister-in-law! You battering-ram. . . . "

"A sister-in-law! You are a man. . . . "

"Yes, I am; I am a man. But you are a well-read gentleman and a fool, do you hear?—you battering-ram—you regular battering-ram! That's what you are! I am not talking about your jokes; but there are jobs such that all of a sudden they are done away with. And Demid—do you hear?—Demid Vassilyevitch says that the post will be done away with. . . . "

"Ah, bless you, with your Demid! You sinner, why, you know. . . . "

"In a twinkling of an eye you'll be left without a post, then you'll just have to make the best of it."

"Why, you are simply raving, or clean off your head! Tell us plainly, what have you done? Own up if you have done something wrong! It's no use being ashamed! Are you off your head, my good man, eh?"

"He's off his head! He's gone off his head!" they all cried, and wrung their hands in despair, while the landlady threw both her arms round Mark Ivanovitch for fear he should tear Semyon Ivanovitch to pieces.

"You heathen, you heathenish soul, you wise man!" Zimoveykin besought him. "Senka, you are not a man to take offence, you are a polite, prepossessing man. You are simple, you are good . . . do you hear? It all comes from your goodness. Here I am a ruffian and a fool, I am a beggar; but good people haven't abandoned me, no fear; you see they treat me with respect, I thank them and the landlady. Here, you see, I bow down to the ground to them; here, see, see, I am paying what is due to you, landlady!" At this point Zimoveykin swung off with pedantic dignity a low bow right down to the ground.

After that Semyon Ivanovitch would have gone on talking; but this time they would not let him, they all intervened, began entreating him, assuring him, comforting him, and succeeded in making Semyon Ivanovitch thoroughly ashamed of himself, and at last, in a faint voice, he asked leave to explain himself.

"Very well, then," he said, "I am prepossessing, I am quiet, I am good, faithful and devoted; to the last drop of my blood you know . . . do you hear, you puppy, you swell? . . . granted the job is going on, but you see I am poor. And what if they take it? do you hear, you swell? Hold your tongue and try to understand! They'll take it and that's all about it . . . it's going on, brother, and then not going on . . . do you understand? And I shall go begging my bread, do you hear?"

"Senka," Zimoveykin bawled frantically, drowning the general hubbub with his voice. "You are seditious! I'll inform against you! What are you saying? Who are you? Are you a rebel, you sheep's head? A rowdy, stupid man they would turn off without a character. But what are you?"

"Well, that's just it."

"What?"

"Well, there it is."

"How do you mean?"

"Why, I am free, he's free, and here one lies and thinks. . . . "

"What?"

"What if they say I'm seditious?"

"Se—di—tious? Senka, you seditious!"

"Stay," cried Mr. Prohartchin, waving his hand and interrupting the rising uproar, "that's not what I mean. Try to understand, only try to understand, you sheep. I am law-abiding. I am law-abiding to-day, I am law-abiding to-morrow, and then all of a sudden they kick me out and call me seditious."

"What are you saying?" Mark Ivanovitch thundered at last, jumping up from the chair on which he had sat down to rest, running up to the bed and in a frenzy shaking with vexation and fury. "What do you mean? You sheep! You've nothing to call your own. Why, are you the only person in the world? Was the world made for you, do you suppose? Are you a Napoleon? What are you? Who are you? Are you a Napoleon, eh? Tell me, are you a Napoleon?"

But Mr. Prohartchin did not answer this question. Not because he was overcome with shame at being a Napoleon, and was afraid of taking upon himself such a responsibility—no, he was incapable of disputing further, or saying anything. . . . His illness had reached a crisis. Tiny teardrops gushed suddenly from his glittering, feverish, grey eyes. He hid his burning head in his bony hands that were wasted by illness, sat up in bed, and sobbing, began to say that he was quite poor, that he was a simple, unlucky man, that he was foolish and unlearned, he begged kind folks to forgive him, to take care of him, to protect him, to give him food and drink, not to leave him in want, and goodness knows what else Semyon Ivanovitch said. As he uttered this appeal he looked about him in wild terror, as though he were expecting the ceiling to fall or the floor to give way. Every one felt his heart soften and move to pity as he looked at the poor fellow. The landlady, sobbing and wailing like a peasant woman at her forlorn condition, laid the invalid back in bed with her own hands. Mark Ivanovitch, seeing the uselessness of touching upon the memory of Napoleon, instantly relapsed into kindliness and came to her assistance. The others, in order to do something, suggested raspberry tea, saying that it always did good at once and that the invalid would like it very much; but Zimoveykin contradicted them all, saying there was nothing better than a good dose of camomile or something of the sort. As for Zinovy Prokofyevitch, having a good heart, he sobbed and shed tears in his remorse, for having frightened Semyon Ivanovitch with all sorts of absurdities, and gathering from the invalid's last words that he was quite poor and needing assistance, he proceeded to get up a subscription for him, confining it for a time to the tenants of the flat. Every one was sighing and moaning, every one felt sorry and grieved, and yet all wondered how it was a man could be so completely panic-stricken. And what was he frightened about? It would have been all very well if he had had a good post, had had a wife, a lot of children; it would have been excusable if he were being hauled up before the court on some charge or other; but he was a man utterly insignificant, with nothing but a trunk and a German lock; he had been lying more than twenty years behind his screen, saying nothing, knowing nothing of the world nor of trouble, saving his half-pence, and now at a frivolous, idle word the man had actually gone off his head, was utterly panic-stricken at the thought he might have a hard time of it. . . . And it never occurred to him that every one has a hard time of it! "If he would only take that into consideration," Okeanov said afterwards, "that we all have a hard time, then the man would have kept his head, would have given up his antics and would have put up with things, one way or another."

All day long nothing was talked of but Semyon Ivanovitch. They went up to him, inquired after him, tried to comfort him; but by the evening he was beyond that. The poor fellow began to be delirious, feverish. He sank into unconsciousness, so that they almost thought of sending for a doctor; the lodgers all agreed together and undertook to watch over Semyon Ivanovitch and soothe him by turns through the night, and if anything happened to wake all the rest immediately. With the object of keeping awake, they sat down to cards, setting beside the invalid his friend, the drunken cadger, who had spent the whole day in the flat and had asked leave to stay the night. As the game was played on credit and was not at all interesting they soon got bored. They gave up the game, then got into an argument about something, then began to be loud and noisy, finally dispersed to their various corners, went on for a long time angrily shouting and wrangling, and as all of them felt suddenly ill-humoured they no longer cared to sit up, so went to sleep. Soon it was as still in the flat as in an empty cellar, and it was the more like one because it was horribly cold. The last to fall asleep was Okeanov. "And it was between sleeping and waking," as he said afterwards, "I fancied just before morning two men kept talking close by me." Okeanov said that he recognized Zimoveykin, and that Zimoveykin began waking his old friend Remnev just beside him, that they talked for a long time in a whisper; then Zimoveykin went away and could be heard trying to unlock the door into the kitchen. The key, the landlady declared afterwards, was lying under her pillow and was lost that night. Finally—Okeanov testified—he had fancied he had heard them go behind the screen to the invalid and light a candle there, "and I know nothing more," he said, "I fell asleep, and woke up," as everybody else did, when every one in the flat jumped out of bed at the sound behind the screen of a shriek that would have roused the dead, and it seemed to many of them that a candle went out at that moment. A great hubbub arose, every one's heart stood still; they rushed pell-mell at the shriek, but at that moment there was a scuffle, with shouting, swearing, and fighting. They struck a light and saw that Zimoveykin and Remnev were fighting together, that they were swearing and abusing one another, and as they turned the light on them, one of them shouted: "It's not me, it's this ruffian," and the other who was Zimoveykin, was shouting: "Don't touch me, I've done nothing! I'll take my oath any minute!" Both of them looked hardly like human beings; but for the first minute they had no attention to spare for them; the invalid was not where he had been behind the screen. They immediately parted the combatants and dragged them away, and saw that Mr. Prohartchin was lying under the bed; he must, while completely unconscious, have dragged the quilt and pillow after him so that there was nothing left on the bedstead but the bare mattress, old and greasy (he never had sheets). They pulled Semyon Ivanovitch out, stretched him on the mattress, but soon realized that there was no need to make trouble over him, that he was completely done for; his arms were stiff, and he seemed all to pieces. They stood over him, he still faintly shuddered and trembled all over, made an effort to do something with his arms, could not utter a word, but blinked his eyes as they say heads do when still warm and bleeding, after being just chopped off by the executioner.

At last the body grew more and more still; the last faint convulsions died away. Mr. Prohartchin had set off with his good deeds and his sins. Whether Semyon Ivanovitch had been frightened by something, whether he had had a dream, as Remnev maintained afterwards, or there had been some other mischief—nobody knew; all that can be said is, that if the head clerk had made his appearance at that moment in the flat and had announced that Semyon Ivanovitch was dismissed for sedition, insubordination, and drunkenness; if some old draggle-tailed beggar woman had come in at the door, calling herself Semyon Ivanovitch's sister-in-law; or if Semyon Ivanovitch had just received two hundred roubles as a reward; or if the house had caught fire and Semyon Ivanovitch's head had been really burning—he would in all probability not have deigned to stir a finger in any of these eventualities. While the first stupefaction was passing over, while all present were regaining their powers of speech, were working themselves up into a fever of excitement, shouting and flying to conjectures and suppositions; while Ustinya Fyodorovna was pulling the box from under his bed, was rummaging in a fluster under the mattress and even in Semyon Ivanovitch's boots; while they cross-questioned Remnev and Zimoveykin, Okeanov, who had hitherto been the quietest, humblest, and least original of the lodgers, suddenly plucked up all his presence of mind and displayed all his latent talents, by taking up his hat and under cover of the general uproar slipping out of the flat. And just when the horrors of disorder and anarchy had reached their height in the agitated flat, till then so tranquil, the door opened and suddenly there descended upon them, like snow upon their heads, a personage of gentlemanly appearance, with a severe and displeased-looking face, behind him Yaroslav Ilyitch, behind Yaroslav Ilyitch his subordinates and the functionaries whose duty it is to be present on such occasions, and behind them all, much embarrassed, Mr. Okeanov. The severe-looking personage of gentlemanly appearance went straight up to Semyon Ivanovitch, examined him, made a wry face, shrugged his shoulders and announced what everybody knew, that is, that the dead man was dead, only adding that the same thing had happened a day or two ago to a gentleman of consequence, highly respected, who had died suddenly in his sleep. Then the personage of gentlemanly, but displeased-looking, appearance walked away saying that they had troubled him for nothing, and took himself off. His place was at once filled (while Remnev and Zimoveykin were handed over to the custody of the proper functionaries), by Yaroslav Ilyitch, who questioned some one, adroitly took possession of the box, which the landlady was already trying to open, put the boots back in their proper place, observing that they were all in holes and no use, asked for the pillow to be put back, called up Okeanov, asked for the key of the box which was found in the pocket of the drunken cadger, and solemnly, in the presence of the proper officials, unlocked Semyon Ivanovitch's property. Everything was displayed: two rags, a pair of socks, half a handkerchief, an old hat, several buttons, some old soles, and the uppers of a pair of boots, that is, all sorts of odds and ends, scraps, rubbish, trash, which had a stale smell. The only thing of any value was the German lock. They called up Okeanov and cross-questioned him sternly; but Okeanov was ready to take his oath. They asked for the pillow, they examined it; it was extremely dirty, but in other respects it was like all other pillows. They attacked the mattress, they were about to lift it up, but stopped for a moment's consideration, when suddenly and quite unexpectedly something heavy fell with a clink on the floor. They bent down and saw on the floor a screw of paper and in the screw some dozen roubles. "A-hey!" said Yaroslav Ilyitch, pointing to a slit in the mattress from which hair and stuffing were sticking out. They examined the slit and found that it had only just been made with a knife and was half a yard in length; they thrust hands into the gap and pulled out a kitchen knife, probably hurriedly thrust in there after slitting the mattress. Before Yaroslav Ilyitch had time to pull the knife out of the slit and to say "A-hey!" again, another screw of money fell out, and after it, one at a time, two half roubles, a quarter rouble, then some small change, and an old-fashioned, solid five-kopeck piece—all this was seized upon. At this point it was realized that it would not be amiss to cut up the whole mattress with scissors. They asked for scissors.

Meanwhile, the guttering candle lighted up a scene that would have been extremely curious to a spectator. About a dozen lodgers were grouped round the bed in the most picturesque costumes, all unbrushed, unshaven, unwashed, sleepy-looking, just as they had gone to bed. Some were quite pale, while others had drops of sweat upon their brows: some were shuddering, while others looked feverish. The landlady, utterly stupefied, was standing quietly with her hands folded waiting for Yaroslav Ilyitch's good pleasure. From the stove above, the heads of Avdotya, the servant, and the landlady's favourite cat looked down with frightened curiosity. The torn and broken screen lay cast on the floor, the open box displayed its uninviting contents, the quilt and pillow lay tossed at random, covered with fluff from the mattress, and on the three-legged wooden table gleamed the steadily growing heap of silver and other coins. Only Semyon Ivanovitch preserved his composure, lying calmly on the bed and seeming to have no foreboding of his ruin. When the scissors had been brought and Yaroslav Ilyitch's assistant, wishing to be of service, shook the mattress rather impatiently to ease it from under the back of its owner, Semyon Ivanovitch with his habitual civility made room a little, rolling on his side with his back to the searchers; then at a second shake he turned on his face, finally gave way still further, and as the last slat in the bedstead was missing, he suddenly and quite unexpectedly plunged head downward, leaving in view only two bony, thin, blue legs, which stuck upwards like two branches of a charred tree. As this was the second time that morning that Mr. Prohartchin had poked his head under his bed it at once aroused suspicion, and some of the lodgers, headed by Zinovy Prokofyevitch, crept under it, with the intention of seeing whether there were something hidden there too. But they knocked their heads together for nothing, and as Yaroslav Ilyitch shouted to them, bidding them release Semyon Ivanovitch at once from his unpleasant position, two of the more sensible seized each a leg, dragged the unsuspected capitalist into the light of day and laid him across the bed. Meanwhile the hair and flock were flying about, the heap of silver grew— and, my goodness, what a lot there was! . . . Noble silver roubles, stout solid rouble and a half pieces, pretty half rouble coins, plebeian quarter roubles, twenty kopeck pieces, even the unpromising old crone's small fry of ten and five kopeck silver pieces—all done up in separate bits of paper in the most methodical and systematic way; there were curiosities also, two counters of some sort, one napoléon d'or, one very rare coin of some unknown kind. . . . Some of the roubles were of the greatest antiquity, they were rubbed and hacked coins of Elizabeth, German kreutzers, coins of Peter, of Catherine; there were, for instance, old fifteen-kopeck pieces, now very rare, pierced for wearing as earrings, all much worn, yet with the requisite number of dots . . . there was even copper, but all of that was green and tarnished. . . . They found one red note, but no more. At last, when the dissection was quite over and the mattress case had been shaken more than once without a clink, they piled all the money on the table and set to work to count it. At the first glance one might well have been deceived and have estimated it at a million, it was such an immense heap. But it was not a million, though it did turn out to be a very considerable sum—exactly 2497 roubles and a half—so that if Zinovy Prokofyevitch's subscription had been raised the day before there would perhaps have been just 2500 roubles. They took the money, they put a seal on the dead man's box, they listened to the landlady's complaints, and informed her when and where she ought to lodge information in regard to the dead man's little debt to her. A receipt was taken from the proper person. At that point hints were dropped in regard to the sister-in-law; but being persuaded that in a certain sense the sister-in-law was a myth, that is, a product of the defective imagination with which they had more than once reproached Semyon Ivanovitch—they abandoned the idea as useless, mischievous and disadvantageous to the good name of Mr. Prohartchin, and so the matter ended.

When the first shock was over, when the lodgers had recovered themselves and realized the sort of person their late companion had been, they all subsided, relapsed into silence and began looking distrustfully at one another. Some seemed to take Semyon Ivanovitch's behaviour very much to heart, and even to feel affronted by it. What a fortune! So the man had saved up like this! Not losing his composure, Mark Ivanovitch proceeded to explain why Semyon Ivanovitch had been so suddenly panic-stricken; but they did not listen to him. Zinovy Prokofyevitch was very thoughtful, Okeanov had had a little to drink, the others seemed rather crestfallen, while a little man called Kantarev, with a nose like a sparrow's beak, left the flat that evening after very carefully packing up and cording all his boxes and bags, and coldly explaining to the curious that times were hard and that the terms here were beyond his means. The landlady wailed without ceasing, lamenting for Semyon Ivanovitch, and cursing him for having taken advantage of her lone, lorn state. Mark Ivanovitch was asked why the dead man had not taken his money to the bank. "He was too simple, my good soul, he hadn't enough imagination," answered Mark Ivanovitch.

"Yes, and you have been too simple, too, my good woman," Okeanov put in. "For twenty years the man kept himself close here in your flat, and here he's been knocked down by a feather—while you went on cooking cabbage-soup and had no time to notice it. . . . Ah-ah, my good woman!"

"Oh, the poor dear," the landlady went on, "what need of a bank! If he'd brought me his pile and said to me: 'Take it, Ustinyushka, poor dear, here is all I have, keep and board me in my helplessness, so long as I am on earth,' then, by the holy ikon I would have fed him, I would have given him drink, I would have looked after him. Ah, the sinner! ah, the deceiver! He deceived me, he cheated me, a poor lone woman!"

They went up to the bed again. Semyon Ivanovitch was lying properly now, dressed in his best, though, indeed, it was his only suit, hiding his rigid chin behind a cravat which was tied rather awkwardly, washed, brushed, but not quite shaven, because there was no razor in the flat; the only one, which had belonged to Zinovy Prokofyevitch, had lost its edge a year ago and had been very profitably sold at Tolkutchy Market; the others used to go to the barber's.

They had not yet had time to clear up the disorder. The broken screen lay as before, and exposing Semyon Ivanovitch's seclusion, seemed like an emblem of the fact that death tears away the veil from all our secrets, our shifty dodges and intrigues. The stuffing from the mattress lay about in heaps. The whole room, suddenly so still, might well have been compared by a poet to the ruined nest of a swallow, broken down and torn to pieces by the storm, the nestlings and their mother killed, and their warm little bed of fluff, feather and flock scattered about them. . . . Semyon Ivanovitch, however, looked more like a conceited, thievish old cock-sparrow. He kept quite quiet now, seemed to be lying low, as though he were not guilty, as though he had had nothing to do with the shameless, conscienceless, and unseemly duping and deception of all these good people. He did not heed now the sobs and wailing of his bereaved and wounded landlady. On the contrary, like a wary, callous capitalist, anxious not to waste a minute in idleness even in the coffin, he seemed to be wrapped up in some speculative calculation. There was a look of deep reflection in his face, while his lips were drawn together with a significant air, of which Semyon Ivanovitch during his lifetime had not been suspected of being capable. He seemed, as it were, to have grown shrewder, his right eye was, as it were, slyly screwed up. Semyon Ivanovitch seemed wanting to say something, to make some very important communication and explanation and without loss of time, because things were complicated and there was not a minute to lose. . . . And it seemed as though they could hear him.

"What is it? Give over, do you hear, you stupid woman? Don't whine! Go to bed and sleep it off, my good woman, do you hear? I am dead; there's no need of a fuss now. What's the use of it, really? It's nice to lie here. . . . Though I don't mean that, do you hear? You are a fine lady, you are a regular fine lady. Understand that; here I am dead now, but look here, what if—that is, perhaps it can't be so—but I say what if I'm not dead, what if I get up, do you hear? What would happen then?"

SELECTED LETTERS

Translated by
S. S. Koteliansky and J. Middleton Murry

SELECTED LETTERS

Translated by
S. S. Koteliansky and J. Middleton Murry

LETTER TO HIS BROTHER

The following is the full text of Dostoevsky's letter, written on the day he was sentenced to death, December 22, 1849, to his brother Mihail. Only the first paragraph of the letter has been published before. It is now published in full for the first time. It is a document of exceptional importance.

The original letter cannot now be traced. But a copy of it, made by Madame Dostoevsky, is now kept in the Central Archives. It has now been made public.

Mihail Dostoevsky was, after all, allowed to see Fiodor before his departure for Siberia. In his *Reminiscences* (1881), A. P. Miliukov relates that Fiodor said to his brother at parting:

"During these three months I have gone through much; I mean, I have gone through much in myself; and now there are the things I am going to see and go through. There will be much to be written."

The Peter and Paul Fortress,
December 22, 1849.

MlHAIL MlHAILOVICH DOSTOEVSKY,

Nevsky Prospect, opposite Gryazny Street,
in the house of Neslind.

Brother, my precious friend! all is settled! I am sentenced to four years' hard labour in the fortress (I believe, of Orenburg) and after that to serve as a private. To-day, the 22nd of December, we were taken to the Semionov Drill Ground. There the sentence of death was read to all of us, we were told to kiss the Cross, our swords were broken over our heads, and our last toilet was made (white shirts). Then three were tied to the pillar for execution. I was the sixth. Three at a time were called out; consequently, I was in the second batch and no more than a minute was left me to live. I remembered you, brother, and all yours; during the last minute you, you alone, were in my mind, only then I realised how I love you, dear brother mine! I also managed to embrace Plescheyev and Durov who stood close to me and to say good-bye to them. Finally the retreat was sounded, and those tied to the pillar were led back, and it was announced to us that His Imperial Majesty granted us our lives. Then followed the present sentences. Palm alone has been pardoned, and returns with his old rank to the army.

I was just told, dear brother, that to-day or to-morrow we are to be sent off. I asked to see you. But I was told that this was impossible; I may only write you this letter: make haste and give me a reply as soon as you can. I am afraid that you may somehow have got to know of our death-sentence. From the windows of the prison-van, when we were taken to the Semionov Drill Ground, I saw a multitude of people; perhaps the news reached you, and you suffered for me. Now you will be easier on my account. Brother! I have not become downhearted or low-spirited. Life is everywhere life, life in ourselves, not in what is outside us. There will be people near me, and to be a *man* among people and remain a man for ever, not to be downhearted nor to fall in whatever misfortunes may befall me—this is life; this is the task of life. I have realised this. This idea has entered into my flesh and into my blood. Yes, it's true! The head which was creating, living with the highest life of art, which had realised and grown used to the highest needs of the spirit, that head has already been cut off from my shoulders. There remain the memory and the images created but not yet incarnated by me. They will lacerate me, it is true! But there remains in me my heart and the same flesh and blood which can also love, and suffer, and desire, and remember, and this, after all, is life. *On voit le soleil!* Now, good-bye, brother! Don't grieve for me!

    Now about material things: my books (I have the Bible still) and several sheets of my manuscript, the rough plan of the play and the novel (and the finished story *A Child's Tale*) have been taken away from me, and in all probability will be got by you. I also leave my overcoat and old clothes, if you send to fetch them. Now, brother, I may perhaps have to march a long distance. Money is needed. My dear brother, when you receive this letter, and if there is any possibility of getting some money, send it me at once. Money I need now more than air (for one particular purpose). Send me also a few lines. Then if the money from Moscow comes,—remember me and do not desert me. Well, that is all! I have debts,* but what can I do?

    Kiss your wife and children. Remind them of me continually; see that they do not forget me.

    Perhaps, we shall yet meet some time! Brother, take care of yourself and of your family, live quietly and carefully. Think of the future of yoi children.... Live positively. There has nevei yet been working in me such a healthy abundance of spiritual life as now. But will my body endure?

---

* Money owed by Dostoevsky to Krajevsky was paid by *A Child's Talc*.

I do not know. I am going away sick, I suffer from scrofula. But never mind! Brother, I have already gone through so much in life that now hardly anything can frighten me. Let come what may! At the first opportunity I shall let you know about myself. Give the Maikovs my farewell and last greetings. Tell them that I thank them all for their constant interest in my fate. Say a few words for me, as warm as possible, as your heart will prompt you, to Eugenia Petrovna.* I wish her much happiness, and shall ever remember her with grateful respect. Press the hands of Nikolay Apollonovich† and Apollon Maikov, and also of all the others. Find Yanovsky. Press his hand, thank him. Finally, press the hands of all who have not forgotten me. And those who have forgotten me—remember me to them also. Kiss our brother Kolya. Write a letter to our brother Andrey and let him know about me. Write also to Uncle and Aunt. This I ask you in my own name, and greet them for me. Write to our sisters: I wish them happiness.

And maybe, we shall meet again some time, brother! Take care of yourself, go on living, for the love of God, until we meet. Perhaps some time we shall embrace each other and recall our youth, our golden time that was, our youth and our hopes, which at this very instant I am tearing out from my heart with my blood, to bury them.

Can it indeed be that I shall never take a pen into my hands? I think that after the four years there may be a possibility. I shall send you everything that I may write, if I write anything, my God! How many imaginations, lived through by me, created by me anew, will perish, will be extinguished in my brain or will be spilt as poison in my blood! Yes, if I am not allowed to write, I shall perish. Better fifteen years of prison with a pen in my hands!

Write to me more often, write more details, more, more facts. In every letter write about all kinds of family details, of trifles, don't forget. This will give me hope and life. If you knew how your letters revived me here in the fortress. These last two months and a half, when it was forbidden to write or receive a letter, have been very hard on me. I was ill. The fact that you did not send me money now and then worried me on your account; it meant

---

* Eugenia Petrovna was the mother of the poet Apollon Maikov, Dostoevsky'a friend.
† N. A. Maikov, the father of A. N. Maikov.

you yourself were in great need! Kiss the children once again; their lovely little faces do not leave my mind. Ah, that they may be happy! Be happy yourself too, brother, be happy!

But do not grieve, for the love of God, do not grieve for me! Do believe that I am not downhearted, do remember that hope has not deserted me. In four years there will be a mitigation of my fate. I shall be a private soldier,—no longer a prisoner, and remember that some time I shall embrace you. I was to-day in the grip of death for three-quarters of an hour; I have lived it through with that idea; I was at the last instant and now I live again!

If any one has bad memories of me, if I have quarrelled with any one, if I have created in any one an unpleasant impression—tell them they should forget it, if you manage to meet them. There is no gall or spite in my soul; I should dearly love to embrace any one of my former friends at this moment. It is a comfort, I experienced it to-day when saying good-bye to my dear ones before death. I thought at that moment that the news of the execution would kill you. But now be easy, I am still alive and shall live in the future with the thought that some time I shall embrace you. Only this is now in my mind.

What are you doing? What have you been thinking to-day? Do you know about us? How cold it was to-day!

Ah, if only my letter reaches you soon. Otherwise I shall be for four months without news of you. I saw the envelopes in which you sent money during the last two months; the address was written in your hand, and I was glad that you were well.

When I look back at the past and think how much time has been wasted in vain, how much time was lost in delusions, in errors, in idleness, in ignorance of how to live, how I did not value time, how often I sinned against my heart and spirit,—my heart bleeds. Life is a gift, life is happiness, each minute might have been an age of happiness. *Si jeunesse savait!* Now, changing my life, I am being reborn into a new form. Brother! I swear to you that I shall not lose hope, and shall preserve my spirit and heart in purity. I shall be reborn to a better thing. That is my whole hope, my whole comfort!

The life in prison has already sufficiently killed in me the demands of the flesh which were not wholly pure; I took little heed of myself before. Now privations are nothing to me, and, therefore, do not fear that any material hardship will kill me. This cannot be! Ah! To have health!

Good-bye, good-bye, my brother! When shall I write you again? You will receive from me as detailed an account as possible of my journey. If I can only preserve my health, then everything will be right!

Well, good-bye, good-bye, brother! I embrace you closely, I kiss you closely. Remember me without pain in your heart. Do not grieve, I pray you, do not grieve for me! In the next letter I shall tell you how I go on. Remember then what I have told you: plan out your life, do not waste it, arrange your destiny, think of your children. Oh, to see you, to see you! Good-bye! Now I tear myself away from everything that was dear; it is painful to leave it! It is painful to break oneself in two, to cut the heart in two. Good-bye! Good-bye! But I shall see you, I am convinced—I hope; do not change, love me, do not let your memory grow cold, and the thought of your love will be the best part of my life. Good-bye, good-bye, once more! Good-bye to all!

Your brother Fiodor Dostoevsky.

Dec. 22, 1849.

At my arrest several books were taken away from me. Only two of them were prohibited books. Won't you get the rest for yourself? But there is this request: one of the books was The Work of Valerian Maikov: his critical essays—Eugenia Petrovna's copy. It was her treasure, and she lent it me. At my arrest I asked the police officer to return that book to her, and gave him the address. I do not know if he returned it to her. Make enquiries! I do not want to take this memory away from her. Good-bye, good-bye, once more!

Your F. Dostoevsky.

On the margins:

I do not know if I shall have to march or go on horses. I believe I shall go on horses. Perhaps!

Once again press Emily Fiodorovna's hand, kiss the little ones. Remember me to Krayevsky: perhaps . . .

Write me more particularly about your arrest, confinement, and liberation.

LETTERS TO A. N. MAIKOV

The eight hitherto unpublished letters written by F. M. Dostoevsky to A. N. Maikov are taken from the originals kept in the Poushkin Department of the Russian Academy of Sciences in Petersburg. These letters are preserved there, together with Dostoevsky's other letters to Maikov which have already been published.

The letters here published are of great interest, chiefly owing to their outspoken tone, but also as containing many facts bearing on Dostoevsky's life abroad during the period 1867–1871.

Maikov was a great friend of Dostoevsky's, and their friendship, which dated from before 1848, was the greater because of the affinity of their political views.

Owing to that affinity 'the friends understood each other from their letters, just as well as by personal contact.' That is why the letters have a special significance. Furthermore, they contain Dostoevsky's most intimate convictions and utterances about Russia and the Russian people, his prognostications of the future destinies of Russia, and his opinions about the 'disintegrated' West.

These letters also tell the history of Dostoevsky's creation of *The Idiot*, and the author's own opinion of that work; they afford a clear and concise explanation of the idea of *The Devils* (called *The Possessed* in the English translation); they contain Dostoevsky's account of the psychology of his creative activity; they also include his literary judgments and opinions of certain writers, such as Leo Tolstoy, Turgenev, Schedrin, and Danilevsky.

I

To A. N. Maikov

Geneva, January 12th, 1868.
December 31st, 1867.

My dear and good friend, Apollon Nicolayevich, the time has come, at last, when I can write you a couple of pages! What have you thought of me? That I have forgotten you? I know you won't think that. Believe me: *I have not had a single hour* of time; I mean literally. I have forgotten all. What is my poor Pasha* doing; to whom I have sent no money now for two months? (I have not had, literally, a farthing *to send him*!) I write to you and shall describe everything, and shall await your answer with morbid impatience. Being in the dark is killing me.

And as for me, this is my story: *I worked and was tortured.* You know what it means to *compose*? No, thank God, you do not know! I believe you have never written to order, by the yard, and have never experienced that hellish *torture*.—Having received in advance from the *Russky Viesinik* so much money (Horror! 4500 roubles), I fully hoped in the beginning of the year that poesy would not desert me, that the poetical idea would flash out and develop artistically towards the end of the year, and that I should succeed in satisfying every one.

---

* Dostoevsky's stepson, Pavel Alexandrovich Isayev, the son of hie first wife by her first marriage.

Moreover, this seemed to me the more likely inasmuch as many creative ideas are always flashing through my brain and my soul, and being conceived. But then these are only flashes, and they need a complete realisation, which invariably comes unexpectedly and all of a sudden. It is impossible, however, to calculate when it is going to come. Only afterwards when one has received a complete image in one's heart can one start artistic composition. And then one may even calculate without mistake. Well: all through the summer and all through the autumn I selected various ideas (some of them most ingenious), but my experience enabled me always to feel beforehand the falsity, difficulty, or ephemerality of this or that idea. At last I fixed on one and began working, I wrote a great deal; but on the 4th of December (new style) I threw it all to the devil. I assure you that the novel might have been tolerable; but I got incredibly sick of it just because it was tolerable, and not *positively good*. I did not want that. Well, what was I to do? The 4th of December! And meanwhile the conditions of our existence can be described as follows.

Did I tell you, I don't remember (indeed, I remember nothing), that, finally, when all my means had come to an end, I wrote to Katkov* asking him to send me one hundred roubles a month? I believe I did tell you. He agreed and began sending punctually. But in my letter to Katkov, thanking him, I confirmed positively, on my honour, the assurance I had given him that he should have the novel, and that in December I would send a considerable part of it to the office. (I promised the more readily, because the writing had gone well and so much had been written!) After that I wrote to him saying that my expenses were extra-ordinary and asking whether he could send me out of the agreed sum (500 roubles) one instalment of 200 instead of 100 (for December). His consent and the money came in December, just at the moment when I had destroyed the novel. What was I to do? All my hopes were shattered. (I had realised at last that all my real hopes are set on my work and writing novels, that, were I to write a decent novel, I could pay off my debt to the Editor, and to you, send a biggish sum to Pasha and to Emily Fiodorovna,† and myself be able to live. Were I, however, to write a really good novel,—I could sell the book-rights and

---

* Editor and publisher of the monthly review *Russkp Viestnik*.
† The widow of Dostoevsky's brother, Mihail Mihailovich.

manage to get some money, pay half or two-thirds of my debts and return to Petersburg.) But everything went smash. On receiving the 200 roubles from Katkov, I confirmed my promise that the novel would arrive without fail in time for the January number; I regretted that theirs* part would reach the editorial office late. But I promised it without fail for January 1st (old style), and I begged him not to bring out the January number of the Russky Viestnik without my novel (as the review never comes out before the middle of the month).

After that (since all my future turned on this) I began tormenting myself with thinking out a new novel. The old one I would not go on with for the world. I could not. I thought from the 4th till the 18th December (old style) inclusive. On the average, I fancy I turned out six plans (at least six) every day. My head became a mill. How it was I didn't go off my head, I don't understand. At last on December 18th I sat down to write the new novel; on the 5th January (new style) I sent off to the Editor five chapters of Part I (about five printed sheets) with a letter in which I promised to send the remaining two chapters of Part I on January 10th (new style). Yesterday, the 11th, I despatched those two chapters and so have delivered the whole of Part I,—about six or six and a half printed sheets.

The first parcel they ought to have received before December 30th (old style), and the second they will get by January 4th; consequently, if they like they can still publish Part I in the January number. Part II (of which of course I have not yet written a line) I gave my word to send to the Editor by February 1st (old style), punctually and unfailingly.

Do understand, my friend; how could I have thought of writing letters to any one, and there is the further question, what could I have written about? And therefore, like the humane man you are, understand, and, as a friend, forgive me my enforced silence. Besides, the time itself was a very hard one.

Now about the novel, so as to make an end of that. In the main I myself cannot tell what the thing I sent off is like. But as far as I can form an opinion—it is not very ship-shape and not at all effective. I have long been troubled by a certain idea, but I have been afraid to make a novel of it; for the idea is too difficult, and I am not ready for it, although the idea is perfectly alluring and I love it. That idea is—to depict a thoroughly good man. In my opinion, there can be nothing more difficult than this, above all in our time. Certainly you will absolutely agree with this. At one time this assumed a partial creative form; but only a partial one, when a complete one was needed. My desperate position alone compelled me to make use of this abortive idea. I took my chance as at roulette: 'Perhaps the idea will develop under the pen!' That is unpardonable.

On the whole the plan has been created. Details occur in the subsequent development, which tempt me very much and keep up the ardour in me. But the whole? But the hero? For the whole turns on the figure of the hero. So it has posited itself. I am obliged to posit a figure. Will it develop under the pen? And imagine what horrors presented themselves: it turned out that besides the hero there was also a heroine, consequently two heroes! And apart from these heroes there are two more characters—absolutely front-rank characters—that is to say, nearly heroes. (Sub-sidiary characters, to whom I am greatly in debt—a great multitude; besides, the novel is in eight parts.) Out of the four heroes—two are firmly outlined in my soul, one is not yet outlined at all, and the fourth, the principal, the first—is extra-ordinarily faint. Perhaps in my heart he dwells firmly enough; but—he is terribly difficult. At any rate I should need twice as much time (this is a minimum) in order to write it.

The first part, in my opinion, is weak. But it seems to me there is still hope for it: the hope is in this, that nothing is yet compromised and that the subsequent parts are capable of satisfactory development. (At least I hope they are!) Part I is, essentially, a mere introduction. One thing is necessary: that it should arouse a certain curiosity about what is going to follow. But of this I positively can't judge. I have one reader only—Anna Gregorevna [Dostoevsky's wife]; she likes it very much; but she is no judge in my business.

In Part II everything must be definitely posited (but still far from being explained). Then there will be one scene (one of the vital ones), but how is it going to turn out? Yet I have it written in the rough, and well.

On the whole all this is still in the future; but from you I expect a strict judgment. Part II will decide everything: it is the most difficult; but write to me also about the first part (although I know in my heart that it is not good, write to me nevertheless). Besides, I implore you, let me know immediately the Russky Viestnik is out—whether my novel is published there? I am still terribly afraid it may have arrived too late. And that it should appear in January is to me of the utmost necessity. Let me know, for the love of God, let me know instantly, even if you send only two lines.

When I sent Katkov Part I, I told him almost exactly the same as I have told you about my novel. The novel is called The Idiot, Yet no man can judge himself, especially when he is hot from the work. Perhaps Part I also is not so bad. If I have not developed the principal character, this was necessary by the laws of my whole scheme. That is why I await your opinion with such eager impatience. But enough about the novel. All the work I have done since the 18th of December has put me into such a fever that I can neither think nor speak of anything else. Now I'll say a few words about our life here from the time I left off writing to you.

My life certainly is work. But we have this to the good that, thanks to the monthly receipt of a hundred roubles, we are in want of nothing. Anna Gregorevna and I live modestly, but quite comfortably. But expenses are impending and a small sum, if only a very small one, must always be kept in reserve. In a month and a half Anna Gregorevna (who bears up excellently) is going to make me a father. You realise what expenses are impending. But during that period I shall ask for 200 roubles per month, and the Editor will send it. I have already sent him the equivalent of nearly a thousand roubles. And by February 5th I shall have sent the equivalent of another 1000 (and perhaps better stuff, more solid, more effective); consequently I am entitled to ask for a somewhat larger sum. By the way, my dear fellow, but for the destruction of the novel, I could certainly have paid you what you lent me by the New Year. But now I ask you to wait another couple of months; for I can't ask the Editor for a considerable sum until I have delivered Part II. But then I will pay you without fail. But my chief, but my most terrible obsession is the thought of what is happening to Pasha? My heart bleeds and the thought of him, added to all my literary torments in December, drove me simply to despair! What is he doing? In November and in December I sent him no money; but even before November he had left off writing to me. With the last allowance I made to him (60 roubles from Katkov), sent through you, I wrote him a long letter, and also asked him to make an inquiry, very important to me, and quite easy for him. I implored him to answer me. Not a single line from him. For the love of God, do give me some news of him. Does he hate me, does he? What for, why? Is it because I strained my resources to the very utmost to send him money and wait with burning impatience for the moment when I can send him more? It is impossible that he should hate me. I put it all down not to his heart, but to his lightmindedness and to his incapacity to make up his mind even to write a letter, just as he could not make up his mind to learn even the multiplication table till he was twenty.

He lived in the same house with Emily Fiodorovna and got into debt in spite of the fact that up to November I was sending him quite enough. It was through you that I paid that debt to Emily Fiodorovna. But how were they all in November and December? They themselves are in want. Fedya* works, but he can't keep them all, and I can't send any money for a month (through you, of course; I implore you, my dear friend, it is to you that the money from Katkov will come. Don't disdain my request and don't be annoyed with them. They are poor. And I will be your servant all my life long, I will prove to you how much I value what you have done for me). To-morrow I shall write to Fedya. Are they still living in Alonkin's house? I expressly asked Pasha to send me Alonkin's Christian name and his father's name (I forgot it) so that I could write to him. Alonkin trusts me, but he will turn them out of the flat, if he does not hear from me; since I had made myself responsible to him for it. Neither from Pasha, nor from Emily Fiodorovna have I had an answer about the man's Christian name and his father's name. And how can I write a letter to Alonkin without that? He is a merchant, he will be offended.

But perhaps I may be able to send them money before; although I am in awful need of money in expectation of my wife's confinement. Although we rub along without denying ourselves the prime necessities, yet our things are constantly being pawned. Every time I receive money I redeem them; but towards the end of the month we pawn them again. Anna Gregorevna is my true helper and comforter. Her love to me is boundless; although there is a great deal of difference in our characters. (She sends her best greetings to you and to Anna Ivanovna [Maikov's wife]. She loves you awfully because you value her mother, whom she adores. She values you both very highly, you and Anna Ivanovna, and esteems you deeply, with sincere, with the sincerest feeling.)

---

* Fiodor—Bon of Mihail Mihailovich, Dostoeveky's brother.

Above all we have suffered real discomfort in Geneva from the cold. Oh if you only knew, what a stupid, dull, insignificant, savage people it is! It is not enough to travel through as a tourist. No, try to live there for some time! But I can't describe to you now even briefly my impressions: I have accumulated too many. Bourgeois life in this vile republic has reached the nee plus ultra. In the administration, and all through the whole of Switzerland—there are parties and continuous squabbles, pauperism, terrible mediocrity in everything. A workman here is not worth the little finger of a workman of ours. It is ridiculous to see and to hear it all. The customs are savage; oh, if you only knew what they consider good and bad here. Their inferiority of development: the drunkenness, the thieving, the paltry swindling, that have become the rule in their commerce! Yet they have some good traits which after all place them immeasurably above the Germans. (In Germany I was above all struck by the stupidity of the people: they are infinitely stupid, they are immeasurably stupid.) Yet with us—even Nicolay Nicolayevich Strahov,* a man of high intellect, even he does not want to understand the truth: 'The Germans,' he says, 'have invented gunpowder.' But it is their life that settled it for them! And we at that very time were forming ourselves into a great nation, we checked Asia for ever, we bore an infinity of sufferings, we managed to endure it all, we did not lose our Russian idea, which will renew the world, but we strengthened it; finally, we endured the German, and yet after all our people is immeasurably higher, nobler, more honest, more naive, abler; full of a different idea, the highest Christian idea, which is not even understood by Europe with her moribund Catholicism and her stupidly self-contradictory Lutheranism. But I shan't go on about that! But it is so difficult for me to live without Russia, I have such a yearning for the country that I am positively wretched! I read the Moscowskya Viedomosti and Golos, every number to the very last letter! Good luck to the Golos for its new policy. I could say much, a great deal, to you, my friend; and what a mass of things have accumulated! But perhaps this year I shall embrace you. But I await your letters without fail. For the love of God, do write, my dear fellow. In my gloomy and tedious isolation—this is my sole

---

* Dostoevsky's friend and biographer.

comfort. Anna Gregorevna finds herself happy because she is with me. But I need you also, I need also my country.

In Switzerland there are still enough forests, there are still on its mountains incomparably more forests than there are in other countries of Europe, although they are diminishing terribly with each year. And now imagine: five months in the year there is awful cold and bises (north winds breaking through the chain of the mountains). And for three months—almost the same winter as we have. Everybody shivers from the cold, they don't take off their flannels and cotton-wool (they have no public baths—imagine now the uncleanliness to which they are accustomed); they don't provide themselves with winter clothes, they run about almost in the same clothes as in the summer (and flannel alone is quite insufficient for such a winter), and with all this—not a grain of understanding how to improve their houses! Why, what use is a fireplace burning coal or wood, even if you were to keep it going all day long? And to keep it going all the time costs two francs a day. And what a lot of wood is consumed;—even then there's no warmth. Why, if they had only double windows—then even with an open fireplace it might be tolerable! I won't ask them to introduce stoves; then all these forests could be saved. In twenty-five years' time nothing will be left of them. They live like veritable savages! But still they can put up with things! In my room, even when heated to the extreme, it is only 5° Centigrade (five degrees of warmth)! I sat in my overcoat, and in that cold waited for money, pawned things and thought out the plan of the novel—isn't it pleasant? They say that in Florence this winter there were nearly 10 degrees of cold. In Mont-pellier there were 15° Centigrade. In Geneva the cold did not rise higher than 8°; but still it is just as bad, if the water in the room freezes. Now I have lately changed my rooms, and we have now two nice rooms, one always cold, the other warm. Since therefore it is constantly 10° or 11° in the warm room life is tolerable. I have written so much, but have not managed to say anything! That is why I don't like letters. The chief thing—I am awaiting a letter from you. For the love of God write as soon as you can: a letter to me, in my present depression, will have almost the value of a good deed. Yes, I have forgotten to ask you: don't tell any one what I have written you about the novel, for the time being. I don't want it to reach the Russky Viestnik by any chance; for I have told them a fib, having said that I had written a good deal in the rough and that I am now only reshaping and copying it. I shall manage to do it and—who knows?—perhaps on the whole it will turn out not a bad novel. But again about the novel; I tell you—I have gone mad about it.

My health is very satisfactory. I have fits only very rarely, and now it is two and a half or three months on end since I had any. My sincerest greetings to your parents.—Remember me also to Strahov when you see him. And tell him to remember me to Averkiev and Dolgomostiev, particularly to Dolgomostiev. Haven't you met him?

I embrace and kiss you.—Your true and loving

F. Dostoevsky.

My particular greetings to Anna Ivanovna.

I have had a letter from Yanovsky. He is a very good man, at times wonderful. I love him deeply.

II

To A. N. Maikov

Geneva, February, 18th 1868
March, 1st 1868.

My good, precious and only friend—(all these epithets are applicable to you and I am happy in applying them)—don't be cross because of my unconscionable silence. Judge me with the same understanding and the same heart as before. My silence was unconscionable; but I almost literally could not answer you—although I did try several times. I have got stuck—my head and all my faculties—in Part II [of The Idiot], trying to complete it in time. I did not wish to spoil it definitely,—too much depends on its success. But now I don't want even success. I only want to avoid complete failure: in the subsequent parts I may still improve, for the novel is turning out a long one. I have at last sent off Part II also (I was too late, but I believe it will get there in time). What shall I tell you? Myself I can't say anything. So much so, that I am incapable of any opinion. I like the finale of Part II, but it is only myself who likes it; what will the readers say? As to all the rest, it is just as in Part I, i.e. I think it flags rather. For me it would be quite enough if only the reader read it without great boredom,—I no longer claim any other success.

My dear friend, you promised me immediately after reading Part I to write your opinion of it to me here. And now I haunt the post office every day, but there is no letter, and you have probably had the Russky Viestnik. I draw the clear conclusion: the novel is weak, and since thanks to your delicacy you are too shy and sorry to tell me that truth to my face, you are postponing your reply. And I need just that truth! I long for any opinion. Without it it is pure torture. True, you wrote me two letters before the review was out; but it can't be that you, in such a matter, should be exacting about letters! But enough of that. If you knew, my friend, with what happiness I re-read your last letter again and again! If you only knew what my life here is like, and what the receipt of a letter from you means to me! I see nobody here, I hear of nothing, and from the beginning of the New Year even the newspapers (Moscowskya Viedomosti and Golos) have not been arriving. Anna Gregorevna and I live all by ourselves; but, although we live fairly harmoniously and love one another and besides are both busy, yet I, at least, am weary. Anna Gregorevna maintains perfectly sincerely (I am convinced of it) that she is very happy. Imagine, up till now we have not yet been blessed, and the expected gentleman has not yet come into the world. I expect him every day, because there are all the symptoms. I expected him yesterday, on my birthday; he did not come. I await him to-day, but to-morrow he is sure to come.

Anna Gregorevna is waiting reverently, loves the coming guest boundlessly, and bears up cheerfully and firmly; but just recently her nerves have got on edge and at moments dark thoughts come to her: she is afraid she may die, etc. So that the situation is rather anxious and troublesome. Of money we have the very tiniest bit; but at any rate we are not in distress, though expenses are on the way. Yet in that state Anna Gregorevna has written shorthand and copied for me, and has also managed to sew and to prepare everything that is needed for the baby. The worst of all is that Geneva is too bad; a gloomy place. To-day is Sunday; there is nothing gloomier and nastier than their Sunday. To move to another place now is impossible; owing to my wife's illness we shall have to stay here for another five weeks, and then I am still in the dark as to money. The coming month will be a difficult one to me: my wife's illness, and Part III, which although it may be delayed, must be sent off regularly. And then comes Part IV; only then can I think of leaving Geneva, towards May. It is a good thing that the winter here has become milder. The whole of February here was warm and bright, exactly as in Petersburg in April, on a bright day.

I am always, incessantly, interested in everything you may write to me here. In the newspapers I am always looking for something of the same kind, as it were for a needle in a bundle of hay—reflecting and conjecturing. The abomination and vileness of our literature and journalism I sense even here. And how naive all that trash is! The Sovremennik and the others try their hardest with the same old Saltykovs and Eliseyevs—and the same old stale hatred for Russia, and the same old French Workers' Associations, and nothing but that. And Saltykov attacking the Zemstvo—all just as it should be. Our Liberals cannot help being at the one and same time inveterate enemies of Russia—conscious ones. Let anything succeed in Russia, let there be any profit for her—and their venom overflows. I have observed it a thousand times. Our extreme Radical party plays exactly the same game as the Viest [an extreme reactionary paper], nor can it be otherwise. And the cynicism and filthiness of all that riff-raff,—this I learn at times from the newspapers.

The editorial office sent me No. 1 of the Russky Viestnik. I have read it from the first page to the last. There is nothing of yours there—you must have been either too late, or they keep you to adorn the February number—and in the January number there is Polonsky (a very fine poem), and Turgenev—with a very weak story [The History of Lieutenant Yergunov]. I read the review of Tolstoy's War and Peace. How much I should like to read it all. I have read only half. It must be a capital thing; though it is a pity that there are so many small psychological details in it. There should be a wee bit less. Yet owing to those details what a lot of good there is in it!—For the love of God, write me oftener about literary matters. You mentioned the Viestnik Europa (is it Stasyulevich's ?). It seems to me that we have quite enough reviews with those ideas.—Imagine: I know nothing about the Moskva, about the Moskvich.—Your Sophia Alexeyevna is a perfect beauty; but a thought flashed across me: how fine it would be, if such a 'Sophia Alexeyevna' could appear as an episode in a whole poem about those times, I mean, in a poem about the Raskolniki [a religious sect], or in a verse-novel about those times! Has such a design never entered your head? Such a poem would produce an enormous effect. Well now, well, what about your Slovo o Polku Igoreve—you do not say where it is going to be published? In the Russky Viestnik, probably. In that case I shall read it! You can imagine with what impatience I await it. Apart from the reading which you have mentioned,—have you read it anywhere in public? Tell me all about it. What did you read at the Krylov anniversary, apart from what you sent me? I read about it in the papers; but it is not clear.

There seems to have been lately a kind of lull in Russia. I've read lately only about the subscriptions for the famine-stricken. Slavdom and Slav aspirations must arouse a whole host of enemies among Russian Liberals. When will these obsolete and retrograde dregs be washed away! For a Russian Liberal can't be considered as anything but as obsolete and retrograde. The so-called 'educated society' of old is a motley collection of everything that has separated itself from Russia, that has not understood Russia and has become Frenchified,—that is what a Russian Liberal is, and that is why he is a reactionary. Recall the best Liberals—recall Bielinsky: isn't he a conscious enemy of his fatherland, isn't he a reactionary?

Well, they can go to the devil! Here I only meet filthy little Poles in the cafes, in huge crowds;—but I enter into no relations whatsoever with them. With the priest here [A. K. Petrov] I am not acquainted. But when the child is born, I shall have to meet him. But remember, my friend, that our priests, I mean those abroad, are not all like the Wiesbaden one, of whom I spoke to you when I left Petersburg. (Have you met him? He is a rare creature; worthy, humble, with a sense of personal dignity, of an angelic purity of heart, and a passionate believer.) Well, God grant that the local one turns out a good one, although he must be spoilt by the aristocracy. Here, in Geneva (according to the Journal des Etrangers), there is a terrible number of Russian aristocrats; it only makes it the stranger that they have been wintering not in Montreux, for instance, but in Geneva where the climate is not good.

If I move anywhere, it will be to Italy; but this is still in the future, and at any rate I shall let you know immediately so that there should be no delay about the address. And you, for the love of Christ, write to me—I can't say that my health is very good. Since the spring my fits have been more frequent.—I read your account of your having served on a jury, and my heart thrilled with excitement.

Of our courts (from all that I have read) I have formed this opinion: The moral nature of our judges, and above all of our jurymen, is infinitely higher than the European; and crime is regarded from a Christian point of view. Even Russian traitors abroad agree about this. But one thing has not yet been really settled; in that humanity towards the criminal there still seems to me to be a great deal of the theoretical, Liberal, non-independent. It does appear now and then. But judging at this distance I may be badly mistaken. At any rate in this respect our nature is infinitely higher than the European. And generally all our conceptions are more moral, and our Russian aims are higher than those of the European world. We have a more direct and noble belief in goodness, goodness as Christianity, and not as a bourgeois solution of the problem of comfort. A great renewal is about to descend on the whole world, through Russian thought (which, you are quite right, is solidly welded with Orthodoxy), and this will be achieved in less than a hundred years,—this is my passionate belief. But in order that this great object may be achieved, it is essential that the political right and supremacy of the Great-Russian race over the whole Slav world should be definitively and incontestably consummated. (And our little Liberals preach the division of Russia into federal states!)

I have again a most enormous favour to ask you, or rather two favours, and I hope for everything from your good heart and your brotherly sympathy to me. This is what it is about. I wrote to Katkov when I sent him Part II, asking him for 500 roubles. It is terrible—but what can I do? I can't help asking. At first I had these dreams: (1) To write the four parts (i.e. 28–24 folios), and (2) to write well,—and only then to approach Katkov with my great request. But I repeat—I can't help asking. Now, with Part II, I have sent to the office altogether 11½ folios,—it means approximately 1700 roubles. Altogether I owe them 4560 roubles (oh!), it means then I still owe them 2860 roubles, and in this state of affairs I am asking again for 500 roubles, i.e. raising my debt again to $2860 + 500 = 3360$ roubles. But there is this to keep in view that by May 1st I shall again deliver the equivalent of 1700, and therefore there will still remain a debt of about 1700 roubles. I worried terribly, when sending that request for 500 roubles. If only the novel were good! Then it would be more pardonable to ask. Will they send it me, or not,—I do not know. But however, in any case, I am telling you all about it and along with this come my two great requests. Request No.

1: I asked Katkov, if he agreed to let me have the 500 roubles, to send me 300 roubles here, and 200 roubles to Petersburg, to you personally. And yet, in spite of the fact that you may perhaps receive these 200 roubles, I still remain a scoundrel towards you and can't pay you (who are certainly in need) not as much as a farthing! Myself and Anna Gregorevna are so tormented by it that at times we speak of it at night; but still my request is— wait a little longer and thereby you will save me from awful sufferings. And my sufferings consist in this—request No. 2,—that I can't even imagine without horror what is happening now to Emily Fiodorovna. She has her son Fedya; but is it not cruel and is it not indecent on my part to rely and to throw all the burden of the family on this young man? He is young and timid and ought not to be allowed to waste his young years and certainly may lose patience,—and that leads to a wrong path. It might very, very easily lead there. I must help them: I am obliged to. Even if only a little. Besides them there is Pasha. There again it's the same story: it is impossible for a young boy, a minor, to live by his own work,—it is impossible, absurd, and indecent on my part. Cruel! It means pushing him to perdition; he won't stand the strain. To me it was that Marie Dmitrievna [Dostoevsky's first wife] bequeathed him, it was her last request. And therefore I implore you, in case you receive the 200 roubles, to do this: give one hundred roubles to Emily Fiodorovna, and one hundred to Pasha, but give Pasha at first only 50 roubles (without telling him that you have another 50 roubles for him), and in two months' time give him the other 50 roubles. (Besides board and lodging, he must have a new supply of underwear, and clothes, he needs some other little things, in a word he must have 50 roubles at once.) Those 200 roubles, if Katkov agrees, you will receive in a fortnight, or if he is late it may take a month. I shall tell Pasha not to call on you too early. You wrote me that on the former occasion they worried you very much; forgive them, my dear friend! To Emily Fiodorovna deliver the money yourself, or let her know through Pasha that she is to call on you to receive it. All this, of course, if you receive the money; I shall write to them. Well, that is my second request, I worry you extremely; but, my friend, save me from these sufferings.

To imagine their situation is such a pain to me that I would rather bear it myself. And to think that everything, my whole fate depends on the success of the novel! Oh, it's hard to be a poet in such conditions! Now how different, for instance, are Turgenev's circumstances, and how dare he after that appear with his Yergunov ! He himself literally told me that he was a German, and not a Russian, and he considered it an honour to reckon himself a German, and not a Russian,—this is the literal truth.

Good-bye for the present, my friend. What more than anything else makes me glad on your account is that you do not allow your spirit to be idle. Desires, ideals, and aims are fermenting in you. That's a great deal. In our time, if a man is seized with apathy, he is lost, dead, and buried. Good-bye, I embrace you closely and wish you all that is best. Write me, write me if only a few words about my novel. Even the tiniest thing.

I constantly read all the political news. There is an infinitude of lies; but I am terribly scared by the weakening and lowering of our foreign policy lately. Apart from this in Russia herself the Sovereign's reforms have many enemies. The only hope is in him. He has already proved his firmness. God grant he may rule long!

Anna Gregorevna greets you, Anna Ivanovna and Eugenia Petrovna. I also; please remember me to them. I somehow believe a Misha or a Sonia is going to make his appearance to-day,—this has already been settled.*— Good-bye, my dear friend.

Wholly your F. Dostoevsky.

III

To A. N. Maikov

Geneva, March, 3rd 1868
February, 20th 1868.

Now I'm again writing you a few lines, my dear friend Apollon Nicolayevich, and again to make an extraordinary request. (Did you receive my letter of yesterday in which I wrote to you that Katkov might perhaps send you in two or three weeks' time two hundred roubles? I asked you most earnestly to help me and to divide that money (one hundred to Emily Fiodorovna, fifty

---

* Sophie or Sonia Dostoevsky was born 22nd February 1868.

to Pasha at once, and to keep the remaining fifty (also for Pasha), without telling him about it, and to hand it over to him after two months). Owing to an urgent cause and an important reason I must dispose of the money differently. Namely: hand over one hundred to Emily Fiodorovna, and fifty to Pasha now; give the remaining fifty roubles, my dear friend, to Anna Nicolayevna Snitkin, Anna Gregorevna's mother. You may let her know through Pasha that she should call on you to get it. Or rather we ourselves will write to her, and she will call on you. When leaving Petersburg we pawned, I believe, all our movables, all our furniture, and all our things. For a whole year Anna Nicolayevna paid the interest (a very high one too) for us out of her pocket; but now she herself has great expenses, and although she does not ask us for money to pay the interest and continues to pay it as before,—we must help her now and just at this moment. And Pasha, I will send to somehow, if I have money later, in two months' time.

Don't disappoint me, my precious friend, don't disappoint me; but do all these commissions which have a most vital importance for me, I earnestly entreat you. I shall try my best to prevent them all from worrying you much; I will ask them. Good-bye for the present. I embrace you closely.

Wholly your F. Dostoevsky.

P.S.—Last night I had a fit, so violent, that I have not recovered yet and I am aching all over; in particular my head aches unbearably.

P.S.—I am so distracted, everything is muddled up in my head because of the fit. I wrote a letter to Pasha, a most urgent one; but, although he has given me his address, I am afraid to send it to him, because he may have moved again to new rooms, and I ask you to hand over the letter to him. My dear friend, Apollon Nicolayevich, forgive me for all this unconscionable trouble I am giving you; but the letter to Pasha, which I enclose here, is so highly important to me and it deals with a question so affecting my heart and soul that nothing can be more important to me than its speedy delivery. Be my benefactor. You have only to send this letter to him through some one at the Address-Office. It is close to where you live and you will find it at once.—In any event, I also inscribe on the letter the address of Pasha's late rooms, which also are not far from your house. Be my benefactor and deliver it to him immediately.

IV

To A. N. Maikov

Geneva, March, 2nd 1868 / March, 14th 1868.

Most kind and true friend, Apollon Nicolayevich, I received your letter, thank you extremely. But I am in the most terrible agitation and anxiety; for I have received a letter (from Anna Nicolayevna, my wife's mother) with strange news: that Pasha had called on her, ridden the high horse, said that 'he does not want to know whether I am in need, that I am obliged to keep him'; that since a good deal of money was expected from Katkov, he was going to Moscow, would see Katkov personally, would explain to him his position and ask him for money, on my account. Anna Nicolayevna positively informs me that he has already left for Moscow (on the 5th February, old style), and that he has quarrelled with his chiefs and she is afraid of his being dismissed.

    Can you imagine now my situation? What is my position in the eyes of Katkov? Myself I blush for my affairs, and each time I am positively afraid to apply to Katkov because they have treated me so decently and well, and this ties my hands terribly. Without having yet seen a single line, they have trusted me to the extent of 500 roubles in advance (me, a sick man, abroad; and, as ill-luck would have it, I have just asked for another 500 roubles!). How terrible to think of Pasha coming and interrupting Katkov in his occupations, which are really enormous, and beginning to shout, and perhaps even to be insolent, and of course blackening my character as much as he can!—Finally. Yesterday I pawned my last coat. I have thirty francs only, and forty to pay to the nurse; I have to pay the midwife 100 francs, 120 francs for the rooms and attendance due by March 20th, i.e. in six days' time (prices this month are higher), and 300 francs I owe for the things pawned. In six days at the latest my 30 francs will come to an end, and then—not a brass farthing, nothing to pawn, and my whole credit exhausted. My whole hope was that Katkov would agree to my request about the 500 roubles, would send you two hundred (as I had written), and would send me 300 roubles here, and those 300 would come here by March 20th, that is, in six days' time. Now what shall I do if Pasha makes him angry and finally exhausts his patience (for any man may lose patience at last in certain circumstances), and he answers me with a refusal. Well, what shall I do then? Then I am done for, absolutely done for, because my wife has now been confined and is ill. And at this moment I receive your letter. The date is not put down; but on the envelope is the mark of the Petersburg post office dated February 26th.

In that letter you say not a single word about this. Then perhaps it is untrue. And yet Anna Nicolayevna asserts it positively. In that case, it is perhaps true; but you are not aware of it (for it is indeed difficult for you to know, just for the reason that if he had made up his mind to do this, he certainly would have avoided meeting you). I sit now crushed and broken and do not know what to do. I had thought of writing to-day to Katkov and apologising to him, by explaining to him the whole circumstances; for, firstly, as regards Katkov personally I feel so ashamed that I could sink into the ground, and secondly, as regards the money I am afraid that he may get cross and not send it. On the other hand, suppose I send the letter, and all this turns out untrue? I had better make up my mind to write to-morrow and to send to-morrow (the letter to Katkov). If only some news would arrive to enlighten me! But there is no news coming from anywhere! But to wait is dangerous, and also difficult. At any rate I implore you, my dear friend: investigate this business and send me news immediately, or I shall die of anguish. But if it is not true, if Pasha only talked, but did not act, I mean, did not go to Moscow, did not speak to Katkov and did not even write to him (it is almost the same thing, writing and seeing him personally),—then please do not tell Pasha that I have learnt it from Anna Nicolayevna. I am afraid he will be very rude to her. In a word, in any event, not a word to him about Anna Nicolayevna. I regard you as my Providence. I'll send Katkov a letter after all; I must. If Pasha is not to blame,—if he did not go to Katkov, certainly what I write won't do him any great harm: the prank of a young man who is not known there at all. For my own part I must tell you that I am sorry for Pasha; I do not blame him very much: indeed, it's a case of youth and lack of self-control. It must be excused, and he should not be treated harshly; for, being such a little fool, it won't take him long to go to the dogs. And I imagined that he had grown sensible and realised that he was already nearly 21 years old, and ought to work, since there was no capital. I thought that having obtained employment he at last realised that honest work was his duty, just as it is the duty of every one, and that he must not act stubbornly and without listening to any one, as though he had made a vow to do nothing and would not stir. And he, as I see it now, imagined that he was doing me a favour by having secured employment. And who put it into his head that I was obliged to keep him for ever, even after 21? His words to Anna Nicolayevna (which must certainly be true)—'I don't want to know whether he is himself in need; he is obliged to keep me'—are too significant in a certain sense to me. This means that he does not love me. Certainly I am the last to blame him, and I know how little an impulse or an arrogant word may mean, that is, I know that a word is not an act. All my life long I will help him and I want to do so. But there's the point: has he done much for himself? It is only for the last three months that he has had no allowance from me. Yet during these three months he received from me 20 roubles in cash, and I paid his debt of 30 roubles to Emily Fiodorovna. And so, really what he has not received only amounts to one month's allowance! And already he has managed to get into a fever about it! It means, then, that the man must be incapable of doing anything for himself! It is not a comforting thought. Out of my very last resources I am now sending money both to him and to Emily Fiodorovna. And yet I am convinced that at Emily Fiodorovna's they are running me down for all they are worth. And added to all this I am a sick man. What would happen if I were unable to work—what then?

My dear friend, you alone are my Providence and true friend! Your letter of yesterday revived me. I have never had anything harder and more difficult to bear in my life: on February 22nd (old style)—my wife (after awful pains lasting 30 hours) bore me a daughter and is still ill, and you can consequently imagine how my nerves are on edge. The least bit of unpleasant news has to be kept back from her; for she loves me so much. Sonia, the baby, is a healthy, big, handsome, lovely, superb baby: positively half the day I kiss her and can't go away from her. This is good; but what is bad is this: all the money I have is 30 francs; everything to the very last rag, mine and my wife's, has been pawned. My debts are urgent, pressing, immediate. My whole hope is in Katkov, and the incessant thought: suppose he does not send? The exasperating news about Pasha; my terrible and continuous fear which does not allow me to sleep at night: what if Anya falls ill? (To-day is the tenth day.) And I have no means of calling in a doctor or of buying medicine; Part III of the novel, which is not yet begun, which I undertook on my word of honour to deliver to the Editor by the first of April (old style); the whole plan of Parts III and IV radically altered last night, for the third time (and therefore, at least, another three days needed for the thinking out of the new arrangement); the increased strain on my nerves and the number and violence of my fits,—there you have my condition!

In addition to all this,—up to the coming of your letter,—complete despair on account of the failure and badness of my novel, and consequently, without mentioning my anguish as an author,—the conviction that all hopes have vanished, for all my hopes were fixed on the novel! Imagine, then, how your letter gladdened me; am I not right now in calling you my Providence? Indeed in my present circumstances you are just the same to me, as my dead brother Misha was.

And so you gladden me with the news of my success. It gives me new heart. Part III I shall complete and send off by April 1st. Haven't I written as much as 11½ folios in two months! I implore you, my dear friend, when you have read the finale of Part II (i.e. in the February number), write me immediately. Believe me, your words to me are a well-spring of living water. I was inspired when I wrote that finale and it cost me two fits one after another. But I may have exaggerated and lost my sense of proportion, and therefore I await your impartial criticism. Oh, my dear friend, do not condemn me for this anxiety, as if it were the anguish of ambition. Ambition, of course, there is, could one do without it?—But here my chief motives, I call God to witness, are different. In the case of this novel too much is at stake, in every way.

Your letters always stimulate me and for several days on end act as leaven on everything in me. I should awfully like to have a talk with you about certain things. This time I have confined myself to family trifles; wait till next time. Surely it is the same Danilevsky, the late Fourierist, who was mixed up in our affair? Yes, he has a strong head. But in the Journal of the Ministry of Education! It has a small circulation, it is little read. Can't it be published separately? Oh, how much I should like to read it! . . .

Write me about yourself as much as you can. My greetings to all yours. My wife loves you deeply and sends her greetings to Anna Ivanovna. She is in ecstasies over her work, and I too. As regards The Idiot, I am so much afraid, so much afraid,—that you can't even imagine my fear. A kind of unnatural fear even; which has never beset me before! . . . What depressing, trifling letters I am writing you! I embrace you closely.

Wholly your F. Dostoevsky.

Anyhow I shall write more often now.

Anya burst into tears when she read in your letter about the success of The Idiot. She says that she is proud of me.

V

To A. N. Maikov

Geneva, March, 20th 1868 / April, 2nd 1868.

Kindest and good friend, Apollon Nicolayevich, first of all I thank you, my dear friend, most deeply for the execution of all my commissions which have turned out so troublesome, and in doing which you have had to run about so much. Forgive me for worrying you; but indeed you are the only man on whom I can rely (which is no excuse at all for worrying you). Secondly—I thank you for your greetings, congratulations, and wishes of happiness for us three. You are right, my good friend, you have described from nature the feeling of being a father, and you have taken your beautiful words from nature: all is perfectly true. I have had, now almost for a month, feelings utterly new and hitherto completely unknown to me; from the moment when I saw my Sonia for the first time up to this minute when we have just been washing her, by our common efforts, in the tub. Yes, an angelic soul has flown into our house too. But I shall not describe to you my sensations. They grow and develop with each day. Now, my dear friend: last time when I wrote to you in such anxiety, I forgot (!) to tell you that as far back as last year in Dresden, Any a and I had agreed (and she scolded me terribly for having forgotten to tell you) that you are to be Sonia's godfather. My dear friend, don't refuse! It is now nearly ten months since we decided on it. If you refuse, it will bring Sonia unhappiness: the first godfather and he refused! But you will not refuse, dear friend. I add, that this will not cause you the least possible trouble; and as to our becoming related by compaternity—so much the better. The godmother is Anna Nicolayevna. Did she tell you? For the love of God let me know your answer as soon as possible—for it is needed for the christening. It is now nearly a month, and she is not yet christened! (Could it be like that in Russia ?) And your god-daughter (I am sure she is your goddaughter)—I inform you—is very good-looking in spite of the fact that she takes after me impossibly, even ridiculously—to the verge of strangeness even. I would not believe it if I did not see it myself. The baby is only about a month old; but she has perfectly my expression of face, my complete physiognomy,—up to the wrinkles on her forehead,—she lies in her cot as though she were composing a novel! I don't speak about the features. Her forehead is like mine, even strangely so. It should of course follow that she is not very good-looking (for I am a beauty only in the eyes of Anna Gregorevna—and seriously a beauty to her, I tell you !). But you, an artist yourself, know excellently well that it is possible to look exactly like a plain person, and yet to be very lovely. Anna Gregorevna is extremely keen on your being godfather. She loves you and Anna Ivanovna very much and respects you boundlessly.

You are too much of a prophet: you prophesy that now that I have new cares I shall become an egoist, and this, unfortunately (since anything else was impossible), has come true. Imagine: all this month I have not written a single line! My God, how am I treating Katkov, my promises, my words of honour, my obligations! I was incredibly glad when, because of my confession that I might be late in view of my wife's confinement, the Russky Viestnik announced at the end of Part I of my novel, that the continuation would follow in the April, not in the March number. But, alas! even for getting it ready for the April number only twenty days remain now (I am awfully behind!), and not a single line is written. To-morrow I am writing to Katkov to apologise,—but they can't make a fur coat out of my promises. And yet I must manage to have it ready for the April number, although the time is so short. And mean-while, apart from all the rest, all my existence (as regards money) depends on them. In truth a desperate position! But what can I do: the whole month has passed in extraordinary fears, troubles and anxieties. And I have not slept for whole nights on end, not only on account of moral anxieties, but because I could not help myself. And with epilepsy it is awful. My nerves are upset now to the last degree. March here was disgustingly bad,—with snow and frost, almost as bad as in Petersburg. Anna Gregorevna was terribly upset physically (don't for the world tell Anna Nicolayevna, for she will imagine God knows what. Simply that Anya could not recover for a long time, and added to this, she nurses the child herself). She has little milk. We also use the bottle. Still the baby is very healthy (touch wood!). And Anya is beginning to go out for walks. It is now the third day of wonderful sunny weather and the first shoots of green. I can hardly recover yet from all this. Then there's the awful trouble,—money. They have sent us 300 roubles. This, owing to the exchange, is 1025 francs. But we have almost nothing left. Expenses have increased, we had to pay our former debts, to redeem the pawned things, and exactly three weeks from now great expenses are imminent on account of our having to move into other rooms (they are turning us out of these because of the baby's crying), and, besides, certain payments must be made,—terrible! And we have also, beginning from to-day, to exist for at least two months before we can hope to receive any more money from the Russky Viestnik. But I can get nothing from the R.V. until I have delivered Part II, and when am I going to write it? Again perhaps in 18 days, the time it took me to write the instalment published in the January number? Your disposition of the money was very good. And though it is too bad of me to trouble you, do send me the remaining 25 roubles here, to Geneva, if possible at once. The last extreme of need! (N.B.—Simply put a 25-rouble note in a letter, register it, so that it shall not be lost, and send it to my address.)

I am very glad that you handed over to Pasha 50, and not 25 roubles. That is good. I am awfully glad that he has got employment. My dear friend, look him up, if only now and then! When I write to him, I shall tell him that, having learnt from you that you have given him 25 roubles on credit, I have already repaid you. But I want to know this: isn't Pasha going to write me anything and congratulate me about Sonia? Others have congratulated me: you, Strahov, the Moscow people, Petersburg friends of Anna Gregorevna; but Pasha—not only have I received nothing from him lately, but I have had no reply to the letter I sent him about six weeks ago, addressed to you (did you receive it? Somehow you did not mention it). On this point, extremely important: After all I do not know whether he was in Moscow or not? Did he go to Katkov? It is very important for me to know. Remember, I sent Katkov a long letter of apology, solely on that account! I must know. Can't you get to know the truth about it, my dear friend, for the love of Christ! . . . (Emily Fiodorovna I have officially, solemnly notified that a daughter has been born to me; but nothing, no reply from her!) Moreover, on the previous occasion, she sent me no answer to my extremely important question about their flat and Alonkin the landlord. It surprises even me. Indeed it is quite disgustingly rude!

As regards my will and all your other advice, I have always been of exactly the same opinion myself. But, my friend, my sincere and devoted friend (perhaps my only one!),—why do you consider me so good and generous? No, my friend, no, I am not so good as all that, and this troubles me. And Pasha—poor Marie Dmitrievna gave him into my charge on her deathbed! How could I desert him? (You yourself didn't advise it.) No, no, I must help him, moreover, I love him sincerely; indeed for over ten years I brought him up in my house! He is like a son to me. We lived together. And to leave him to his own resources so young, and alone,—how can I possibly do it? After all, however poor I may be, help him I must. True, he is a great lazybones; but in truth I myself, at his age, was perhaps even worse (I remember it). Now he should be supported. To leave a good and pleasant impression on his heart now will help him in his later development. And that he is now employed and works for himself,—I am awfully, awfully glad of it,—let him do some work. And you I embrace and kiss as a brother for having gone to Rasin and secured the post for him there. . . . As for Emily Fiodorovna, there again my dead brother Misha is concerned. And indeed you do not know what he was to me—all my life, from my first conscious moments! No, you don't know! Fedya is my godson, moreover he is a young man, who is earning his bread by hard work. And in his case, if only it is possible, I must help at times (for he is a young man; everything ought not to be thrown on his shoulders,—it is too hard). And yourself, my dear friend, why do you make yourself out to be so practical and egotistical: didn't you lend me 200 roubles and didn't you lose nearly 2000 roubles by my brother Misha's death and the failure of the review! Yet I should not have broached these subjects. At any rate, I consider your advice perfectly correct.—And as for myself, there's a very appropriate proverb: 'Don't boast when going to war.' And I say this because I have been harping on my obligation to help and so on. And how can I tell what is going to happen to myself?

However ugly, however beastly living abroad has become to me, do you know that at times I think with fear of what will happen to my health when it pleases God to permit me to return to Petersburg? If my fits occur here so often,—what would it be like there? I am positively losing my mental faculties, for instance, my memory. . . . All that you write about Russia, and especially your mood (rose-coloured), makes me very happy. It is perfectly true that it is not worth while paying attention to various particular cases: it is only the whole that should be considered, its impetus and aim, and all the rest is bound to come as part of the tremendous regeneration which is taking place under the present great Sovereign. My friend, you really look at things exactly as I do, and you have at last expressed what I was saying, saying aloud three years ago, at the time I was editing the review; but it was not understood, namely: that our constitution is the mutual love of the Monarch for the people and of the people for the Monarch. This principle of the Russian State, the principle of love not of strife (which I believe was first discovered by the Slavophils), is the greatest of all ideas, an idea on which much will be built. This idea we shall proclaim to Europe, which does not understand anything at all about it. Our wretched, uprooted tribe of clever ones, alas! was sure to end like that. They will die like that, they can't be reborn. (Take Turgenev, now!) But the newest generation—it is there we have to look. (Classical education might be of great assistance. What is Katkov's Lyceum?) While here abroad, with regard to Russia I have finally become sTconiple'te moliarcmst. If any one has (lone anything in Russia, it is obviously the Tsar alone. (But not on this account only, but simply because he is the Tsar, beloved by the Russian people, beloved for himself and because he is the Tsar. With us the people have given and give their love to every Tsar, and only in him do they finally believe. To the people it is a mystery, a priesthood, an anointment.) Our Westerners understand nothing about this; they pride themselves on basing themselves on facts, and they overlook the primary, the greatest fact of our history. I like your idea of the pan-Slav significance of Peter the Great. It is the first I have heard of this idea and it is a perfectly true one. But there: I read the Golos here. Terribly distressing facts are at times described in it. For instance, about the chaotic state of our railways (the newly constructed ones), about affairs in the Zemstvos, about the awful condition of the colonies. The dreadful misfortune is that we still have so few men of executive capacity. Talkers there are, but men who do things—you can count them on your fingers. Of course I'm not referring to administrators in high positions, but simply to officials of all kinds in general, a whole host of whom is needed, and who are not there. For the courts, for the juries, perhaps there are plenty of men. But what about the railways? And the other public services? It is a terrible conflict of new men and new demands with the old order. I do not speak of inspiring them with an idea: freethinkers we have in plenty, but Russian men are but few. The chief thing—the self-realisation of the Russian man in oneself—that is what is needed. And how greatly publicity helps the Tsar and all Russians,—even the hostile publicity of the Westerners. I long for us to have political railways soon (the Smolensk-Kiev railway: as soon as possible), and also new guns as soon as possible! Why is Napoleon increasing his army, and thus running the risk of making himself unpopular with his people, at such a critical moment? The devil knows why. But it won't end well for Europe. (I'm deeply convinced of this somehow.) Awkward, if we get mixed up in it. If they would only wait a couple of years. Nor is it Napoleon alone. Apart from Napoleon the future is threatening, and we must be prepared for it. Turkey is on its last legs; Austria is in much too abnormal a state (I only analyse the elements, but form no judgment); there is the damned problem of the proletariat, in its acute stage, in the West (which is not even mentioned in the politics of the day!), and, lastly, chiefly, Napoleon is an old man in indifferent health. He won't live long. As long as he lives he will be involved in more failures, and the Buonapartes will become still more loathsome to the French,—what will happen then? For this contingency Russia must prepare herself without fail and without delay; for it may come to pass very soon.

How glad I am that the Heir Apparent has revealed himself to Russia in such a good and noble manner, and that Russia testifies her hopes in him and her love for him, as to a Father. God grant that our Alexander live happily for another forty years. He alone has done for Russia almost more than all his predecessors taken together. And the most important thing is that he is so much loved. This is now the mainstay of the whole Russian movement; on it alone all regeneration is based. Oh, my friend, how I should love to come back, how sickening my life is here! A bad life. And, above all, my work does not go right. If only I could finish the novel satisfactorily, how good it would be! This is the beginning of my whole future. Anna Gregorevna does not feel homesick, and sincerely says she is happy; but I am nauseated. I go nowhere and see no one. And even if I had acquaintances I don't think I should go to them, I have completely lost my bearings,—and yet my work does not come off. At five o'clock every day I leave the house for two hours and go to the cafe to read Russian newspapers! I know no one here, and I 'm glad of it. It is horrible to meet our clever ones. Poor! Insignificant! Rubbish, puffed up with self-love! Sh . . .! Loathsome! By chance I met Herzen in the street; we talked for ten minutes in a hostile-polite tone, mockingly, and then parted. No, I shan't go. How far behind the times, how terribly backward they are, and they understand nothing! And puffed up, how terribly puffed up they are! I read here greedily the announcements in the papers about the appearance of the numbers of the reviews and the lists of contents. How strange are the titles and lists of contents of publications like the Otechestvennya Zapiski! Yes, rags instead of flags, that is true! My dear friend, don't give them anything, wait. And the question as to where to publish your things seems to worry you. Don't be worried, my friend. I am writing hastily now, or I would have a good talk with you. I have an idea for you; but its exposition would require a whole letter, and now I have no time. I will write soon. This idea I conceived apropos your 'Sophia Alexeyevna.' And believe me, it is serious, do not laugh! I will expound it to you. It is neither novel nor poem. But it is so deeply needed, it is so necessary, and so original and new and of such an urgent, Russian tendency, that you yourself will be surprised! I shall expound the programme to you. It is a pity I must do it in a letter and not do it in friendly talk. Through it you might become famous, and it is important that you should bring it out as a book, after having previously published a few fragments. The book should sell enormously.—So you have finished your translation of the Apocalypse? And I thought you had given it up. Certainly it cannot possibly escape the ecclesiastical censorship, not possibly; but if you have translated perfectly accurately, then of course it will pass. I received a letter from Strahov. It made me happy. I want to answer him as soon as possible; but as he did not give his address (he forgot!) I shall answer him through you. And I shall ask you to let him have the letter.

My dear friend, do write to me more frequently. You can't believe what your letters mean to me! To-day is already the third of April of the new style, and the 25th is the last day (absolutely the last) for the delivery of the novel, and I have not a line, not a single line written! Lord, what shall I do? Well, good-bye, I kiss and embrace you. Anya greets you, and we both greet Anna Ivanovna.

Wholly your F. Dostoevsky.

P.S.—For the love of God, tell me everything you hear (if only you do hear) about The Idiot. I must, must, must know without fail! For the love of God! The finale of Part II—about which I wrote to you—is the same as that published at the end of Part I. And I relied on it so much! Though I still believe in the perfect fidelity of the character of Nastasya Filipovna. By the way, many little things at the end of Part I are taken from life, and certain characters are simply portraits,—for instance, General Ivolgin and Kolya. But perhaps your opinion is quite true.

VI

To A. N. Maikov

Florence, $\dfrac{\text{May, 15th 1869}}{\text{May, 27th 1869.}}$

What a long, long time I have refrained from replying to your good sincere words, my good and only friend! But you are right; for of all those whom I have happened to meet and to live with for the last forty-eight years, you and you alone I consider as a man after my heart. Of all those I have met, during all these forty-eight years, I have hardly one, hardly a single one like you (I do not speak of my dead brother). You and I, although we do not mix in the same society, yet in heart, in soul, in our cherished convictions and in our cordial intercourse, are almost chums. Even our intellectual conclusions and those derived from our experience have of late begun to be strangely similar, and I think the ardour of our hearts is the same. Judge, for instance, from this fact, my dear friend. Do you remember last year, I believe it was in the summer and I believe exactly a year ago (as far as I remember, before the summer holidays), I wrote you a letter (to which I received no answer from you for three or four months; at that point our correspondence was interrupted, and when it started again in the autumn, we began to write about completely different things and forgot where we had stopped in the summer). Well, in that letter, at the end, I wrote you, full of serious and profound rapture, of a new idea that had occurred to me, strictly for you, for your use. (The idea occurred by itself, as something independent and as a complete whole; but as I could not possibly regard myself as the person who ought to realise that idea, I naturally destined it, or wished to destine it for you. So perhaps it was born in me for you, indeed, as I have already said, or rather indissolubly connected with your image, as a poet.) If you had answered me immediately then, in the summer, I would have sent you a comprehensive explanation of the idea, with full details; I had then thought out what to write to you to the last line. But I think it is as well that you did not reply then. Judge: my idea consisted then in this (I'll say only a few words about it now) that a series of legends, ballads, songs, little poems, romances—call them what you like—might be composed in attractive, fascinating verses, in such verses as can be learnt by heart without the least effort,—which is always the case with profound and beautiful verses; here the essence and even the metre depend on the soul of the poet, and they come suddenly, completely ready in his soul, even independently of himself. . . . I 'll make a long digression: a poem, in my view, makes its appearance like a virgin precious stone, a diamond, completely ready in the poet's soul, in all its essence; and that is the first act of the poet, as creator and maker; the first part of his creation. If you like, it is not even he who is the creator, but life, the mighty essence of life, the God living and real, concentrating his power in the diversity of creation here and there, and most often in the great heart and in the great poet, so that if the poet himself is not the creator (and one ought to agree that he is not, especially you, a master and poet yourself; for indeed the creation comes suddenly out of the poet's soul far too completely, far too definitely, far too finished)—well, if the poet himself is not the creator, then at any rate his soul is that very same mine, which begets diamonds and without which they cannot be found anywhere. Then follows the poet's second act less profound and mysterious, but that in which the poet is concerned as artist,—the business of cutting and polishing the diamond which he has obtained. Here the poet is almost a jeweller. Now, in this series of legends in verse (in thinking of those legends I thought at times of your poem, Clermont Cathedral) should be depicted from the very outset—with love and with our thought,—and with a Russian conception,—the whole of Russian history, those moments and points being distinguished in which at certain times and in certain places it as it were concentrated itself and manifested itself, all of it, suddenly, in its complete wholeness. Such all-revealing moments can be found, throughout the ages, ten at least, perhaps even rather more. Well now, to seize those points and to tell them in a legend, to all and sundry, but not as a simple chronicle, no, but as a sincere poem, even without strict adherence to the facts (but with extraordinary clarity); to seize the chief point and to relate it so that men can see out of what idea the poem was begotten, with what love and pain it was brought to light. But without egoism, without words from oneself, but naively, as naively as possible, with love for Russia streaming forth as from a living spring,—and nothing else. Imagine to yourself that in the third or fourth legend (I composed them all in my mind then and went on composing them long afterwards) I took the capture of Constantinople by Mahomet II (and this came directly and involuntarily as a legend from Russian history, by itself and without design; afterwards I wondered, at the way—without hesitation, reflection, or conscious thought—it had occurred to me to connect the capture of Constantinople with Russian history, without the faintest doubt). To relate all that catastrophe in a naive and concise account! The Turks closely investing Tsargrad (Constantinople); the last night before the assault at dawn; the last Emperor walking in the Palace. . . .

('The King pacing with long strides.')

The prayer before the image of Our Lady; the prayer; the assault; the fight; the Sultan with a bloody sword entering Constantinople. At the Sultan's command the body of the last Emperor searched for and found among a heap of the slain; and recognised by the eagles embroidered on his boots; Saint Sophia, the trembling Patriarch, the last Mass, the Sultan on his horse dashing up the stairs into the middle of the Church (historique). Having reached the middle he stops his horse in confusion, looks round musingly, anxiously, and utters the words: 'Here is the house of prayer for Allah!' Whereupon the ikons and the Communion table are thrown out, the altar is destroyed, a mosque is erected, the corpse of the Emperor is buried; and the last of the Palaeologi appears in the Kingdom of Russia with a double-headed eagle for her dowry; the Russian wedding; Ivan III in his wooden hut, instead of a palace, and into this wooden hut passes the great ideal of the pan-Orthodox significance of Russia, and there is laid the first stone of the future hegemony of the East; there the circle of Russia's future destinies is extended; there is laid down the idea not only of a great state, but of a whole new world, which is destined to renew Christianity by the pan-Slav, pan-Orthodox idea and to introduce a new idea to mankind. Then comes the disintegration of the West, a disintegration which will occur when the Pope distorts Christ finally and thereby begets atheism in the defiled humanity of the West.

Nor is this idea concerned with that epoch alone; I had another idea, along with the picture of the wooden hut and of the wise Prince—cherishing a grand and profound ideal, of the Metropolitan, in poor clothes, sitting with the Prince, and of 'Fominishna,' gladly settled in Russia.—Suddenly, in another ballad, we pass to a description of the end of the 15th and of the beginning of the 16th century in Europe, Italy, the Papacy, art in the churches and Raphael, the worship of Apollo Belvedere, the first rumours of the Reformation, of Luther, America, gold, Spain and England,—a whole vivid picture, parallel to all the preceding Russian pictures,—but with hints of the future of that picture, of future science, of atheism, of the rights of man. realised in the Western way, and not in ours,—all which serve as the source of all that is and will be. In my ardent musings I also thought that the legend ought not to end with Peter the Great, for instance, on whom a specially fine utterance and fine poem is needed,—a legend based on a bold and frank point of view, on our point of view. I would go as far as Biron and Katherine and even further,—I would go as far as the liberation of the peasants and up to the wanderings of the aristocrats all over Europe with their last paper rouble notes, and their ladies copulating with the Borghesans, up to the preaching of atheism by seminary students, up to the appearance of omni-human citizens of the world, up to the Russian Counts who write criticisms and stories, etc. etc. The Poles would have to occupy much space. Then I would finish with imaginary pictures of the future: of Russia after two centuries, and alongside with her—of the eclipsed, lacerated, and brutalised Europe, with her civilisation. Here I would not stop at any imagination. . . . You consider me at this moment certainly mad, strictly and chiefly because I have written so much; for all this ought to be spoken of personally and not written about. For in a letter one can't say anything intelligibly. But I have become excited. You see, when I read in your letter that you were writing those ballads, I was struck with wonder: I wondered how it is that to us, separated for so long, the same idea, of the same poem, has occurred? I was made happy by this and then I began to think: Do we understand this properly, in the same way? You see, my idea is that the ballads could become a great national work and would contribute mightily to the regeneration of the consciousness of the Russian. Why, Apollon Nicolayevich, every schoolboy will know and learn these poems by heart. But having learnt a poem, he will also learn the idea and attitude, and as this attitude is true, it will abide in his soul all his life long. Since the verses and poems are comparatively short, the whole reading world of Russia will read them, as they read your Clermont Cathedral, which even now many know by heart. And therefore—it is not only a poem and a literary work,—it is science, it is preaching, it is an heroic act. When last year I wanted to write to you and urge you to set to work on that idea, I thought to myself: How shall I tell it him so that he will understand me completely ?—And suddenly, a year later, you yourself become inspired with the same idea and find it necessary to write it! It means, then, the idea is true! But one thing, one thing is needed, without fail: the poems must have an extraordinary poetic charm, they must carry the reader away, carry him away without fail, carry him away to the point of being involuntarily learnt by heart. My friend! remember, that perhaps all your poetical career up till now was only a preface, only an introduction, and that only now you will have the power to utter the new word, your new word! And therefore look at the matter more seriously, more deeply, and with more enthusiasm. And above all,—simplicity and naivete! And remember this too: write in rhymes, and not in the old Russian metre. Do not laugh! It is important. Rhyme now is simplicity, and the old Russian metre is academism. Not a single poem in unrhymed verse is learnt by heart. The people no longer compose songs in the old metre, but compose in rhymes. If there are to be no rhymes (and no ballad metre),—really you'll ruin the thing. You may laugh at me; but I tell you the truth! The crude truth!

About Yermak [the conqueror of Siberia] I can't say anything; you certainly know better than I. In my notion, there is at first the Cossack daredevilry, vagabondage and brigandage. Then is shown the man-genius under a sheep-skin coat; he divines the magnitude of his work and its future significance; but only when his whole work has made a favourable start and is running smoothly. There is born a Russian feeling, an orthodox feeling of being one with the Russian root (and it may even be a direct feeling, something of a nostalgia), and thence comes his embassy and homage to the great Russian King who completely expresses, in the popular conception, the Russian people. (N.B.—The chief and completest expression of that conception reached its full, ultimate development, do you know when, to my thinking? In our century. Certainly I am speaking of the people, and not of putrefied seminarists and aristocrats.)

But enough of this now. I only believe this: that you and I agree in ideas, and I am glad of it. Please send me something of what you have written, and if possible, send me a good deal. I shall not misuse it. You yourself can see that it interests me to the point of agitation.

You will ask: why didn't I write to you for so long? But I have been silent for so long, that I find it difficult even to answer the question. Chiefly—nostalgia; but were I to speak and to explain further, then there would be a great deal to tell. But my nostalgia is such, that if I were by myself, I should fall ill of anguish. It is a good thing that I am with Anna Gregorevna, who as you know is again expecting to be confined. These expectations agitate us both. (We have Anna Gregorevna's mother staying with us now, and in Anna's present state this is necessary.) It was a great disappointment to me to have to remain in Florence, when a month ago we had decided to move to Dresden. All this happened for lack of money.

It ended in my promising a story (it will be a very short one*) to the Zarya. My dear Nicolay Nicolayevich [Strahov] (who is perhaps cross with me now) arranged that affair (he gave 125 roubles to Marie Gregorevna Svatkovsky to pay interest (60 roubles), and the remaining 65 roubles he divided between Pasha (25 roubles) and Emily Fiodorovna (40 roubles); and besides he promised to send me here, to Florence, 175 roubles by a definite date). Now I relied on receiving the money by that date for the means of moving to Dresden. But there was a little contretemps. Instead of sending the money by registered post, the Zarya sent it through an agency, and I received it ten or twelve days late. (Because it was not posted, I almost missed getting it altogether; for the agency might have failed to find me at all in Florence.) Thus, for a fortnight, expecting money, we spent some more money, and we had not enough to take us to Dresden. I sent a request for relief to the Russky Viestnik. By January I shall send off a novel to the Russky Viestnik.† In Dresden I shall work without lifting my head from the grindstone. But generally there's a mass of troubles and worries. The heat in Florence is getting awful; it is a suffocating city, burning hot. The nerves of all of us are on edge,—which is particularly bad for my wife. We are crowded at the present moment (and all this en attendant) in the smallest, tiniest little room, facing the market. I am sick of this Florence, and now because of the heat and the overcrowding I can't even sit down to work. On the whole, terrible nostalgia, the worse for being in Europe; everything here makes me feel like a beast. I have decided at all costs to return to Petersburg next spring (when I finish the novel),—even if they put me in the debtors' prison. I do not mention spiritual interests; but even my material interests suffer here, abroad. Imagine, for instance, this circumstance: no matter how, my works (all of them) have gone into a third, fourth, and fifth edition. The Idiot (whatever he is, I shall not argue now) is anyhow good merchandise. I know for certain that a second edition will be sold out in a year. Why not publish it then? It's just the time now, and chiefly—I want to for one special reason. What did I do? Six weeks ago I gave Marie Gregorevna Svatkovsky the following commission: to call on A. F. Basunov [book-seller and publisher] (with a

---

* *The Eternal Husband*, published in Nos. 1 and 2 of Zarya, 1870.
† The novel is *The Possessed*, which, however, did not begin to appear in the *Russky Viestnik* until January 1871.

letter of introduction from me) and to give him this message: Won't he undertake to bring out The Idiot? (It would be ready by next winter, if he took it up now.) The price—2000 roubles (I even thought of letting him have it for 1500, if he paid the money down). The legal and formal aspects of the agreement need not postpone matters: for I could send a formal and duly certified authorisation from here. I asked Marie Gregorevna just to ask Basunov, without specially urging him, to say yes or no, and let me know here. If the answer is no (although he is quite aware how my books have been selling hitherto and what sort of merchandise they are),—then it is all right, I don't mind. I shall publish it myself when I come back and I shan't be the loser by it. It seems that my commission was not a difficult one, was it? It could have been done in two minutes, by two words with Basunov. What then? It is now six weeks and I have not heard a word from Marie Gregorevna. Yet I asked her to do this (the first request in my life) simply because she herself eagerly offered to do any commissions for me in Petersburg, when she was in Switzerland last year. Thus my interests obviously suffer, solely because I am abroad. And not only this one thing! A great number of things, which I cannot do without, have been left behind in Russia! Did I or did I not tell you that I had a certain literary idea (a novel, a parable on atheism), compared with which all my previous literary career has been negligible, a preface merely, and to which I am going to devote all my subsequent life? But I cannot write it here; utterly impossible; I absolutely must be in Russia. Without Russia I can't write it. . . .

And what a mass of troubles! What a mass of worries! If only they were spared me! Apollon Nicolayevich, for the love of God, write to me about Pasha and about his quarrels with Emily Fiodorovna! It may be nonsense: but it is important to me. Yet Emily Fiodorovna has not written me a word about Pasha, but she sent me a letter the other day full of reproaches. They have queer notions. True, they are poor, but I can do only what I can. . . . Listen, Apollon Nicolayevich, I have a favour to ask you. If you can—do it, if not—refuse to do it. And for the love of God don't trouble yourself. Yet the trouble is not great; but my request is a delicate one. It's about that same Basunov. I beseech you to call on him at his shop and to ask him: Is he or is he not disposed to publish The Idiot, and to give me 2000 roubles for it? (I don't want to take less.) With Alexander Fiodorovich Basunov, as perhaps you know, you may talk frankly. Moreover, you are to make no efforts, and particularly don't try any special coaxing,—only—in a friendly way—if a conversation arose—Basunov likes asking advice—say a good word for The Idiot. But above all—don't show any particular eagerness. Having learnt what he says—write to me. That's all I ask. I'm sure, I'm sure you won't refuse my request (it's a very important thing to me, in spite of the fact that I do not wish to reduce the price; and if he says 'no,'—well, that's as he pleases, I shall not lose, I'll publish it myself, or I'll wait). But there is one delicate point in the affair. It is this. I had commissioned Marie Gregorevna to do this very thing, and made her promise secrecy, although I informed her at the same time that I was going to write to you about it. Won't she be offended by my asking you and passing her over? At the same time, why should she be offended? Especially as she knows that. you were to hear about it from me. And besides—she hasn't replied to me, although the time is passing, and the business is important to me. If she would only write to say that she did not want to undertake the commission, then at least my hands would not be tied; but I've had no word from her. At all events I think it's quite all right; I mean, it wouldn't be a bad idea if you were to call on Basunov, for instance, and ask him: whether he had received any proposal from me about publishing The Idiot? And then, if you thought the conversation was taking a good turn, if you spoke to him about the terms. Well now, this is my earnest request to you, Apollon Nicolayevich! If you can, do it, I beseech you. I do not ask you to conclude the business (it cannot be concluded, for an agreement and a power of attorney are necessary), but only to begin it, and to let me know about it, if only a line. Only please do not scold and reproach me for troubling and worrying you constantly.—I consider it necessary, though, to tell you that one of these days I am going to write to Marie Gregorevna and to ask her to proceed no further in the matter with Basunov, and to consider my request as never having been made. I should have written this to her, even if I had not intended to ask you about Basunov. But the best of all, the best of all—would be if you would take the trouble to see Marie Gregorevna herself and simply ask her: Has she done anything in my business, or has she forgotten about it? But I am afraid to trouble you; it means too much running about for you.

    I still hope to leave this place soon and go to Dresden again. Letters addressed to me in Dresden Will be forwarded to me to Florence, if I remain in Florence; for I have already written about it to the Dresden post-office. But this is an extreme supposition; I really do hope to leave soon for Dresden, and therefore if you wish to write me (I shall be eagerly expecting a letter), write to me at the poste restante, Dresden.

In truth we have to move to Dresden for many urgent reasons, and chiefly because it is a city familiar to us, and comparatively cheap; we even have friends there, and it is the place where Anna Gregorevna hopes to realise her expectations (it will be towards the beginning of September). Anna Gregorevna thanks you deeply for your good words; she often remembers you and feels homesick. I am very glad that her present occupation will to some extent dispel her homesickness. Good-bye, my friend. I have written three sheets, and what have I told you? Nothing. We have been separated too long, and because of the separation we have lost touch with one another on many questions. Some idea of all that is taking place in Petersburg reaches me. I have the Russky Viestnik, Zarya, and I read the Golos which is taken in by the local library. How do you like Danilevsky's Russia and Europe? In my opinion the book is important in the extreme; but I am afraid it has not received enough attention in the reviews. I consider Averkiev's Comedy the best work of the year. At the first reading I was in raptures; now after the second I've begun to regard it a little more cautiously. I press your hand firmly and embrace you.—Wholly and ever your

F. Dostoevsky.

VII

To A. N. Maikov

Dresden, August, 14th 1869 / August, 26th 1869.

I am absolutely delighted by your opinion and shall certainly write without waiting for your long letter, my dearest and precious friend Apollon Nicolayevich. (But remember, remember, dear man, that you promised me a long letter soon!) Firstly, I thank you for your thought about me and my interests.* ...

Next year (even if I have to go to the debtors' prison) I must return to Russia. Yes, things have now taken such a turn that it's better for me to sit in the debtors' prison in Russia than to remain abroad. My health is quite good, leaving aside my fits, and I can bear all kinds of trouble; but if I were to remain here a year longer, I should be surprised if I were able to write anything; I don't mean write it well, but write it at all—I've got so out of touch with Russia. I feel it. Anna Gregorevna also longs for Russia, I can see it. Besides, the loss of one child (a child such as I have never seen, so strong, beautiful, so full of understanding and feeling) was due solely to the fact that we could not fall in with the foreign way of feeding and rearing babies. If we lose the one which is expected, we both shall fall into real despair. Anna Gregorevna expects her confinement in three weeks at the latest.† I am terribly afraid for her health. Her first confinement she bore courageously. This time it is a completely different thing: she is seedy all the time, and besides she feels nervous and anxious; she's become impressionable and, added to this, she's seriously afraid of dying in childbirth (when she remembers the pains of the first childbirth). Such fears and anxieties are truly dangerous in natures which are not timid and weak, and therefore I am very anxious. By the way: my wife greets you and your wife affectionately. She remembers you often and passionately, she thanks you for your congratulations on my novel, and we decided, eight months ago, to ask you to stand godfather again. Pray, Apollon Nicolayevich, do not refuse; it is our great fixed desire. (The godmother as before is to be Anna Nicolayevna, whom you know,—my wife's mother.)

In general I am having a very worrying time and an awful lot of troubles; nevertheless I have to sit down to write—for the Zarya [The Eternal Husband], and then begin a long thing for the Russky Viestnik [The Possessed]. . . . It is eight months since I wrote anything. I shall certainly start writing in a fever; but what will happen later? Ideas I have of some sort; but I need Russia.

---

* The letter then enters into details about a will made by Dostoevsky's aunt which are omitted here.
† The second child, Lubov or Aimee, was born at Presden, on September 14, 1809.

Of course I know better than you how you spend the summer, and I knew beforehand that you would not write to me before the autumn. Yet there was one point about which I did expect to receive two lines of information from you. I don't mean it as a reproach. It was with regard to Basunov and the publication of The Idiot,—simply a matter of 'Yes' or 'No'; I did not even dare dream of putting on you, my dear man, the whole burden of the business; and it wouldn't have been decent on my part to trouble you in such a way. Still, just the 'yes' or 'no,' with Basunov's views, would have been interesting; though I am not very keen on selling the work now. Later on—it may perhaps suit me better—and apart from this, in any case, I now have other aims and intentions; for, come what may, I have decided to return to Russia next year.

One more favour, my dear friend! Write me a word about Pasha! I am in anguish and torment, thinking and pondering over him. I know he has his salary—if only he continues his work; but I should like to help him awfully. At the present moment I haven't a penny to spare; but in a month or five weeks I shall send my story to the Zarya, which, owing to its length, will, I believe, fetch more than I've had in advance from the Zarya. Then I shall again be able to give Pasha a small sum (a little is better than nothing). God knows how much I shall need money myself by that time. The Dostoevskys have probably received some money and will not need help from me for some time. Write to me about that, my dear friend.

Write to me also about yourself. Write me the promised long letter. I think by the time this letter reaches Petersburg you will have returned from the country.

I press your hand firmly, I greet your wife. Do you know, at times I have an idea that we have lost touch with one another much more than we think, and that it is already difficult to communicate our ideas fully in letters.—Wholly and ever your

F. Dostoevsky.

VIII

To A. N. Maikov

Dresden, October, 9th 1869
October, 21th 1870.

Your letter, my dear and much-esteemed Apollon Nicolayevich,—a letter which delighted and surprised me,—I've left unanswered till now because I have been sitting down to some troublesome work, and wished to finish it at all costs. And therefore I not only failed to answer several letters, but didn't even read anything all that time (except newspapers, of course). The work which I've taken so long over is only the beginning of the novel for the Russky Viestnik [The Possessed] and I shall have to write day and night for another six months at least; so that I am sick of it beforehand. There is of course something in it which draws me to write it; but speaking generally—there is nothing in the world more disgusting to me than literary work, I mean strictly, the writing of novels and stories—that is what I have come to! As for the idea of the novel, it is not worth explaining. In the first place, to express it fully in a letter is quite impossible, and you will be punished enough if you are inclined to read the novel, when it is published. Then why should I punish you twice?

You wrote a great deal about St. Nicholas—the Miracle-Worker. He will not desert us, because St. Nicholas is the Russian spirit and stands for Russian unity. We are no longer children, you and I, much-esteemed Apollon Nicolayevich; we know, for instance, this fact: that in case,—not only of a Russian disaster, but in case merely of Russian troubles,—the most un-Russian part of Russia,—a Radical—a Petersburg official, or a student—even they become Russians, begin to feel themselves Russians, although they may be ashamed of admitting it. Last winter I happened to read a serious admission in a leading article in the Golos—that 'we almost rejoiced during the Crimean War at the success of the Allied arms and at the defeat of our own.' No, my Radicalism did not go so far as that; at that time I was still serving my time in the galleys and did not rejoice at the success of the Allies; but together with my comrades, the unhappy ones* and their soldier-guards, I felt myself a Russian, I wished success to Russian arms and,—although I still retained a strong leaven of scabby Russian Liberalism, preached by . . . like the dung-beetle Bielinsky and the rest,—I did not consider myself inconsistent, when I felt the Russian in myself. True, the facts showed that the disease which had attacked cultured Russians was much more violent than we ourselves had imagined, and that the matter had not ended with the Bielinskys, Krayevskys, etc. But then came the miracle testified by St. Luke. The devils had entered into the man and their name was legion, and they asked Him: Suffer us to enter into the swine, and He suffered them. The devils entered into the swine, and the whole herd ran violently down a steep place into the sea and were drowned. When the people came out to see what was done they found the man, out of whom the devils were departed, sitting at the feet of Jesus, clothed and in his right mind, and those who saw it told them by what means he that was possessed of the devils was healed. Exactly the same has happened with us in Russia. The devils went out of the Russian and entered into a herd of swine,—into the Nechayevs, Serno-Solovio-viches, etc. [terrorists]. These are drowned and will be drowned, and the healed man, from whom the devils had been cast out, is sitting at the feet of Jesus. So it ought to happen. Russia has spewed out the abomination on which she has been surfeited, and certainly nothing Russian was left in those spewed-out scoundrels. And observe this, my dear friend: he who loses his people and nationality, loses also the belief of his fathers, and God. Well, if you want to know,— this is precisely the theme of my novel. It is called The Devils [called The Possessed in the existing English translation], and it is a description of how these devils entered into a herd of swine. Beyond all doubt I shall write it badly; being more of a poet than an artist I have always taken themes beyond my powers. But since not one of all the critics who have passed judgment on me has denied me a certain talent, then in this long novel too there are likely to be passages that are not so bad. Now that's all.

And in Petersburg there still seem to be many clever people who, although they are horrified by the scoundrels into whom the swine have entered, still go on dreaming how fine it was during the liberal-humane times of Bielinsky, who still think that the enlightenment of that time

---

* The convicts and exiles in Siberia are called 'unhappy ones' by the people.

should be brought back. Now, this idea can be seen even in the newest nationalist converts, etc. The old fellows do not give in: the Plescheyevs, Annenkovs, Turgenevs, and whole journals like the Viestnik Europa are of this school. They go on giving prizes in girls' schools, distributing to the girls books like the works of Bielinsky, in which he bewails the fact that Tatyana remained faithful to her husband. No, it won't be uprooted for a long time, and therefore, it seems to me, we have nothing to fear from external political commotions, such as, for instance, a European war on behalf of the Slavs; although it is strange: we are alone, and they are all of them together. The present position allows us two or three years of certain peace—shall we realise our position? Shall we prepare? Shall we build enough railways and fortresses? Shall we get another million rounds of ammunition? Shall we settle firmly on the border territories, and will reforms be introduced into the poll-tax and the recruiting for the army? These are the things that are needed, and the rest, that is, the Russian spirit, unity,—all this exists and will endure, and it will be so strong, it will have such wholeness and sacredness that even we are impotent to fathom the whole depth of that force, to say nothing of foreigners; and—my idea is that nine-tenths of our power consists just in the fact that foreigners do not understand and never will understand the depth and power of our unity. Oh, how clever they are! I have been assiduously reading for the last three years all the political papers, that is, the most important of them. How remarkably well they know their own affairs! How they can foretell events! What a knack they have of hitting the nail exactly on the head! (Compare them with our political papers, with their imitative rubbish, all imitation—with the exception perhaps of the Moscowskya Viedomosti.) What then? No sooner do they touch on Russia,—than they start muttering the devil knows what, like a feverish man in the dark! In Europe I think they know the star Sirius more thoroughly than they know Russia. And this very thing, for a time, is our power. And the other power will be our own belief in our individuality, in the sacredness of our destiny. The whole destiny of Russia lies in Orthodoxy, in the light from the East, which will suddenly shine forth to Western humanity, which has become blinded and has lost Christ. The cause of the whole misfortune of Europe, everything, everything without exception, has been that they gained the Church of Rome and lost Christ, and then they decided that they would do without Christ. Conceive now, my dear friend, that even in such superior Russians as, for instance, the author of Russia and Europe, I have not met with this idea about Russia—this idea of her exclusive Orthodox mission to mankind. And if this is so,—then it is really early as yet to demand independent thought from us.

But I have gone too far into the wood, and I am on the fourth page already. I live somehow, try to work, I am too much behind everywhere in delivering my work, everywhere I have broken my promises,—and suffer because of it. Anna Gregorevna too is depressed; so that I do not know what to do. I ought to return in the spring;—but I have still no money,—not only not enough to pay my debts, but not enough even to get back home. I have few acquaintances here, yet there are as many Russians in Dresden as there are Englishmen. Rubbishy people, these Russians are, generally speaking, I mean. . . . And, my God, what trash there is among them! And why do they wander about?

My little girl is healthy, well-nourished, weaned, she begins to understand well and even to speak; but she is a very nervous child, so that I am afraid for her, although she is healthy. My greatly respected friend, why do you give me so few details when you write about Pasha, about such an event as his marriage? For the love of Christ, tell me if you know. I have had no news from Pasha. And he is dear to me. Of course, it would be ridiculous on my part, at this distance, after a separation of three years, to claim to have an influence on his decisions. Still it is sad. I have a cousin, Misha, who married when he was still younger than Pasha; but he is a very intelligent boy, a boy of character. But Pasha is different—in character, and in the smallest matter of self-discipline.

If you can write anything to me, you will make me very, very grateful. My wife greets you. Luba kisses you. Good-bye, keep well and happy.

Wholly your F. Dostoevsky.